Beyond the Borders of Baptism

†
STUDIES IN WORLD CATHOLICISM

Beyond the Borders of Baptism

Catholicity, Allegiances, and Lived Identities

EDITED BY
Michael L. Budde

CONTRIBUTORS

Braden P. Anderson
Maria Clara Lucchetti Bingemer
Michael L. Budde
Matthew Butler
William T. Cavanaugh
Jose Mario C. Francisco, SJ
Peter Galadza
Stanley Hauerwas
Daniel Izuzquiza, SJ

Slavica Jakelić
Pantelis Kalaitzidis
Eunice Karanja Kamaara
Emmanuel Katongole
Dorian Llywelyn, SJ
Martin Menke
Agbonkhianmeghe E. Orobator, SJ
A. Alexander Stummvoll

CASCADE Books • Eugene, Oregon

BEYOND THE BORDERS OF BAPTISM
Catholicity, Allegiances, and Lived Identities

Studies in World Catholicism

Copyright © 2016 Wipf and Stock Publishers. All rights reserved. Except for brief quotations in critical publications or reviews, no part of this book may be reproduced in any manner without prior written permission from the publisher. Write: Permissions, Wipf and Stock Publishers, 199 W. 8th Ave., Suite 3, Eugene, OR 97401.

Cascade Books
An Imprint of Wipf and Stock Publishers
199 W. 8th Ave., Suite 3
Eugene, OR 97401

www.wipfandstock.com

PAPERBACK ISBN: 978-1-4982-0473-6
HARDCOVER ISBN: 978-1-4982-0475-0
EBOOK ISBN: 978-1-4982-0474-3

Cataloguing-in-Publication data:

Names: Budde, Michael L.

Title: Beyond the borders of baptism : catholicity, allegiances, and lived identities / edited by Michael L. Budde.

Description: Eugene, OR: Cascade Books, 2016 | Series: Studies in World Catholicism | Includes bibliographical references and indexes.

Identifiers: ISBN 978-1-4982-0473-6 (paperback) | ISBN 978-1-4982-0475-0 (hardcover) | ISBN 978-1-4982-0474-3 (ebook)

Subjects: LCSH: Church and the world. | Christianity and politics. | Globalization—Religious aspects—Christianity. | Identification (Religion) | Christian sociology.

Classification: BR115.W6 B439 2016 (print) | BR115.W6 B439 (ebook)

Manufactured in the U.S.A.   AUGUST 31, 2016

Contents

Acknowledgments | *vii*

Introduction by Michael L. Budde | 1

PART ONE: Identities, Allegiances, and Theological Reflections

1: Thinking Theologically about Identities and Allegiances:
Parables of a New "We" | 13
EMMANUEL KATONGOLE

2: Thinking Theologically about Identities,
Allegiances, and Discipleship | 28
DORIAN LLYWELYN, SJ

3: Church Matters | 47
STANLEY HAUERWAS

PART TWO: History, Context, Theology, and Eschatology: Notes, Experiences, Suggestions, and Possibilities

A: Europe, West and East

4: Engaging European Contexts and Issues: Some Reflections | 65
DANIEL IZUZQUIZA, SJ

5: The Challenge of Being a Catholic in Liberal Secular Europe | 77
A. ALEXANDER STUMMVOLL

6: Multiple Caesars? Germany, Bavaria,
and German Catholics in the Interwar Period | 91
MARTIN MENKE

7: Catholicism and Belonging, in This World | 104
SLAVICA JAKELIĆ

8: Multiple Belongings and Transnational Processes
of Catholic Formation in an Eastern Catholic Church | 123
PETER GALADZA

9: Baptismal and Ethnocultural Community: A Case Study of
Greek Orthodoxy | 141
PANTELIS KALAITZIDIS

B: Africa: Catholicity and Incarnated Identities

10: African Cases and Theological Reflections | 168
AGBONKHIANMEGHE E. OROBATOR, SJ

11: Cases and Controversies from Africa | 180
EUNICE KARANJA KAMAARA

C: Latin America

12: Poverty, Injustice, and Plurality:
A Complex Question for Catholics in Latin America | 199
MARIA CLARA LUCCHETTI BINGEMER

13: A Crown of Counterrevolutionary Thorns?
Mexico's Consecration to the Sacred Heart: January 6, 1914 | 214
MATTHEW BUTLER

D: North America

14: Kenotic Identities:
Political Self-Emptying and Redefined Belongings | 246
BRADEN P. ANDERSON

15: Is Catholicism a Religion? Catholics and Nationalism in America | 262
WILLIAM T. CAVANAUGH

E: Asia

16: Imagining Identity/Community as Christian/Filipino:
Implications for Doing Theology in East Asian Contexts | 279
JOSE MARIO C. FRANCISCO, SJ

PART THREE: In Lieu of a Conclusion

17: Loyalties, Allegiances, and Discipleship: Facing the Challenges | 301
MICHAEL L. BUDDE

Bibliography | 323
Subject/Name Index | 351
Scripture Index | 357

Acknowledgments

This book required the attention and support of many people. I am grateful for the support and encouragement provided by the Center for World Catholicism and Intercultural Theology (CWCIT) at DePaul University. The Center sponsored the conference from which this book is derived, and allows me the pleasure to serve there as a senior research professor. Both its past director (Peter Casarella) and current director (William Cavanaugh) supported this volume from its conceptual beginnings through its completion. I am indebted to the Center and to the leaders at DePaul University who appreciate the value of a research institution focused on Christianity as a worldwide phenomenon. Collaborative scholarship is supposed to look something like what goes on here.

I am also thankful for the tireless work of Francis Salinel, the Center's administrative coordinator, and of Karen Kraft, the Center's communications coordinator. It would have been impossible to gather the worldwide conversation of scholars that led to this volume without their diligence and creativity. That this book has found its way into print is itself a testimony to the editorial support of Ms. Kraft, whose professional skill, attention to detail, and patience were absolutely essential in bringing this book to life.

Finally, I am grateful to the contributors to this project for their work, witness, and willingness to share their work with one another and with readers of this volume. The editors and staff at Cascade Books continue to demonstrate their professional skill and interpersonal congeniality at every turn. *Beyond the Borders of Baptism* is the first volume in a series, Studies in World Catholicism, published by Cascade, with more entries to follow in the months ahead; the series is in good hands with such publishing partners as Cascade and Wipf and Stock.

Introduction

MICHAEL L. BUDDE

No wonder ours is a confused age. We are offered a thousand different ways to think of ourselves—as consumers of athletic shoes, as online supporters of a petition drive, as parents of children with a sports enthusiasm, as a member of a beleaguered ethnic or sexual community, as partisan supporters of one of ten thousand ideologically normed media or communications outlets, and much more.

At the same time, claims are forced upon us about which most people have no choice, or have little awareness of having selected or affirmed. We may be claimed by a nation, a state, a tribal group, an ethnic community, a socioeconomic class, and so much more. Cultural celebrations of postmodernism point to the plurality of identities and belongings, the fluidity of allegiances and the permeability of dogmatic and ideological silos of truth and awareness. Yet this same celebration and elevation of hyper-individuality and hybridity operate alongside and within a regimenting discipline that enables nationalism and other collective identities, militarism, the dogmas of capital, and the myths of states, empires, tribes, and subcultures.

These are profound issues for everyone, but profoundly challenging to those who call themselves Christians. As followers of Jesus Christ, those called to live as disciples in between the age that is and the age to come, Christians have special questions to ask regarding identities, allegiances, and notions of belonging. What does it mean to be part of the Body of Christ, God's new creation from among the nations, in a world filled with nations aplenty? There is no escape from such questions, no easy answer waiting in a book (or The Book)—no time at which Christians got it completely right, and to which we merely need make a return. "Who—and whose—are we?" is a question for Catholics and Protestants of all flavors, for the traditions of Orthodoxy and the entrepreneurs of Pentecostalism. All parts of the global church face similar questions with different inflections, divergent grooves cut by the plows of history, and varied neighbors, imperatives, and opportunities. And the stakes are high: matters of war and peace, exclusion and inclusion, who starves and who does not, the credibility of the Gospel itself—all of these and more are caught up in the whirl of identities, allegiances imposed or refused, and what "the church" might possibly mean in such circumstances.

This book is one modest contribution to discussions underway in many parts of the church, in some sectors of the academy, and elsewhere. These chapters began life as presentations at a conference titled "The Borders of Baptism: Multiple Belongings and Transnational Processes of Catholic Formation," April 14–17, 2013, at DePaul University in Chicago. The conference invited, but did not require, participants to consider some of the issues raised in my book *The Borders of Baptism: Identities, Allegiances, and the Church* (Cascade, 2011); some found that book helpful as a resource, others as a foil for criticism, and still others did not bother with it at all. They did just what the organizers hoped, in other words.

This conference was sponsored by DePaul's Center for World Catholicism and Intercultural Theology (CWCIT), a research institute focusing on the global nature of Christianity as it becomes more thoroughly a movement of the so-called Global South. Despite the Center's name, it does not consider Catholicism alone in exploring Christianity in its worldwide diversity, nor does it limit itself to a single region or era. One of the strengths of the Center, in my view, is its willingness to keep the ecumenical and interreligious dimensions of Christianity as essential concerns while simultaneously taking Catholicism seriously as the largest and most diverse of Christian communities in the world.

Real life has a way of intruding on events like this. Two of the participants (one from Africa, one from Asia) were unable to revise their presentations for publication due to war and civil unrest that made working for peace and defending the poor more pressing matters than working on a book manuscript. Another colleague with heavy administrative responsibilities excused himself from the volume due to time constraints. What remains are the products of our intentionally broad questions put to participants in our letters of invitation:

> *In this conference we will explore the following questions: What difference does "being a Catholic Christian" make in a world of powerful institutions and processes that shape identities, loyalties, and allegiances? Has Catholicism's embrace of nationalism and other powerful forms of political/cultural identity limited, inhibited, or thwarted the call of the Gospel to form communities of discipleship across human borders and divisions? How can the Church respect the diversity of its*

members—many nations, cultures, and communities—while maintaining a coherent witness to the Kingdom of God that is not undermined by more parochial ideologies or priorities?

This project explores theological, political, and pastoral issues related to the Catholic encounter with processes and institutions that form politically salient loyalties and identities in the modern and postmodern world. As people worldwide inescapably find themselves part of multiple and overlapping communities of identity and belonging (e.g., racial, political, cultural, sexual, ideological), it is far from obvious how these can and should stand in relative importance to the unity in Christ effected in baptism and sustained by the Eucharist.

Structure of the Book

In Part One of this book, three world-renowned Christian theologians provide important starting points for reflection on matters of identity, allegiance, and Christian discipleship.

In his chapter, Emmanuel Katongole suggests that just as an earlier generation of Christian theology asserted the need to situate all work "after Auschwitz," so our generation now stands "after Rwanda"—the 1994 genocide in which more than eight hundred thousand Christian Rwandans were murdered by their fellow Christian Rwandans under the labels of Hutu v. Tutsi. A Ugandan theologian and Catholic priest now at the University of Notre Dame, Katongole explores how to relate so-called natural identities (family, tribe, nation), which contrary to their self-presentation are always also political, to the "new we" that Christ creates among humanity and has named as the church.

For his part, Dorian Llywelyn, SJ, invites readers into "Thinking Theologically about Identities, Allegiances, and Discipleship." Llywelyn is a lecturer in theology and philosophy at Heythrop College at the University of London, and the author of the foundational book *Toward a Catholic Theology of Nationality* (Lexington, 2010). In this chapter, Llywelyn offers a substantive definition of discipleship (all too often missing or vague in much contemporary theology), along with the challenges in trying to come to terms with concepts as fluid as "identity," especially inasmuch as "identity" is not a typical theological category (unlike the concept of "person," for example). While noting the areas of conflict and contestation between discipleship and other claims on Christian persons, Llywelyn wonders what a set of identities or allegiances healed by Jesus's Incarnation might look like in the world.

This section concludes with "Church Matters," an extended reflection on the need for Christian formation via the cultivation of particular and Christ-centered patterns of speech and action. This contribution by Stanley Hauerwas, the Gilbert T. Rowe Emeritus Professor at Duke Divinity School, emphasizes that "the church is a material reality that must resist the domestication of our faith in the interests of societal peace" (49), even as he notes that bad theology on this score makes Christianity impotent in the face of nationalism and militarism.

The majority of chapters in this book present themselves in Part Two, "History, Context, Theology, and Eschatology: Notes, Experiences, Suggestions, and Possibilities." Given that there is no way to provide comprehensive treatment of issues so large, we opted instead to provide something of a sampler for readers—varied regions, historical periods, and questions—in hopes of encouraging deeper exploration and conversation. While geographic categories often obscure as much as they illuminate regarding the diverse experiences of Christians worldwide, we used a loose regional template—Europe, North America, Latin America, Asia, and Africa—to allow authors to reflect on those questions of prime importance to them. In addition, this section gives space for exploration of Christianity and nationalism in the Orthodox context—where such are explosive issues theologically and politically—and among Eastern Catholics (those churches similar in rite and history to the Orthodox churches, but in communion with the Bishop of Rome).

The Spanish Jesuit Daniel Izuzquiza has seen the transformations of European Catholicism from the street (as former director of Pueblos Unidos, a center serving undocumented immigrants) and from the academy (as professor of theology at Comillas Pontifical University) in Madrid. In "Engaging European Contexts and Issues: Some Reflections," Izuzquiza describes contemporary Europe as illustrative of "embodied identity and universal catholicity." While the success of the European integration project is apparent on some levels, he sees the fracturing of identities (with profound implications for the churches), especially as the poor are excluded from political, economic, and cultural space.

The modern European Union, of course, has its roots in the work of persons trying to overcome the continent's propensity to tear itself apart in regular bouts of warfare. Where some scholars begin "after Auschwitz" in trying to understand Christianity in the contemporary world, Martin Menke explores the divided loyalties of German Catholics in the interwar period, divisions that prevented a coherent stand as the Nazi party rose in prominence. In "Multiple Caesars? Germany, Bavaria, and German Catholics in the Interwar Period," Menke (professor of history and political science at Rivier University) looks at nationalism as divisive not only between countries but within them—in this case, the divisions between Catholics identifying first with Bavaria and those committed to the success of the Weimar regime. These antagonistic relations, Menke notes, "complicate the question of the relationship between identities defined by religion, nation, and region" (92).

Several of the contributors to this volume give voice to the tensions, if not outright conflict, between strong ethno-national notions of identity and the christological and ecclesiological convictions that undergird a robust notion of discipleship—the latter of which relativizes ethnic, political, and other collective identities. In "Catholicism and Belonging, in This World," Slavica Jakelić stands up for what she calls "group-oriented Catholicisms"— those that she says typify or name an entire ethnic or national group, e.g., Polish Catholicism, Mexican Catholicism, where group and religious identities interpenetrate broadly and deeply. An associate fellow at the Institute for Advanced Studies in Culture at the University of Virginia and assistant professor of humanities and social thought at Valparaiso University's Christ College, Jakelić notes the major objections to close Christian-national identities even as she provides examples where such give testimony to the Gospel demands to make peace and reconcile with enemies. In this her use of the example of Franciscan communities in Bosnia, as well as the better-known case of Solidarity in Poland, is well worth considering in other contexts and traditions.

Considerations of Christian identities and allegiances in Europe would be incomplete without some attention to the near complete collapse of this longtime cultural intermixture. Alexander Stummvoll—a young, cosmopolitan scholar, urbane and erudite—notes that most of his European peers cannot believe that anyone "like him" could still be a Catholic or any sort of Christian anymore. Declaring, with others, that "European Catholics are an endangered species," Stummvoll asserts that the only worthwhile future for Catholics in Europe lies neither in conservative restoration nor in liberal accommodation, but as "diverse, smaller yet spiritually vibrant communities, spiritual centres, and pilgrimage sites" (78). Separating Catholicism from the political and cultural identities of Europe will make for a church with less power and prestige, which—rather than something to be feared—may "provide a welcome opportunity [for generating] pastoral strategies in order to transform a declining and complacent status-quo church into a more vigorous missionary Church" (79).

A native of Austria, Stummvoll completed postdoctoral work at the Institute of Political Science at the Pontifical Catholic University in Chile, and then began his current work as district director in Baden-Baden, Germany for a member of German Parliament (Bundestag).

While the question of allegiances and identities has been explored in the Western spheres of Christianity, in many ways, it is an especially powerful and controversial matter in the Orthodox traditions of Christianity worldwide. In fact, the nature of Christianity's relationship with national identity and national political allegiance is a hotly debated, often contentious topic among theologians in the Orthodox world—all too often, however, this debate is ignored by scholars more focused on Christianity in the "West" and "South." With more than two hundred million Christians in the Orthodox family of churches, this is no minor constituency.

Pantelis Kalaitzidis, director of the Volos Academy for Theological Studies in Greece, is among the most important scholars in the Orthodox world who is re-examining the complex historical and theological intertwining of nationality and Christianity (expressed in Greek Orthodoxy, the Russian Orthodox Church, the Serbian Orthodox church, and others). In "Baptismal and Ethnocultural Community: A Case Study of Greek Orthodoxy," he offers a careful recapitulation of scriptural and early Christian sources regarding the unity of the church, its existence as an eschatological community distinct from all "natural" ones and formed by baptism and affirmed in Eucharist. He then explores the contentious case of nationalism in the contemporary Orthodox world, using Greece as a case study in which Christianity became inextricably tied to the Greek nation. In some ways, his contribution offers something of a contrast to Jakelić's view of inherited national-cultural collectivistic religions. As he writes,

> We Orthodox remain so spellbound and trapped in the premodern, medieval, or romantic communitarian model that we seem to have forgotten that acceptance of the gospel message and inclusion in the body of the church cannot be understood on the basis of collectives—such as that of a people, a nation, a language, a culture, etc.—but on the basis of a completely personal act, free of every kind of biological, cultural or ethnic pre-determination (159).

Some church traditions, of course, find themselves straddling the divide between the Catholic/Protestant "West" and the Orthodox "East"—namely, those churches rooted in the liturgical and spiritual traditions of Orthodoxy but also in ecclesial community with the Bishop of Rome. From this family of traditions we have a creative chapter from Peter Galadza, the Kule Family Professor of Liturgy in the Sheptytsky Institute of Eastern Christian Studies and the Faculty of Theology at Saint Paul University in Ottawa, Ontario. In some ways his chapter, "Multiple Belongings and Transnational Processes of Catholic Formation in an Eastern Catholic Church," serves as a useful complement both to the work of Kalaitzidis and to the contributors who focus on Western Europe on matters of nationality, identity, and the church.

A leader in the Ukrainian Greco-Catholic Church (one-fifth of whose members now live outside Ukraine, as do half of its bishops), Galadza offers a chapter that is one part primer, one part nuanced explanation of the nuanced interactions of war, Vatican politics, Vatican II, and the politics of Orthodox Christianity. His is a fascinating and important contribution, especially for persons unfamiliar with the world of Eastern Catholic churches and the lessons their experiences have for Christians in other parts of the world. Galadza offers interesting interpretations on matters of discipleship and pacifism, ethno-dogmatic nationalism and a healthy love of country, and the need to make subtle distinctions in the midst of messy and confusing (and shifting) transnational experiences.

While Orthodox scholars like Kalaitzidis hope to confront a once-seamless intertwining of ethno-nationalist and Christian identities, the African theologian Agbonkhianmeghe Orobator—the president/principal of Hekima University College Jesuit School of Theology and Institute of Peace Studies and International Relations in Nairobi—notes that in Africa the religious person by necessity operates between multiple religious polarities that shape his or her identity. In other words, religious identity is not a matter of simple affiliation or adherence, practice of beliefs, or profession of faith. Rather, it involves a complex combination of factors, intersections of processes, and overlapping points of reference.

The diversity of religious traditions and ethnic and tribal groups means that, with reference to Catholics in many parts of Africa, "Catholic identity is incarnated at multiple levels or loci of religious practice . . . Catholic enclaves are rare; rarer still are Catholic ghettos." This produces "an economy of identities that allows for flexibility and fluidity in delineating the borders of religious belief, practice, and allegiance" (168).

Orobator offers a fraternal critique of *The Borders of Baptism* by insisting that the natural ties of clan, family, and ethnicity ensure that baptism is insufficient in putting Christian identity and community in a primary location; moreover, he finds much that is positive and adaptive in the African adoption of multiple religious identities and affiliations. At a minimum, he suggests, the sort of church unity sought in *The Borders of Baptism* requires a deep Eucharistic sensibility to be materially relevant in the lives of believers: "Alone baptism cannot withstand the tsunami of multiple and competing identities . . . Hence baptism *and* Eucharist play a mutually reinforcing role" (178). In this Orobator hits two notes that may be in tension with one another, or simply two goods worth affirming: the benefits of religious multiplicity and the requisites of church unity.

From another starting point, the Kenyan theologian Eunice Karanja Kamaara approaches questions of Christian and Catholic identity and allegiance with special attention to African Traditional Religions (ATRs), and feminist consciousness and perspectives. Given the role of the churches in the colonial era—taking land, labor, and culture from Africans as part of the imperial "civilizing" project—she says it is no easy matter to frame the question, "to whom should Africans be loyal, and where should their allegiances lie?"

Kamaara here offers a framing of the problem distinct from other contributors to this volume—not focusing on Catholicism or Christianity in conflict with rival claimants like nationalism, tribalism, or the modern state, but on certain Roman Catholic practices like celibacy that clash with authentic and valued parts of African cultural identity. She prefers and celebrates the latter over the former, and in this explores the question of Christianity and its loyalties by way of an examination of a splinter "Reformed Catholic Church" that eschews celibacy as part of a blending of "African" and "Catholic" ways of being.

Questions of religious plurality are inescapable in the world today, even in those regions that were once thought to exemplify religious homogeneity. Brazilian theologian Maria Clara Lucchetti Bingemer offers a wide-ranging set of reflections on this changing context in "Poverty, Injustice and Plurality: A Complex Question for Catholics in Latin America." She notes how hybridity, pluralism, and the colonial legacy affect questions of Christianity and allegiances/identities in contemporary Latin America, a place where the outward domination of Catholicism masked the enduring diversities of Portuguese and Spanish, African and indigenous, racially mixed and segregated, and many more.

Complementing Bingemer's broad overview, which reviews Catholic reforms of the twentieth century from Vatican II to Medellín, Puebla, Aparecida, and the emergence of Pope Francis, historian Matthew Butler looks in detail at a case where religious and state loyalties interacted in complex and sometimes violent ways. In "A Crown of Counterrevolutionary Thorns? Mexico's Consecration to the Sacred Heart: January 6, 1914," Butler offers a fine-grained exploration of the conflicting ideas of Mexican cultural and political identity proffered by anticlerical state modernizers and conservative Catholic leaders in revolutionary-era Mexico. An historian at the University of Texas-Austin, Butler fleshes out a picture of church-state conflict and church-society interactions that has been obscured by some accounts and overshadowed in others.

Considerations of church and nationalism in the United States receive extended consideration in "Kenotic Identities: Political Self-Emptying and

Redefined Belongings," by Braden Anderson. Anderson, a Protestant theologian and author of *Chosen Nation: Scripture, Theopolitics, and the Project of National Identity* (Cascade, 2012), here offers a serious engagement with Catholic social teaching and especially its translation into the "faithful citizenship" rhetoric of the United States Conference of Catholic Bishops. In a series of statements over several years (culminating, in 2011, with *Forming Consciences for Faithful Citizenship: A Call to Political Responsibility from the Catholic Bishops of the United States*), the bishops encourage political participation and civic engagement as essential aspects of what it means to be a Christian. Anderson notes that the rhetoric chosen, the frameworks presumed, and even the graphic design of printed and online materials together constitute a sort of "nationalism by *omission*," a narrative distorted by the *absence* of theological content in favor of explicit commitments to America and to our patriotic duties as its citizens. It is an account of one community, the church, whose salvation narrative seems to entail the church's safeguarding of the culture and political institutions of our properly *political* community, America. The statement selectively appropriates the Christian salvation narrative by using terms like "mission" and "baptismal commitment" to refer to "responsible citizenship" and political participation, not in any sense of transnational ecclesiality, but rather in the specifically American context. This selective appropriation leaves out the biblical roots of church identity and mission.

In contrast to the sort of overt championing of Christianity and Americanism conjoined in much rhetoric from the (mostly Protestant) "religious right" in the United States, Anderson finds the U.S. Catholic sort no less problematic given how much the latter leaves implicit rather than explicit.

The noted Catholic theologian William Cavanaugh offers a chapter that extends Anderson's work by attending to the contradictions that emerge from the Catholic embrace of nationalism in the United States. In "Is Catholicism a Religion? Catholics and Nationalism in America," Cavanaugh tells the story of a lay Catholic school teacher who gets fired for refusing to lead his students in the Pledge of Allegiance. In Cavanaugh's treatment, this episode opens to an exploration of the "aura of unspeakability, untouchability, obedience, [and] transcendence" associated with the venerations Americans are taught regarding the symbols and practices of the nation-state.

The unexplored context of Christianity and nationalism in the United States, according to Cavanaugh, is one in which neither the churches nor the society name American patriotism as a religious phenomenon, even though it exhibits most of the traits commonly associated with a "religion"; indeed, much rides on denying that nationalism is an object or agent of veneration and worship. As Cavanaugh notes wryly with reference to the lay teacher fired from his job, "The Diocese treated the flag as something sacred, while firing [the teacher] for saying so" (263).

While Anderson and Cavanaugh offer a challenging theological case from the context of the United States, Jose Mario Francisco, SJ, shows how nationalism and Christianity have interacted in the church's engagement with Asian peoples, histories, and religions. In "Imagining Identity/Community as Christian/Filipino: Implications for Doing Theology in East Asian Contexts," Francisco (a professor of philosophical and systematic theology at Ateneo de Manila University) works through the ambiguous history of the Philippines as the only Christian-majority country in Asia. He traces the winding path of identity construction that, beginning in the sixteenth century, moved indigenous peoples from being "native" to being "colonized and Christian." This culminated in the development of Filipino nationalism, Catholic identity, and the idea of the "Catholic Philippines"—a label that conceals as much as it reveals.

While noting the contributions to social development made possible by the notion of a "Christian nation," Francisco notes the costs both to the church and the Filipino people attendant to this sort of identity. He calls for a process of "dis-imagining the religious nation" as in the best interests of all concerned with the welfare of the Filipino people and the integrity of the church.

The book ends with an inconclusive concluding chapter. In "Loyalties, Allegiances, and Discipleship: Facing the Challenges," I offer a restatement of an ecclesiology that sees the church as a new community created by God's invitation through Jesus Christ, one very different in its ends and means from "the nations" in every age. Not simply an oppositional identity, Christian discipleship embodies God's hopes for the entire human family, despite the failings of the church to reflect those eschatological hopes; indeed, in its embrace of forgiveness and reconciliation, the failures of the church offer formative processes of community that do not require the exclusions, dominations, and violence intrinsic to the modern process of state- and nation-building and maintenance. This final chapter also offers a few thoughts prompted by some of the criticisms of *The Borders of Baptism* and similar moves to prioritize "being a Christian" over other claims on the identities and allegiances of followers of Christ. The issues involved are large enough, important enough, and difficult enough to benefit from further exploration, fraternal correction, and ecclesial experimentation in the many contexts and circumstances in which Christianity finds itself as a movement that extends beyond borders of many sorts even as it incarnates itself in the myriad contexts and cultures of the world.

PART ONE

Identities, Allegiances, and Theological Reflections

1

Thinking Theologically about Identity and Allegiances: Parables of a "New We"

EMMANUEL KATONGOLE

Do not conform yourself to this age, but be transformed by the renewal of your mind, that you may discern what is the will of God, what is good and acceptable and perfect. (Rom 12:2)

Introduction: Nyamata, 1998

The question of identity, allegiance, and being a Christian is not a speculative theological question. It is a concrete and urgent question, particularly in our time, living as we are after the 1994 Rwandan genocide. In less than a hundred days, close to a million Rwandans—mostly Tutsis—were killed by their neighbors and countrymen (mostly Hutus). The greatest irony of this genocide of our time is that it happened in one of the most Christianized countries in Africa, where at least 70 percent of the population was Catholics and 15 percent Protestant.[1] This means that almost all of the victims and their killers were Christians, who had been baptized and often worshipped in the same churches where a number of the killings took place. The church of Nyamata was one such killing field. I visited the church of Nyamata in the summer of 1998, on my first visit to Rwanda after the genocide. Even though it had been four years since the genocide, the empty church carried fresh

---

1. Most accounts put the Christian population of Rwanda prior to the genocide between 85 and 90 percent. See, e.g., Rittner et al., *Genocide in Rwanda*, xi; Longman, *Christianity and Genocide in Rwanda*, 4. See also Katongole, "Christianity, Tribalism and the Rwanda Genocide," 95–117.

memories of what had happened here. The corrugated tin roof was pierced by bullet holes and bore visible bloodstains; the church basement, accessible down steep steps in the back, had been converted into a permanent catacomb. On either side of its very narrow hallways were racks of skulls, bones, coffins, and personal belongings of the more than eight thousand people who had been killed inside the church. The expansive main area of the church was empty. The altar's white sheet covering still bore bloodstains. The tabernacle stood wide open; the marble baptismal font was chipped in a number of places, obviously by machetes intended for some of the victims.

As I stood in horrified silence in the empty church, a number of questions ran through my head. How could this have happened in this beautiful and deeply Christian country? Why was the Catholic Church never able to provide a bulwark against the slaughter of Rwandans by their neighbors, being instead, as some cases indicated, a contributing factor in the killing?[2] The fact that the genocide started during Easter week added more irony and contradiction. For obviously, many of the victims had celebrated Christ's Resurrection from the dead, thus becoming the first fruit of God's new creation, here in this very church, together with the killers. Was all the talk of new identity, new life with God—words that describe the life of the Christian—nothing but mere *spiritual* platitudes that actually meant very little in the "real" world? What, then, is the relationship between one's biological, national, racial, or ethnic identity and the reality of baptism? Does the blood of tribalism run deeper than the waters of baptism?

I begin with the vivid memory of Nyamata for two reasons. First, it is to make the point that any reflection about identity, allegiance, and being a Christian cannot proceed in an abstract fashion. It must always draw attention to a particular place (America, Africa, Rwanda—to the extent these notions are places) and begin by paying attention to the contradictions within which Christians find themselves as they engage the politics of their nations. But I also begin with the memory of Nyamata because it is now clear that what happened in Rwanda in 1994, while extreme and particularly intense, is by no means exceptional. For as Michael Budde notes, Christians readily kill other Christians in service to the claims of state, ethnicity, or ideology.[3] Moreover, such killing has become so commonplace that we no longer see this as a scandal to the Christian gospel.[4] That is why Rwanda does serve

---

2. For some of these cases, see Katongole and Wilson-Hartgrove, *Mirror to the Church*, especially 9–26.

3. Budde, *Borders of Baptism*.

4. Ibid., 5. A key aspect of modern tribalism, as Budde describes, is that we have found ways to "explain away" and obscure the scandal of Christians killing other Christians: "World War I is described as interstate rivalry run amok, not the industrial

well as a mirror—indeed, as a metaphor—for the modern forms of tribalism that habituate Christians to live in ways that assume that bonds of tribalism, nationalism, racism, or ethnicity run much deeper than the waters of baptism.[5] Accordingly, reflecting on Rwanda might provide us with much-needed lessons for learning how to think theologically about identity and belonging in our time.

Learning to Think Theologically about Identity: The Dialectical Task

Learning to think theologically about identity involves two interrelated tasks, an intellectual as well as a practical one. These interconnected tasks are nicely captured by Paul's words in his letter to the Romans, when he warns his audience, "Do not conform yourself to this age, but be transformed by the renewal of your mind, that you may discern what is the will of God, what is good and acceptable and perfect" (Rom 12:2).

Time and occasion do not allow us to get into the historical, hermeneutical, and literary issues connected with Paul's letter to the Romans and this particular recommendation. What is clear is that, comprised of both Jewish and Gentile Christians, the church of Rome experienced some "tensions." In writing this encouraging letter to the Romans, Paul highlights the new life of hope and freedom in Christ that God's love has given to all through God's unmerited justification. As bearers of this new life, Roman Christians must learn to think of themselves in a "new" way—not as Gentile and Jewish in the first place, but as God's new people, made such through God's unmerited grace. It is within this context that he urges them to "not conform to this age" but to live transformed lives. What is of particular significance for us here is the way that Paul suggests that Roman Christians might be able to go about the business of "being transformed." They do so, according to Paul, in two interconnected ways. First, it is by the "renewal of your minds." What Paul recommends here is not a one-time "making up" of their minds but a "renewal," which is to say an ongoing (trans)formation of their minds, which is realized through cultivation of the relevant habits of

---

butchering by Christians of one another; Rwanda symbolizes the ugliness of ethnic conflict rather than Catholics massacring Catholics; the U.S. wars in Central America are charged to the Cold War account instead of Christians in the United States abetting the killing of Nicaraguan, Salvadoran, and Guatemalan Christians by one another. That no one describes these events as a scandal to the gospel, a cruel inversion of the unity of the body of Christ, is among the most embarrassing charges against contemporary Christianity."

5. I make this argument more explicitly in *Mirror to the Church*.

mind. This renewal is about developing the necessary mental capacities and categories to enable them to think rightly—that is, in a manner consistent with their new status as God's people, made thus not through the law (the old categories) but through God's grace.

Second, Paul shows that learning to think properly—while it is about developing the right mental capacities and categories—is not a detached intellectual exercise. Rather, it is dialectically connected to, and at the same time made possible by, relevant patterns of living. It is connected with the ability to "discern what is the will of God, what is pleasing, perfect, and true." The key term here is "discern," which various translations render differently: "to test and approve what God's will is" (New International Version); "to learn and know God's will" (English Standard Version); "to prove what the will of God is" (New American Bible).

What the various translations confirm is the practical dimension of discernment as a form of living out the will of God: what is good, acceptable, and perfect. Moreover, if these different expressions ("test," "learn," "know," and "prove") seem to reflect a certain tentativeness in Paul's recommendation, they point to a crucial dimension of ad hoc discernment, experimentation, an ongoing negotiation of their new identity, which requires the formation of both relevant mental capacities and practical disciplines. These disciplines are at once as subversive (i.e., do not conform to the patterns of this world) as they are revelatory of what is good, pleasing, and perfect. Moreover, this way of understanding who they are and living in the world is a form of politics ("politics" here understood as the configuring of bodies in space and time).[6] That is why, in the end, thinking correctly about Christian identity is about learning to see one's body as both the site of resistance and the revelation of that new reality of God's justification. Thus, in the opening words of Romans 12, which immediately precede the exhortation not to conform to this age, Paul states, "Therefore, I urge you, brothers and sisters, in view of God's mercy, to offer your bodies as a living sacrifice, holy and pleasing to God—this is your true and proper worship" (Rom 12:1 NIV).

This is what learning to think theologically about identity, allegiance, and being a Christian is about. But I realize I have jumped ahead of myself. My intention in drawing attention to Paul's exhortation to the Romans here was to highlight the two dialectical requirements of Christian identity: the cultivation of relevant mental capacities and categories on the one hand and, on the other, the formation of relevant practical skills and postures that enable one to negotiate one's Christian identity in the world. Let me now try

---

6. For this understanding of politics, see particularly Cavanaugh, "The World Reconciled." For my response to, and a more extended discussion of, Cavanaugh's essay, see Katongole, "A Blood Thicker than Tribalism."

to highlight each of these dialectical requirements by drawing some crucial lessons from the Rwandan genocide, so as to provide more concrete and specific suggestions of what these might look like for us today.

Christian Identity as "Political" Identity

Rwanda forced me to rethink issues of ethnicity and nationalism and, overall, the status of so-called natural identities. The way the genocide in Rwanda was explained by Western media (and governments)—a myth that was reproduced throughout the world, including in Africa—was that the genocide in Rwanda was nothing but the playing out of age-old animosities between Tutsi and Hutu tribes or ethnicities. The impression of this pervasive explanation was that the Tutsi and Hutu were culturally and historically distinct communities, each with a different origin, and they shared little in common other than their long-standing hatred for one another. This actually is not true. For not only did Hutu and Tutsi speak the same language, live on the same hills, intermarry and intermingle, they also shared the same culture and the same religious traditions. In fact, prior to European colonialism, as Philip Gourevitch notes, "There are few people in Europe among whom one finds these three factors of national cohesion: one language, one faith, one law."[7]

What soon became clear through extended research on Rwanda was the fact that the categories of Hutu and Tutsi did not conform to the standard categories of race, tribe, or ethnicity, even though each of these had been subsequently used to describe Rwanda.[8] But what also became clear was that even though Hutu and Tutsi continued to live on the same hills, speak the same language, and share the same cultural traditions, by 1994, Hutu and Tutsi had become two distinct and mutually exclusive "political" communities united by their hatred and fear of each other and thirst for revenge. By 1994, Hutu and Tutsi had become exclusive "political" identities. In particular, the work of the Ugandan Muslim scholar Mahmood Mamdani showed how Tutsi and Hutu had become political identities, produced and reproduced through the political formation of the modern Rwanda by highlighting a crucial distinction between "cultural," "market," and "political" identities. Cultural identities reflect something of the past (a shared history, language, customs, beliefs, etc.); "political" identities are in

---

7. Gourevitch, *We Wish to Inform You*, 55.
8. See Katongole, *Sacrifice of Africa*, especially 64–86.

view of a future political project (realizing specific political goals or allocating access, privileges, etc.).[9]

Mamdani's conclusion—that Hutu and Tutsi did not merely reflect biological, racial, or cultural differences but rather were *formed* identities in view of particular political goals and aspirations—proved to be revolutionary for my thinking about identity. In the first place, it led me to begin to see that there was something naïvely wrong in assuming that one's national, ethnic, or racial identity is one's "natural" and therefore primary identity, on which one's being Christian builds. This rather widespread view is reflected in many ways, from assumptions that our "ethnicity" is the way God made us, and nothing can be done about that,[10] to more theological arguments that invoke Aquinas' dictum that "grace builds upon nature" to suggest that Christian formation does not radically change or interrupt our natural identities but simply builds on these.[11] But such formulations do not allow

---

9. "We will need to distinguish political identity from both cultural and market-based identities. Political identities exist in their own right. They are a direct consequence of the history of state formation, and not of market or cultural formation. If economic identities are a consequence of the history of development of markets, and cultural identities of the development of communities that share a common language and meaning, political identities need to be understood as a specific consequence of the history of state formation. When it comes to the modern state, political identities are inscribed in law. In the first instance, they are legally enforced" (Mamdani, *When Victims Become Killers*, 22).

10. See, e.g., Buconyori, *Tribalism and Ethnicity*. The 2009 Gathering of Christian Leaders in Reconciliation of the East African Great Lakes Initiative, organized by the Duke Center for Reconciliation and its partners in Bujumbura in January 2009, had as its theme "Identity, Community and the Gospel of Reconciliation." Most leaders assumed as a starting point that the issue of ethnicity is a matter of biological givenness about which nothing can be done. The challenge, as many expressed it, was not "tribe" but "tribalism," which is the exclusive concern for one's tribe alone and hatred for anyone from another tribe. The gathering sought to show that the issue of "tribalism" was far more complex, and at any rate often involves a call to live in a way that might involve "betraying" one's people. See Katongole, "Identity, Community and the Gospel of Reconciliation," the workbook for the 2009 gathering.

11. I am aware, of course, that a great deal of African theological reflection was born out of an attempt to reclaim the African traditional heritage as a positive starting point—a veritable *preparation evangelion* for Christianity in Africa. African Christian theologians argued that African Christian identity does not start from a tabula rasa but remains in continuity with (and thus builds on) the positive elements within the African Christian's traditional heritage. See e.g., Bediako, *Theology and Identity*. While I am greatly sympathetic to this historical moment of African theological reflection and applaud much of it—particularly the early contributions to the movement of African theology—my concern is that more recent contributions in the enculturation or indigenizing approach have the point of African tradition heritage as a "starting point" not as an end—*terminus ad quem*—of Christian identity. Thus, more recent contributions seem to be more interested in merely dressing up Jesus in African garb—making

for the full political reality of Christian identity. For once it has been accepted that our biological, national, racial, or ethnic identities are our primary identities, then the best that Christianity might be able to do is to provide either inner spiritual dynamism to bolster those so-called natural identities, or ethical guidelines to civilize and check the excessive tendencies of racism, tribalism, or nationalism. Christianity is left without any resources to question or interrupt the political goals and expectations toward which these so-called natural identities are directed.

That is why, in view of Mamdani's analysis, what became clear to me was the fact that Christian identity is political identity; that is to say, it is a form of belonging that seeks to advance specific political visions of life and expectations. That is why the decisive practical and theological challenge has to do with clarity about the political ends (the "toward what?") of Christian identity and, connected with that, finding ways to realize these goals within the space of other contending political goals and expectations. It now became clear to me that, since the Christian always finds herself located within other forms of belonging (nation, race, ethnicity) that claim her allegiance in pursuit of specific political goals and aims, it might be more useful to speak of Christian identity not in terms of a stable "given" or realized essence but as an ongoing journey that involves constant negotiation in relation to existing political expectations and formations. Given the prevailing tribalism through which Christians have become acculturated to live as though the bonds of race, tribe, nation, and ethnicity are more primary than the waters of baptism, a more specific conclusion was that Christian identity needs to be viewed as form of "interruption" that will always have, in the words of Sam Wells, a "certain mischievous and subversive character"[12] within the existing political, national, ethnic, or racial formations. In view of this conclusion, I saw the contemporary urgency of Paul's exhortation to the Romans, which I began to paraphrase thus:

> Brothers and sisters, do not be naïve about the politics of your nations; do not just fit within the forms of belonging as defined

---

Jesus simply one of us. For an extended critique of enculturation theology within the context of Rwanda, see Katongole, "Christianity, Tribalism and the Rwanda Genocide"; Katongole, "Of Faces of Jesus and *The Poisonwood Bible*."

12. Wells, *Improvisation*, 19. In this book, Sam Wells uses the notion of drama and performance to depict Christian life. Using Wells's characterization in this context might suggest that we learn to view Christian baptism as a note or tune—somewhat off-key, and even jarring given its strangeness—whose goal is not simply to "interrupt" the well-rehearsed symphonies of cultural and national identities but rather to reframe and point these compositions within a totally different telos, thus creating a new musical composition and performance.

by your race, ethnicity, nationality or class, but be transformed by the renewing of your minds, so that you learn to negotiate what is perfect, true and good.

Negotiating Christian Identity: Parables of a "New We"

God is determined to form a new people in the world. Baptism and the entire range of Christian practice are meant to reflect and to advance this political reality. Time, space, and occasion do not allow for a full explication of this claim, but by describing God's purpose as "political," I want to make clear that the Kingdom of God is not merely a "spiritual" reality (that dwells within the interiority of the Christian conscience) or a mystical reality that wafts above the concrete forms of everyday life and belonging. It is a real, concrete form of being in the world, of which the church is a sacrament. As a sacrament, the church is both the visible re-presentation (a kind of "demonstration plot") and a sign of (and, thus, only points to) the full reality that is yet to come. Given this sacramental nature, it is perhaps not surprising that, in the gospels, Jesus speaks about the Kingdom of God using parables.[13] Accordingly, since Christian identity is in view of the politics of the Kingdom of God, it calls for parables that are able not only to capture its reality in our time but also to illumine the opportunities and possibilities, and the tactics and skills, that are needed to negotiate the practical and social requirements of Christian identity in the context of other forms of belonging in the world. In the remaining section of this paper, let me suggest four such parables.

Ephesian Moments of a "New We"

God is determined to form a new people in the world. Christian identity seeks to create, realize, and reflect "Ephesian moments" of this movement of God in the world. Paul writes that God's purpose in Christ was to create, out of many, "one new man" (Eph 2:15), so that Jewish and Gentile Christians now share "one Spirit" (2:18), "one hope" (4:4), "one Lord, one faith, one

---

13. For Jesus, using parables was at once a modality of communication—a form of analogy, through which he tried to capture a reality that was here and yet not here—and a form of social critique. In this sense, the focus of Jesus's parables was not only a vision of the reign of God but also the gory details of the dominant structures that obscured and resisted the reign of God. For this understanding of Jesus's parables, see e.g., Herzog, *Parables as Subversive Speech*. In line with Herzog, I use "parables" here as both a form of social analysis and a form of theological reflection, as both an exercise in teleological exposition and social critique.

baptism, [as they are all children of] one God and Father of all" (4:5-6). For Paul, these are not simple "spiritual" platitudes but concrete possibilities that the Christians of Ephesus have already begun to experience and live out. Accordingly, Andrew Walls, the famed historian of world Christianity, rightly notes that the original Ephesian moment was the coming together for the first time of Jewish and Gentile Christians. It is this coming together of two communities historically separated—the breaking down of the wall of separation brought about by Christ's death (2:13-18)—that Paul celebrates in his letter to the Ephesians. Jewish and Gentile Christians are "no longer strangers and sojourners, but . . . fellow citizens" and "members of God's household" (2:19). Thus, if the letter to the Ephesians recognizes the cultural and political realities of being Jew and Gentile, this is not what Paul celebrates, but rather the fact of their "coming together"—of their being "made alive" together (2:5), of being raised up together and seated together (2:6). Jewish and Gentile Christians "belong together" as "bricks being used in the construction of a single building—the temple where the One God would live" (2:19-22). They do not constitute two separate communities but one community, of which they are both members, constituting as it were (and now Paul uses another image: the body) different parts of a single body of which "Christ is the head, the mind, the brain, under whose control the whole body works and is held together" (4:15-16).[14]

Three elements of Walls' description of the original Ephesian moment speak directly to an appreciation of Christian identity. First, involved in the Ephesian moment is the realization that, on their own, Jewish and Gentile Christians remain but "fragments" of God's purpose. Together—and only together—can the fragments come to the "very height of Christ's full stature." Thus, on our own—as American, Asian, African, White, Black, etc., Christians—we remain but "fragments." It is only by coming together that these different fragments reflect the church's maturity—the very height of Christ's full stature. Connected with this observation is the realization that the coming together of Jewish and Gentile Christians creates something new. "The full height of Christ's full stature" that Paul celebrates is about this new and odd communion of believers that is neither Jewish nor Gentile. This is what is going on in Antioch, where the term "Christian" was first used. In a unique Ephesian moment, Jews and Gentiles came together. Their coming together created a "new we" that required a new name. No one had needed such a term when they existed independently as only Jew and Gentile. Thirdly, as Walls notes, the expression and test of that coming together was the meal table: "two cultures historically separated by the meal table

---

14. Walls, "Ephesian Moment," 77.

were now able to come together at table to share the knowledge of Christ."[15] Thus, the meal table—the institution that had once symbolized the ethnic and cultural division—now became the hallmark of Christian living. It is this experience that was reproduced at Antioch, Jerusalem, and other places as "one of the most noticeable features of life in the Jesus community," for "the followers of Jesus took every opportunity to eat together."[16]

An appreciation of Christian identity in our time requires creating and finding opportunities for eating together across national, racial, tribal, and ethnic boundaries. It is these opportunities that not only "break down the dividing walls of hostility" but also create forms of catholicity that both reflect and reveal something of the "very height of Christ's full stature." It is something of the Ephesian moment that is glimpsed in the story of Fr. André Sibomana, who narrowly survived the genocide in Rwanda. In the aftermath of the genocide, he mobilized his Christians for the reconstruction of schools, public places, and houses for genocide survivors. The Christians were both Hutu and Tutsi. At the beginning, the Hutu and Tutsi did not speak to one another. But the communal work helped build bridges. At the inauguration of the first two hundred houses, on August 21, 2005, Hutu and Tutsi drank banana beer from the same jug.[17]

The Future Is Mestizo

Christian identity presses toward a Mestizo[18] existence. Nobody has captured this reality as well as Fr. Virgilio Elizondo. "The core of our existence," Elizondo writes, "is to be other," to embrace a "new identity"; it is to live "in between" cultures—neither this nor that but fully both,[19] always straining ("journeying") toward the fuller reality of a new humanity that Jesus himself represents. Speaking of his own hyphenated life as a Mexican-American and what that has taught him about the Christian identity, Elizondo writes, "Mestizos are part of both while not being exclusively either":

> Yet in neither am I ever considered one of the group. I am always both kin (at home) and foreigner at the same time. This

15. Walls, "Ephesian Moment," 78.
16. Ibid., 77.
17. Sibomana, *Hope for Rwanda*, 131–32.
18. This Spanish word was first used to describe the children of the violent encounter between European fathers and Amerindian mothers; neither European nor Indian, these children belonged to a new people, a people of mixed heritage. See Elizondo, *The Future Is Mestizo*.
19. Elizondo, *Future Is Mestizo*, 26.

"in-between" is the pain and potential, the suffering and the joy, the confusion and the mystery, the darkness and the light of Mestizo life. As I claim this ambiguity and recognize it for what it truly is, I become the bearer of a new civilization that is inclusive of all the previous ones. No longer do I carry the burden of the shameful news, but rather become the bearer of the good news of the future that has already begun in us.[20]

This in-between, far from being negative, has tremendous advantage: "I am an insider-outsider of both and thus have the ability of knowing both from within and from the outside... I can know them in ways that they can never know me or suspect. I can truly become the interlocutor who will help both to see and appreciate themselves and each other in ways they have never before suspected."[21]

Even more significantly, Elizondo notes that Mestizo is, by its very nature and origin, a radical transvaluation (to use a Nietzschean term) of all biological, cultural, and political categories, as "the mestizo 'in-between' keeps expanding as the 'frontera' keeps expanding both north and south at the same time; it keeps including more and more peoples, more ethnicities, and races."[22]

It is this future as Mestizo, as in-between, that is glimpsed in the story of the confused Hutu boy who, during the Rwandan genocide, fled to the bush with the Tutsis. After two or three weeks, the Tutsis pointed out to him that he was Hutu and so could be saved. He left the marshes and was not attacked. But the mixed-up boy had spent so much time with Tutsis in his early childhood that he was confused. He didn't know how to draw the "proper" line between ethnic groups. Afterward, when he returned to his village, he did not get involved in the killings. The *interahamwe* militias tried to force him to participate but eventually gave up on him because his mind was, in their words, "clearly overwhelmed."[23] The challenge and invitation of Christian identity in our time is about forming such confused, overwhelmed, Mestizo Christians.

Ecclesial Solidarity

Negotiating Christian identity in our time requires Christians to pursue a radical form of solidarity that cuts across national, racial, ethnic, and

20. Ibid., 129.
21. Ibid.
22. Ibid., 128–29.
23. Katongole and Wilson-Hartgrove, *Mirror to the Church*, 45–46.

cultural boundaries. Among other things, this means that Christians need to understand our membership in the Body of Christ as our primary identity. I find Michael Budde's characterization of this notion of "ecclesial solidarity" quite illuminating. Christians, Budde writes, need to think of themselves as joined first and foremost to one another, and only secondarily, or derivatively, to other corporate claimants on their affections and allegiances.

> When Christians take ecclesial solidarity as their starting point for discernment—political, economic, liturgical, and otherwise—it makes them members of a community broader than the largest nation-state, more pluralistic than any culture in the world, more deeply rooted in the lives of the poor and marginalized than any revolutionary movement, more capable of exemplifying the notion of *e pluribus unum* than any empire past, present, or future. Seeing oneself as a member of the worldwide body of Christ invites communities to join their local stories to other stories of sin and redemption, sacrifice and martyrdom, rebellion and forgiveness unlike any other on offer via allegiance to one's tribe, gendered movements, or class fragment.[24]

The fact that the suggestion of ecclesial identity as primary identity may today strike many as strange just goes to confirm the extent to which modern political allegiances have succeeded in fragmenting the body of Christ along national, racial, and ethnic forms of belonging, thereby helping perpetuate the "spiritualization" of Christian baptism and identity, and making it impossible to counteract the reproduction of tribalism in its many current forms. This development, however, is a recent (modern) one. For, as Budde notes,

> The earliest Christians would have found nothing exceptional in the idea of "ecclesial solidarity." Early Christians saw themselves, and were seen by others, as more than just a new "religious" group, more than a new idea unleashed in the ancient world, and more than a voluntary club like other social groupings of associations . . . Early Christians were more often seen as part of a new ethnic group, even a new race of people, in the Roman world.[25]

Moreover, this new race was unique because not only was it able to redefine Roman notions of race as fixed identity but also because becoming part of this new race or ethnic community was available to all regardless

---

24. Budde, *Borders of Baptism*, 4.
25. Ibid., 7. See also Buell, *Why This New Race?*, 2–3.

of their communities or identities of origin. "Conversion" was the process through which one became a member of this new race. That is why, within this context, conversion is best seen "not as a private matter of individual conscience resulting in an individual's affiliation with a religious movement, but explicitly as becoming a member of a people, with collective and public consequences."[26]

It is this kind of "solidarity"—membership into a new people, drawn from but much deeper than any nation, race, tribe, or ethnicity—that is glimpsed in the story of the Muslim Nyamirambo community. In his account of the Rwandan genocide, Gérard Prunier contrasts the widespread involvement of Christian churches in the genocide with the case of the Muslim community on the outskirts of Kigali: "The only community that was able to provide a bulwark against barbarity for its adherents was Islam. There are many testimonies to the protection of members the Muslim community gave each other, and their refusal to divide themselves ethnically."[27] There might have been many reasons for the solidarity that this community exhibited. One reason I find particularly telling is quite powerful in illuminating the ecclesial solidarity that being a Christian ought to be about, but at which the church often fails. The solidarity of the Muslim community, Prunier notes, came from the fact that "being Muslim in Rwanda, where Muslims are a very small (0.2 percent) proportion of the population, is not simply a choice dictated by religion: it is a global identity choice. Muslims are often marginal people and this reinforces a strong sense of community identification, which supersedes ethnic tags, something the majority Christians have not been able to achieve."[28]

A Living Sacrifice

Negotiating Christian identity calls for postures of resistance against modern forms of tribalism, and therefore the willingness to offer one's body as a "living sacrifice." In the opening words of the section of Paul's letter to the Romans to which we have already pointed, Paul appeals to the Romans: "Therefore, I urge you, brothers and sisters, in view of God's mercy, to offer your bodies as a living sacrifice, holy and pleasing to God—this is your true and proper worship" (Rom 12:1). It is this kind of courage and sacrifice to which the story of Sr. Félicité Niyitegeka of Gisenyi bears witness. A Hutu nun aged about sixty, Sr. Félicité Niyitegeka was the director

26. Budde, *Borders of Baptism*, 8.
27. Prunier, *Rwanda Crisis*, 253.
28. Ibid.

of an orphanage, the Centre Sainte-Pierre in Gisenyi. She sheltered refugees during the genocide. When her brother, a colonel in the Rwandan army, instructed her to leave to escape being killed, she wrote the following letter to him:

> Thank you for wanting to help me. I would rather die than abandon the forty-three persons for whom I am responsible. Pray for us, that we may come to God. Say "goodbye" to our old mother and our brother. When I come to God, I shall pray for you. Keep well. Thank you for thinking of me. If God saves us, as we hope, we shall see each other tomorrow. Yours, Sr. Félicité Niyitegeka.[29]

Sr. Félicité and her sisters continued to shelter refugees and save others by helping them across the borders. When the militia arrived on April 21, they transported the remaining Tutsis together with Sr. Félicité and her sisters to an already prepared mass grave. They shot to death more than twenty refugees and six of the sisters, leaving Sr. Félicité for last. "I have no reason to live," she said, "now that you have killed all my sisters." The militia leader asked her to pray for him before he shot her.

Conclusion

It is stories like these that point to what it means to think theologically about identity, allegiance, and being a Christian, which, as my analysis here shows, is about learning to live in a way that defies tribalism in its many forms. The stories illumine the form and shape of Christian baptism as incorporation into a new social reality, a new form of belonging to a community that extends beyond boundaries of time and geography, of ethnicity, race, and nationality, and even beyond terrestrial and celestial boundaries. For it was only by locating herself as a member of this "new we" that includes those who have already gone before us that Sr. Félicité was willing to offer her body, knowing that her life is not wasted but is gathered up as a fragrant offering, a living sacrifice, holy and pleasing to God. That she willingly accepted death rather than surrender the refugees is an indication that, throughout her life, in her calling and serving, she was able to understand herself as already a member of that immense crowd, the "multitude that no one could count, drawn from every nation, tribe, people, and language, standing before the throne and before the Lamb" (Rev 7:9). Her story, just like the other stories,

---

29. Shorter, *Christianity and the African Imagination*, 13. See also J. Martin, *This Our Exile*, 188.

is both the argument and evidence that Christian identity is not merely a mystical or spiritual reality, but a concrete, historical, and social reality that has been made possible through the death and resurrection of Christ. Moreover, it is these kinds of stories or parables that point to what it means—and how exactly one might be able—to heed Paul's exhortation to the Roman Christians: "Do not conform yourself to this age, but be transformed by the renewal of your mind, that you may discern what is the will of God, what is good and acceptable and perfect." Only by developing the relevant mental capacities and categories and the concomitant skills of living in the world in a manner consistent with our new identity as God's new people will we be able to resist the pervasive forms of modern tribalism, for which the Rwandan genocide is a metaphor, and thus show that the waters of baptism run deeper than the blood of tribalism.

2

Thinking Theologically about Identities, Allegiances, and Discipleship

DORIAN LLYWELYN, SJ

Theology, in the classic Anselmian definition, is faith in search of understanding. In other words, it is the work of seeking, rationally and responsibly, to make sense not only of one's prime Christian commitment but also of the world in which that faith is lived. In the task of thinking theologically about identities, allegiances, and discipleship, the stress falls ineluctably on the search rather than the answer. In these unwieldy and tangled matters, any claims to a Grand Unified Theory are likely to be hubristic.

Discipleship involves *inter alia* receiving and owning an identity that has aspects that are inseparably—though distinctively—individual and collective. (Tertullian's famous dictum *solus Christianus, nullus Christianus* comes to mind.) The conscious owning and appropriation of that identity indicates that being a Christian is also an allegiance, a free choice to take up responsibilities. All of that is to say that the three categories of identity, allegiance, and discipleship are profoundly interrelated and indeed can all be broadly construed under the category of relationship or, to speak in theological patois, *koinonia*. The complexities, challenges, and gifts of that relationship have to do with the relative importance and claims on us of other aspects of our identity—including culture, family, gender, sexual orientation, nationality, politics, economics, social class, and ideological bents—and the relative possibility of integrating them with who we are as Christians.

En route to Auschwitz in 2006, Benedict XVI told reporters, "We must always learn that we are Catholic, and thus that one's nationality is inserted, relativized, and also carefully located in the great unity of the Catholic communion."[1] For "nationality," one could also substitute many other forms of identity and allegiance. Pope Benedict's statement raises two questions, respectively epistemological and ethical: first, *how* to understand and evaluate these forms of being and concomitant stances before the world, and from there, how to "insert, relativize and carefully locate" them in one's own life as well as in the Catholic communion.

The initial description of the conference at which this paper was originally given stated somewhat restrainedly that integrating "multiple and overlapping communities of belonging [with] . . . unity in Christ" is "far from obvious." Responding to the complex influence of global patterns in our contemporary context appears to demand a dauntingly large application of theological imagination. Where might we begin? Any number of places in Scripture and theological tradition might offer themselves as a starting point for an ethics of identity or allegiance. However, to begin with ethics would be to attempt to answer "how should we be?" before thinking about "who are we?" To reference the old Irish joke, "If I were you, I wouldn't start from here."

The Problematics of Identity

In fact, even before thinking theologically—let alone ethically—about identity, it is worth considering the identity of identity. The question is, of course, an ancient philosophical topos. There is broad consensus, at least in the mainstream of Western thought, that there exists such a thing as personal identity, even if agreeing on a list of its essential ingredients is a harder task. Part of that difficulty derives from different disciplinary perspectives. There exist vast libraries of scholarly writing on the theme, in which philosophers, psychologists, social scientists, historians, anthropologists, as well as theologians all have significant investments, while "identity" has also entered the lexicon of popular psychology. Different academic dialects and registers do not employ the term in the same manner and are also likely to be based on a variety of lurking and silent anthropological presuppositions. In fact, for theology, dialogue with other perspectives on the topic of identity is especially difficult due to the fact that it is not a native theological category. "Person" is, however, an indigenous theological term, which at least allows the possibility of thinking theologically about "personal identity." (The category "social identity," however, presents some challenges for theological thought, as this article will argue below.)

---

1. Quoted in Llywelyn, *Toward a Catholic Theology*, 16.

Clearly, in the Judeo-Christian imaginary, to be a person is to be an image and likeness of God. My clone and I would be different persons, even if we shared identical DNA. Even if, in parallel universes, we occupied the same physical space and shared the exact same thoughts and experiences, we would not share the same identity. To be a person is to be gifted with a uniqueness and unrepeatability that is more than physical or psychological, but which exists at the most profound level of being.

One obvious way of defining identity, whether personal or social, is by way of differentiation and contrast: to be X is not-Y, to be me is to be not-you, to be a Democrat is to be not-Republican. And from that negative concept of identity derives a relative, negative ethics: because I am X, I don't do Y-things. However, potential problems swarm if we attempt to theologize identity in this privative sense as our primary lens. Human identity in Christian terms cannot be fundamentally an identity-by-difference, a not-being. This is especially true for Christian identity: we are saved by Christ, rather than not-damned, and primarily saved *for* rather than saved *from*. Nor is that religious identity something that is ultimately contingent on our moral action or choice. Rather, the freedom belongs to God, and the identity is God's gift, bestowed on us in our baptism that conforms us to Christ, in the Church. Where human action is called upon, however, is in appropriating that identity, the work of freely building our allegiance to Christ. That certainly includes rejecting all other claims on our ultimate loyalty, but this is also, once again, a positive stance: the choice for Christ that brings in its train turning away from everything that is spiritually inauthentic and re-ordering our attitudes to and use of everything that is not God, so that we may serve and love him in all things.[2]

A second popular definition of identity is conformity to a set of defining characteristics. Hispanic identity, for example, would be defined by one's having a Spanish name and browner skin and speaking Spanish. Clearly, attention to questions of power demands noting a number of things here: who compiles that set of characteristics and who is excluded from that process; which characteristics are held to be primary and which secondary; and not least, the degree of historical variation and evolution that is admitted.

The doyen of nationality studies, Anthony D. Smith, notes two broad approaches in the study of ethnic identity. A "Heraclitean" approach focuses on the emergence and dissolution of ethnic identity. "Parmenidean" sensibilities, on the other hand, give weight to those unchanging cultural aspects

---

2. See Ignatius of Loyola, "Principle and Foundation," no. 23.

that identify particular human groups—their religion, way of life, language and communal memories, values, and territory.³

Heraclitean skepticism raises important questions for Parmenidean essentialism. In multicultural societies in particular, individual and social identities build on characteristics that are necessarily fluid and tend toward the fragmented: if someone, for example, does not speak Spanish, or is Jewish, or has a Japanese mother and a Chilean mother, is she still Hispanic, or less authentically Hispanic? Personal identity can be navigated and negotiated almost by the minute, according to the most salient characteristic: depending on context, a person may variously think of herself—or be thought of—as a Filipina, a mestiza, a vegetarian, a sister, a judge, a Catholic.

In practice, the more culturally heterogeneous a society, the more the question of identity becomes convoluted. One's sense of self, and how one wishes to be categorized by others, becomes a matter that shouts out for political attention—and gets it. A *self*-identity (the notion of identity frequently employed in popular discourse) is, in effect, an identity-by-individual-choice. Despite his white mother, President Obama has reputedly "checked only the racial box that says: 'Black, African Am., or Negro.'"⁴ The overlapping senses of identity of the postmodern denizen of a globalized world may also be potentially conflictive. I may hold two passports and have two native languages. But will someone perceive me as fully American if I am Muslim?⁵ Can someone be Catholic in her religious identity and, at the same time, Buddhist in cultural identity?⁶ Such personal questions require careful consideration, and their importance increases by geometrical progression when the personal becomes communal and political.

In the specific case of Christian identity, the logical problem with identity-by-essential-characteristics is that if all (or most) As are Bs, or if they do B things, the reverse is not necessarily true. Typically "Christian" characteristics such as love, joy, peace, patience, kindness, generosity, faithfulness, gentleness, and self-control (Gal 5:22–24) also abound among non-Christians, from atheists to Zoroastrians. Clearly, there do exist defining characteristics of what it is to be Christian—faith in Christ being the most nonnegotiable. But within Christianity as outside it, defining what characteristics constitute an identity is problematic. A *longue durée* historical perspective shows Heraclitean flow as well as Parmenidean stability. Moreover,

---

3. Smith, *Ethnic Origins*, 207.
4. Avila, "Obama's Census-Form Choice."
5. See, for example, Yazbeck Haddad, *Not Quite American?*
6. This would be, broadly speaking, a claim for "multiple religious belonging." See Phan, "Multiple Religious Belonging."

what are characteristic elements of an identity may not necessarily be essential ones. It is, after all, possible to be Catholic in one's allegiance and identity without a strong personal devotion to the Virgin Mary.

Mass v. Count

The title of this paper refers to identit*ies*, in the plural. Whether one speaks of identity or identities is not an innocent question, and it is also a potential tare among the wheat. The mass noun "identity" is a universal: it suggests an essential unity that has a potentially limitless subhierarchy of related expressions of the one foundational identity. The claim that, along with one faith and one baptism, there is one Christian identity, however, carries a potential virus: that of conflating unity with uniformity, of identifying one expression of Christian life as the overarching model for all. At the opposite pole, where identity is used as a count noun—as in the plural "identities"—questions of diversity, difference, pluralism, and antihierarchical taxonomy occupy our attention. The concomitant danger is fragmentation into atomized identities, which champions particularity at the expense of commonality. There, we would have only Christianities, Catholicisms, and discipleships. The provocative title of Bart D. Ehrman's *Lost Christianities: The Battles for Scripture and the Faiths We Never Knew* emphasizes above all difference, context, pluralism, and subjective viewpoints. It challenges, moreover, not only the hierarchy of ideas and doctrinal orthodoxy but also their very possibility. In a contemporary expression of the ancient "the one and the many" question, Ehrman claims that the diversity of contemporary Christian practice renders it "difficult to know whether we should speak of Christianity as one thing or lots of things, whether we should speak of Christianity or Christianities."[7] At the same time, he refers, nonetheless, to "forms of Christianity," and "varieties of ancient Christianity," a plurality he champions under a modern value-concept of "diversity." Clearly, from a Catholic point of view that sees Christianity as essentially one faith, such thinking does not easily convince.

Overemphasis on either front—unilateral insistence on unity or difference—leads too easily to disengagement from the mission of unity that involves making, or making manifest, loving relationship. Logically, the practice of *koinonia*, which seeks to integrate difference harmoniously, requires that there be difference to resolve. Hence, it seems obvious that Christian identity, whether personal or collective, does require the existence of a variety of other embodiments of that same identity. On the other hand,

---

7. Ehrman, *Lost Christianities*, 1.

there has to be some normative essence of Christian discipleship lest individual expressions of Christian allegiance—personal or collective—become so idiosyncratic as to make even the idea of unity impossible.

First Persons

Another complication in the consideration of identity comes from an important semantic slippage. Identity has both individual and social aspects, but we should not assume that they function in the same way. What is true of me is not necessarily true of us, or vice versa, and if it happens to be true, then it is not necessarily true in the same way or to the same degree. The term "social identity" is misleadingly ambiguous. As my birth, upbringing, and language are Welsh—and those realities are part of how I think, feel, and interact with others—then it seems cogent to claim that my social identity is Welsh. However, when the category "social identity" is used collectively to apply to whole groups of people, such as ethnic communities or nations, it often has another meaning, one that is related but also distinct. It is the idea that there is such a thing as X-ness (manliness, for example), a diachronic and diatopic essence that would be found in various degrees in the individuals who currently compose a particular polity, yet which at the same time would not be radically dependent on them for its existence. In other words, this notion of social identity posits a collective "us" that is different from and more than the current sum of its parts. I have suggested above that some of the secular academic uses of the term "identity" can be broadly approximated to the Christian notion of "person," which allows us to treat "individual personal identity" as a theological category. However, what is harder by far is to come up with a theologically responsible way of talking about the second, collective sense of social identity. In most Christian theology, a person is an individual human being, not a collective. Theologizing about collective social identity—the identity of groups of people *as groups*—is no easy task.[8]

One can argue, of course, that there is one exception: in Scripture, dogma, and doctrine, quasi-personal identity is effectively attributed to the Church. Ecclesiological metaphors for the Church include collective images ("the people of God"), individual terms ("the Bride of Christ, the sacrament

---

8. There exist many historical studies of the interrelation between religious and other collective identities (e.g., Grosby, *Biblical Ideas of Nationality*; Barker, *Religious Nationalism in Modern Europe*), as well as on Christianity and cultural identity (e.g., Loades and Walsh, *Faith and Identity*; Hutchison and Lehmann, *Many Are Chosen*; Myhill, *Language, Religion, and National Identity*). In Catholic theology, however, the topic seems to have been studied as a subset of theological ethics or political theology.

of salvation"), and epithets that combine both individuality and collectivity ("the body of Christ"). The Church is indeed different from the sum of its constituent parts, yet exists in and as them. Murkier by far—for doctrinal and political reasons—is the attribution of collective personhood to other social groups, such as clerisy or empire. Does the term "Christian nation" mean, for example, anything more than the fact that most of a nation's members profess Christianity? Following Prince Vladimir's conversion in 988, the inhabitants of Kievan Rus' accepted Christianity, an event referred to in Russian religious literature as "the baptism of Rus.'" If this is merely an extravagant poetic trope, no damage is done. However, by its very nature, a metaphor tends to be slippery, holding in tension two realities each of which tends to want to de-metaphoricize it, dragging imagery into the orbit of literalism. If "the Baptism of Rus" is taken to suggest that this mass conversion wrought an ontological change in the Russian nation—conforming it to Christ, prophet, priest and king, and turning it into a "kingdom of priests, a holy nation"—then the specter of politico-religious national messianism begins to take chilling form. Much then depends—doctrinally and politically—on how metaphorical the metaphor of "social identity" is.

Theseus's Ship on Heraclitus's River

Individual personal identity combines fluidity with fixity. My body looks radically different than it did thirty years ago, but I experience myself as fundamentally the same "me" as that younger man. Theologically speaking, each of us is still the same person that we became when sperm met egg. However, the interplay of continuity and change does not necessarily play out in the same way in the matter of collective identities. The ancient conundrum of the ship of Theseus relates how, over the course of years, that venerable ship was gradually replaced, plank by plank, until nothing of the original parts remained. Was it or was it not still Theseus's ship?[9] In theological parlance, a communal personal identity such as a nation or a religious group might be called a *traditio*, meaning something handed on for safekeeping. Tradition, in Catholic theology, is both the static content of what is received and handed on, and the dynamic act of reception and transmission. Understood in this way, a sociocultural *traditio* both shapes and is shaped by individuals. It also depends on them for its continuance: being the last of the Mohicans effectively means the end of Mohican being. In this way, individual identities and collective ones, and the social and individual aspects of personal identity, cannot really be radically separated: there be-

---

9. Plutarch, *Lives*, 49.

ing a "me" implies that there is also an "us," and vice versa. Discipleship involves inseparable identification with allegiance to fellow humans as well as to God.

Being a Christian is not only a question of who and what one is, but also how one is. Ontology begets ethics. The specific *modus operandi* of Christian identity is faith, which can be rendered as "loyalty" or "allegiance," or how one lives in relationship-to. It is self-evident that the ancient Mediterranean world gave far more weight to the sphere of the communal, the collective, and the social than is common in our post-Kantian Western context. For practical reasons at the least, personal survival meant being dependent and belonging to others. Only through being rooted—and especially through being perceived by others as being rooted—in extended family, kin group, and place of origin could one find a place within the warp and weft of the wider society. In that world, without an "us," the self would be sorely diminished: the most vulnerable among all the *anawim* were such people as widows or lepers who were de-connected from the social mainstream.

But Jesus also replaced the cultural sovereignty of family and clan solidarity with belonging to the new, eschatological community of his disciples.[10] In the ancient Mediterranean world, gathering a following was a common occurrence. A group that gathers for a specific common enterprise for a limited time is referred to by some social scientists as a "coalition."[11] Jesus, however, is a founder of a "faction," one specific kind of coalition that focuses on a leader who has a grievance and who gathers around him others—"followers" or "disciples"—who share that grievance and who give him their fealty.

Loyalty, commitment, and solidarity are the cluster of values that Jesus invites his followers to embrace. Primarily, of course, these virtues should be directed to the God of Israel. Jesus himself is praised for his loyalty to God (Heb 3:1–3) and obedience to him (Heb 5:8). But Jesus also demanded allegiance to himself and his project. It is worth pausing to consider the fact that the word "allegiance" has its distant etymological roots in a Germanic term for "serf." Time spent with Jesus results in seeking to live like Jesus, in the company of others who desire to do the same. Being one of Jesus's faction involves serving God in serving others.

Matters of service and community raise the central matter of the relationship between Christian identity and those other loyalties that may also demand solidarity and commitment. The renunciations of family bonds demanded by Jesus do not so much reject other kinds of claims on the hearts

---

10. See Mark 12:50; Matt 19:29; Luke 14:26.
11. See Duling, "Recruitment to the Jesus Movement."

and minds of disciples as relativize them: the Jesus event does not necessarily destroy other forms of identity and allegiance. As the *Epistle to Diognetus* famously states, "Christians are indistinguishable from other men either by nationality, language, or customs. They do not inhabit separate cities of their own, or speak a strange dialect, or follow some outlandish way of life . . . They pass their days upon earth, but they are citizens of heaven."[12] Aquinas's dictum that "grace builds on nature"[13] should warn us away from a reactive, pessimistic *fuga mundi* espoused by many forms of Christianity over the millennia. Instead, it invites us to live in a certain tension with the world in which tares and wheat grow together.

The tension between Christian discipleship vis-à-vis other allegiances and forms of identity touches on some very foundational theological considerations. Paul reminds the Philippians that "our citizenship is in heaven." But at the same time that the Prologue to the Gospel of John teaches that "the world did not know him," it also affirms that the Word "made his dwelling among us." Christians cannot, of course, reject *à parti pris* other human relationships and institutions. The fact that God has forbidden us to worship the things of this world—including our own nations, cultures, and communities—does not mean that we may not love them. Rather, our creed demands that Catholics practice judicious discernment about how we engage with our other communities of belonging.

Trinity: The Real Value of Real Diversity

A foundational tension in being a Catholic Christian "in encounter with institutions that form politically salient loyalties and identities in the modern and postmodern world"[14] derives from the very order of creation. Humans are made in the image and likeness of the Triune God. As an earthy creature—*adam* (man) made out of *adamah* (earth)[15]—infused with the breath of God, the proto-human has in himself something both of this world and of the world of heaven.

Trinitarian considerations lend themselves not only to explaining that tension but also to living it well: there is a direct correspondence between how we construe the inner life of God and our ideals of human relationship.

---

12. *Epistle to Diognetus*, 5.1–2, 9, cited in Davies, *Gospel and the Land*, 368.

13. Aquinas, *Summa Theologiae* 1–2.3.

14. "The Borders of Baptism: Multiple Belongings." See project description online: http://events.depaul.edu/event/opening_plenary_the_borders_of_baptism_multiple_belongings_of_transnational_processes_of_catholic_formation#.V4QJ21f722o.

15. Gen 2:7.

There is real distinction of persons: Father, Son, and Holy Spirit are not merely modes of being, nor are they parts of God. There is also a unity of love and being between those persons. The standard patristic opinion derived from Augustine is that, within the Trinity, it is the loving, self-giving relationship between the persons that constitutes them as persons. At the same time, Father, Son, and Holy Spirit must each be endowed with something that belongs to that person alone, in order that it may be freely communicated to the other two persons. The *primum analogatum* of this is the human experience of giving and receiving love, an act that requires selfhood, in order that one's self may be freely shared with others and unity nurtured. If human relationships are to be rooted in justice, and if the Trinity is the supreme model of loving, then the existence of an identity that is real in and of itself (rather than one that is merely privative) is a logical prerequisite to both justice and charity. There is a Trinitarian corollary to the legal principle of *nemo dat quod non habet*, which is "if you've got it, love demands that you share it."

Naturally, the domestic arrangements of the Trinity are beyond our experience or capacity to understand totally, but the notion that the Trinity is the source and model of the Church is theologically uncontroversial. Within God, there is identity of nature: all persons are fully and co-equally divine. The ecclesial implications are practical and immediate. The Spanish proverb goes, "Dime con quién andas y te diré quién eres": tell me whom you keep company with, and I'll tell you who you are. In other words, community reflects and makes identity. I would like to expand the application of the Trinitarian model of loving—in Bishop Zizioulas's phrase, "being-as-communion"[16]—beyond the confines of the Church, and to propose it as the model for all kinds of relationship that seek to combine legitimately diverse and autonomous elements with an essential unity. Where such difference is practiced as Trinitarian communion, it strengthens the distinctive identities of the partners, rather than vitiating them.

If self-giving love is demanded of all humans, as images and likenesses of God, then it has to be required *a fortiori* of Christians. Jesus prays to the Father for his disciples that "they may be one, as we are one."[17] Love requires both someone to give it and a recipient. Nothing in Scripture suggests that love can and should be practiced between individuals alone. If Trinitarian love, involving communion of uniqueness of persons, is to be practiced by individual Christians, then it can and indeed should be also practiced by Christians collectively, who will be known and recognized as Christians

16. Zizioulas, *Being as Communion*. Particularly relevant to this topic are chs. 1–2.
17. John 17:11.

(our social identity) because of that love. This logic suggests the necessity of there being such a thing as a collective Christian being, something as incarnated in all individual Christians who are currently alive, yet which is not radically dependent on them for its being. In Catholic terms, that someone is the Church, the object of whose charity can and should include other communities of identity belonging as well as individuals.

However, employing the Trinity in this way, as the ideal model of love, is limited by one important reason: there is a significant difference between being within the Trinity and being as it occurs within creation. In the Trinity, being and self-giving are the same thing. In the world, this is not so. Within the Trinity, the existence of the persons is always dependent on each other. In the order of creation, each of us is certainly morally and practically dependent on other people. Aquinas, following Aristotle's *Politics*, asserts that human community is not only a practical need, but also a prerequisite of human flourishing.[18] However, no person or social group is dependent for her or its very being on the existence of any other person or social group. Own lives are not *ontologically* dependent on anyone else's.

But being Christian is a moral process as well as an ontological state. Even though we are limited as creatures in how we can mirror the interior life of the Creator, our mission is nonetheless to become more like the Trinity. It is important to continue to insist that Trinitarian doctrine has significant practical implications when it comes to living out our other identities and allegiances as Catholics. Discipleship is made in the crucible that marries universal brotherhood with individual personhood. In the Church, diversities between persons and groups are the concrete opportunity and the raw material of the building blocks of the body of Christ. That tension inheres in the Church itself, at an individual level: "the very differences which the Lord has willed to put between the members of his Body serve its unity and mission."[19] But that same potential for unity and disunity exists in the Church's very DNA, in the relationship between the Church and the churches. It is out of the particular churches "that the one and unique Catholic Church exists."[20]

The coincidence of opposites—unity of nature and difference of persons—exemplified par excellence in the metaphysics of the Trinity, presents itself as the ideal of a series of analogous relationships, secular as well as religious: between individuals and the Church; between individuals and any given society; between local (or even separated) churches and the Church;

---

18. See Aquinas, *On Law, Morality, and Politics*, 282–83.
19. *Catechism*, 873.
20. Paul VI, *Lumen Gentium*, 23.

and between the various kinds of social organizations and the community of humankind. In each of these binaries, difference and unity should balance each other. *Should*, rather than *do*, for each of them offers the serious possibility of violent discord as well as harmony. Within the immanent Trinity, the diversity of persons and the undivided unity of the divine nature inhere in each other, as co-absolute and co-implicating principles. In the world, although diversity and unity are proximate values, each being equally subordinate to salvation, they are also perennially susceptible to seeking to become ends in themselves. A myopic overemphasis on either diversity or unity will destroy the possibility of healthy equilibrium between the two. When particularity degenerates into particularism, the individual elements become autonomous and solipsistic, and communication between people or ideas that are different from each other is avoided or rendered impossible. At the other pole, where there is no or little distinction between the parts, loving respect is also precluded; there is no freedom to love when there is no real other.

The exemplars of these two dangers are many. One of the neuralgic points of questions of nationality, for example, concerns the relationship of particularity to universality. Both political and cultural forms of nationalism champion particularity, belonging, and distinctiveness.[21] Yet, giving a disproportionate stress on the cultural uniqueness of a nation can render unity with other societies impossible. Conversely, where unity is confused with uniformity, the value of diversity will be downplayed or not recognized. Politically, forms of disunity include aggressive patriotism and claims of ethnocultural superiority. At the other extreme, social homogenization has many faces: totalitarian, imperialist, and colonialist. Within the Church, forms of atomization include heresies and schisms, as well as claims of special divine election. On the other side, history shows many attempts at the centralization of ecclesial power and responsibility, including the drive to standardize religious practice to such a degree that there is little room for expressing particular cultural identities in a world Church. In all of these situations of potential deviancy, love patterned on the Trinity will obviate the twin extremes of fragmentation and homogenization.

Within the Trinity, distinct persons and identical nature coincide to complement each other. Analogously, we can argue that individual societies (including nations) require the existence of the larger principle of the universal destiny of all created things lest they become ends in themselves. On the other hand, in order that the large and abstract ideals that universal

---

21. The philosophical roots of the drive to particularism are explored in Vincent, *Nationalism and Particularity*.

principles represent—"the call of the Gospel to form communities of discipleship across human borders and divisions . . . [and] the unity in Christ effected in baptism and sustained by the Eucharist"[22]—may become incarnated, they must be expressed in the particular, the specific, the local, and the temporal: these are the very arenas where our "natural" identities and allegiances—with all their tremendous emotional, volitional, and political heft, their potential blessings as well as their limitations—must coexist with our religious hearts and minds.

Son of God and Son of Mary

Person and nature, the key terms that express difference and unity within God, are of course also the building bricks of Christology. In the christological debates of the early centuries, Christian thinkers struggled to answer not so much "who do you say I am?" but "what do we say he is?" Pressing practical issues forced the impassioned debates: how people understand who and what Jesus is has direct effects on how we construe our discipleship, our other commitments, and the relationship between the two.

A brief recap on the question of social identity is useful at this point. As images of the Trinity, we are made for communion: *solus homo, nullus homo*. If we believe that Jesus is fully human, then we have to consider *his* social identity, the role of *his* political, cultural, and religious identities in the Incarnation.[23] From there, we can proceed to look at the role of our political, cultural, and religious identities in the scheme of salvation.[24]

Clearly, Jesus's life and death cannot be understood apart from his own social, political, religious, and cultural context—but there is something greater here than mere exegesis. According to the popular patristic adage, "what was not taken up was not healed," that is, Jesus's human nature—we might argue, his human identity—was part of the Incarnation. But we cannot take that to mean that our salvation requires us to be first-century Palestinian Jews, especially since, in Christ, there is "neither Jew nor Greek, neither slave nor free person, there is not male and female" (Gal 3:28). In the Incarnation, what is "taken up" and brought into unity with Jesus's divinity

---

22. "The Borders of Baptism: Multiple Belongings."

23. See Meier's series, *A Marginal Jew*.

24. Two important studies of early Christian attitudes about social identity are Grosby, "Early Christianity and Second-Century Judaism," and Buell, *Why This New Race?*

is all that is constitutively human. That includes both sociocultural and individual aspects of personal identity.[25]

A parallel with Jesus's gender and our own might help clarify the implications of this for Christian anthropology. Gender, like sociocultural identity, is a marker of real humanity.[26] Despite there being in Christ "neither male nor female," neither Incarnation, nor baptism, nor redemption eradicates our—or Jesus's own—gender.[27] Although Jesus was male, the Incarnation surely did not happen "for us *men* and our salvation" alone. Rather, what is changed by the Christ event is the significance of gender in the order of salvation: the Incarnation both affirms yet transcends the importance of gender. The same re-signification, I would argue, has to be true for sociocultural identities and allegiances.

Pope Benedict called for "relativizing" nationality within the Catholic communion. But do the Incarnation, the Paschal Mystery, and the presence of the Spirit in the world and Church—and the Christian discipleship that is their consequence—do anything to our other identities and allegiances apart from relativize them? Gregory of Nazianzus expands the insight of Athanasius and others ("what is not assumed is not healed") to affirm that what is united to Jesus's divinity is healed.[28] What might "healing" other identities and allegiances involve? If indeed "grace builds on nature and perfects it," then intimacy with God does not negate or destroy anything of our God-given human nature. Being a disciple may involve choosing to abandon our natural attachments. It certainly involves tempering them, or "locating them and carefully inserting" them in our membership of the Church catholic. But it cannot involve necessarily abandoning them as a universal, *sine qua non* prerequisite, were that even possible. Rather, grace elevates, purifies, brings order where there was disorder, and leads to completion. The transformation involved in *theosis* comes about when divine grace harnesses human effort: grace opens and invites into relationship, through our free, careful, and loving response to the gift of God, and seeks the integral conversion of *all* aspects of one's being (Ps 103:1). If we agree that "no phenomenon of the finite reality of this world, including human beings, is appropriately understood so long as it is seen apart from its relationship to God,"[29] then the command of the Shema to "love the Lord, our God, with

---

25. For a more detailed discussion of this, see Llywelyn, *Toward a Catholic Theology*, ch. 4.

26. A point famously made in Steinberg, *Sexuality of Christ*.

27. *Pace* Mark 12:25 and parallels, and Matt 19:12.

28. Gregory of Nazianzus, *Epistle 101*.

29. Pannenberg, *Human Nature*, 50.

our whole hearts, and with our whole being, and with our whole strength" surely includes all aspects of our identity and all our natural loyalties.

Concretely, how might Christians respond to other forms of identity and belonging, particularly when these are potentially inimical to discipleship? If Christ is the perfect human, then it is to Christ that we must look for the answer. A rough Christo-normative proposal such as I am making here involves moving rapidly through several centuries of history of dogma. At the Council of Chalcedon in 451, the gathered bishops proclaimed as orthodoxy faith in "one and the same Son, our Lord Jesus Christ, one in being with the Father in his divinity, and one in being with us in his humanity... one and the same Christ... to be acknowledged in two natures, *inconfusedly, unchangeably, indivisibly, inseparably*. The union between those two natures by no means does away with the distinction between them; rather, the property of each nature is preserved and comes together in one Person."[30] The famous four Chalcedonian adverbs were directly targeted at heterodox Christologies. *Inconfusedly* was a whack across the nose of Arianism, which held that Jesus was a semidivine creation of God. *Unchangeably* refutes the monophysite notion that, in the Incarnation, Jesus's human interiority was absorbed into his divinity, or else by a human nature unlike ours. *Indivisibly* refutes Nestorianism, which tended to envisage the body as containing two persons, human and divine, with no more than a moral link between them at best. *Inseparably* corrects the Docetist belief that Jesus's divinity became unhinged from his body at the time of his suffering.

Chalcedon's language is abstruse. But its ideas about the "how" of the union of the divine and the human in Jesus serve as one useful map of congruity between many other related binaries: grace and nature; eternity and historicity; the universal and the local; transcendence and immanence; faith and culture; psychology and spirituality; belonging to Christ and belonging to the world; and love of God and love of neighbor. The analogues for the views Chalcedon seeks to correct are, therefore, legion. However, rather than suggesting in this article precisely how the Church might "respect and celebrate the diversity of its members—many nations, cultures and communities—while maintaining a coherent witness to the Kingdom of God that is not undermined by more parochial ideologies or priorities,"[31] I am going to propose, along the lines of the four Chalcedonian adverbs, all of them negative as they are, how *not* to do this.

The problem with Nestorianism is its implications for salvation. If Jesus did not fully take on the human condition, it is hard to see how humans

---

30. Denzinger, *Enchiridion symbolorum*, 301–2.
31. "The Borders of Baptism: Multiple Belongings."

could ever reach intimacy with God. A semidivine savior could only bring about semi-salvation. A "confused" Arian Christology takes analogous form in those homogenized socioreligious identities where Christian and other loyalties are mashed up into something that is less than the sum of its parts, such as integrist Catholicism, religious nationalisms, or the forms of "civil religion," in which the Church functions as state, or the state plays at being church. Such *tertium quid* positions are often, too, the discrete substrate of those positions that reduce redemption to political liberation,[32] or faith to its expression as social justice. In such cases, the resulting position tends toward diminution of the fullness of salvation: the underlying conviction of Arianism is reticence about the degree of God's action in the world and his willingness to enter into the human condition. "Quasi-Arian" projects do not respond to the otherness of the Kingdom that is not of this world. At the same time that we remember that "the joys and the hopes, the griefs and the anxieties of the men of this age, especially those who are poor or in any way afflicted . . . are the joys and hopes, the griefs and anxieties of the followers of Christ,"[33] it is also important to note that "earthly progress must be carefully distinguished from the growth of Christ's kingdom."[34] Indeed, Christians must "discern carefully between the Reign of God and the progress of the culture and society in which they are involved."[35]

In a *changeable* Christology, redemption would mean leaving behind our humanity. As a consequence, Christian discipleship would be unable to find a place in Benedict's "great union of the Catholic communion" for any other than supernatural goods. Since, in this scheme, grace overrides nature, pietistic spirituality would wipe out psychology. Such things as family life, marriage, and human affect would lose their legitimate secular value yet not find a place in redemption. Changeable soteriologies deny the reality and the autonomy of reason and science, or the value of culture. This is Niebuhr's paradigm of "Christ above culture." Here, Christian discipleship could be expressed only as a *contemptus mundi*, and collective Christian identity would take the form of sect.

Divisible Christologies have their parallels in divided loyalties. Here, for individuals and societies alike, church and state, religion and politics, occupy different spheres of life, hermetically isolated one from another. "I am," said John Kennedy famously, "the Democratic Party's candidate for president, who happens also to be a Catholic . . . Whatever issue may come before me as president, I will make my decision . . . in accordance with

32. See Catholic Church, "Instruction on Certain Aspects," 867–77.
33. *Gaudium et Spes*, 1.
34. *Gaudium et Spes*, 39.
35. *Catechism*, 2820.

what my conscience tells me to be the national interest, and without regard to outside religious pressures or dictates."[36] Yet, according to *Gaudium et Spes*, "the earthly and the heavenly city penetrate each other."[37] That interpenetration is a multidimensional and organic relationship—literally, a *perichoresis*—in which each reality exists "totally through the other; when one goes . . . into the other, without merging, but rather creating an interior relationship which does not come about when substances are merely joined together."[38] The innate dignity of the human person as image and likeness of God and the God-given nature of human activity render it impossible to cordon off the religious and the secular into neatly separate pens, relatively private and public.

Finally, a *separable* Christology, in sidestepping the problem of a suffering God, also avoids the question of the meaning of human suffering, a necessary corollary of interpersonal engagement. It cannot, therefore, engage in building solidarity with or among nations, communities, and cultures, nor involve itself significantly in encounters with the religious, political, or cultural other. Under threat of sacrifice, a *separable* discipleship retreats to a pietism that seeks to limit sacrificial love—the self-emptying love of Christ.

Heresies and How to Love Them

Far from being *a priori* exercises in willful stupidity, heresies are the result of faith in search of understanding. Like orthodox creeds, they too are the result of seeking responses to the question, how should we live? In fact, many heresies are not so much wrong as insufficient and partial stances, and not infrequently reactive plays when another party has taken just one element of the truth too far. So it is important to remember that the four Chalcedonian adverbs seek to hold together within one faith a number of tendencies that, when they are embraced too enthusiastically or unilaterally, can result in inauthentic discipleship and identity. To that extent, mitigated forms of what would be heretical positions, were they pushed to an extreme, are necessary checks on one another.

Witnessing to the City of God in the City of Man involves holding in tension a set of opposites that are mutually corrective. A legitimate degree of "Nestorian" division between the autonomous competencies of church and

---

36. Kennedy, "Address to Greater Houston Ministerial Association."

37. *Gaudium et Spes*, 40.

38. J. R. Jones, "Cydymdreiddiad iaith a thir," translated in Llywelyn, *Sacred Place, Chosen People*, 70.

political community, for example, keeps us away from the "monophysite" confusions of caesaropapism or theocracy: it is the basis for both religious freedom and the legitimate autonomy of the state. On the other hand, the realms of the secular and the sacred require—at least in this world—each other's presence, so that both may live out their legitimate autonomies. The real value of diversity needs to be tempered by a real and universal solidarity that may demand renouncing or tempering our attachment to good things that we hold dear—such as preference for family, ethnic group, or nation, or political or ideological groups—in favor of the common good or the greater good of unity. At the same time, in the logic of the Incarnation, there is a perennial value to the scandal of the particular, the soil of unity. The tent of encounter with the God who is above all place and time is the locally and the historically particular. Where true particularity degenerates into parochial particularism, it loses its virtue. But we should not confuse the two. Particularity derives its theological significance from the Incarnation. Its ugly stepsister is mere vulgar ideology.

St. Teresa of Ávila insisted on the importance of keeping before the mind the humanity of Jesus.[39] The Spanish mystic wrote out of the sapiential experience that Jesus's divinity is present in his humanity and vice versa. It is through the incarnate, particular God that we gain access to the Trinity, or in the far older formulation of Athanasius, "God became human so that humans might become divine."[40] In other words, in the same dispensation by which the interpenetration of the human and the divine in Jesus opens a gateway to the life of the Trinity, so too the life of the world, in those "things counter, original, spare, strange," is the place of encounter with the life of God.

Theologically, the world—place of our "other" identities and allegiance—might be defined as "that in which the Triune God is present and can be encountered." In the Trinity, there is no being without communion, and vice versa. Among the consequences, therefore, for discipleship of the logic both of the Incarnation and of life patterned after the Trinity is the necessity of the other: Christian discipleship needs the world—those other racial, political, cultural, sexual, and ideological communities of belonging—much as leaven needs dough in order to be able to make bread: without the world, there is no Church; without earth, no salt of the earth. The reverse is not necessarily true. Other communities of identity, most political

---

39. See, for example, Teresa of Ávila, *Interior Castle*, Sixth Mansion, ch. 8, and *The Life*, chs. 22–23.

40. Athanasius, *Incarnation* 54:3.

and cultural allegiances, do not need the Church in order to exist. Yet, without Christianity, what kind of world would the world be?

Precisely how we evaluate "Catholicism's embrace of . . . forms of political/cultural identity" in "the call of the Gospel to form communities of discipleship across human borders and divisions," and how we treat those "theological, political, and pastoral issues related to the Catholic encounter with processes and institutions that form politically salient loyalties and identities in the modern and postmodern world"[41] will depend significantly on how we understand the relationship between creation, on the one hand, and Incarnation and redemption, on the other—as connected moments of the same divine plan, or as radically different interventions of God. The primal commandment that God gives to humanity in Gen 1:28 is "to be fertile, and multiply, to fill the earth and subdue it." This *mission civilizatrice*, the prelapsarian cultural imperative to make use of the gifts of nature, belongs to the original constitution of humanity. The eschatological mission given by Jesus—"to make disciples of all nations, baptizing them in the name of the Father, and of the Son, and of the Holy Spirit, teaching them to observe all that I have commanded you" (Matt 28:19–20a)—is the fulfillment and full flowering of that Edenic proto-mission. The specifically evangelical mandate does not supersede the cultural, but rather it flows out of it, includes it, and brings it to completion.

The challenge for the Church involves more than "respecting and celebrating the diversity of its members," that late twentieth-century Western obsession. Rather, its mission extends beyond the borders of baptism, and is at the same time theological and cultural, political and pastoral—inconfusedly, unchangeably, indivisibly, inseparably so. Christian discipleship involves keeping together in one solidarity and two related missions: earthing the gospel, and gospelling this earth, home to many identities and many allegiances.

---

41. "The Borders of Baptism: Multiple Belongings."

3

Church Matters[1]

STANLEY HAUERWAS

The Theological Politics of the "And"

I am a Christian. I am even a Christian theologian. I observe in my memoir, *Hannah's Child*, that you do not need to be a theologian to be a Christian but I probably did. Being a Christian has not and does not come naturally or easy for me. I take that to be a good thing because I am sure that to be a Christian requires training that lasts a lifetime. I am more than ready to acknowledge that some may find that being a Christian comes more "naturally" but that can present its own difficulties. Just as athletes with natural gifts may fail to develop the fundamental skills necessary to play their sport after their talent fades, so people naturally disposed to faith may fail to develop the skills necessary to sustain them for a lifetime.

By training I mean something very basic such as acquiring habits of speech necessary for prayer. The acquisition of such habits is crucial for the formation of our bodies if we are to acquire the virtues necessary to live life as a Christian. For I take it to be crucial that Christians must live in such a manner that their lives are unintelligible if the God we worship in Jesus Christ does not exist. The training entailed in being a Christian can be called, if you are so disposed, culture. That is particularly the case if, as Raymond Williams reminds us in *Keywords*, culture is a term first used as a process noun to describe the tending or cultivation of a crop or animal.[2] One of the challenges Christians confront is how the politics we helped cre-

---

1. In honor of Stan Grenz who, from an evangelical perspective, helped us see why the church matters.

2. Williams, *Keywords*, 77–78.

ate has made it difficult to sustain the material practices constitutive of an ecclesial culture to produce Christians.

The character of much of modern theology exemplifies this development. In the attempt to make Christianity intelligible within the epistemological conceits of modernity, theologians have been intent on showing that what we believe as Christians is not that different than what those who are not Christians believe. Thus MacIntyre's wry observation that the project of modern theology to distinguish the kernel of the Christian faith from the outmoded husk has resulted in offering atheists less and less in which to disbelieve.[3]

It should not be surprising, as David Yeago argues, that many secular people now assume that descriptions of reality that Christians employ are a sort of varnish that can be scraped away to reveal a more basic account of what has always been the case. From a secular point of view it is assumed that we agree, or should agree, on fundamental naturalistic and secular descriptions of reality, whatever religious elaborations may overlay them. What I find so interesting is that many Christians accept these naturalistic assumptions about the way things are because they believe by doing so it is possible to transcend our diverse particularities that otherwise result in unwelcome conflict. From such a perspective it is only a short step to the key sociopolitical move crucial to the formation of modern societies, that is, the relegation of religion to the sphere of private inwardness and individual motivation.[4]

Societies that have relegated strong convictions to the private, a development I think appropriately identified as "secularization," may assume a tolerant or intolerant attitude toward the church, but the crucial characteristic of such societies is that the church is understood to be no more than a "voluntary association" of like-minded individuals.[5] Even those who identify as "religious" assume their religious convictions should be submitted to a public order governed by a secular rationality. I hope to challenge that assumption by calling into question the conceptual resources that now seem to be given for how the church is understood. In particular, I hope to

---

3. MacIntyre, *Religious Significance of Atheism*, 24.

4. Yeago, "Messiah's People," 147–48.

5. I have no intention to enter into the never-ending debates about secularization and the corresponding discussions concerning the demise of "religion." Suffice it to say I am in general sympathetic with David Martin's contention that secularization is best understood in terms of social differentiation correlative of the division of labor with the result that discrete sectors of social life are assumed autonomous. See D. Martin, *Future of Christianity*, 124.

convince Christians that the church is a material reality that must resist the domestication of our faith in the interest of societal peace.

There is a great deal going against such a project. For example, in his book *Civil Religion: A Dialogue in the History of Political Philosophy*, Ronald Beiner argues that in modernity the attempt to domesticate strong religious convictions in the interest of state control has assumed two primary and antithetical alternatives: civil religion and liberalism. Civil religion is the attempt to empower religion not for the good of religion but for the creation of the citizen. Indeed, the very creation of "religion" as a concept more fundamental than a determinative tradition is an indication that, at least in Western societies, Christianity has become "civil."[6] Rousseau, according to Beiner, is the decisive figure who gave expression to this transformation because Rousseau saw clearly that the modern state could not risk having a church capable of challenging its political authority.[7] In the process, the political concepts used to legitimize the modern state are, at least if Carl Schmitt is right, secularized theological concepts.[8]

In contrast to civil religion, the liberal alternative rejects all attempts to use religion to produce citizens in service to the state. Liberalism, in its many versions, according to Beiner, seeks to domesticate or neutralize the impact of religious commitment on political life.[9] Liberalism may well result in the production of a banal and flattened account of human existence, but such a form of life seems necessary if we are to be at peace with one another. In other words, liberalism as a way of life depends on the creation of people who think there is nothing for which it is worth dying. Such a way of life was exemplified by President Bush, who suggested that the duty of Americans after September 11, 2001, was to go shopping. Such a view of the world evoked Nietzsche's bitter condemnation, ironically making Nietzsche an ally of a Christianity determined by martyrdom.[10]

An extraordinary claim to be sure, but as Paul Kahn has observed, the Western state exists "under the very real threat of Christian martyrdom: a threat to expose the state and its claim to power as nothing at all."[11] The martyr does so, according to Kahn, because when everything is said and done sacrifice is always stronger than murder. The martyr wields a power

---

6. William Cavanaugh provides an invaluable account of how the creation of "religion" was a correlative of the modern state. See his *Myth of Religious Violence*, 60-71.
7. Beiner, *Civil Religion*, 1-7.
8. Schmitt, *Political Theology*, 5, 35.
9. Beiner, *Civil Religion*, 301-5.
10. Ibid., 374-94.
11. Kahn, *Liberalism*, 82.

that defeats the murderer because the martyr can be remembered by a community more enduring than the state. That is why the liberal state has such a stake in the domestication of Christianity by making it but another lifestyle choice.

In contrast, the modern nation-state, Kahn argues, has been an extremely effective sacrificial agent able to mobilize its populations to make sacrifices to sustain its existence as an end in itself. The nation-state, therefore, has stepped into the place of religious belief, offering the individual the possibility of transcending finitude. War becomes the act of sacrifice by which the state sustains the assumption that, though we die, it can and will continue to exist without end.[12]

I have earned the description of being a "fideistic, sectarian tribalist" because of my attempt to imagine an ecclesial alternative capable of resisting the politics Beiner (and Kahn) describe.[13] For as Yeago observes, most churches in the West, with the possible exception of the Roman Catholics, have acquiesced in this understanding of their social character and have therefore collaborated in the eclipse of their ecclesial reality.[14] As a result, the church seems caught in a "ceaseless crisis of legitimation" in which it must find a justification for its existence in terms of the projects and aspirations of that larger order.[15]

In his extraordinary book *Atheist Delusions: The Christian Revolution and Its Fashionable Enemies*, David Bentley Hart observes that the relegation of Christian beliefs to the private sphere is legitimated by a story of human freedom in which humankind is liberated from the crushing weight

---

12. Kahn, *Liberalism*, 276–77. I am indebted to Sean Larson for suggesting the importance of Kahn's understanding of liberalism for the argument I am making in this paper.

13. Kahn argues that there is a liberalism of the will that can and does demand sacrifice. Liberalism of interest and reason, however, cannot acknowledge the sacrifices required by the state. The result is what Kahn calls the "paradox of democratic self-government," that is, "the more the nation believes itself to be a product of the will of the popular sovereign, the less democratic it becomes—if, by democratic, we mean subject to control through broadly participatory electoral mechanisms." Kahn suggests this is the modern form of Rousseau's distinction between the general will and the will of all (*Liberalism*, 161).

14. For an extremely informative comparison of the Catholic and Protestant responses to secularization, see D. Martin, *Future of Christianity*, 25–44. Perreau-Saussine's *Catholicism and Democracy* is a fascinating account of the rise of the political importance of the papacy after the French Revolution, at once the manifestation as well as the result of the Catholic agreement with the liberal presumption that there is "something irreducibly secular about the modern state" (2).

15. Yeago, "Messiah's People," 148–49.

of tradition and doctrine. Hart, whose prose begs for extensive quotation, says the story goes like this:

> Once upon a time . . . Western humanity was the cosseted and incurious ward of Mother Church; during this, the age of faith, culture stagnated, science languished, wars of religion were routinely waged, witches were burned by inquisitors, and Western humanity labored in brutish subjugation to dogma, superstition, and the unholy alliance of church and state. Withering blasts of fanaticism and fideism had long since scorched away the last remnants of classical learning; inquiry was stifled; the literary remains of classical antiquity had long ago been consigned to the fires of faith, and even the great achievements of "Greek science" were forgotten until Islamic civilization restored them to the West. All was darkness. Then, in the wake of the "wars of religion" that had torn Christendom apart, came the full flowering of the Enlightenment and with it the reign of reason and progress, the riches of scientific achievement and political liberty, and a new and revolutionary sense of human dignity. The secular nation-state arose, reduced religion to an establishment of the state . . . and thereby rescued Western humanity from the blood-steeped intolerance of religion. Now, at last, Western humanity has left its nonage and attained to its majority, in science, politics, and ethics. The story of the travails of Galileo almost invariably occupies an honored place in this narrative, as exemplary of the natural relation between "faith" and "reason" and as an exquisite epitome of scientific reason's mighty struggle during the early modern period to free itself from the tyranny of religion.[16]

This "simple but thoroughly enchanting tale" is, Hart observes, captivating in its explanatory power. According to Hart, however, there is just one problem with this story. The problem is that every detail of the story, as well as the overarching plot, just happens to be false.[17] Hart's book provides the arguments and evidence to sustain that judgment. What I find so interesting, however, is that even if the narrative is false in every detail, it is nonetheless true that believer and unbeliever alike assume, though they may disagree about some of the details, that the main plot of the story is true.

That this story now has canonical status has deep significance for how Christians should understand the relation between faith and politics. Put

16. Hart, *Atheist Delusions*, 33–34.
17. Ibid., 34.

even more strongly, in the interest of being good citizens, of being civil, Christians have lost the ability to say why what they believe is true. That loss is, I want to suggest, a correlative of the depolitization of the church as a community capable of challenging the imperial pretentions of the modern state. That the church matters is why I resist using the language of "belief" to indicate what allegedly makes Christians Christian.[18] Of course Christians "believe in God," but far more important for determining the character of Christian existence is that it is constituted by a politics that cannot avoid challenging what is normally identified as "the political." For what is normally identified as "the political" produces dualisms that invite questions such as, what is the relation between faith and politics? If I am right, that "and" prematurely ends any serious theological reflection from a Christian perspective.

As I have already indicated, to make this argument necessarily puts me at odds with the attempt to make Christian convictions compatible with the epistemological and moral presumptions of liberal social orders. That project presumed a story very much along the lines suggested by Hart. Theologians trimmed the sails of Christian convictions to show that even if the metaphysical commitments that seem intrinsic to Christian practice cannot be intellectually sustained, it remains the case that Christianity can claim some credit for the creation of the culture and politics of modernity.

In particular, Christian theologians sought to justify Christian participation in the politics of democratic societies. The field of Christian ethics, the discipline with which I am identified, had as one of its primary agendas to convince Christians that their "beliefs" had political implications. The determinative representative of this mode of Christian ethical reflection was Reinhold Niebuhr. Thus his claim that "the real problem of a Christian social ethic is to derive from the Gospel a clear view of the realities with which we must deal in our common or social life, and also to preserve a sense of responsibility for achieving the highest measure of order, freedom and justice despite the hazards of man's collective life."[19] Niebuhr reminded Christians that we do not live in a world in which sin can be eliminated, but we nonetheless must seek to establish the tentative harmonies and provisional equities possible in any historical situation.

18. In his magisterial book *The Unintended Reformation*, Brad Gregory observes that the Reformation placed an unprecedented emphasis on doctrine for identifying what made Christians Christian. Such an emphasis led Protestants and Catholics alike to emphasize the importance of an "interior assent to the propositional content of doctrinal truth claims, whatever they were." Gregory observes that this development "risked making Christianity seem more a matter of what one believed than how one lived—of making the faith a crypto-Cartesian matter of one's soul and mind, rather than a matter of what one does with one's body" (155).

19. Niebuhr, *Politics*, 153.

Niebuhr, who prided himself for being a sober realist challenging what he took to be the unfounded optimism of liberal thinkers such as John Dewey, would have in like manner called into question the optimism of the story Hart associates with the celebration, if not the legitimization, of modernity. But Niebuhr's support of liberal democratic political arrangements drew on a narrative very much like the one Hart identifies as the story of modernity.[20] The result is ironic, a category Niebuhr loved, because Niebuhr's arguments for political engagement by Christians presupposed a narrative that legitimates a political arrangement that requires the privatization of Christian convictions—one of the consequences being the loss of any attempt to say what it might mean for the gospel of Jesus Christ to be true.

For instance, one of the curiosities associated with the "new atheists" is their assumption that the most decisive challenges to the truthfulness of Christian convictions come from developments in the sciences, or perhaps more accurately put, the "method" of science. Such a view fails to appreciate that the most decisive challenge to the truthfulness of Christian convictions is political.[21] The politics of modernity has so successfully made Christianity but another lifestyle option that it is a mystery why the new atheists think it important to show that what Christians believe is false. Such a project hardly seems necessary given that Christians, in the name of being good democratic citizens, live lives of unacknowledged but desperate unbelief just to the extent that they believe what they believe as a Christian cannot be a matter of truth. As a result, Christians no longer believe that the church is an alternative politics to the politics of the world, which means they have lost any way to account for why Christians in the past thought they had a faith worth dying for.

The Witness of Karl Barth

I need an example of what the connection between the truthfulness of Christian speech and politics might look like. An example is necessary because I am not sure we know what Christianity so understood would look like. I think, however, we have the beginnings in the work of Karl Barth.

20. For a fuller defense of this account of Niebuhr, see Hauerwas, *Wilderness Wanderings*, 32-62, and Hauerwas, *With the Grain of the Universe*, 87-140.

21. David Martin nicely shows that the assumption that science makes theological claims unintelligible is simply not sustainable. See his *Future of Christianity*, 119-31. Brad Gregory observes that "empirical investigation of the natural world has not falsified any theological claims." Much more troubling for the status of the truthfulness of Christian convictions, according to Gregory, were the unresolved disputes between Protestant and Catholic concerning the meaning of God's actions (*Unintended Reformation*, 47).

Barth, more than any other theologian in modernity, recognized that the recovery of the language of the faith entailed a politics at odds with the world as we know it. For Barth there is no kernel of the Christian faith, because it begins and ends with the extraordinary claim that what we mean when we say "God" is to be determined by Mary's willingness to be impregnated by the Holy Spirit.

That is not where Barth began. Barth began by presuming the work of Protestant liberal theologians was a given. It was, however, a political event that called into question Barth's liberalism. On a day in early August 1914, Barth read a proclamation in support of the war policy of Wilhelm II signed by ninety-three German intellectuals. To Barth's horror, almost all of his venerated theological teachers were among those who had signed in support of the war. He suddenly realized that he could no longer follow their theology or ethics. At that moment, the theology of the nineteenth century, the theology of Protestant liberalism, came to an end for Barth.[22]

Barth characterized the theology he thought must be left behind—a theology identified by figures such as Schleiermacher and Troeltsch—as the attempt to respond to the modern age by underwriting the assumption that Christianity is but an expression of the alleged innate human capacity for the infinite. From such a perspective, Christianity is understood to be but one particular expression of religion. Such a view of the Christian faith presumed that the primary task of Christian theology is to assure the general acceptance of the Christian faith for the sustaining of the achievements of Western civilization. Barth observed that theology so conceived was more interested in humanity's relationship with God than in God's dealings with humanity.[23]

For Barth, however, a theology understood as the realization in one form or another of human self-awareness could have no ground or content other than ourselves: "Faith as the Christian commerce with God could first and last be only the Christian commerce with himself."[24] The figure haunting such an account of Christianity is Feuerbach, whom Barth thought had powerfully reconfigured the Christian faith as a statement of profound human needs and desires.

Drawing on Kierkegaard, Dostoevsky, and Overbeck, as well as his discovery of what he characterized as "the strange new world of the Bible,"

22. Barth, *Humanity of God*, 14.

23. Ibid., 24. Barth noted, however, that theology so understood could be in continuity with Melanchthon's emphasis on the benefits of Christ. So there is no reason that an attempt should not be made to develop a Christian anthropocentrism in which theology is done, so to speak, from the bottom up.

24. Ibid., 26.

against the theology of his teachers, Barth proclaimed, "God is God."[25] Barth did not think such a claim to be redundant but rather to be the best expression of who God is; it is a response to the particularity of a God who has initiated an encounter with humankind. Barth says, "The stone wall we first ran up against was that the theme of the Bible is the deity of *God*, more exactly God's *deity*—God's independence and particular character, not only in relation to the natural but also to the spiritual cosmos; God's absolutely unique existence, might, and initiative, above all, in His relation to man."[26]

So Barth challenged what he characterized as the accommodated theology of Protestant liberalism using expressions such as God is the "wholly other" who breaks in upon us "perpendicularly from above." There is an "infinite qualitative distinction" between God and us, rendering any presumption that we can know God on our terms to be just that—a presumption based on sinful pride. Thus Barth's sobering claim that God is God and we are not means that it can never be the case that we have the means to know God unless God first makes himself known to us.

Barth will later acknowledge that his initial reaction against Protestant liberal theology was exaggerated, but any theology committed to clearing the ground for a fresh expression of the Christian faith could not help sounding extreme. Barth acknowledged that his first salvos against Protestant liberalism seemed to be saying that God is everything and humanity nothing. Such a God, the God that is wholly other, isolated and set over against humanity, threatens to become the God of the philosophers rather than the God who called Abraham. The majesty of the God of the philosophers might have the contradictory results of confirming the hopelessness of all human activity while offering a new justification of the autonomy of humanity. Barth wanted neither of these results.

In retrospect, however, Barth confesses he was wrong exactly where he was right, but at the time he did not know how to carry through with sufficient care the discovery of God's deity.[27] For Barth the decisive breakthrough came with the recognition that "who God is and what He is in His deity He proves and reveals not in a vacuum as a divine being-for-Himself, but precisely and authentically in the fact that he exists, speaks, and acts as the *partner* of man, though of course as the absolute superior partner."[28]

---

25. Timothy Gorringe suggests that Barth may well have seen *A Midsummer Night's Dream*, whose "Well roared, Lion" he liked to use to characterize his reaction against Protestant liberalism. See Gorringe, *Karl Barth*, 25.

26. Barth, *Humanity of God*, 41.

27. Ibid., 44.

28. Ibid., 46.

In short, Barth discovered that it is precisely God's deity that includes and constitutes God's humanity.

We are not dealing with an abstract God, that is, a God whose deity exists separately from humanity, because in Jesus Christ there can be no isolation of humanity from God or God from humanity. In Barth's language: "God's deity in Jesus Christ consists in the fact that God Himself in Him is the *subject* who speaks and acts with sovereignty . . . In Jesus Christ man's freedom is wholly enclosed in the freedom of God. Without the condescension of God there would be no exaltation of man . . . We have here no universal deity capable of being reached conceptually, but this concrete deity—real and recognizable in the *descent* grounded in that sequence and peculiar to the existence of Jesus Christ."[29]

I am aware that this all too brief account of Barth's decisive theological turn may seem but a report on esoteric methodological issues in Christian theology. But I ask you to remember that Barth's discovery of the otherness of God, an otherness intrinsic to God's humanity, was occasioned by his recognition of the failure of the politics and ethics of modern theology in the face of the First World War. I think it not accidental, moreover, that Barth was among the first to recognize the character of the politics represented by Hitler. Barth was a person of unusual insight, or as Timothy Gorringe describes him, a person of extraordinary vitality who was a profoundly political animal.[30] But his perception of the threat the Nazis represented cannot be separated from his theological turn occasioned by his reaction against his teachers who supported the war.

Gorringe rightly argues in his book *Karl Barth: Against Hegemony* that Barth never assumed his theology might have political implications because his theology was a politics. That way of putting the matter—that is, "his theology was a politics"—is crucial. The very structure of Barth's *Dogmatics,* Gorringe suggests, with its integration of theology and ethics displayed in his refusal to separate law from gospel, was Barth's way of refusing any distinction between theory and practice. Barth's christocentrism meant that his "theology was never a predicate of his politics, but [it is] also true that politics is never simply a predicate of his theology."[31]

Gorringe's argument that Barth was a political theologian was confirmed in 1934, the same year in which Barth wrote the Barmen Declaration, by Barth's response to a challenge by some American and English critics that his theology was too abstract and unrelated to actual lives. Barth begins his

---

29. Ibid., 48.
30. Gorringe, *Karl Barth*, 11.
31. Ibid., 9.

defense by observing that he is after all "a modern man" who stands in the midst of this age. Like his questioners, he too must live a life not merely in theory but in practice in what he characterizes as the "stormy present." Accordingly, he tells his antagonists that "exactly because I was called to live in a modern world, did I reach the path of which you have heard me speak."[32]

In particular, Barth calls attention to his years as a pastor, during which he had the task of preaching the gospel in the face of secularism. He was confronted with the modern world, but he was also confronted with the modern church. It was a church, a church of great sincerity and zeal with fervid devotion to deeds of charity, too closely related to the modern world. It was a church that no longer knew God's choice to love the world by what Christians have been given to do in the light of that love, that is, to be witnesses to the treasure that is the gospel. The problem, according to Barth, is that the church of the pious man—this church of the good man, of the moral man—became the church of man.[33] The result was the fusion of Christianity and nationalism.[34]

Consequently, the modern church is a near relative to the godless modern world. That error, Barth suggests, had begun two hundred years before with Pietism's objections to orthodoxy. In the Reformation the church heard of God and of Christ, but love was not active.[35] The fatal error was the Christian response: they did not say, let God be even more God and Christ be even more the Christ, but instead they said, let us improve matters ourselves. Reverence for the pious man became reverence for the moral man, and finally, when it was found that man is of so large an importance, it became less important to speak of God, of Christ, of the Holy Spirit. Instead, men began to speak of human reason.[36]

---

32. Barth, *God in Action*, 133. This little gem of a book contains lectures Barth gave in response to the Nazis in 1934.

33. The role of Pietism for the development of Protestant liberal theology as well as the legitimating discourse for the subordination of the church to the state is a story in itself. It is not accidental that Barth was the great enemy of Pietism. David Martin suggests that Pietism was the ultimate working out of the implications of the Protestant Reformation for the development of the centralized sovereignty necessary to legitimate the formation of the nation-state. He observes, "German Pietism inculcated disciplines that helped ensure the smooth running of the state" (*Future of Christianity*, 199).

34. Barth, *God in Action*, 134-35.

35. In his book *The Unintended Reformation*, Brad Gregory convincingly argues that "the Western world today is an extraordinarily complex, tangled project of rejections, retentions, and transformations of medieval Western Christianity, in which the Reformation era constitutes the critical watershed." The secularization that was the result of the Reformation was, according to Gregory, unintended but no less a reality (2).

36. Barth, *God in Action*, 137.

Barth then directly addresses his questioners, whom he identifies as "friends," to tell them he is well aware of what is happening and that is exactly why he insists that he must speak of God. He must speak of God because he must begin with the confession, "I am from Germany." Because he is from Germany he knows that he stands in a place that has reached the end of a road, a road that he acknowledges may be just beginning for social orders like America and England. Yet Barth claims he is sure that what has been experienced in Germany, that is, the remarkable apostasy of the church to nationalism, will also be the fate of those who think Barth's theology to be a retreat from political engagement. Thus Barth's challenge to his critics: "If you make a start with 'God *and* . . .' you are opening the doors to every demon."[37]

Barth early recognized such a demon had been let loose in the person of Hitler. He was able to do so because Hitler's attempt to make Christianity a state religion through the creation of the German Church meant that the free preaching of the gospel was prohibited. Theological speech and politics were inseparable. It is, therefore, no accident that Barth in the Barmen Declaration challenged the "German Christians" on christological grounds.[38] He does so because Barth assumes that Jesus's claim "I am the way, and the truth, and the life; no one comes to the Father, but by me" (John 14:6) is the defining politics of Christianity. Barth writes,

> Jesus Christ, as he is attested for us in Holy Scripture, is the one word of God which we have to hear and which we have to trust and obey in life and in death. We reject the false doctrine, as though the Church could and would have to acknowledge as a source of its proclamation, apart from and beside this one word of God, still other events and powers, figures and truths, as God's revelation.[39]

The witness that is Karl Barth—that is, how such a life fits into the ongoing story we must tell as Christians of our faithful and unfaithful living out of the gospel—means there is no way we can avoid making clear to ourselves and to the world that we believe a new world began in the belly of Mary.

---

37. Ibid., 138.

38. The Barmen Declaration was the statement of protest by the Confessing Church, that is, the church in opposition to Hitler's formation of the German Christian Church. The synod met in Barmen on January 4, 1934. Though the Barmen Declaration was a joint effort of several theologians, Barth was the primary author.

39. I am quoting from Cochrane, *Church's Confession*, 172–78.

Where Are We Now? Where Do We Need to Go?

You may be rightly wondering, if not worried, where all this has gotten us. I should like to be able to say more about where we are now and where we need to go, but I am unsure who the "we" or the "us" may be. I have assumed I should speak—or perhaps more truthfully, I can only speak—from a first-person perspective, but hopefully it is one shaped by my Christian identity. Yet just as Barth confessed that he was German, so I must acknowledge that I am American. Indeed, it may be I am more American than Christian and thus tempted to confuse the Christian "we" and the American "we." That confusion tempts Americans to assume we represent what any right-thinking person should say because our "we" is the universal "we."

American presumption is always a problem, but the problem is deeper than my American identity. For I think none of us can assume an agreed-upon "we" or "us" to be a manifestation of the cultural and political challenges that are the subject of this conference. Given the difficulty of locating the "we," some may worry that directing attention to Barth in order to show the political character of Christian convictions is morally and politically the exemplification of a profoundly reactionary position. In Nazi Germany, a Barmen Declaration may have seemed "prophetic," but "after Hitler," a Barmen-like account of the politics of Christian convictions suggests theocracy.[40]

I confess I often enjoy making liberal friends, particularly American liberal friends, nervous by acknowledging I am, of course, a theocrat. "Jesus is Lord" is not my personal opinion; I take it to be a determinative political claim. So I am ready to rule. The difficulty is that following a crucified Lord entails embodying a politic that cannot resort to coercion and violence; it is a politic of persuasion all the way down. A tiring business that is slow and time-consuming, but then we, that is, Christians, believe that by redeeming time Christ has given us all the time we need to pursue peace. Christ, through the Holy Spirit, bestows upon his disciples the longsuffering patience necessary to resist any politic whose impatience makes coercion and violence the only and inevitable response to conflict.

For fifteen hundred years, Christians thought Jesus's lordship meant that they should rule the world. That rule assumed diverse forms, some beneficial and some quite destructive. "Constantinianism" or Christendom

---

40. During a visit to the Holocaust Museum in Washington, DC, my wife and I encountered school children wearing shirts emblazoned with the slogan "Celebrate Diversity." There is much good, no doubt, in training the young to enjoy difference, but I worry for those who think the celebration of diversity an adequate response to a movement like National Socialism.

is a description of the various ways that Christians sought to determine the cultural and political life of the worlds in which they found themselves. Some Christians look with nostalgia on that past, seeking ways to recapture Christian dominance of the world. That is obviously not my perspective.

For as David Hart observes, Christianity's greatest historical triumph was also its most calamitous defeat. The conversion of the Roman Empire in which it was thought the faith overthrew the powers of "this age" found that the faith itself had become subordinate to those very powers. Like Hart, I have no reason to deny the many achievements of Christendom. I think he is right to suggest that the church was a revolution, a slow and persistent revolution, a cosmic sedition, in which the human person was "invested with an intrinsic and inviolable dignity" by being recognized as God's own.[41] But this revolution, exactly because it was so radical, was absorbed and subdued by a society in which nominal baptism became the expression of a church that was reduced to an instrument of temporal power and the gospel was made a captive to the mechanism of the state.[42]

In *The Stillborn God: Religion, Politics, and the Modern West*, Mark Lilla has written in defense of what he calls "the great separation" of politics and religion represented by Hobbes. He observes that though Christianity is inescapably political, it has proved incapable of integrating this fact into Christian theology.[43] The problem, according to Lilla, is that being a Christian means being in the world, including the political world, but somehow not being of it. Such a way of being, Lilla argues, cannot help producing a false consciousness. Christendom is the institutionalization of this consciousness just to the extent the church thought reconciliation could be expressed politically.[44] Politics so constituted cannot help suffering from permanent instability.

Lilla, I think, is right that the eschatological character of the Christian faith will challenge the politics of the worlds in which it finds itself. But that is why, even at times when the church fails to be true to its calling to be a

---

41. Hart, *Atheist Delusions*, 167.

42. Ibid., 194. It is true, nonetheless, as Gregory argues in *The Unintended Reformation*, that the church was never coextensive with or absorbed by any secular political entity. A thousand years after Constantine, from the papacy to the parishes into which Christendom was parceled, the church remained distinct from secular political entities such as medieval kingdoms, principalities, duchies, and cities and city-states (136–37). One of the great virtues of Gregory's book is his treatment of the often ignored Anabaptists. He rightly understands the Anabaptists to represent a political alternative to the magisterial Reformers just to the extent the latter led to the increasing control of the church by the state.

43. Lilla, *Stillborn God*, 85.

44. Ibid., 169.

political alternative, God raises up a Karl Barth. For as Barth insisted, this really is all about God, the particular God of Jesus Christ. The humanity of that God, Christians believe, has made it possible for a people to exist who do in fact, as Nietzsche suggested, exemplify a slave morality. It is a morality Hart describes as a "strange, impractical, altogether unworldly tenderness" expressed in the ability to see as our sister or brother the autistic or Down syndrome or disabled child—a child "for whom the world can remain a perpetual perplexity"—or the derelict or broken man or woman who has wasted life, or the homeless, the diseased, the mentally ill, criminals, and reprobates.[45]

Such a morality is the matter that is the church. It is the matter that made even a church in Christendom uneasy. From the church's standpoint today, Christendom may be a lamentable world now lost, but it is not clear what will replace or shape the resulting culture or politics. Hart observes that when Christianity passes from a culture, what remains may be worse than what might have been had Christianity never existed. Christians took the gods away, and no one will ever believe them again. Christians demystified the world, robbing good pagans of their reverence and hard-won wisdom derived from the study of human and nonhuman nature. So once again, Nietzsche was right that the Christians shaped a world that meant that those who would come after Christianity could not avoid nihilism.[46]

Why this is the case is perhaps best exemplified by how time is understood. Christians, drawing as they must on God's calling of Israel to be the promised people, cannot help believing that time has a plot, that is to say, Christians believe in history. A strange phrase to be sure, but one to remind us of how extraordinary it is for Christians to believe we come from a past that will find its fulfillment in the future. Accordingly, we believe that time has a narrative logic, which means time is not just one damn thing after another. The story of creation is meant to remind us that all that exists lends witness to the glory of God, giving history a significance otherwise unavailable. Creation, redemption, and reconciliation are names for Christians that we believe constitute the basic plot line that makes history more than a tale told by an idiot.[47]

Yet the very assumption that history has a direction is the necessary condition that underwrites the story of modernity earlier characterized by Hart—the story that has underwritten the new atheists' presumption that, if history is finally rid of Christianity, we will discover that through

---

45. Hart, *Atheist Delusions*, 213–14.
46. Ibid., 229–30.
47. Ibid., 201–2.

unconstrained reason our politics can be made more just and humane. Thus Hart speculates that the violence done in the name of humanity, a violence that is now unconstrained, might never have been unleashed if Christianity had not introduced its "peculiar variant of apocalyptic yearning into Western culture."[48] Hart rightly observes that such a judgment is purely speculative given the reality that past great empires prior to Christianity claimed divine warrants for murder. Yet Hart thinks that the secularization of Christian eschatological grammar is the "chief cause of the modern state's curious talent for mass murder."[49] An exaggerated claim, perhaps, but it is at least a reminder that it is by no means clear why the killing called war is distinguishable from mass murder.[50]

This last observation, I hope, draws us back to Karl Barth's theological work. I suggested Barth exemplifies the politics of speech that is at the heart of Christian convictions. At the heart of Christian convictions is the belief in "the humanity of God," a humanity made unavoidable by our faith in Jesus Christ as the second person of the Trinity. Christ's humanity means no account of the church is possible that does not require material expression that is rightly understood as a politic. Church matters matter not only for the church; we believe that what is a necessity for the church is a possibility for all that is not the church.

I suspect humans always live in times of transition; what is time if not transition? But I believe we are living in a time when Christendom is actually coming to an end. That is an extraordinary transition whose significance for Christian and non-Christian has yet to be understood. But in the very least, it means the church is finally free to be a politic. If I may summarize what I take to be one appropriate response to this observation, it is quite simply this: let Christians make the most of it.

48. Ibid., 222–23.
49. Ibid., 223–24.
50. In a blog post titled "Bend Your Knee," Noah Berlatsky defends my arguments for pacifism against Eric Cohen's critique of my book *War and the American Difference*, which appeared in the conservative magazine, *First Things*. Cohen described my views as "a form of eschatological madness"—a description that Berlatsky quite rightly suggests I would happily accept. Berlatsky suggests that Cohen missed my argument that war produces its own logic and morality. In fact, according to Berlatsky, Cohen's defense of war as a heroic story exemplifies the view of war I was criticizing; when war becomes a "heroic story," it becomes idolatry. He observes that, though I would like to get rid of war, what I really want to get rid of is a church of war. What Cohen missed is that my argument is aimed at Christians. He then makes what was for me the surprising claim that he finds this to be a relief for someone like him because he is an atheist, so he can cheerfully continue to support Caesar. Yet he observes there is a bit of discomfort, because if Christians were to take up nonviolence—and he hates to have to say it—"it would be hard to escape the suspicion that that might actually be the work of God."

PART TWO

*History, Context, Theology, and Eschatology:
Notes, Experiences, Suggestions, and Possibilities*

4

Engaging European Contexts and Issues: Some Reflections

DANIEL IZUZQUIZA, SJ

Introduction

Exactly one hundred years ago, in 1913, Marc Chagall painted his famous work *The Fiddler*. This picture offers a good introductory framework for my contribution on "Engaging European Contexts and Issues," because it shows, in a direct and clear way, the complexity of identities and their current relevance. When we think of Chagall and his own personal identity, shall we say that he is a Russian painter, or French, or Jewish, or . . . ? Is he a migrant, a refugee, a cosmopolitan artist?

If we look closely at *The Fiddler*, we see that his right foot is resting on the roof of a house—hence the inspiration for the well-known movie *The Fiddler on the Roof*—while the left foot seems to be floating in the air. This can be seen as a symbol of how a person combines territorial specificity, on the one hand, with universal expansion, on the other. Embodied identity and universal catholicity. Not surprisingly, the picture was painted in Paris, but it reflects the landscape of Chagall's native Vitebsk, in what is now Belarus. When we talk about embodied identities—and this appears clearly in the case of Marc Chagall and from a European perspective—we must consider the biographical aspects alongside the sociocultural dimension. Not only does Chagall's personal biography speak about complex identities, but also the very landscape of the painting does: the houses of the Jewish families amidst the Russian Orthodox churches, the warmth of home and footprints in the snow, social inequality, forced migration . . . One foot is anchored in concrete and tangible history, while the other foot is tapping to the beat of a music that transcends borders. Embodied identity and universal catholicity.

I still want to make two introductory references to other contemporary authors who offer helpful perspectives for our reflection. First, I refer to Manuel Castells, a European sociologist living in California, who some fifteen years ago published the trilogy *The Information Age: Economy, Society and Culture*. He argues that the central question of our time is the tension between the local and the global, between the sphere of identity and the sphere of flows, between the individual and the systemic. Current societies live "a fundamental division between an abstract, universal instrumentalism and particularist identities with historical roots. Our societies are becoming ever more structured around a bipolar tension between the network and the self."[1] In this context, Castells distinguishes three types of identity: the legitimizing identity, which reproduces and sustains the dominant system; the resistance identity, which has a reactive character and arises among marginal groups; and the project identity, which aims at creating a collective social force through which individuals can grasp a fuller meaning of their experience. The first two types, for different reasons, tend to become closed identities, and so can hardly be compatible with Christian identity, which, anchored in the project of the Kingdom, is by definition catholic, universal, and open.

Our next reference may help us understand and clarify what we mean by identity. Is there, perhaps, such a thing as a closed identity, a culture with neatly defined borders, a tradition in which the group consensus is unquestioned? Reality is much more complex than that; such pure identities exist only in books or in the ideological imaginations of certain biased persons. Writer Amin Maalouf has depicted such pure identities as "killer identities,"[2] and he seems to be right, even for those of us whose cultural identity is not as clearly amalgamated as Maalouf's. He is Christian by birth, with a Protestant father and a Catholic mother; he received a Jesuit education in a Muslim context; Lebanon is his birthplace; his native language is Arabic; and he is a naturalized French citizen. In this global world, we are all—especially Christians—called to combine our local roots with our global belonging to a broader reality that surrounds us and surpasses us.[3]

---

1. Castells, *Information Age*, 1:3. In fact, the first volume of this trilogy is titled *The Rise of the Network Society* and analyzes the flow spaces that carry us to global interconnection by way of technology and community; in the second volume, however, he recalls "the power of identity," based on community, self, and interpersonal relations.

2. See Maalouf, *In the Name of Identity*. For her part, Benhabib in *Claims of Culture* has defended a narrative foundation of cultures, rejecting cultural essentialism and affirming their internal plurality, the changing dynamics, and their porous boundaries.

3. See Häring et al., "Creating Identity," 173–328.

Context

Since we want to address the issue of Catholicity and incarnated identities from a European perspective, we need now to say a few words about this specific context. In the next section, we shall look at three main challenges that stem from this political, economic, and cultural context and from a broader European situation.

Political Context

On October 12, 2012, Thorbjørn Jagland, chairman of the Norwegian Nobel Committee, announced the granting of the Nobel Peace Prize to the European Union (EU) with these words: "The Union and its forerunners have, for over six decades, contributed to the advancement of peace and reconciliation, democracy, and human rights in Europe . . . The division between East and West has to a large extent been brought to an end; democracy has been strengthened; many ethnically-based national conflicts have been settled."[4]

But this award coincides with the worst financial crisis the EU has suffered in its fifty-five-year history and with a succession of conflicts in neighboring countries in North Africa and the Middle East. In this context, a number of EU institutions' decisions—social cuts, bailouts, and international actions—have been highly controversial. Perhaps anticipating criticism, the Nobel Committee statement says, "The EU is currently undergoing grave economic difficulties and considerable social unrest. The Norwegian Nobel Committee wishes to focus on what it sees as the EU's most important result: the successful struggle for peace and reconciliation and for democracy and human rights. The stabilizing part played by the EU has helped to transform most of Europe from a continent of war to a continent of peace." We must not forget, of course, the deep Catholic convictions of three of the main architects of this process: the Italian Alcide De Gasperi, the Frenchman Robert Schuman—whose cause for beatification is in progress—and the German Konrad Adenauer.

The ambiguities of the European project, in its concrete realization, are obvious. There is a tension between the granting of the Nobel Prize to the EU and the building of a "Fortress Europe" that turns its back to—sometimes at the expense of—the impoverished peoples of the earth. There is also an internal tension between the desire to strengthen social cohesion as a true linchpin of the European project and its concrete realization in a

---

4. See Norwegian Nobel Committee, "Announcement."

two-speed process, which leaves excluded people and marginal countries in Southern or Eastern Europe out of the decision-making and shared benefits of the Union. Finally, a collision is detected between the true dynamics of political unification and particular interests leading to disintegration.

Economic Context

Although the European Union has provided, over the second half of the twentieth century, one of the longer periods of social stability and economic prosperity in its history, it is also true that it currently suffers a deep and extended crisis. The financial situation has led to an economic and social crisis with very serious consequences for large sections of the European population. Rising unemployment and increased poverty are truly alarming from the social point of view and unacceptable from the point of view of ethics. Just to mention a single figure, in Spain, we are suffering more than five hundred house evictions daily, which means that more and more persons (even whole families) are becoming homeless—strictly speaking, without a home.

Different research publications show that there is "a general pattern since the mid-1980s in European countries at the national level where top deciles capture an increasing part of the income generated in the economy, while the poorest 10 percent are losing ground."[5] This fact is not just incidental or merely circumstantial; it is directly linked to the core of the European project. What we are facing is a battle between wealth and inequality, between the welfare state and increasing poverty. The way we manage this economic crisis may lead Europe to strengthen its solidarity model or, on the other hand, it may provoke the dismantling of it. Those who are most in need are the ones who will suffer the hardest consequences, but it will be the European society as a whole that may lose its solidarity networks, which belong to its basic identity.

Cultural Context

Throughout the centuries, Europe has been the source of countless cultures and frequent interactions between them. Despite being a small geographical territory, its cultural variety and the dynamism of its creativity have been impressive. Even now, around 225 languages are spoken in Europe. Twenty-four of them are official languages recognized as such by the EU, and all of

---

5. Fredriksen, "Income Inequality," 18.

them are considered to be working languages at all European institutions. Quite often, difference has been the occasion of division. In fact, conflict and war have been part of European history very frequently—sometimes led by economic, political, or religious interests. It is also true that the European integration process promoted since the second half of the twentieth century has attempted to correct or reverse this trend, trying to move toward a stronger common integration.

However, here we face again a new tension in the design of this project that intends to build and strengthen a European identity. How can it be done without destroying local cultures? How can specific identities be respected, particularly those of minority groups? Is it possible to achieve a flexible and open identity, or does the European project necessarily lead to a self-enclosed identity—one that is homogenizing at home and neocolonial abroad? Regarding local identities, do they become fixed or blurred when they join this new European identity?

There are many questions we cannot adequately resolve, partly because this is an open discussion, with different views and interests. In fact, unifying tendencies—perhaps dominated by economic interests—coexist along with more stable dynamics. For example, discussions regarding the European Constitution in 2004 were unable to reach a positive agreement between the different actors on (among other issues) defining a European identity and, more specifically, on referencing its Christian roots. After the French and Dutch referendum results, the ratification of the Constitution treaty was finally delayed *sine die*. A second example refers to the political voting tendencies in the European Parliament: very frequently, members of Parliament align themselves according to national background and not according to the political party to which they belong. That is, local identities or narrow allegiances seem to play a stronger role than ideologies or global projects.

Challenges

Within this context, we can now look at the main challenges Europe is facing regarding its own identity. Moreover, we want to focus on how Catholicity can become incarnated in this particular context. Before we move on, we must keep in mind the contrast between the "secular Trinity" that forms the skeleton of the European project—nation-state allegiances, social and economic class interests, and cultural homogeneity—and the social implications of Christian Trinity—universal brother- and sisterhood, the option for the poor, and diversity, corresponding to God the Father, Jesus Christ the Son, and the Holy Spirit. Keeping this framework in mind, we can now address these three challenges: secularization, injustice, and pluralism.[6]

The Challenge of Secularization

Our cultural context is characterized by unbelief. Now, at the dawn of the twenty-first century, rather than using the term *atheism* or *agnosticism*, it might be better to refer to this phenomenon as *indifference*. This is the term Monsignor Rino Fisichella, president of the Pontifical Council for the Promotion of the New Evangelization, widely uses to describe the situation, particularly in Europe.[7] Religion has ceased to be significant for most of the people around us, not only in terms of individual behavior, but also in the social structure and the formation of culture, as a mentality shared by a certain group of people. Interestingly, this coexists with a religious revival, which seems to indicate some longing or nostalgia, but lacks significance and social relevance. Another way of expressing the same is through the phrase "death of God." Among our contemporary neighbors, there are many who think that God is dead. And in the actual life of many, God *is* dead—or he seems dead, since he has absolutely no influence on their lives. Whatever the reason—either because they do not listen or because they feel that God does not listen to them amidst their suffering and anguish—there is no communication or personal relation between God and these individuals.

The Challenge of Injustice

The second aspect of our context is the heartbreaking situations of global injustice that tear apart our world, turning it upside down. Although in recent decades theological reflection has engaged the challenges posed by this reality, the fact is that the situation continues to worsen for the victims of injustice. Moreover, the twentieth and twenty-first centuries have seen how utopias fall, and how major historical projects fail. We are taking refuge in the flat little story of everyday life. Decades ago, we could refer to a working class as the historical subject of the revolution, or perhaps we could see the impoverished masses as the new people of God on their way to the new exodus. Right now, however, we must focus on the reality of the so-called Fourth World. First, at the global level, an entire continent (Africa) remains at the margins of global economic flows and, in pure economic "logic,"

---

6. See Izuzquiza, *Rincones de la ciudad*, 35–42.
7. Fisichella, *New Evangelization*.

could disappear without a problem. Second, as affluent societies in Europe, we are facing an increasing and contemporary "lumpenproletariat"—masses of people turned into nonpersons. A number of terms are used to refer to them: excluded, marginalized, illegal, *sans-papiers*, undocumented, etc. In the words of Uruguayan writer Eduardo Galeano, they are "los nadies," the nobodies.[8] Probably the most striking example of this reality in Europe refers to migration, specifically irregular migration. All over Europe—in Italy, France, Germany, the United Kingdom, Spain, and so on—different measures have been put in place to limit health care for irregular migrants, thus violating a basic and universal human right.

The Challenge of Pluralism

Another feature of our sociocultural situation is the emergence of religious pluralism. In global terms, this fact is quite clear not only for statistic or geostrategic reasons—that is, the increasing role of religions in the global political realm. And it is not just an effect of global networks of communication, as if the only difference is that we are now more aware of a plurality that has always been there. It is more than that. Actually, we are living in a new paradigm. Particularly in Europe, a "Christian region" throughout the centuries, immigration and other changes in society have modified our religious landscape. Although it is not easy to find accurate figures since they vary significantly according to different sources, there is a significant and increasing presence of Muslim populations in Europe. According to the Pew Forum on Religion and Public Life, the total number of Muslims in Europe in 2010 was slightly more than forty-four million (6 percent), excluding Turkey. The total number of Muslims in the EU in 2010 was about nineteen million (3.8 percent).[9] Less numerous and even more difficult to quantify is the presence of Buddhism,[10] whose influence can be connected with new forms of spirituality apart from organized religions. Besides religious pluralism, there is a persistent and increasing general pluralism. In this context, former Pope Benedict XVI often stressed the dangers of relativism and reiterated the need for the Church to make its voice heard in the public realm—one among the others, humbly but firmly, a Christian voice must enter the public conversation.

---

8. Galeano, *Libro de los abrazos*, 52.
9. Pew Forum and Pew-Templeton, *The Future of the Global Muslim Population*.
10. See Fuss, "The Emerging Euroyâna."

Proposals

Thus situated, we can now address the question that guides our reflection: How do we foster Catholicity and strengthen an incarnated identity in this context, facing these challenges? To this aim, we offer four proposals, which take their inspiration from this well-known passage in the Letter to the Ephesians: "I pray that you may have the power to comprehend, with all the saints, what is the breadth and length and height and depth, and to know the love of Christ that surpasses knowledge, so that you may be filled with all the fullness of God" (Eph 3:17–19).

This means going higher, lower, deeper, and wider. Each of these aspects is deployed in a dynamic and creative tension between two poles. What appears to be an opposition or a contradictory polarization is discovered, from a Christian logic, as a fruitful paradox that energizes existence. It is therefore the logic of the Paschal mystery, the wisdom of the Cross, the Eucharistic key to a full life.

Going Higher

A first feature of an incarnated Catholic identity should lead us higher, above the flat life that surrounds us and in which we live. This means we need to embody the tension between silence and speech. This tension is not just two essential dimensions of the human, expressed in the ability to speak and the ability to listen; nor is it simply a key element of Christian life in general. Of course, all of this is true, but we are also facing a specific response to a particular challenge—that of secularism, which, as we saw, is a central characteristic in the European cultural context.

Secularism limits human reality to certain areas, preventing other facets or dimensions of life to be fully developed, explained, and displayed in public. The result is an impoverished life and society. It is true that there are secular forms of nonreligious spirituality,[11] but it is also true that European society seems to have lost much of its ability to hear the reality beyond what science, technology, and economics tell. We need to hear other voices, and thus we need other voices to be present in society. In short, we need a higher vision, one that exceeds the shallowness of what is already known, a way of looking that goes beyond the quantifiable. Of course, Christian identity cannot accept pushing God out of society, but it should bring its word—one more voice in the midst of a pluralistic society—so that the religious dimension can be heard in the public discourse.

---

11. See, as a significant and recent example, Ferry, *La révolution de l'amour*.

Going Lower

If we need to go higher, we also need to go lower. As already mentioned, secularization comes together with injustice, inequality, and social exclusion. This cannot be surprising at all, since global capitalism is but one form of secularism—nowadays, the dominant one. In other words, capitalism is the economic expression of secularization in the world of thought. It is by no means an accident that secularization is only a major tendency among the elites of the world, not among the popular masses in history and humanity.[12] Therefore, we say that we must go down, lower, closer to the poor.

If we want to develop an authentic Catholic identity, we need to combine a universal vision with a preferential option for the poor. As noted by some authors, the only way to live universality is from below, from the poor.[13] Not only for spiritual purposes but also for practical, economic, and ecological reasons: the current system of consumption is not sustainable, and it is impossible to extrapolate it beyond privileged minorities to reach the whole of humanity or, at least, the majority. Therefore, we say that only from below is a Christian globalization possible. We need to combine action and passion. Passion first, because it is necessary to share the life, the desires, and the sufferings of the poor people of the earth, crucified like Jesus, and also because it is necessary to live passionately in the struggle to improve this world. Therefore, together with this passion, action appears. To put it another way, Catholic identity must be embodied in the lives of the poor and in the fight against poverty. In a world as unequal as ours, Christian identity cannot remain indifferent in the face of global capitalism and the injustice and suffering that come along with it.

Going Deeper

A third element, connected to the one already mentioned, refers to the shallowness of life. If the first aspect we have indicated—going higher in the face of secularization—seems to require a particular religious view of the world, and the second aspect—going lower against injustice and inequality—seems to imply a certain ideological approach, then in going deeper we simply need to discover a true appreciation of humanity. Much of our world, our relationships, and our way of understanding reality is dominated

---

12. See, for instance, the data and reflections of a Spanish sociologist of religion in Elzo, *Los cristianos*.

13. Sobrino, *Fuera de los pobres*.

by an extreme superficiality. And this leads to an existential boredom, a meaningless life.

Too often, we humans—and I think this is especially true in my particular European context—become dominated by work, activism, and productivity. Honestly, a very poor life horizon. Furthermore, as a lifestyle, it is quite impoverishing. We tend to forget other key dimensions of life, which humanize us and put us in contact with the specifically human: relationships, dialogue, coexistence, public action for the common good, and so on. Thus, we need to nurture and to develop a new polarity: understanding life as a gift and, at the same time, as a task (in German, *Gabe* = gift, and *Aufgabe* = task). In our world, we often live alternating hard work with indifference and lack of responsibility. On the one hand, we work too hard in a productivist manner; on the other hand, we are insufficiently committed. There is an error in this approach, which leads to destroying the person and which does not build a humane society. By contrast, the Christian point of view understands life as an undeserved gift that we receive gratuitously and, for that reason, as a commitment of our own freedom in the task of making the world more livable for everyone. This means going deeper.

Going Wider

Finally, the fourth dimension we must address leads us wider than we have seen so far. Surely, Christian identity is anchored in the concrete, embodied in a local territory, linked to personal stories. But it is not reduced to them. It opens, from there, to the universal. It expands itself. It becomes wider. As one famous nineteenth-century hymn has it, "There's a wideness in God's mercy." The Christian way of self-understanding is always universal and catholic, precisely because it is received from Godself, who is unbounded amplitude.

These are not purely devotional or generic issues, but they relate very directly to a society often dominated by the "politically correct." A society that has narrowed its views, that has limited the horizon of the possible, has deleted utopia from its thought and action. Facing this situation, it is essential to rediscover another way of standing before life, with a broader, more open, more inclusive approach. This is a more divine and, for the same reason, more human horizon, because all human beings fit there—no one is excluded. Borrowing a classical expression from the Catholic Worker movement, we must rediscover hospitality and resistance. On the one hand, hospitality with the stranger, the poor, the other, the very concrete suffering person before us. On the other hand, resistance against all unjust and oppressive systems that create this very suffering. We need to widen our hearts in order to welcome the other, to be hospitable. And we need to widen our communities and societies so that, in practice, no one is excluded from God's mercy.

In sum, using Paul Tillich's words, the dynamic tension between Catholicity and incarnated identities is shown in "the tension that exists between the absolutely concrete and the absolutely universal." Tillich recognizes that "it seems paradoxical if one says that only that which is absolutely concrete can be absolutely universal and vice versa," but he also notes that it is precisely here where "Christian theology emerges, the point which is described as 'Logos became flesh.'" He specifies, in a footnote, that "the Logos doctrine is misunderstood if the tension between the universal and the concrete is interpreted as a tension between the abstract and the particular . . . Christian theology moves between the poles of the universal and the concrete, but not between the poles of the abstract and the particular."[14] Only Jesus Christ can solve this tension, as he is the incarnation of God, in whom the absolutely concrete and the absolutely universal become united.

Conclusion

At this point, it may seem too difficult to embody Catholicity in the European territory. We may even feel that we are living in minority, isolated. For this reason, as a final reflection, I refer to one of the best-known European comics, *The Adventures of Asterix and Obelix*. In my opinion, these characters—Gauls living in a village on the ancient Brittany coast, always surrounded and threatened by the powerful Roman empire—shed some light on what it means to flesh out a Christian identity in twenty-first-century Europe.[15]

First, I focus on Obelix, strong and simple as a standing stone, authentic and tender as the boars. You may remember that he received his supreme strength when, as a child, he fell into a kettle full of a magic potion that Getafix the Druid had prepared. What a baptism by immersion! Immersed in the potion, Obelix was, from that point forward, a special being, forever marked with an unknown strength. As Christians, "we have been buried with him by baptism into death, so that, just as Christ was raised from the dead by the glory of the Father, so we too might walk in newness of life" (Rom 6:4). Immersed in Christ and in the life of the Trinity, we are new

---

14. Tillich, *Systematic Theology*, 1:16–17.
15. See Izuzquiza, "Astérix y Obélix," 52.

creatures. Do we really live according to our baptism, or are we "conformed to this world" (cf. Rom 12:2)?

Asterix, on the other hand, helps us capture the effect of the Eucharist in our lives. Agile, intelligent, dynamic, creative, kind . . . his smallness is transformed with an overwhelming power whenever he partakes of the magic potion. He is not changed once and forever—as Obelix was by his "baptism"—but he assumes progression in life and the need to go back once and again to daily food. Like the manna in the wilderness (see Exod 16), daily Eucharist gives us the strength to walk some distance at a time, every day, and thus it gradually transforms us.

The characters' Gallic village, as such, also offers some insights that help clarify our identity as a Christian community. I highlight only two. First, their shared communal character allows them to interact with the Romans without succumbing to their threats, while at the same time, they are also able to interact with various peoples without diluting themselves. It might be possible that they require overcoming "resistance identity" in order to open themselves to an identity-project, but meanwhile, at least, these Gauls are not swallowed by the empire. Certainly, European Christians must be "in the world but not of the world"—that is, we should not allow ourselves to be kidnapped by it.

Finally, readers may recall the final scene of every episode of the adventures of Asterix: the whole village is gathered around the table for a banquet that they all celebrate together. We can find here a reference to the Eucharist. The Eucharist is always local, always universal.[16] It is never a mere individual devotion but an act of the community; it not just strength to carry on but also a joyous, festive, and overflowing celebration. For this reason, any Catholic identity that is born and nourished by the Eucharist will be a transformed and transformational identity—an identity that can dive into the thick of the real (secularism, injustice, pluralism; economic, political, and cultural crisis) and, from there, an identity that can push reality to higher, lower, deeper, and wider levels. That is, it is an identity that becomes more catholic and more incarnated at the same time.

---

16. See Cavanaugh, *Theopolitical Imagination*, 112–22; Cavanaugh, *Being Consumed*, 59–88.

5

The Challenge of Being a Catholic in Liberal Secular Europe

A. ALEXANDER STUMMVOLL

Introduction

European Catholicism—the faith, piety, and religious tradition that historically have helped shape Europe's culture and values more than any other religious belief system or political ideology—is under great pressure.[1] The galloping secularization of Europe, plummeting church attendance rates, and an ever-growing disconnect between popular culture and religion are pointing toward a far-reaching and radical transformation of European Catholicism. Given today's postmodern pluralism, faith is becoming an important yet difficult personal choice rather than a widely shared heritage that is part and parcel of European identity.

As a young European Catholic who has studied, lived, and worshipped in Austria, Germany, the United States, Wales, France, England, Belgium, Italy, and Chile, I often get smiles from people when they find out I am a practicing Catholic. In Europe, I sometimes get asked—amusingly, if not disparagingly—"How can a young, intelligent, cosmopolitan man like you *still* adhere to such an outdated thing as the Catholic faith?" Occasionally, people express their admiration. In contrast to similar conversations in North or South America, however, I never leave such encounters with the feeling that it simply is normal to be a Catholic Christian in Europe. In the secular and highly diverse context of today's Europe, what, if any, future

---

1. I gratefully want to acknowledge helpful comments on this paper provided by Mariano Barbato; Josef Hien; Fearghas Ó Béara; Justinus Pech, OCist; and Jodok Troy.

does European Catholicism have, especially for young people? Can it be saved from what appears to be an unprecedented and inevitable demise?

In this chapter, I want to discuss the relationship between liberal secularism and Catholicism in Europe, particularly the challenge the former poses to the latter. I will make the admittedly pessimistic argument that European Catholics are an endangered species. In a nutshell, Catholicism in Europe is in a crisis whose long-term cultural, theological, and political transformations are still difficult to foresee. In fact, the erosion of European Catholicism dates back to the Enlightenment and the French Revolution. However, whereas secularization was largely an elite-driven phenomenon in the past, it has now become a mass phenomenon that increasingly puts the onus of justification on the Christian believer rather than the nonbeliever.

Cultural and geographical context matters when discussing the theological, political, and personal problem of faithfully living out the Catholic Christian tradition in a world where many different ideologies and groups also expect loyalty and commitment. In contrast to Stanley Hauerwas and Michael Budde, who warn us about the seductive temptations of capitalism and nationalism in a North American context—or Emanuel Katongole, who is concerned about the way the blood of tribalism often trumps the water of baptism—I argue that the biggest problem facing European Catholics is liberal secularism. Together with a strong commitment to pragmatism and materialism, the contemporary liberal secular European mind exalts the autonomy of the individual, thus transforming faith into an increasingly challenging personal choice rather than a cultural fact that traditionally had rather naturally been passed on from one generation to the next.

Existing secular and liberal structural pressure makes it highly unlikely, if not impossible, to save European Catholicism as we know it, because both secularization and liberalism make it increasingly difficult to choose and live out the Catholic tradition. The Catholic Church will neither regain its former hegemonic grip on European culture and values, as conservative Catholics hope, nor will it conform to the postmodern *Zeitgeist*, as liberal Catholics wish. Rather, current trends suggest that Catholic life is increasingly coalescing not around the traditional parish but around diverse, smaller yet spiritually vibrant communities, spiritual centers, and pilgrimage sites. The European Church is still very rich in financial terms, especially in Germany and Austria. Evidence suggests, however, that the future Church will become materially poorer and constitutional privileges will be increasingly difficult to defend. European Catholicism will take an increasingly critical stance vis-à-vis the surrounding culture and will have to be a missionary Church in an indifferent, if not hostile, environment. These structural changes should be neither feared nor demonized. In fact, they provide a welcome opportunity for evolution as European Catholics have become too lazy in their personal missionary zeal and as ecclesial institutions urgently need to revamp pastoral strategies in order to transform a declining and complacent status-quo Church into a more vigorous missionary Church.

The Disconnect between Culture and Christianity in Europe

In his book *The Borders of Baptism: Identities, Allegiances, and the Church*,[2] Michael Budde argues that if Christians only took "ecclesial solidarity" more seriously—that is, their allegiance to Jesus Christ and their bonds to fellow Christians around the world as well as humanity at large—politics as usual would become radically converted. Rival sources of identity—Budde is particularly concerned with the idolatries of patriotism, capitalism, and racism—would then have less, if any, impact on the attitudes and practices of baptized Christians. Such a change of heart, Budde claims, is imperative, as "the inability of churches across confessional divides to form people into more than nominal or cultural Christians is one of the scandals of our age." The Catholic Church, Budde regrets, is actually the trailblazer as the "least effective in forming the affections, dispositions, and priorities of its would-be adherents."[3]

Writing from a North American perspective that broadly converges with similar thoughts expressed in the field of political theology by eminent thinkers such as Stanley Hauerwas, William Cavanaugh, and Emanuel Katongole, Budde deplores that Christianity tends to be too comfortable with patriotism and neoliberal capitalism, thus reducing itself to an integral part of mainstream culture, rather than being an independent prophetic force that critically examines popular beliefs and prevailing policies in the light of the gospel. While Budde is critical of the convergence between culture-as-it-is and Christianity-as-it-is, he makes the normative argument that there should be a divergence between culture-as-it-is and Christianity-as-it-ought-to-be. Underpinning this normative argument are two important implicit assumptions: first, Christianity is an attractive way of life, and second, Christianity actually enjoys a meaningful presence, even if only in a nominal manner. While both assumptions hold true for the United States, a bleaker and more complicated picture emerges if we try to apply this argument to a European context.

2. Budde, *Borders of Baptism*.
3. Ibid., 99–100.

The secular and liberal pressure on the Catholic Church is considerably stronger in Europe than it is in the United States. This does not mean that there is an elite-driven conspiracy to push religion out of the public sphere. The pressure is both deeper and more powerful as it takes place on a structural level. In the past, Europeans were Catholic, Protestant, Orthodox, Anglican, or Jewish, with some pockets of Muslims in the Balkans. With some exceptions, such as the Jewish ghettos, the surrounding culture and religion formed part of a coherent whole. While we should not fall into the trap of overgeneralizing or overestimating the religious literacy of past generations, it is safe to assume that it was generally much easier to be religious in the past. It was considerably more difficult—at dark times, even deadly—to reject purposely the religion of one's culture.

A series of complex political, economic, and social upheavals, transformations, and changes increasingly drove a wedge into this intrinsic linkage between religion and mainstream culture. The 1789 French Revolution sowed the seeds of a strong anticlerical tradition and put man rather than God at the center of political philosophy. Nineteenth-century philosophers such as Karl Marx, Ludwig Feuerbach, and Sigmund Freud provided the first powerful intellectual reasons for modern atheism and agnosticism. Nazism subjected the Jewish population to genocide, and Communism led to a persecution of Christianity. The sexual revolution of the 1960s led to a questioning skepticism vis-à-vis the moral authority of the Church whose credibility has recently further suffered from the child abuse scandal. The blatant gap between professed values and actual practices scandalized Christians and non-Christians alike.

Europe is experiencing what Charles Taylor refers to as "a secular age." We have moved "from a society where belief in God is unchallenged and indeed, unproblematic, to one in which it is understood to be one option among others, and frequently not the easiest to embrace."[4] More specifically, to apply Taylor's secularization argument to the situation of European Catholic Christianity, European culture is de-Christianizing itself. God, religion, and the Church move to the background, whereas individual autonomy moves to the forefront. This does not mean that liberal secularism automatically results in ethical relativism. Rather, liberal and secular values contest, replace, and compete with Christian values, particularly on issues of sexual ethics and family values. Our liberal secular friends are anything but lukewarm about the values they confess. The problem, then, is not a clash between Christian values and a confused postmodern wilderness but a clash between Christian values and liberal secular values, although a clash

---

4. Taylor, *Secular Age*, 3.

on sexual ethics and family values coexists with a convergence on sociopolitical issues such as the fight against poverty and social injustice. Church leaders across Europe have tried hard to stem this tide. But the liberalization of popular attitudes and state policies on contraception, abortion, and, more recently, same-sex marriage highlights the limits of the Church's cultural influence. Often the Church's power is imagined to be much greater than its actual impact on public policies.

What further complicates analysis of the tension between liberal secular values and Catholic values is the way this tension often is misused and exploited by the extreme political right for their xenophobic, Islamophobic, anti-Semitic, anti-European, and homophobic policies rather than for a faithful and authentic concern about the role of Christianity in Europe. During the 2009 electoral campaign for the European Parliament, for example, Heinz-Christian Strache, the leader of the far-right Austrian Freedom Party (FPÖ), held up a cross during a rally against plans to build a mosque, which prompted the archbishop of Vienna, Cardinal Schönborn, to publicly state that the cross "must not be misused as a fighting symbol against other religions."[5] It is a Christian imperative, then, for the Catholic Church and its members to critically ask *who* is advancing arguments in favor of Europe's Christian identities and for *what kind of political purpose* in order not to be co-opted by the extreme right for their un-Christian and often anti-Christian worldviews.

The disconnect between culture and religion in Europe means that the Church increasingly cannot identify itself with the surrounding European culture, which it historically helped create and sustain. At the same time, secularized Europeans find the Church's stance on hot-button issues odd, outdated if not unjustifiable, and discriminatory. Secularism has not canceled out religion, though, Olivier Roy warns. Rather, secularism is helping reshape and reformat religion as an autonomous category largely independent of the sphere of culture, society, and politics.[6] Religious people are also implicit in the move toward a "purer" concept of religion as the standards of what it means to be a good Catholic are becoming increasingly higher. It is neither sufficient nor possible to simply receive the sacraments, show up at church on Sundays, and be carried through life by a largely supportive surrounding culture. Rather, a deeper personal faith coupled with a commitment to Christian practices, even if they involve painful countercultural positions, are becoming the new imperative for ordinary Catholics but especially for Catholics in leading positions in both church and politics.

5. *BBC News*, "Far Right Riles Austrian Church."
6. Roy, *Holy Ignorance*.

Historically, arguments about the de-Christianization of Europe are not new and have surfaced during the eighteenth-century French Revolution, the nineteenth-century conflict between Catholicism and liberal modernity, and the twentieth-century persecution of the Church in the age of totalitarianism. What is a novelty, though, is the extent to which the de-Christianization of Europe is not predominantly the result of an oppressive hostility by outside forces but is also driven by a conscious voluntary policy of exculturation. This process, Oliver Roy explains, occurs when a hegemonic religious tradition retreats from a culture to which it hitherto had been organically linked but which it now increasingly perceives to be contaminating, negative, or pagan rather than simply non-sacred, that is, profane.[7] Whereas Europeans are forgetting about their Christian heritage, there is an ongoing debate among European Christians on the question of how to deal with this growing disconnect between culture and religion. Should Christianity be modernized, or should Europe be (re)Christianized?

Changing the Church or Changing the World?

The typical reaction of liberal Catholics is to call for a more "modern" form of Catholicism, in line with the "spirit" of the Second Vatican Council (1962–65) during which Catholic bishops from around the world came together to discuss the question of what it means to be a Catholic in the modern world. Traditional Catholics, on the other hand, worry that distorting interpretations of the actual Council texts have already made the Church too "worldly." In their view, renewed emphasis has to be put on re-evangelizing society in accordance with traditional papal teaching. Ultraconservative Catholics, such as followers of Archbishop Marcel Lefebvre, founder of the controversial Society of St. Pius X, would even claim that the papacy, in the aftermath of the Council, made too many compromises with modernity and can no longer speak legitimately on behalf of Catholic orthodoxy.

European liberal Catholics, for their part, like to blame the "restorationist" policies of Pope John Paul II and Pope Benedict XVI for the demise of the Catholic Church in Europe, especially their hard stance on abortion, contraception, gay marriage, divorce, and female priests. One of the most prominent liberal Catholic critics of the Church is the Swiss theologian Hans Küng. Together with Joseph Ratzinger, who, in 2005, became Pope Benedict XVI, Küng was the youngest theological expert advisor during the Second Vatican Council. In the late 1960s, both served together as theology

---

7. Ibid., 115–19.

professors in Tübingen, Germany, before Ratzinger returned to his native Bavaria, having become wary of the intellectual atmosphere in Tübingen, which became dominated by the 1968 student movement and Marxism.

Küng and Ratzinger personify two very different strands of Catholicism that fundamentally diverge in their diagnosis of the causes of the Church's contemporary problems and in their prescriptions for how to move forward. In his 2011 book *Ist die Kirche noch zu retten? (Can We Save the Catholic Church?)*, Küng blames Pope John Paul and Pope Benedict for failing to continue the project of the Second Vatican Council. Liberal Catholics such as Küng insist on the importance of radical internal Church reforms, which should include an end to mandatory celibacy for priests, allowing women to serve as deacons if not even as priests, relaxing moral rules on contraception, allowing remarried Catholics to receive communion, and permitting intercommunion services between Catholics and Protestants.[8] A progressive group of Austrian priests, the so-called Priests' Initiative, even expressed a public "call for disobedience" to foster these ends.[9] Elsewhere, Küng warned about a "Putinization" of the Vatican and went as far as arguing that the sidelining of critics, the promotion of former associates, the disempowerment of the Russian parliament and the Synod of Bishops, and the resistance to "real reform" revealed striking parallels between Putin's Kremlin and Benedict's Vatican.[10]

Pope Benedict XVI, on the other hand, following St. Augustine, views the world much more critically as a sphere of selfishness, widespread moral relativism, and global injustice. As God's people, the Church's task is to sanctify and heal the world. He consequently puts the stress on reforming and changing the world rather than the Church, and he emphasizes the need for permanent individual conversion, celebrating the sacraments, personal commitment to Church teaching, maintaining Church discipline and unity, and evangelizing. Ratzinger's recently published collected writings on ecclesiology reveal that his emphasis on changing the world rather than the Church is a thread that has permeated his writings for many decades.[11] As early as 1958, Ratzinger warned that the Catholic Church in Europe had become a "church of pagans," that is, it had become too worldly. In contrast to earlier times, the pagans were now in the midst of the Church rather than outside it. In the early church, faith was based on an act of conversion and deep personal faith in Jesus Christ, which led to an "authentic, living

---

8. Küng, *Ist die Kirche noch zu retten?*
9. See the Pfarrer-Initiative's Web site: http://www.pfarrer-initiative.at/.
10. Doerry et al., "Theologian Hans Küng on Pope Benedict."
11. Ratzinger, *Kirche-Zeichen* (2010a, 2010b).

community of the faithful." Well before secularization fully accelerated in Western Europe, Ratzinger already deplored that Christianity had ceased to be a personal decision and became a more or less random political-cultural characteristic of the Occident. To move forward, Ratzinger suggested tighter sacramentary discipline, as "sacraments without faith are useless," and a stronger distinction between "Church" and "non-Church" as a prerequisite for renewed missionary efforts to convert new pagans.[12]

"The call for reform is virtually universal, while the terms of reform are comprehensively disputed," George Weigel rightly notices in his prologue to his latest book, *Evangelical Catholicism*.[13] Indeed, reform is a key concept in the theology of both Hans Küng and Joseph Ratzinger. However, while the former understands reform in terms of structural, institutional change and a modernization of teaching, the latter defines "true reform" primarily in terms of a personal spiritual conversion. "Liberal" and "conservative" are perhaps concepts that are too politically charged and too polarizing to serve as helpful labels for understanding how European Catholics come down on different sides of an important ongoing debate. The Vatican's emphasis on fighting social injustice, combating climate change, deepening disarmament, protecting migrants, and promoting fairer economic relations between North and South can hardly be classified as "conservative." Moreover, "liberal" priests and lay people are often much more committed to "conserving" conventional local parish structures than their "conservative" counterparts who believe that the Church first may have to shrink again to a vibrant, small, and healthy size before it may once more expand in the future.

Pragmatically speaking, the liberal Catholic vision of making the Church conform to the liberal *Zeitgeist* is a pipe dream, as this project enjoys no support among key decision-makers inside the Vatican and little enthusiasm in the Global South. In this context, it will be fascinating to see how long the liberal Catholic honeymoon with Pope Francis will last. The Holy Father's interest in a poor church, in being close to the poor, and his humble style have been very well received. On a deeper level, as John Allen explained, the Church in the Global South tends to be morally even more conservative on issues such as abortion, homosexuality, and traditional family values. The liberal issues that tend to dominate Church debates in Europe—celibacy, female priests, sexuality, divorce, abortion, secularism, relations with Protestantism—are not the key issues for Catholics in the Global South, whose concerns have more to do with material survival,

---

12. Ratzinger, *Kirche-Zeichen* (2010b), 1143–58.
13. Weigel, *Evangelical Catholicism*, 1.

development, fighting poverty and social injustice, and dealing with the effects and causes of war, migration, unbridled capitalism, and the growth of rival evangelical movements or Islam.[14] The conservative vision for how to move the European Church forward suffers from a different, more nostalgic illusion. Rather than realizing and accepting that the mainstream culture of contemporary Europe is fundamentally disconnecting itself from Christianity, there is a strong tendency to sulk and to look backward to Europe's "Christian roots" rather than forward to the future. The outcry over the omission of a reference to God in the preamble of the EU Constitution and, following its failed ratification, in the Treaty of Lisbon serves as a case in point. Descriptively, at least, the Treaty's reference to the "cultural, religious, and humanist inheritance of Europe" is a compromise solution that reflects more the current realities and belief patterns of Europeans than wishful thinking about Europe's Christian identity.[15]

In sum, not only is the Catholic Church in Europe subject to strong secular and liberal pressure, there is also a strong division among European Catholics with regard to the question of what kind of reforms are necessary and whether the object of reform should be individual hearts, Church teachings, or the world.

Current Trends

After centuries in which Catholicism, in tandem with its Protestant twin, was the cultural hegemon of Western and Central Europe, Catholics have to learn what it means to live in a secularized mission territory rather than in the traditional heartland of Christianity. This structural change has far-reaching pastoral, theological, social, and political consequences. Five trends are particularly worthy to note.

First, *the traditional model of the local parish is becoming either outdated or is in need of radical transformation.* Given the decline in the number of practicing Catholics as well as the ensuing decrease in the number of vocations to the priesthood, larger and different organizational models of bringing Catholics together for praying, worshipping, and celebrating the sacraments will be necessary. This process is already underway in Germany and Austria. The Archdiocese of Vienna, for example, under the leadership of Cardinal Schönborn, recently launched a development process called Acts of the Apostles 2.1 with a view to helping create more

---

14. Allen, *Future Church*.

15. For a good overview of the institutional role of religion in the European Union, see Leustean, *Does God Matter?*

conducive structures for missionary activities and to proactively respond to the priest shortage and more limited financial resources.[16] The core idea behind such restructuring processes is the realization that the Catholic Church in Europe simultaneously needs larger administrative units and smaller faith-driven communities. Larger territorial units are needed to reduce administrative redundancies, to ensure better cooperation, to create more collegiality among priests, and to sell hundreds if not thousands of buildings that no longer serve any essential purposes. Smaller faith-driven communities, led by lay people on a voluntary basis, will be essential for keeping and spreading the faith in a personal manner in close proximity to people on the ground.

Second, *the most creative and dynamic spiritual and pastoral centers no longer tend to be found in traditional parishes but are linked to diverse groups, movements, pilgrimage sites, ecclesial events, and monasteries* such as the ecumenical community in Taizé with its youth gatherings, the Focolare Movement, Communion and Liberation, the Camino de Santiago in Spain, the World Youth Days, or the Cistercian monastery of Heiligenkreuz in Austria with its award-winning monks singing Gregorian chants in Latin.

Third, *in the long run, the Church in Europe will become poorer and is facing the probability of losing further material and constitutional privileges.* Whereas the number of baptisms, marriages, and priests is declining dramatically, the Church's income in Germany is the only statistical indicator that has grown—from 4.3 billion Euros in 1995 to 5.2 billion in 2012—largely thanks to macroeconomic reasons.[17] However, given the ongoing decline in Church membership and the general aging of Europe's population, in twenty years German dioceses will probably face a budget deficit of 20 to 30 percent.[18] Constitutional or symbolic privileges such as the presence of crucifixes in classrooms or state aid in collecting church taxes are increasingly difficult to defend. Pope Benedict, in a speech in Freiburg during his 2011 apostolic journey to Germany, recommended a "profound liberation of the Church from forms of worldliness" (*Entweltlichung*) so that the Church becomes a more credible witness and regains her worldly poverty. Such a less worldly attitude, the pope argued, is especially important to counter "a contrary tendency . . . namely that the Church becomes self-satisfied,

---

16. See the Web site of the Roman Catholic Archdiocese of Vienna for information on its "Diocesan Development Process" [Diözesaner Entwicklungsprozess]: http://www.erzdioezese-wien.at/pages/inst/25473874.

17. See the official statistics provided by the German Bishops' Conference, "Nettoaufkommen an Kirchenlohn- und -einkommensteuer."

18. See the analysis provided by McKinsey & Company Senior Director Thomas von Mitschke-Collande, *Schafft sich die Katholische Kirche ab?*, chapter 2.5.

settles down in this world, becomes self-sufficient, and adapts herself to the standards of the world."[19] Rather than seeing its material riches as an asset, Pope Benedict conceded that even though the "Church in Germany is superbly organized" and has "more than enough by way of structure," it has "not enough by way of spirit."[20] Providing a strong, implicit critique of the liberal argument that the Church needs to change in order to modernize its teaching, Pope Benedict put the emphasis on an individual change of heart. While the German bishops did not believe that Benedict's argument about *Entweltlichung* questioned the government's collection of church tax, there is a curious shared opposition among secular liberals and conservative Catholics who wish to see this practice come to an end. The former see an inappropriate confluence of church and state activities. The latter, outraged that a failure to pay church tax actually leads to a *de facto* excommunication from the Church, supports stifling bureaucratic structures of Catholic institutions and the kind of worldliness that Benedict XVI warned about.

Fourth, *after centuries in which Europeans sent out missionaries and priests to other continents, we are now beginning to experience "reverse" missionary activities where priests from countries such as India or the Philippines will come to Europe to serve local Catholics.*[21] In an ideal world, foreign missionaries would be an exciting personification of the global Church and help revitalize a spiritually tired continent. The move away from small parishes and the import of priests from abroad will not be without tension, as people will probably have to attend Sunday Mass further away from their homes and as cultural and spiritual differences between foreign priests and local congregations could cause conflict. Also, priests from the Southern hemisphere may require special training to come to grips with the condition of material abundance and spiritual poverty that tends to be the exact opposite of conditions in the Global South. In the same context, it is also important to note how lay migrants change the demographic composition of European Catholics in cosmopolitan cities such as London.[22] Whereas European Catholics brought the cross to the rest of the world in the missionary era, they now increasingly rely on non-Europeans to reinvigorate their dry faith.

Fifth, *the European Church is losing its dominant role in the global Church*. It is already anachronistic that 52 percent of all cardinal electors come from Europe, whereas European Catholics represent only 23.8 percent

---

19. Benedict XVI, "Address at Meeting with Catholics Engaged in the Life of the Church and Society."
20. Benedict XVI, "Address at Meeting with the Catholic Lay Faithful."
21. Allen, *Future Church*, 44–45.
22. Cacciottolo, "Papal Visit."

of all baptized Catholics. Europe deserves much less representation in the College of Cardinals if we measure importance in terms of its share of the global number of Catholics. The numbers of the official Statistical Yearbook of the Church, published by the Vatican, are revealing:[23]

1973

Continent	Total Population	Catholics	Percent of Total Population	Percent of Total Number of Catholics	Cardinal Electors (Oct. 1978)	Percent of Cardinal Electors
Africa	378,935,000	44,200,000	11.6	6.4	13	11.7
Americas	535,813,000	326,300,000	60.9	46.9	31	27.9
Asia	2,213,127,000	56,000,000	2.5	8.1	7	6.3
Europe	655,812,000	263,600,000	40.1	37.9	56	50.5
Oceania	20,312,000	4,900,000	24	0.7	4	3.6
Total	3,803,999,000	695,000,000	18.3	100	111	100

2010

Continent	Total Population	Catholics	Percent of Total Population	Percent of Total Number of Catholics	Cardinal Electors (2013)	Percent of Cardinal Electors
Africa	1,015,544,000	185,620,000	18.3	15.5	11	9.6
Americas	927,021,000	585,998,000	63.2	49.0	33	28.7
Asia	4,156,096,000	129,661,000	3.1	10.8	10	8.7
Europe	713,397,000	284,924,000	39.9	23.8	60	52.2
Oceania	36,492,000	9,468,000	26.0	0.8	1	0.9
Total	6,848,550,000	1,195,671,000	17.5	100	115	100

A comparison of these tables shows that, in 1973, Europeans constituted 37.9 percent of all Catholics. In 2010, Europe was home to only 23.8 percent of global Catholics, yet by the time Pope Benedict resigned in 2013, its share of cardinal electors had actually slightly increased to 52.5 percent compared with 50.5 percent at the October 1978 conclave that elected Pope

23. Catholic Church, *Annuarium*, 1973 and 2010.

John Paul II. In fact, all other continents increased their share of global Catholics over the last forty years, with Europe being the sole and dramatic exception.

Looking Forward

It is highly unlikely, if not impossible, to save European Catholicism as we commonly know it as a dominant, culture-shaping religious force in Europe. Secular and liberal structural pressures that go back to the Enlightenment, the French Revolution, and the emergence of modern forms of atheism and agnosticism underpin the ongoing de-Christianization of Western Europe. The Catholic Church in Europe is divided over how to react to this ever-growing disconnect between culture and religion. The different models for incarnating Catholic identity—or living out Catholic tradition—vary significantly. Liberal Catholics believe the answer lies in reconciling Catholicism with liberal modernity. To bridge the gap between the Church and the world, far-reaching "change" is necessary. Conservative Catholics, on the other hand, are much more optimistic about the Church and pessimistic about the world. They want the Church to stay truthful to tradition in order to re-evangelize a "sinful world." While this distinction might be too simplistic, and while there are many shades of grey, there is an important cleavage among European Catholics and no widely shared recipe for how to react to the galloping secularization and liberalization of values in Europe.

We are likely to see increased tensions between the Catholic Church, on the one hand, and government authorities and popular culture, on the other. To the extent that mainstream European culture and Christianity will alienate themselves from each other, it would not come as a surprise to see American-style culture wars enter into a European context. We are likely to see a Church that will enjoy fewer constitutional privileges but will be more involved in political opinion-shaping and cultural interventions. We will see a Church that will have to come to grips with its new minority situation. European Catholics will have to be missionaries, or they will not *be*. If the Catholic faith is not being incarnated, passed on, and promoted, it will gradually wither away, as it is no longer sustained by a supportive surrounding culture. Christianity will become a continuous and highly personal choice, challenge, and journey that only begins rather than ends with baptism, first communion, and confirmation.

More radical, more personal, and more authentic forms of discipleship will be a *sine qua non* for European Catholics. However, amidst all structural transformations, the big temptation to avoid is to reduce Christianity to an elite project of the committed few rather than present it as a source of salvation for all. Put differently, the Church in Europe must not become a scared subculture but a sacred counterculture. Sociologically, it is understandable that a Church under cultural siege shores up its identity. Pastorally, however, the Church must not scare away the huge middle ground of people, especially young people, who are neither principled atheists nor practicing Catholics but who may be culturally drawn to Christianity while having questions and doubts. In the past, the inherent connection between Christianity and culture in Europe ensured that there were sufficient points of contact. In the present and future, these contemporary doubting Thomases will drift even further away and will have no chance of personally encountering the risen Christ if there is no pastoral outreach, or if they encounter nothing but judgmental, elitist, or inward-looking attitudes on the part of practicing Catholics. Pope Francis's recommendation that the Church should not get stuck in the sacristy and become self-absorbed by internal debates but cast itself out into the gutters of poverty and suffering provides a very helpful and timely warning in this regard.

Neoclericalism cannot be the answer to the evaporating Catholic identity of Europe. As Catholics, we must never believe that Christians are better than nonbelievers or people of other religions. As Catholics, we must never believe that God works only through Christians and abandons nonbelievers. As Catholics, we must believe that by serving, loving, and being with the poor, the marginalized, the oppressed, and the nonbelieving, we follow the message and person of Jesus Christ. It will not be easy to become or remain a Christian in twenty-first-century Europe, especially for young people, but it certainly will not be boring.

6

Multiple Caesars? Germany, Bavaria, and German Catholics in the Interwar Period

MARTIN MENKE

Living faithful to God in the world has never been easy, especially when earthly demands and those of God come into conflict. Choosing correctly is difficult, as there are many potent earthly distractions. Already in Joshua, God reminds us to choose wisely when, confronted with false gods, Joshua proclaims, "Now if you are unwilling to serve the Lord, choose this day whom you will serve, whether the gods your ancestors served in the region beyond the River or the gods of the Amorites in whose land you are living; but as for me and my household, we will serve the Lord."[1] Ever since, it has been difficult to make this choice. When Jesus told the Pharisees to give unto God what is God's but unto Caesar what is Caesar's, he knew what choice they had already made.[2] Finally, when Pilate demanded of Jesus what earthly power he wielded, Jesus reminded us that Pilate was asking the wrong question, that earthly power is irrelevant in face of a "kingdom not of this world."[3] In other words, what ultimately matters—the basis of the final judgment—is faithful service to God. The measure of all Christian life is whether or not it moves us closer to our transcendent God. Theologian Dorian Llywelyn quotes Benedict XVI's words at Auschwitz: that identities as citizens, as rooted in a certain region, a certain class and culture, must ultimately be reconciled with the identity as Christian.[4] In other words, identities incompatible with Christianity must be rejected or at least modified.

---

1. Josh 24:15.
2. Mark 12:13–17.
3. John 18:33–38.
4. Llywelyn, *Toward a Catholic Theology*, 16. See also Budde, *Borders of Baptism*, 70.

National identity is one of these identities that must be reconciled to Christian identity, but increasingly, national identity itself is a problematic concept. First, as Moritz Föllmer has argued, nationalism can be just as divisive within a country because it appears to imply a high degree of homogeneity, which cannot exist in a pluralistic society.[5] Secondly, Zimmer has defined the process of nation-building as a "competition [among various groups] for the right to interpret and define, for status and prestige in the evolving nation-state. At the heart of this process are nationally bound processes of interaction and interpretation in which various confessional groups actively participate."[6] In other words, religious groups jockey for relevance and even preeminence in each new forming nation-state or in nation-states redefining themselves. A great example of this is the case of German Catholics in the interwar period of the twentieth century. Their experience offers examples with which to complicate the question of the relationship between identities defined by religion, nation, and region.

In the *City of God*, Saint Augustine comforted the people of rapidly declining Rome by pointing to the City of God as the only home that mattered, not the city of man.[7] The most poignant example of this subordination of secular authority to the demands of a transcendent God, however, is Saint Ambrose's admonition to Emperor Theodosius that, despite his imperial title, he remained a child of the Church, before which he must atone in order to regain grace.[8] This notion of life on Earth as transitory and not worth deep engagement faded once the Renaissance began. In the reformations, the scientific revolution, and the Enlightenment, the rise of national churches, explicitly in Protestant states but also in Catholic absolutism, contributed to the rise of the sovereign state. In the definitions of Herder and Abbe Sieyès, the nation was defined culturally and economically as a rejection of noble elites by an incipient bourgeoisie. The French Revolution and the Wars of Liberation against Napoleon reaffirmed both the importance of the state and the notion of nationalism as a countercultural force that threatened the state. The agreements struck at the Congress of Vienna seemed to restore religion and the dynastic state by putting an end to nationalism, but that was not to be. The manipulation of nationalism by the state led to the claim that the nation-state was the culmination of a people's self-expression and self-determination.

---

5. Föllmer, "Problem of National Solidarity," 204.
6. Zimmer, "Nation und Religion," 623.
7. Augustine, *City of God* 14:1.
8. Grant, *Roman Emperors*, 273.

For religion, the fairly new concept of nationalism proved challenging. If the nation and state were self-justifying purposes, then how was this nation to be understood theologically? Like many of the new ideologies, it was difficult to define. There were the definitions of Herder and Sieyès, but also of Fichte and Mazzini.[9] Both Fichte and Mazzini acknowledge an intermediate body between the individual's community and the nation: the *Heimat* or *paese*.[10] The word *Heimat* may well be the most emotionally laden word in the German language, as it goes far beyond *Staat*, *Gemeinschaft*, *Volk*, even *Vaterland*. Fichte acknowledged that *Heimat* is one's home—physically, culturally, and linguistically—and it is not the entire *Vaterland*.[11] In the United States, for example, both a New Englander and a Texan are U.S. Americans, but they have little in common in terms of their home region, their culture, and their language. Furthermore, within the United States, a Texan would be hard-pressed to choose between the nation as a whole and the Lone Star State. Similarly, an Italian is much more interested in the affairs of his or her *paese*, its feast days, its crops and thus its cuisine, etc., than in the country as a whole.

To make the matter even more complicated, the nation-states established or identified as such in the late nineteenth century were separated by boundaries that conflicted with regions identified as *Heimat* or *paese*. Austrians, Swiss Germans, German-speaking Bohemians, Romanians, Hungarians or the Ruthenians, and others all shared *Heimat* regions with other states. The problem of the tension between nation and regions dominated by ethnic minorities became acute in the wake of the Treaty of Versailles, which proved Woodrow Wilson's concept of ethnic and national self-determination impracticable. Czechs and Slovaks were united in a state in which there were more German speakers than Slovaks. The bigger problem, however, was not the tension between regional and national identity of peoples who were clearly defined minorities, but the tension between regional and national identity of groups within a recognized larger nation. For example, in interwar Germany, the largest state of the Reich was Prussia. But Prussia itself was not a state in which a single identity applied to all: East Prussians saw Prussian identity as quintessentially German, quintessentially Protestant, and quintessentially agrarian. In the Rhineland, however, Prussians were Catholic, a mix of urban working class and bourgeois. In the countryside lived Prussia's only grape farmers. For many of them, it was easier to identify with Germany than with Prussia. Saxons, Hessians,

---

9. Barnard, *Herder*; Sieyès, *Tiers état*.
10. Mazzini, *Opere politiche*.
11. Fichte, *Reden an die deutsche Nation*.

Mecklenburgers, all identified first with their region and then with Germany. Upper Silesians identified themselves as Upper Silesian Catholics rather than as Germans or Poles.[12]

In the Weimar Republic, German Catholics living almost anywhere in Germany other than Bavaria chose the German Center Party to represent their national political identity. Before the war, the Center was the only party of German political Catholicism. Rather than merely represent Catholic particular interests, the Center sought to infuse German politics with Catholic values. Already in the Wilhelmine period, the Center had evolved from a party representing Catholic interests to a party infusing the German body politic with Catholic values.[13]

After World War I, German Catholicism offered a useful example of competition based on national and regional identity between Bavarian German Catholics and German Catholics elsewhere. The prewar Catholic party, the German Center Party, played a largely constructive role in the revolution and continued to serve Weimar Germany until its demise. At the war's end in Bavaria, however, fears of a loss of regional autonomy as well as a fundamentally different understanding of the nature of the state and of the church's role in the state led to a split from the national party and, subsequently, the formation of the Bayerische Volkspartei (BVP), the Bavarian People's Party, as the voice of Bavarian Catholicism. Much of its political activity during the Weimar years was directed at both garnering respect for Bavarian autonomy and for the particular Bavarian point of view on national and international politics in all areas of government responsibility.[14] Comparing the Center and the BVP, one sees a case where lacking homogeneity led to disputes about identity, not only about the definition of identity but also about comparative claims to the "right" identity. First, the BVP and most Bavarian Catholics thought of themselves as Bavarians first and as Germans second. Furthermore, they thought of themselves as better Catholics than those elsewhere in Germany.

The Bavarian People's Party distinguished itself from the German Center Party by insisting on Bavarian-inherited rights and traditions that superseded any efforts by the German national government of the Weimar Republic to create a more centralized government. So in understanding what it meant to be Bavarian, for the BVP, regional autonomy and even independence were crucial characteristics. When BVP authors wrote of *unser*

12. Bjork, "Nations in the Parish," 210.
13. Hürten, *Deutsche Katholiken*, 88.
14. For a history of the Center, see Morsey, *Die deutsche Zentrumspartei* and *Der Untergang des politischen Katholizismus*. For the interim period, see Ruppert, *Im Dienste am Staat von Weimar*. For the BVP, see Schönhoven, *Die Bayerische Volkspartei*.

Land, one often is not sure which *Land* they mean—Germany or Bavaria. Also, to distinguish their more conservative *Weltanschauung* from that of the Center Party, the Bavarians denigrated the national party's Catholicism as corrupted by the Enlightenment and as insufficiently righteous by its acquiescence to the Versailles Treaty and to various subsequent foreign impositions. Finally, the BVP used its own self-righteous understanding of Christian values to avoid engaging the messy realities of compromise at the national and international levels.

The split between Center Party and BVP was finalized in 1920 when Center Party politician and Reich Finance Minister Matthias Erzberger introduced a more centralized system of taxation than the highly federal system that had existed during the Kaiserreich. The BVP was Catholic, but it was more conservative than the Center, and it feared that the Weimar would inadequately take into account the rights and needs of the Bavarian minority. Bavaria itself, however, was not a homogeneous state. Much of Franconia, especially around Nuremberg, was Protestant and stressed linguistic and cultural differences from Bavaria. On the left bank of the Rhine, the post-Napoleonic settlements had left much of the Palatinate—Catholic but definitely not Bavarian—in Bavarian hands. Furthermore, while the Center Party's leadership evolved to include almost no nobles and many more Catholic labor representatives, the BVP never made room for the growing number of Catholic laborers and remained much more bound by networks of Bavarian aristocrats and agrarian groups.[15] Nonetheless, the BVP saw itself as the party called to take on political leadership of all Bavarian regions.

In addition to the two political parties, Germany's desire for associations (*Vereine*) of all kinds had led to the formation of the *Volksverein für das katholische Deutschland*, the Popular Association for Catholic Germany, which published everything from short pamphlets to longer works—still cheaply bound to make them accessible—on strictly religious, political, social, cultural, and economic questions.[16] While the *Volksverein* operated in Bavaria, the Bavarian bishops feared its close association with the Center Party and its supposed lack of respect for Bavarian concerns.

The Center Party answered the question of a particularly Catholic definition of the nation by pointing to culture and heritage and to the notion of service. True nationalism is service to the people, not to some abstract ideal. This also meant that nationalism always had to be positively constructive; it did not permit German Catholics, as much as they longed to do so, to

15. Klaus Schönhoven notes that the vote to split from the Center was taken by the BVP leadership against the votes of Bavarian labor leaders and BVP Reichstag deputies (*Die Bayerische Volkspartei*, 36–38).

16. Klein, *Volksverein für das katholische Deutschland*.

stand on their principles of national outrage against Germany's treatment in the postwar era or on the principle of fundamental opposition to partnering with atheist socialists and Protestant nationalists to govern Germany. Center Party leaders had the Reichstag votes to paralyze government or to withdraw from governing responsibility, but their moral imperative prevailed to serve Germans.[17] Center Party deputies argued that while God still had first claim to piety, loyalty, and service, the Fatherland came in a close second. However, contemporary theologian Peter Tischleder made clear the particularly Catholic definition of one's relationship with the Fatherland: "Our admiration of the Fatherland is to be understood, however, as the admiration for one's fellow citizens and of all friends of the Fatherland." Also, following the teaching of Pope Leo XIII, Tischleder argued that Catholics have the duty to resist a government that becomes institutionally and fundamentally immoral in order to provide themselves with a morally sound government.[18] The nation thus was not a Treitschkean or otherwise social Darwinist organism, nor an abstract principle; it was a collection of people.[19] Germany's relevance and importance to Europe stemmed then from its central location and from its commitment to the Christian-Germanic mission of an occidental culture.[20]

While the Center Party's leaders thought in terms of all Germans—and insisted on this in order to defend and protect occupied Rhinelanders, separated Upper Silesians, Germans living abroad, etc.—the Bavarians defined the nation differently. While the Bavarian episcopate often criticized the Bavarian state government's lack of support in matters of public education and public respect for the faith, the bishops supported the BVP's uniquely Bavarian identity. First, in late 1924, Cardinal Michael Faulhaber of Munich gave a lecture on national honor and Christianity. He argued that true love of country manifested itself in

> Obedience to the laws of the state, rejection of all revolution, readiness for fiscal and personal sacrifices, cooperation to promote the welfare of the state and of the people, as demanded by conscience and shaped by the fourth commandment. As is the case for every moral virtue, the love of the fatherland is measured by a stepladder with many rungs, and by the occasional overextension that can become a vice. Love of the Fatherland is calmly acting love, not headless stormy passion. It is clarified

17. Menke, "Thy Will Be Done," 300–320.
18. Tischleder, *Staatslehre*, 144.
19. Ibid., 146.
20. Hugelmann, "Das Abendland," 299.

wine, not eternally fermenting must. German classical authors have often written about the failings in the German character and in German history, and yet they are German classics. Worth more than loud fanfares and parades is the quiet vocational work in service of the people.[21]

Faulhaber's definition of the nation included an important difference from both that of the Center Party and, one could argue, that of Leo XIII. While Faulhaber categorically condemned revolution, the Center had dispensed with that question as a done deal and had moved on to dutiful service of the new government. Leo XIII had argued that if the government threatened the moral welfare of the people, Catholics were compelled to resist and change the government.[22] With his condemnation of revolution, Faulhaber had explicitly distinguished Catholic teaching in Bavaria from that in the rest of Germany.[23] Faulhaber went much further than rejecting revolution, however. During the entire Weimar period, he fought all efforts to limit Bavarian autonomy, to centralize German government, and to acknowledge the legitimacy of the Weimar Republic. For example, commenting on the transfer to Berlin of Eugenio Pacelli, papal nuncio to Bavaria, Faulhaber claimed that "the news had evoked great fear in Bavaria. In those parts where one considers Berlin to be the cemetery of Bavaria, the news led to rather disrespectful comments."[24] Faulhaber also rejected the Reich government's desire for the Bavarian bishops to participate in a newly introduced memorial day for those killed in World War I as incompatible with the Catholic liturgical calendar and, more importantly, as an imposition from the Protestant north and especially from Berlin.[25] He also rejected any attempt to link the negotiations for a new concordat between Bavaria and the Holy See to negotiations for an all-German concordat. He feared that the Reich government secretly only represented Prussian interests.[26] In justifying his desire to exclude the Reich Chancellor, Josef Wirth of the Center Party, from the National Catholic Assembly in Munich in 1922, Faulhaber

21. Faulhaber, *Deutsches Ehrgefühl*, 38.

22. *Sapientiae Christianae*, 10. Earlier, in *Diuturnum*, Leo had admonished Catholics to resist immoral laws only quietly, without tumult (*Diuturnum*, 18).

23. At this time, Germany had two bishops' conferences—one at Freising for Bavaria, and one at Fulda for the rest of Germany.

24. Volk, *Akten Faulhabers*, 1:149.

25. Ibid., 177. Later, Faulhaber rejected an ecclesiastical commemoration of the republic's national holiday, the anniversary of the adoption of the Weimar constitution (ibid., 337–38), of the funeral of Reich President Friedrich Ebert (ibid., 364–65), and of Reich President Paul von Hindenburg's eightieth birthday (ibid., 421–22).

26. Ibid., 197–98.

argued that the reasons for tensions between Bavaria and the Reich were to be sought outside of Bavaria.[27] Faulhaber accused the Center Party of having departed far from the true teachings of the Church and having moved too close to socialism.

For the Bavarians, the homeland—the *Heimat*—was Bavaria. It was, in the words of one party leader, land "that cannot entrust its survival and its statehood to a majority of people who are strangers to our land."[28] The "strangers to our land" were not French or British, but people from the other German states whose Reichstag deputies had the temerity to pass national legislation without according the BVP a veto. As early as spring 1919, the BVP leader Dr. Georg Heim complained in the Reichstag that the states had not been granted veto power over the new constitution.[29] While the Center Party publicly committed itself to the constitution, against fundamental opposition by the German Nationalists, and by and large against a restoration of the monarchy, Bavarians saw this very differently. In 1920, the General Secretary of the BVP, Anton Pfeiffer, explained why Bavarians had such a strained relationship with the rest of Germany and with the Reich government: "The new constitution of August 11, 1919, limited Bavaria's special rights or, more properly, the governmental autonomy of Bavaria in such an extraordinary manner that one can hardly speak of a Bavarian state any longer. We are no longer permitted to call ourselves a state [*Staat*]; we must call ourselves a province [*Land*]."[30] Bavarians convinced themselves that, even more than during the Hohenzollern Reich, the rest of Germany was determined to belittle Bavaria.

At the 1922 national convention of German Catholics, the president of the assembly, Cologne's mayor Konrad Adenauer, provoked an éclat when he claimed to speak for all German Catholics as being committed to a parliamentary republic. Cardinal Michael Faulhaber, archbishop of Munich until after World War II, reminded the assembled that revolution against a well-established Christian monarch was a sin and that the concept of popular sovereignty was blasphemous.[31] In other words, the Bavarian primate was calling for a reversal of the revolution and the restoration of the Wittelsbach House, as if 1918 had never happened. In October 1923, the leader of the BVP, Heinrich Held, complained to Faulhaber that the Nazi movement —the Nationalsozialistische Deutsche Arbeiterpartei, or NSDAP (National

27. Ibid., 275.
28. Eggersdorfer, *Die Krise des staatlichen Lebens*, 8.
29. Ibid., 7.
30. Hauptstaatsarchiv Bayern, *Biographie Anton Pfeiffers*, 22.
31. Stehkämper, *Konrad Adenauer*, 120.

Socialist German Workers' Party)—in Bavaria was led by non-Bavarians.[32] Held implored Faulhaber to make a public statement against the Nazis: "I am sure that a word from your eminence would immediately reawaken our Bavarian Catholic people [*Volk*] and inspire it to act in a Catholic and Bavarian manner." For Held, the priority was Catholic and Bavarian; the troublemakers came from Germany into Bavaria.

Another point of distinction was the Center's position on peace among nations and on international relations generally. Tischleder argued that every people has its place and its purpose in God's divine role.[33] Since God created all Fatherlands, and since the Fatherland produces each individual, we owe the Fatherland everything and must be willing to serve the Fatherland unto our death. Each nation has the right to protect itself as long as the nation promotes moral goodness. A nation must be willing to replace its form of government should the latter prove immoral.[34] Just as God created each nation, so God also created the family of nations. The task of a Christian family of nations is to bring to fruition God's moral order here on Earth.[35] Therefore, it was only logical that the *Germania*, Germany's largest Catholic daily, claimed that national honor is not satisfied with many tanks and battalions but by the knowledge that everyone in the country had enough to eat.[36] The by no means liberal *Kölnische Volkszeitung* argued that while German Catholics were committed to serving the Fatherland, they served the Fatherland within the larger framework of a Christian community of nations.[37] The Center Party, for its part, warned that the BVP's excessive emphasis on nationalist pride and principles was hurting Germany's position abroad, and especially in France.[38]

Bavarian Catholics saw this differently. The Bavarians saw their Christian love of the Fatherland—again without specifying which that might be—as the basis for a Christian international order. For example, they claimed that because they were committed to an international order based on Christian moral principles, they were compelled continuously to raise the question of the war guilt clause, reparations, etc.[39] In fact, reporting on

32. Volk, *Akten Faulhabers*, 314. In that letter, Held mentioned several non-Bavarian Nazi leaders but did not include Hitler among them.

33. Tischleder, *Staatslehre*, 145.

34. Ibid., 145–46.

35. Ibid., 386.

36. "Nationale Ehre," *Germania*, August 29, 1928.

37. *Kölnische Volkszeitung*, "Katholikentag in Frankfurt," September 7, 1921.

38. "Nationalistische Umtriebe und Aktivitäten Bayern," *Germania*, November 6, 1922.

39. Bavarian People's Party, Supplement to *Mitteilungen*, 11.

an address by a pacifist Jesuit and Center Party supporter to the national Catholic assembly, the BVP complained that the overemphasis on Catholic supranationalism would turn off young people instead.[40] Finally, whereas the Center Party supported Germany's accession to the League of Nations, the Bavarian People's Party rejected it as too political an institution, too little based on idealism. Furthermore, any international organization of states should have asked the Holy Father to serve as its head.[41] Thus, the BVP claimed that its fairly obstructionist and certainly impotent position in foreign policy was more legitimate than the engaged, constructive policy of the Center.

While the Center Party certainly had a monarchist wing, especially among its remaining nobles and large landowners, in fall 1924 Wilhelm Marx could note as fact that the majority of Center Party deputies were committed to parliamentary democracy.[42]

Finally, and perhaps most devastatingly, the BVP rejected the Center for its active engagement in politics that were not strictly governed by what the BVP considered to be a legitimate moral basis on Catholic teaching. In other words, the BVP accused the Center of being bad Catholics. The BVP condemned the Center's foreign policy as a failure because the Party had not been able to prevent the various calamities that befell Germany before the mid-twenties. Explicitly, the BVP rejected the left wing of the Center Party, listing its leaders by name: Ignaz Teipel; Friedrich Dessauer; Joseph Joos; of course, Joseph Wirth, the Bavarian professor and publisher of *Hochland*; Carl Muth; and even Peter Tischleder.[43] The BVP did this because it claimed the Center Party's Catholics had fallen prey to the dangers of the Enlightenment, in particular to the notions of Rousseau. The question of majority rule was a modern evil designed to create a tyranny of the majority. Reflecting on ten years of Weimar and ten years of the BVP as an independent party, Regensburg political scholar F. X. Eggersdorfer argued that the reason for the public's exhaustion with Weimar was its birth as an Enlightenment project in which the God-given rights of Bavarians were not respected. Germany was formally a democracy, but in practice it was a tyranny of special interests rather than a true organic democracy in which each element is respected.[44] Eggersdorfer argued that in a constitution adopted solely by a group of parliamentarians in Weimar, all rights became subject

---

40. Geschäftsstelle des Lokalvereins, "Report on 71st General Assembly," 13.
41. Eggersdorfer, *Die Krise des staatlichen Lebens*, 16.
42. Reich Chancellery Archives, "Ministerial Meeting."
43. Eggersdorfer, *Die Krise des staatlichen Lebens*, 6–7.
44. Ibid., 8.

to the Reichstag's approval—all judgments of right and wrong, of religious freedom, etc., were guaranteed only as long as the Reichstag agreed. To this, the BVP could never submit.

In other words, by claiming that the ideals and political positions of the German Center Party were determined not by Catholic teaching and its emphasis on natural law but by an agreement of the majority and on other principles stemming from Rousseau, Kant, and Mill, the BVP claimed that the Center's leaders had forsaken "true" Catholicism in favor of revolutionary secularism and materialism. By denying the Center's adherence to Catholic values, indeed the Center's Catholicity, the BVP could claim the mantel of true Catholicism. This was crucial for the BVP because it had not contributed actively to the resolution of Germany's postwar foreign and domestic problems. The BVP had defended Bavarian interests and the positions of Bavaria's conservative Catholic elites, but that had largely put it in opposition to almost all measures taken by the Reich government, both in the Reichstag and the cabinet. As Klaus Schönhoven notes, the BVP's Reichstag deputies became increasingly exasperated by the desire of party leaders in Munich to determine BVP policy from afar.[45] By 1923, the BVP had lost all political influence at the national level.[46] Thus, it needed to protect its Catholic identity to legitimize its unproductive record. Finally, the BVP's support for the candidacy of the right-wing presidential candidate, former Field Marshal Paul von Hindenburg, against the Center's Wilhelm Marx made it imperative for BVP supporters to believe that their party remained the true Catholic party in Germany. This continued throughout the remaining Weimar years. After accepting the London Agreements of 1924, the party rejected the Locarno Agreements, the entrance into the League of Nations, and the Young Plan, largely because they impinged on Bavarian *Land* interests. The Young Plan, for example, was to be financed in part by a dramatic increase (75 percent) in the Reich beer tax.[47] To Bavarians, this was an unacceptable violation of their rights and interests. Subsequently, in September 1931, the Bavarian bishops voted to express their thanks to the Bavarian minister president and to the leaders of the BVP deputies in the Bavarian state legislature and in the Reichstag for preserving the autonomy of Bavaria.[48] The bishops decided to mount a public information campaign to enlighten the faithful about the dangers of centralism. Especially in

45. Schönhoven, *Die Bayerische Volkspartei,* 80.

46. Ibid., 46.

47. Reich Chancellery Archives, "Minister of Finance to Secretary Pünder."

48. Volk, *Akten Faulhabers,* 568. See also 581–83, where the bishop of Regensburg warned that a unitary reform of the Reich would render Bavaria "an appendage to Greater Prussia" (582).

Bavaria, the Church would lose its concordats, would lose the support of Germany's one Catholic-majority state, and would lose its financial security at a time when the faithful depended more than ever on the ministrations of the Church.[49] The bishops firmly believed that an autonomous Bavaria would guarantee the freedom of the Church throughout Germany, both the faithful and the hierarchy. Bavaria was the last bastion of Catholicism in Germany.

This lay at the heart of the BVP's challenges in defining national and religious interests. Paralyzing the BVP were the refusal to cooperate with other countries without a prior admission by those nations that they had wronged Germany; insistence on the century-old rights of Bavaria; insistence on a level of federalism unsustainable in Weimar Germany; and insistence on an adherence to Catholic values much further down Faulhaber's ladder than those threatening Germany with chaos. In the end, the BVP could only assert Bavaria's superior Catholicism and its heritage as an ancient land—not much older than some of the other German states—to define its identity. In reality, the BVP was using its understanding of religious and national identity to justify Bavaria's special status and to defend its interests. This was possible only by constraining the definition of Catholic identity by claiming that its regional identity superseded Bavarians' identity as Germans. In the end, however, that did not protect the BVP from Nazi electoral gains in Bavaria's state elections of 1932, when it became impossible for the BVP to form a government without either the hated socialists or the feared national socialists.[50] Beyond all the usual fears concerning the Nazis, the BVP feared the centralizing tendencies in the NSDAP and the conservative German National People's Party, the DNVP.[51] Although President von Hindenburg personally assured the ministers president of the German states that the Reich government's coup against Prussia was not designed or expected to be repeated against the other states, especially since there were no communist and socialist dangers in Bavaria, Hindenburg provided no assistance when the time came.[52]

In a larger context, not only was Moritz Föllmer's point about the dangers of nationalism in heterogeneous states proven true in this case, but

49. Ibid., 568.

50. Wiesemann, *Vorgeschichte*, 110.

51. Steber, "Bayerische Volkspartei im Jahre 1933," 71. Steber argues that the BVP failed in part because of its devotion to the Bavarian state and all things Bavarian, especially the autonomy of Bavaria in the Reich, but also because its opposition to the Reich prevented the development of an effective defense against the Nazis (77).

52. Becker, "Ein Dokumentarbericht Heinrich Helds," 424–25. See also Volk, *Akten Faulhabers*, 664–68.

so was Reinhard Richter's point that German Catholics resorted to discussions of nationalism primarily in matters that party leaders feared the party supporters might otherwise not accept.[53] Furthermore, the comparison of Center and BVP shows problems in determining criteria for defining a nation. Otto Dann argues that the nation is primarily a political body in a given territory built around a constitutional consensus.[54] While he argues that national identity is also based on culture, he admits that every national identity is multicultural in some way, and that even the predominant culture of any nation is framed by a transnational context.[55] As this case study has shown, national identity becomes increasingly difficult to explain when groups share neither an understanding of their shared national identity nor of their predominant cultural identity. Ultimately, in the face of the rising National Socialists in October 1932, the journal *Hochland* could only bravely remind its readers that "as God already made clear to Abraham, the people of God stands above all other peoples and cannot tolerate competing ideas of nationhood. People must transition from the peoples of nature into the people of God. The people of Israel is only united by its religion; yet it has survived centuries of persecution. Christianity is no different; it too will survive the pestilence of nationalism."[56] By spring 1933, the BVP's information materials for its election speakers would speak the same language again as the Center party, but by then it was too late.[57] On March 9, 1933, four days after the last partially free elections in Germany, in which the NSDAP for the first time had won the greatest number of Bavarian votes, Nazi party officials and storm troopers occupied Bavarian government buildings in Munich and insisted that the Bavarian government accept the appointment of a Reich Commissioner for Bavaria.[58] That which the Bavarian bishops had always feared the constitutional republican government of Weimar would impose on Bavaria, the Nazis did within weeks.

53. Richter, *Nationales Denken*, 110.
54. Dann, *Nation und Nationalismus*, 9.
55. Ibid., 15.
56. Moock, "Christentum und Nation," 233–43.
57. Bavarian People's Party, *Mitteilungen für die Vertrauensleute*, 11:198.
58. Becker, "Ein Dokumentarbericht Heinrich Helds," 433.

7

Catholicism and Belonging, in This World

SLAVICA JAKELIĆ

The link between Catholicism and collective identity is usually perceived as a problem. For theologians, Catholic identity defined by virtue of one's birth into some specific group is an obstacle for her belonging to a universal community of salvation and a hindrance for the possibility of true catholicity.[1] For social scientists, Catholicism constitutive of collective identity is a problem because it creates sharp boundaries among different groups and can impede the processes of social integration in pluralistic societies.

Both the theological and sociological critiques of the group-oriented Catholicisms often stem from an understanding that such Catholicisms are first and foremost linked to nationalisms. The first part of this essay, which looks at the Polish Catholic Radio Maryja and the Marian pilgrimage site in Međugorje, affirms such critiques in at least one respect: whenever Catholic theology, traditions, and institutional legacies *succumb* to the force of nationalist ideologies, they incite or justify intolerance and social conflicts. In other words, the appraisals of the group-oriented Catholicisms as a theological and sociological problem bring an important insight if such Catholicisms are manifestations of religious nationalism. These appraisals are also valuable because they contribute to the larger point about nationalism and nation-states as the secularizing forces of Western modernity.

But while the importance of such critiques is beyond doubt, one question remains: are all group-oriented Catholicisms reducible to religious nationalism? Are they merely a result of the processes of secularization, the victory of nationalism, or is their phenomenology more complex? I

---

1. For an example of this type of thinking, see Cavanaugh, "If You Render Unto God," 607–19.

raise these questions in the second part of the essay. Here, I again attend to Catholicisms and collective identities in Poland and Bosnia and Herzegovina but this time in the context of the 1980s Solidarity movement and the Bosnian Franciscan community. These two cases are significant because they uncover the multiple meanings of Catholicism as a *collectivistic* phenomenon—as a religious tradition that constitutes collective identities, next to and equally significant as region, language, territory, cultural identity, or nationality. Most importantly, the cases of Solidarity and the Bosnian Franciscan community suggest that Catholicisms connected to national identities do not have to become consumed by nationalism. Rather, they may be able to transcend or even subvert the power of exclusivistic nationalistic ideologies.

The discussion that follows, then, attempts to problematize the usual straightforward and oftentimes reductionist approach to collectivistic Catholicisms as a political phenomenon, a function (or epiphenomenon) of nationalism, and an institutional pillar that supports the power of nation-states. In my reading,[2] the Solidarity and the Bosnian Franciscan Catholicisms expose the limitations of the view that whenever Catholicism is linked to national identity, it reflects the sacred-secular divides that cause Catholicism to lose that which makes it religious. Instead, the essay invites readers to recognize the complicated ways in which "the boundaries of baptism," in the apt phrase of Michael Budde,[3] are embodied and embedded in this world—lived within and through one's sense of cultural identity, with regard to people's histories and ethical notions of solidarity, and by means of people's collective narratives.

Finally, the essay puts forward two broader arguments. First, it maintains that reducing the richness of the group-oriented Catholic identities and narratives to secularization or the politics of secularism is historically and sociologically inaccurate, as well as theologically impoverishing. Second, the essay proposes that seeing collectivistic Catholicisms as just an expression of exclusivistic nationalisms is problematic politically. It runs the danger of dismissing the Catholic identities that shape (to use William Connolly's words) "the visceral register[s] of intersubjectivity" in non-manipulative ways,[4] instead of seeing such identities as vital to any contemporary conversation about pluralism and belonging.

---

2. This reading builds on my historical sociological study of collectivistic Christianities in Europe; see Jakelić, *Collectivistic Religions*.

3. See the title of the conference held at DePaul University in April 2013, where the initial version of this paper was first presented.

4. Connolly, *Why I Am Not a Secularist*, 12–13.

Catholicism and Nationalism in Poland and Bosnia and Herzegovina

The Polish Catholic Nationalism and the Case of Radio Maryja

After five decades of communist rule and religious oppression, the 1990s ushered Poles into the age of democracy. For the Catholic Church, this change signified the full freedom of public activities and, even more importantly, the position of the most powerful and most privileged religious institution in a predominantly Catholic country. To be sure, being "Catholic in a Polish way" did not suddenly become simple and straightforward. Just as in the past, the Polish Catholic Church was internally plural, theologically and politically. Furthermore, while the majority of Poles eagerly embraced religious freedom and demonstrated respect for the Church's courageous stance during the communist rule, more than 70 percent of them did not approve of the manner in which the Church threw itself into the political life of democratic Poland.[5]

These diverse approaches to the religious and national aspect of Polish identity also contributed to the renewed interest in the meaning of the notion *Polak-Katolik*,[6] the idea that asserts the historical inseparability of Catholicism and the Polish national identity. Scholars have long shown that this notion is a modern phenomenon that emerged with the rise of Polish nationalism,[7] after a rich history of religious pluralism and alongside the country's increasing homogenization. But according to popular narratives and the slogan *Polonia semper fidelis* ("Poland Always Faithful"), Poland has been "Catholic" since the baptism of Prince Mieszko I in 966,[8] and Polishness and Catholicism have been mutually constitutive from time immemorial.

The historicity and constructed nature of these narratives did not greatly affect their appeal. To the contrary, during the decades when the Polish Catholic Church was the only institution standing against the atheist ideology of the communist state, the narratives about the inseparability of Polishness from the Catholic faith came to shape the self-understanding of

---

5. Nowicka, "Roman Catholic Fundamentalism," 22.

6. Polak-Katolik means "a Pole is a Catholic," suggesting the interchangeability of the terms.

7. See Wolff, *Vatican and Poland*, 1; Eberts, "Catholic Church and Democracy in Poland," 818. On the modernity of the concept of *Polak-Katolik* identity, see Zubrzycki, *Crosses of Auschwitz*; see also Miłosz, *Native Realm*, 82.

8. On such narratives as affirmed by the Catholic Church, see Mach, "The Roman Catholic Church in Poland."

many Poles. The importance of Catholicism and the power of the Church, which was so clearly displayed in the face of the communist antireligious policies, were captured particularly well in the celebration of Christianity's thousand years in Poland. The celebration started in 1957 and culminated in 1966, when hundreds of thousands of Poles met Cardinal Wyszyński on his tour around the country, greeting him with piety, enthusiasm, and church banners announcing that the "Nation is with the Church." While these events of the "Great Novena" indicated that Catholicism in Poland was strong and alive, they also cemented the view that to be Polish is to be Catholic. What is more, while the boundaries of Polish national identity were political and drawn in opposition to Russia, they were also built around ethical notions of solidarity, human dignity, dignity of work, and freedom.[9]

The homogeneity and defensive aspect of the Polish identity emerged in response to the communist totalitarianism and came into question with the country's democratization. But for the millions of Polish Catholics, it was the moral content and publicness of the *Polak-Katolik* identity that needed a continued defense, this time against the threat of cultural pluralism and globalization. The program of the Catholic radio station Radio Maryja became the main voice of these Polish Catholics. Founded by Father Tadeusz Rydzyk, the radio station began broadcasting locally in December 1991 and grew into a national phenomenon with a true network—from the daily *Nasz Dziennik* (Our Daily) to an association of the station's listeners, Rodzina Radia Maryja (The Family of Radio Marya), which also "has its monthly under the same title, and extensive network of local cells."[10]

Father Rydzyk's media project has had great success. Selling about two hundred thousand copies daily, the *Nasz Dziennik* has been one of the most influential religious papers in Poland. With some five million listeners in the late 1990s,[11] and three million listeners one decade later,[12] Radio Maryja continues to be one of the most popular stations in Poland. The station has also been vocal in public debates about a variety of political and economic questions—from those about the insufficient religious grounding of the Polish constitution and the purpose of Polish membership in the European Union, to disapproval of the sale of land to foreigners and privatization of state-owned companies.[13] The nationalist concern with the foreign influ-

9. For the ways in which the political and ethical aspects of Polish identity became intertwined in communist Poland, see Tischner, *Spirit of Solidarity*; see also Zbigniew Brzezinski's foreword to the same book, viii.
10. See Burdziej, "Voice of the Disinherited?," 208.
11. See Perlez, "Priest Gives Poles Hate Radio."
12. See Puhl, "Polish Populists."
13. See Burdziej, "Voice of the Disinherited?," 208.

ence and presence in Poland here merged with the critiques of capitalism, while the negative stance toward the EU reflected a conviction that cultural pluralism would bring moral relativism.

The program of Radio Maryja, to be sure, is first and foremost religious: it attracts its audience primarily with its religious content, especially the prayers that include daily Mass and the rosary, the Liturgy of the Hours, and religious songs.[14] But the program also garners attention—from its faithful listeners and its critics—because of its political content, particularly its direct promotion of the conservative political parties, its xenophobic attitude, and its anti-Semitism. For Father Rydzyk, for example, the European Union is a conspiracy of Freemasons, while for other Radio Maryja commentators the "Holocaust Industry" wields influence worldwide.[15]

The Polish secular left and liberal Catholics have been equally critical of such messages. Rebukes of Father Rydzyk's radio program also came from the Polish Church hierarchy and the Vatican. Pope John Paul II rejected the station's anti-European orientation and anti-Semitic stance and voiced a strong disapproval of Father Rydzyk's use of Catholicism for narrow political purposes.[16] In 2002, Cardinal Jozef Glemp, the main figure of the Polish Catholic Church, banned "the offices of a radical Catholic radio station from operating" in Warsaw and restricted its fund-raising activities.[17] In 2006, Pope Benedict XVI also issued warnings to Radio Maryja, asking it to quit engaging in politics.[18]

Yet, both the Polish prelates and the Vatican recognized the enormous influence that Father Rydzyk had in the Polish context. In late 2012, at the general audience of the Polish pilgrims to Rome, Pope Benedict XVI especially welcomed the members of the Rodzina Radia Maryja. On this same occasion, Wacław Depo, the archbishop of Częstochowa and president of the Polish episcopate's Council for Social Communications, also demonstrated his approval of Radio Maryja's activities. Depo expressed his

---

14. Ibid., 216.

15. See Puhl, "Polish Populists."

16. According to the *New York Times*, Cardinal Glemp, widely perceived as a conservative part of the Polish Catholic Church, issued a public letter in which he admonished Father Rydzyk "for stirring 'hostility' and for being insubordinate to the church hierarchy." Further, he advised Father Rydzyk to "stop being so brazenly political and asked the head of his order, the Rev. Edvard Nocun, head of the Redemptorist Order, to supervise the priest more closely" (Perlez, "Priest Gives Poles Hate Radio," par. 5). The same article states that the spokesman of John Paul II "expressed his displeasure with Radio Maryja, stressing that the views of the station's correspondent at the Vatican were personal views and not those of the Vatican" (par. 9).

17. Walton, "Polish Cardinal Tackles Radical Radio."

18. See Puhl, "Polish Populists."

concern over the Polish telecommunications laws that "hinder" the activities of religious media such as Radio Maryja,[19] lamented the pushing of faith out of the public sphere, and argued that "it is clear and obvious" that believers should "have the right to mould social life according to [their] faith and convictions." Archbishop Depo finally made a point of greeting the Family of Radio Maryja, "who are praying for their Homeland, for families and for the freedom of expression."[20]

These statements of the Polish prelate established a link between the media laws (seen as antagonistic toward a public expression of faith) and Radio Maryja's patriotism and actions (seen as representative of strong Catholic identity). In so doing, Archibishop Depo contributed to narratives about the threat to the *Polak-Katolik* identity in the postcommunist Polish context. As was the case under the communist regime, these narratives emphasized the moral aspect of Polish Catholicity. But the moral component of postcommunist Polish Catholicism is much narrower than the moral meaning of Polishness in communist Poland. Whereas the latter was intertwined with the humanistic (and personalist) ideals of dignity, solidarity, and freedom—the point on which I will focus in a moment—the postcommunist and especially Radio Maryja's patriotic discourse centered on family values as indistinguishable from national identity. In this narrative framework, for example, the Catholic condemnation of abortion is not just a matter of theological and doctrinal truth; it becomes a call for the preservation of the Polish nation.

In the case of Radio Maryja, the Catholic tradition and faith serve politics and nationalistic agendas. This does not happen because the nation-state appropriates religion for its purposes but because of the role sought by the Catholic Church's representatives and their desire to articulate the *Polak-Katolik* identity for the postcommunist Polish context. Radio Maryja thus underscores the theological and sociological critiques of Catholicism-nationalism links, wherein Catholic faith yields to nationalistic ideologies and justifies intolerance of religious and national others. Most importantly, perhaps, the case of Radio Maryja clearly shows that national identities are not a secular affair. Not only can religious traditions provide some of the most central themes of national narratives, the responsibility for defining the content of these narratives often belongs precisely to religious elites and institutions.

---

19. See Lehnert, "Controversy Involving Radio Maryja."
20. Ibid., par. 5. Depo here quotes Pope Benedict XVI.

The Croatian Catholic Nationalism and the Case of Međugorje

The sight of a big Croatian flag on the towers of the central Catholic Church in Međugorje, the world-famous Marian pilgrimage site in Herzegovina, is not unprecedented. One can also see national flags next to Catholic shrines in the U.S. or Austria, especially on some national holidays. The fact that the local Međugorje believers and Catholics in neighboring Croatia speak of Mary as "the Queen of the Croats" (*Kraljica Hrvata*) is not unusual either: if Mary speaks Croatian in Međugorje, she also speaks French in Lourdes.

But the Croatian flag on the Međugorje church does acquire another layer of meaning when placed in the broader historical and political context of this town and region. From the moment when the apparitions in Međugorje began in the early 1980s to the period of the Bosnian War in the 1990s, this pilgrimage site and Mary as "the Queen of the Croats" stood as a major identity marker for Croatian Catholic identity against a range of others. The apparitions in Međugorje began in 1981, only days after the Orthodox Christian Serbs in this region had commemorated the fortieth anniversary of the killing of their women and children by the Catholic Croats during World War II.[21] As the pilgrimage site acquired its national and international reputation, it also became a powerful symbol of the power of religion against the communist Yugoslav regime.

The significance of Međugorje in defining the boundaries of the Catholic Croatian nationalism in the region, and beyond, was particularly evident in the 1990s with the breakup of communist Yugoslavia. The Republic of Croatia declared its independence on the tenth anniversary of the first of Mary's apparitions in Međugorje, and some Herzegovinian Catholics argued that Croatian independence was a gift from the Virgin Mary.[22] All of this cemented the connection among the pilgrim site, the religious miracle ascribed to it, and the Croatian national struggle—against the communists, against the Serbian Orthodox Christians, and, in the context of the Bosnian War, against the Bosniak Muslims. Thus, over the years, Međugorje acquired not one but several collectivistic meanings.

It is important to note that it was not the secular nationalist ideologues who used the religious symbols and theological narratives of Catholicism surrounding Međugorje for their political agendas. Just as was the case with Radio Maryja, the key role in articulating the Međugorje narratives belonged to the religious elites. This time, the Catholic elite in question were members of the Herzegovinian Franciscan province. The history of

---

21. See Herrero, "Medjugorje," 141–42.

22. See Father Tomislav Pervan, the Herzegovinian Franciscans' provincial, as quoted in Perica, *Balkan Idols*, 173, 295.

the Herzegovinian province offers narratives that have linked Catholicism and Croatian national identity since at least the early twentieth century. For the purpose of our discussions, we focus on the Herzegovinian Franciscan stance in the war in Bosnia and Herzegovina. This war began in the spring of 1992 and centered around the division of a country where three national groups—Bosnian Muslims or Bosniaks,[23] Croats, and Serbs—lived together[24] in nationally "pure" regions. At first, the Bosniaks and Bosnian Croats fought together against the Serbian claims to Bosnia and Herzegovina[25] and jointly defended the country against the Yugoslav Army. Within a year, the war became a conflict between the Serbian and Croatian nationalists, on the one hand, and all the Bosnians whose goal was to preserve Bosnian sovereignty, on the other hand. These Bosnians were primarily Bosniaks, but they were also Bosnian Croats and Serbs who considered Bosnia and Herzegovina their homeland.

Rather than supporting the independence of Bosnia and Herzegovina, the Herzegovinian friars sided with Croatian nationalists, advocating the partition of the country between the Serbs and Croats.[26] For these Franciscans, Catholic religious and Croatian national identity could be fully expressed only within the Croatian state. Within Bosnia, Herzegovinian friars contended, Croatian Catholics would always be in the minority and under threat. The head of the Herzegovinian Franciscan province, Tomislav Pervan, argued that the Bosnian Muslims were organizing an "Islamic state," while the government of the Bosnian state was similar, Father Vinko

---

23. Although the term "Bosniak" has been adopted as a national name for the Bosnian Muslims only recently, for the purpose of clarity, I use it throughout the essay.

24. According to the 1991 census, Bosnia and Herzegovina was comprised of 43.7 percent Bosniaks, 31.3 percent Serbs, 17.3 percent Croats, and 7.7 percent other nationalities and Yugoslavs. Bosniaks were the majority in forty-five municipalities, Serbs in thirty-four, and Croats in twenty, as cited in Kulenović, "Pripreme za početak rata," 92.

25. One of these indications was the referendum about Bosnia and Herzegovina as a sovereign country. In February 1992, 63.4 percent of the Bosnian-Herzegovinian population voted in the referendum on Bosnian independence; 92.8 percent voted for, and 0.19 percent against, independence. The main party of the Bosnian Serbs, SDS, organized a separate referendum in November 1991, after which it was declared that Bosnian Serbs had decided to remain in Yugoslavia. See Magaš and Žanić, *War in Croatia and Bosnia-Herzegovina*, 360, 357.

26. On Boban, see Jergović, "Mate Boban 1940–1997"; on Boban's cooperation with the Bosnian Serbs, see Lovrenović, *Bosna-kraj stoljeća*, 216. Gojko Šušak was the most influential Herzegovinian in the circles of the Croatian president Franjo Tuđman. On the political situation in Herzegovina during and after the war, see also Žanić, "Hercegovački rat i mir," 84–92; on the relationship between Bosnia and Croatia, see, for example, Ćimić,"Bosanska raskrižja," and Banac, *Cijena Bosne*.

Mikolić proposed, to "Turkish occupiers."[27] Another Herzegovinian Franciscan, Jozo Zovko, declared from the Međugorje pulpit that Mary is "calling upon her people to pick up their swords, put on their uniforms, and stop the power of Satan."[28] In the context in which the friars sided with the Croatian nationalists who fought the Bosniak Muslims, the events of the twentieth century merged with the fifteenth-century Ottoman conquest. Zovko's reference was not to be understood biblically but historically—it was a reference to Islam.[29]

The meanings of Međugorje, in other words, were never simply theological, just as has been the case with the Catholic crosses displayed in schools, hospitals, or on the hills above Herzegovinian towns, often next to the Croatian national flag. These crosses symbolize territorial and national claims—a boundary marker that tells the non-Catholic others that this is not their land. Second, just like Mary in Međugorje, these crosses place the Christian narrative of suffering and salvation in the context of the national narrative of suffering and redemption of one specific group—the Bosnian Croats.

For social scientists, religious studies scholars, and theologians, Catholicism in Herzegovina serves as an example of what happens to a religion when it is used for this-worldly identities. Miroslav Volf, a distinguished Yale theologian and a Croatian by birth, wrote that religions in the former Yugoslavia were a problem because they served as a cultural resource rather than an active faith.[30] From this perspective, Catholicism in Herzegovina and in Medjugorje is distorted: it is not about religious identity and religious behavior but embodies a connection between fundamentalism and nationalism. In the words of another scholar, Michael Sells, religions in Bosnia are the source of rejection rather than affirmation of the religious others.[31] Željko Mardešić, the Croatian sociologist of religion[32] and him-

27. See Velikonja, *Religious Separation*, 272.

28. See Herrero, "Medjugorje," 162.

29. Jozo Zovko did state that the Bosnian War "was a political conflict and not a religious war"; see Velikonja, *Religious Separation*, 271. Zovko's other statements, however, gesture toward the responsibility of some religious elites for the perpetuation and justification of the Bosnian conflict.

30. See Volf, Review of *The Bridge Betrayed*, 250–53.

31. See Sells, *The Bridge Betrayed*; also see Sells, "Crosses of Blood," 329. For the argument about the link of religion-nationalism as being at the heart of the problems that caused conflicts in Bosnia, see Mojzes, "Camouflaged Role of Religion"; Cohen, "Bosnia's 'Tribal Gods.'"

32. His numerous books, scholarly articles, and intellectual essays were written under the pseudonym Jakov Jukić or under his real name, Željko Mardešić. The influence of his ideas about the personal, pietistic kind of Christianity is evident in the recent

self a devout Catholic, argued that the only way out of the "vicious circle" in which Catholicism and other religions "fall into the worldly traps" was the affirmation of faith that was not historically grounded but founded in "the personhood of every human being."[33]

These scholars make an important point: much can be said about the direct or indirect roles that Catholicism and representatives of the Catholic Church in Bosnia and Herzegovina (and beyond) had in the Bosnian War. Both Međugorje and Radio Marya give support to the arguments that the links between Catholicism and group identities are a political phenomenon and a problem, theologically and sociologically. First, these cases underscore that one's belonging to a universal community of salvation becomes secondary when religious identity develops an uncritical relationship to a national community and, especially, nation-state. They thus confirm the critiques of the strong connections between worldly and spiritual identities. Second, the cases in question suggest that when Catholicism serves as a national mark, it can quickly become a source of boundaries and antagonism between different religious and national groups, and an impetus for intolerance. Such Catholicisms, succinctly put, show the divisive powers of religious nationalisms in contemporary societies.

At the same time, the Međugorje and Radio Marya cases also complicate the larger view of religious nationalism as a result of secularization—a process in which secular national ideologues use religion and nationalisms swallow up religious traditions. While these claims often point to realities of religious and national experiences, the latter is hardly a matter of theoretical assumption. Rather, it should be subject to empirical consideration. Međugorje and Radio Marya point out the role of church representatives in defining Catholicism as inseparable from the national identities and interests of the Croatian and Polish nation-state, respectively. This last point is important: it discourages any sociological or theological arguments about national identities and nation-states as secular in character.

Another set of stories from the Polish and Bosnian contexts—one about Solidarity and another about the Bosnian Franciscan province, "Silver Bosnia"—further questions a straightforward narrative about group-oriented Catholicisms as a result of the invincible march of the homogenizing and secularizing forces of nationalisms and nation-states.

Manifesto of the Christian Academic Circle, of which Mardešić was one of the founders; see Christian Academic Circle, "Manifesto," 181–90.

33. See Jukić, *Lica i maske svetoga*, 511.

Collectivistic Catholicisms: Embedded Catholicisms Transcending National Ideologies

Polish National Identity and Catholicism in the Context of Solidarity

In 1979, Karol Wojtyła came to his homeland as the newly elected Pope John Paul II. He was greeted by millions of Poles. In thirty-two homilies that the Polish pope gave during his nine-day visit, he spoke of human dignity and freedom.[34] The Poles responded to their pope with hymns and prayers. They carried crosses and sang hymns; they waved national flags. In the midst of the atheist Soviet bloc, and as the communists watched, the Poles shouted, "We want God."

The story of John Paul II, Solidarity, and the fall of communism in Poland is quite well known. But what needs more unpacking is the manner in which the humanistic rhetoric of John Paul II—the rhetoric deeply grounded in the pope's personalist theology—was intertwined with his understanding of Catholicism as inseparable from Polish culture and history. John Paul II's appeals to the dignity of the human person, therefore, did not resonate with Poles in some abstract, theological sense but on the level of their historical experience—their loyalty to Rome and their stubborn opposition to Marxist atheism. For the Poles, the communist regime just confirmed the old truth about Poland as the frontier of the Catholic world—the *antemuralis Christianitatis*—that has been defending the faith over centuries against various non-Christians, non-Catholics, and (now) nonbelievers.

The visit of John Paul II to his homeland is significant for any discussion of Catholicism and group identity because it was not just a one-time explosion of religious fervor. It was an event that released the moral and political energies of the whole Polish nation and, as a number of historians later asserted, gave an impetus to the rise of Solidarity, the first independent trade union in the Soviet bloc. The evidence of Catholicism's influence on Solidarity was everywhere. Pictures of the Polish pope adorned the union's offices, while the Gdańsk workers spent their lunch breaks waiting on their knees for confession and Holy Communion. Furthermore, Solidarity's emphasis on nonviolence and dignified resistance, its call for self-restraint, and its ban on alcohol (in a country where alcoholism was a real problem) pointed to the profound impact that Catholic ethical teachings had on the union's discourse and methods.

---

34. Barnes and Whitney, "John Paul II."

Yet Solidarity was also more than simply a Catholic-inspired labor organization. It was a social movement that unified some ten million Poles of every rank and worldview, from Catholic workers and engineers to secular intelligentsia and clergy. This "tacit alliance" of believers and nonbelievers[35] was surprising to anyone who knew anything about the relations between the Polish secular left and the representatives of the Polish Catholic Church. The secular intelligentsia has long understood the Church in Poland as a conservative force, defined by nationalistic, chauvinistic, and anti-Semitic tendencies. The Polish churchmen for their part distrusted everyone associated with, or sympathetic to, atheism. Yet, despite this history of distrust, secular leftist intellectuals came to advise Solidarity and worked together with some of the most influential church leaders.

To be sure, this secular-religious coalition was neither natural nor easy, and much can be said about the public exchanges between the Catholic and secular intellectuals showing how the distrust never fully disappeared. Nonetheless, the alliance did happen, through both dialogue and quarrel.[36] One reason was pragmatic: the Catholic and secular Poles had a common enemy. The Polish secularists critiqued the Soviet style of communism and advocated a more humanistic version of Marxism. Catholic intellectuals and the Catholic Church saw the communist regime as a hindrance to living a dignified life and as oppressive to faith and believers. And while the secular and religious critiques of the communist regime developed from very different vantage points, they were unified in seeing the regime as an obstacle to a just and sovereign Poland. The central idea of a song whose refrain is "So that Poland shall be Poland," a song that became Solidarity's theme song, "meant that the Polish People's Republic in 1980 was *not* 'Poland,'" because it was under Russian control and because "it was bankrupt, sick, [and] undemocratic."[37]

Aside from the common adversary and shared desire for Poland's political sovereignty, however, the alliance of the religious and secular was also grounded on something more. What everyone shared was a purpose—a vision of the Polish national identity that, as everyone seemed to have admitted, had strong roots in Catholicism but was nonetheless inclusive of all Poles, believers and nonbelievers. The discussions among the workers in the shipyards, the homilies of the Catholic clergy,[38] the writings of

---

35. Garton Ash, *Polish Revolution*, 27.
36. See Tischner, *Marxism and Christianity*.
37. Garton Ash, *Polish Revolution*, 91.
38. On these aspects of Polish Catholicism during the communist period, see, for example, Strassberg, "Post [World] War II Poland."

secular intellectuals—all addressed the ideals and meaning of solidarity, of human dignity and freedom. Under the auspices of Solidarity, workers and intellectuals, priests and secular intellectuals, all equally pointed to the *ethics* of what it meant to be Polish. Two figures, one religious and one secular, illustrate especially well the ways in which the moral and political categories merged in this vision of Polishness—Father Józef Tischner, Polish personalist philosopher and the chaplain of Solidarity, and Adam Michnik, secular activist, intellectual, and an adviser to Solidarity.

In his homilies and philosophical work, Tischner spoke of how the dignity of each person stemmed from her being created in the image of God. At the same time, Tischner's reflections on the necessity of the freedom of individuals; his defense of the human right "to sensible work," "to assemble," and to hope; and his thinking about human solidarity as a source of human dignity[39]—all of these ideas reflected his strong belief that these highest principles could "be saturated with a concrete content" and could gain in substance when placed within the context of the historical experience of the Polish people.

Michnik recognized the Catholic discourse of human dignity as something that was common to all and embracing of all. The secular left and the Catholic Church, Michnik wrote, shared a belief in the freedom of individual conscience, the importance of human dignity for democracy, and the need for a moral renewal of Poland. And precisely in the name of freedom of conscience and the dignity of each individual, Michnik asked his fellow secular Poles to show respect toward their religious others.

There is no doubt that the links between Catholicism, the Catholic Church, and Polish national identity were defined as a political statement against the oppressive and atheist character of the communist regime and Soviet intrusion into Polish national sovereignty. But the vision of Polishness that Solidarity put forward also transcended the realm of politics. In this very particular moment of Polish history, Solidarity gestured toward a possibility that the Catholic ideals of the dignity of human personhood could be seen as complementary to the secular approaches to human rights and freedom of conscience. Yes, for most Poles being Polish in the context of Solidarity meant being Catholic, but it also meant being democratic and in solidarity with all other Poles. In the 1980s, nobody found it surprising that the Polish Cardinal Wyszyński could receive a delegation of pious Catholics and Jewish socialists and hand out to each of them a signed Bible.[40]

---

39. Tischner, *Spirit of Solidarity*, 88.
40. Ibid., 89.

Catholicism, Bosnianism, and Croatian Nationalism in the Context of the Franciscan Province "Silver Bosnia"

Just like Solidarity, the case of the Bosnian Franciscan community calls into question the idea that group-oriented Catholicisms represent a victory of nationalism and secularization over religious identity. If the Bosnian War brought to light the exclusivistic character of religious nationalism of the Međugorje (Herzegovinian) Franciscans, it also pointed to the peacemaking and tolerant Catholicism of the Bosnian Franciscans.

At first sight, and in the larger context of the peacemaking activities of religious communities and organizations, the Bosnian Franciscan province "Silver Bosnia" was not unusual. Its actions consisted of the combination of economic, cultural, and political projects with the goal of alleviating the consequences of the conflict. Moreover, all church elites in Bosnia and Herzegovina provided humanitarian aid, and all claimed to have done so regardless of the national and religious identity of those in need. But the Bosnian Franciscan peacemaking role, its practice, and the ways in which this practice was justified and grounded merit more attention.

Father Ivo Marković is a case in point. One of the greatest spokesmen of reconciliation among the Bosnian Muslims, Orthodox Christians, and Catholics, Marković has been the leader of the Face to Face (*Oci u Oci*) Center for Interreligious Dialogue and the founder of the Pontanima Choir. For this choir, which consists of Catholic, Christian Orthodox, and Muslim singers, learning spiritual songs from a variety of religious traditions is not just an artistic expression. It is a way to overcome the experiences of war and to live once again with members of other religions and national groups. And while Marković was crucial for the initiatives that affirmed interreligious dialogue and coexistence, his role in the Bosnian War went beyond peacemaking projects: he also personally helped refugees of different religious backgrounds escape across enemy lines, and he brought medicines and essential supplies across those same lines.[41]

Marković, in other words, exemplifies the radical nature of the Bosnian Franciscans' peacemaking stance, which is inseparable from the commitment to Bosnian plurality. So is the case with other members of the

---

41. In 1998, Marković received the Peacemaker in Action Award from the Tanenbaum Center for Interreligious Understanding for his "extraordinary heroism in helping refugees escape across enemy lines; bringing medicines and essential supplies across those same lines; as well as [his] continuing efforts to promote interreligious dialogue." Georgette Bennett (President of the Tanenbaum Center), letter to Marković, April 18, 1998; Father Marković's acceptance remarks in Marković, letter to Bennett, April 27, 1998.

province. Father Nikica Miličević, the guardian of an old Franciscan monastery in Fojnice, acted as a representative of Fojnice's Croats in peace negotiations with the Muslims, following his belief that Bosnian Croats "indeed do not have some 'homeland on reserve'" but "belong" to Bosnia. Disregarding the conflicts between Muslims and Catholics, Father Mile Babić taught at the Islamic theological school in Sarajevo. Father Marko Oršolić was one of the founders of Together, an interreligious and intercultural organization that, among other activities, has been assisting people from religiously and nationally "mixed" marriages since 1991.

One of the foundations for Bosnian Franciscans' peacemaking was the universal values of their faith, especially the Franciscan approach to Christology as a source of toleration and forgiveness.[42] But the actions and words of the Bosnian Franciscans during and after the war also revealed the whole province's uncompromising dedication to recovering and preserving the religiously and nationally pluralistic Bosnian society. Contrary to the views of their Herzegovinian brothers, the Bosnian Franciscans held a strong conviction that the Catholic identity of Bosnian Croats was grounded in, and inseparable from, Bosnia as their homeland. It had a full meaning, they asserted, only in relation to their religious and national others. "We [a]re Croats," wrote the Bosnian Franciscan provincial, "in our Bosnian way," and this Bosnianism involves "the right to be Croat," which by its very nature also includes the right of "others to be Serb, Bosniak-Muslim, or something else."[43]

The notion of Bosnianism put forward in these statements was not just a political category. It stemmed from the old historical narratives about the presence and role of the Franciscans in Bosnia. The stories reveal pride in the persistence and even stubbornness that gave the friars the courage to stay in Bosnia and negotiate with the Ottoman rulers after every other Catholic representative had left. These are the narratives about the ways in which the Franciscans secured the Catholic faith's preservation in this region,[44] but they are also about friars as the Bosnian "romantics" who learned how to preserve Catholicism while also being open to Bosnian non-Catholics.

Father Ljubo Lucić's 1993 address to the Bosnian parliament highlighted all of these elements of Franciscan Bosnianism: "I am a Bosnian Franciscan. I emphasize this Bosnian! We have stayed in *our* Bosnia even after the Muslims conquered it. Our monasteries were destroyed, and we

---

42. See, for example, Markešić, *Svjetlo riječi*, 9; Babić, "Kristološko utemeljenje tolerancije," 287–320.

43. Provincial Petar Andjelović as translated in Solic, "The Other Bosniaks."

44. See Jakelić, *Collectivistic Religions*, especially ch. 3.

built new ones. They were persecuting us to leave Bosnia ... but we did not let them. There is no part of Bosnia without our graves ... there is no part of Bosnia where people do not respect and love us because *they recognized us as their own*."[45]

In Lucić's words, Franciscan Bosnianism means historicity, particularity, and tolerance; it means representing Catholics and Croats but also belonging to all other Bosnians. All official speeches, declarations, and actions of the Bosnian Franciscan province during the war have in the background an understanding that Bosnianism is not just an ideal identity of a multireligious society; it is a solution for the roots and consequences of the Bosnian War. For the friars, this Bosnian identity embraces all while it does not abolish any of the specific religious identities. Within the sense of Bosnian self, Catholic and Croatian identities exist *next to and are shaped by* religious and national "others." Or as Bosnian friars declared to the Bosnian-Herzegovinian Croats during some of the worse fights in 1994, "We can realize our religious, cultural, national, and political identities first and foremost in dialogue with the members of other nations, religions, and cultures ... The more we affirm the differences in Bosnia and Herzegovina, the more we affirm its unity."[46]

It is important to note that, in the case of the Bosnian Franciscan province, Catholicism remains connected to the Croatian national identity. However, Catholicism is also constitutive of the larger cultural and political particularity—the Bosnian collective identity. These layers of collective identity—Catholic, Croatian, Bosnian—shape a type of collectivistic Catholicism that is particular yet inclusive of others, group-oriented but also a piece of a larger, Bosnian mosaic. This Catholicism, in other words, represents collectivistic religions but also a type of particularist universalism that, by remaining particularist, also subverts the exclusivistic nature and power of the Croatian national ideologies.[47]

Just like Catholicism in the context of Solidarity, the Bosnian Franciscan Catholicisms thus become an example of rooted faith that deepens, in the words of Pope Benedict XVI, the cultural consequences of religious ideas. The two cases of collectivistic Catholicism, to be sure, differ greatly. Solidarity's Catholicism happened in one very particular moment of Polish history and revealed the possibility of a vision of collective identity that is

---

45. See Lucić, "Govor u Bosansko-hercegovačkom parlamentu"; see also his "Oporuka mrtvog franjevca"; italics are mine.

46. Statement of the representatives of the Bosnian Franciscan province issued in July 1994, as cited in Andjelović, *Vjerni Bogu, vjerni Bosni*, 151.

47. For the notion of particularist universalism, see Seligman, "Particularist Universalism."

based on the affinity between religious and secular ethical ideals of dignity and solidarity. The Catholicism of the Bosnian Franciscans had its roots in everyday life: it developed, in the words of Bosnian writer Ivan Lovrenović, from "the civilizational process that last[ed] daily" and expanded into a sense of alterity, the umbrella of social life for everyone—Bosnian Muslims, Orthodox Christians, and Catholics.[48] These important differences notwithstanding, Solidarity and Bosnian Franciscan Catholicisms share unique collectivistic features: the historical and cultural specificity of Catholic faith, yet the capaciousness to see and affirm the others.

Embedded Catholicisms: Beyond Critique

The cases of Radio Marya and Međugorje reflect the phenomenology of religious nationalism—of religion that not only constitutes, but also succumbs to, the narrow political meanings and boundaries of national identities. The first part of this essay, in other words, pointed out both the realities and problems of religious nationalism. It confirmed some important aspects of critiques of any religion that is linked to national identities. At the same time, this essay also argued that religious nationalism constitutes only one modern aspect of collectivistic religiosity and cannot explain the complexity of collectivistic Catholicisms. This theoretical proposition implies that the relationship between religious and collective identity should always be examined empirically—by looking at all of the dimensions that shape Catholicism and belonging. To use Emile Durkheim's insight, Catholicism as a source of "collective effervescence" creates boundaries that can lead to conflict but can also lead to socially beneficial solidarity.[49] Just like any other type of collective identity, collectivistic Catholicism can be the source of exclusion and conflict but also of integration.

This is an important insight: it compels us to rethink the oft-repeated calls to reject collectivistic Catholicisms as a betrayal of religious tradition and as a source of intolerance. Instead, we are asked to direct our attention toward a more difficult goal: the retrieval of the political, philosophical, and institutional conditions conducive to Catholicisms that shape more virtuous ways of belonging. This belonging is one that enables individuals to affirm the boundaries of baptism, the cultural and historical particularities that shape one's ways of being Catholic, but also the acceptance of others—religious and nonreligious, national or tribal.

---

48. On the notion of alterity, see Lovrenović, "Rat 1992–1995 i nakon njega."
49. See Shilling and Mellor, "Durkheim, Morality and Modernity."

To be able do this, it is necessary to avoid what philosopher Charles Taylor calls the "subtraction" stories of religion in the modern world. In my reading, the claim about the Catholicism-collective identity link as the secularization of religion is one such "subtraction" story, because it assumes a sharp division between modernity and tradition,[50] a divide between the homogenizing and secularizing forces of nationalism and nation-states, and the particularities that defined premodern contexts. The subtraction story in question—embodied in the concept of religious nationalism—carries two problematic premises. First, it understands collective identity *as* national identity, rather than as constituted by religious, territorial, ethnic, national, cultural, or linguistic identities. Second, it carries a modernist bias in thinking about religion and collective identification, which suggests that the emergence of nationalism replaces or displaces religion.[51]

The latter is not just a default view held by social scientists. The American theologian William Cavanaugh mirrors the same subtraction stories that have become common among social scientists when he asserts that the rise of nation-states implies "the triumph of the universal over the particular";[52] argues that the nation-state grooms and disciplines its citizens to cede all of their particular loyalties; and posits that the nation-state domesticates the faith communities that precede it. First, he assumes that the rise of nation-states replaces or displaces particular identities, religious identities included. Second, Cavanaugh maintains that the existence of nation-states leads to the transfer of sacred devotion from the Church to the nation-state.[53]

If his argument is correct, how are we to account for the custom of cross tattoos among Catholic women in Bosnia? Should this custom be understood as a remnant of pagan times and the Illyrian tribes who lived in that region? Is this custom, as it was in the context of Ottoman Bosnian society, a way for Catholic women to publicly and clearly mark their religious identity? Should the cross tattoos that one still sees among the older women of central Bosnia be interpreted as an expression of one's national identity and the political appropriation of Catholic faith? Or is this yet another example of the complex ways in which one's belonging to a particular Catholic

---

50. On the critique of the division between modernity and tradition in the study of ritual, see Seligman et al., *Ritual and Its Consequences*, especially 179–80.

51. For these arguments, see Jakelić, *Collectivistic Religions*, especially ch. 1. On modernism in the study of nationalism, see A. Smith, *Nationalism and Modernism*; for a multilayered critique of the modernist view of religions and nationalisms, see van der Veer and Lehmann, *Nation and Religion*.

52. Cavanaugh, *Theopolitical Imagination*, 99.

53. Cavanaugh, *Migrations of the Holy*.

community becomes embodied—indeed, an example of the complicated interconnections between tradition and modernity and a sign that the past and present collectivistic meanings of Catholicism do not disappear in the late modern age of nation-states?

It is important, in my view, to develop theoretical and theological modes of thinking about Catholicism and collective identity that avoid the traps of the straightforward, epic narratives about the victory of modernization and secularization in our world. Such approaches should be able to appreciate the multiple types of boundaries and identity markers, their simultaneous firmness and fragility, their sovereign power and their porousness. These theoretical and theological tools, in other words, should be able to address and engage liminality—that space in between—that has been and still often is a model of belonging.

The stories of Catholic identity, past and present, are neither straightforward nor uncomplicated. Our task, whether as social scientists or theologians, is not to streamline and impoverish such complex boundaries of belonging. Our task is twofold. First, it is to explore when and how the Catholic identities strongly linked to birth, origins, and groups can allow for—rather than inhibit—the presence of the one and universal Church, fully embedded and lived in this world. And second, our task is to engage such collectivistic Catholic identities to reimagine the contours and institutions of contemporary societies through more virtuous ways of belonging—ways that sustain one's religious particularities while also affirming their different others.

8

Multiple Belongings and Transnational Processes of Catholic Formation in an Eastern Catholic Church

Peter Galadza

Eastern Catholicism comprises more than twenty churches.[1] Here I can treat only one: the Ukrainian Greco-Catholic Church (UGCC), or simply "Ukrainian Catholic" as it is usually, though unfortunately, known in the West.[2] It is a happy coincidence, however—one that makes my task

---

1. For an introduction to these churches, see Galadza, "Eastern Catholic Christianity," and Roberson, *Eastern Christian Churches*, 133–83. A helpful overview of some of the problems pertaining to Eastern Catholicism can be found in Nichols, *Rome and the Eastern Churches*.

2. Until the 1950s, the Church was generally known simply as the "Greek Catholic." This alludes to its Byzantine tradition. In documents, the word "Ruthenian" frequently preceded the term, though members usually described themselves without this prefix. After World War II, with a large influx to the West of political emigrés who had lost Ukrainian statehood twice in twenty-five years, "Ukrainian" came to replace "Ruthenian." And once ethnic categories came to dominate, "Greek" was also eliminated. Paradoxically, in Ukraine, members of this Church continue to refer to themselves simply as "Greek Catholics." Because the latter term is useful, but open to confusion, some, myself included, prefer "Greco-Catholic." This conforms to the original intent of the term, which was never intended by its Habsburg creators to designate an ethnic group.

For a cursory overview of the Church's history in the U.S., for example, see Procko, *Ukrainian Catholics in America*. See also Markus, "A Century of Ukrainian Religious Experience," and Labunka and Rudnytzky, *The Ukrainian Catholic Church, 1945–1975*. For the UGCC in Canada, see Motiuk, *Eastern Christians in the New World*. Discrete sections of the following volume contain information on the Church in other Western countries: Pawliczko, *Ukraine and Ukrainians throughout the World*.

Note, incidentally, that another *sui iuris* Church, the Byzantine Catholic Metropolia of Pittsburgh, is still occasionally identified as the "Ruthenian" Church, though it is distinct from the Ukrainian Catholic Church.

easier—that a conference on world Catholicism, in the American Midwest, has chosen to discuss what effectively describes *the* ecclesiological challenge of the UGCC. The very name "Ukraine" is usually traced to a Slavic term for "borderland." And that territory's "baptism" in 988 AD united two bodies of Christians who nonetheless are not in communion with each other. In spite of the schism, however, a significant part of the two bodies (the UGCC on the one hand, and the Orthodox of Ukraine on the other) occasionally speak of themselves as "Churches of St. Vladimir's Baptism."[3] On that basis, some of them strive for rapprochement. Paradoxically, however, the Roman Catholic Church of Ukraine, which *is* in full communion with the UGCC, is not considered one of the "Churches of St. Vladimir's Baptism." It is not of the Byzantine tradition, so its "belonging" is distinct.

Then there is the transnational question—of particular urgency for Ukrainian Greco-Catholics in the West. Almost a fifth of all Ukrainian Greco-Catholics worldwide, and almost half of their bishops, live outside Ukraine. "Multiple belonging" takes on unique coloration for them not only because their religious tradition, as mentioned already, relates them to the Orthodox, but also because their (sometimes flawed) sense of what it means to be Eastern Catholic can cause *ethnicity* to trump *Christian* "belonging." Many Ukrainian Catholics in the West presume their Church's name actually means "Catholic Church for Ukrainians."

The preceding two paragraphs alone are probably enough to confound most readers. But there is no need to blush from ignorance. Eastern Catholics together account for only 1 percent of Catholics worldwide, and even though they are supposedly the Catholic Church's other lung,[4] they know

---

3. Bendyk, "Церкви Свято-Володимирового Хрещення" [Churches of St. Vladimir's Baptism].

4. John Paul II used this metaphor and encouraged the Catholic Church "to breathe with both lungs." See, for example, par. 54 of his encyclical *Ut unum sint*. It is significant that his most official use of the term is found in a reflection on the Baptism of Kievan Rus'. "The other event which I am pleased to recall is the celebration of the Millennium of the Baptism of Rus' (988–1988). The Catholic Church, and this Apostolic See in particular, desired to take part in the Jubilee celebrations and also sought to emphasize that the Baptism conferred on Saint Vladimir in Kiev was a key event in the evangelization of the world. The great Slav nations of Eastern Europe owe their faith to this event, as do the peoples living beyond the Ural Mountains and as far as Alaska. In this perspective, an expression that I have frequently employed finds its deepest meaning: the Church must breathe with her two lungs! In the first millennium of the history of Christianity, this expression refers primarily to the relationship between Byzantium and Rome. From the time of the Baptism of Rus' it comes to have an even wider application: evangelization spread to a much vaster area, so that it now includes the entire Church. If we then consider that the salvific event which took place on the banks of the Dnieper goes back to a time when the Church in the East and the Church in the West were not divided, we understand clearly that the vision of the full communion to be sought is that of unity in legitimate diversity."

they are a very small "organ"—even if vital in other ways. But in spite of the need for more background, I must leave readers to probe these "Oriental intricacies" on their own.[5]

Several final introductory remarks: the Ukrainian Greco-Catholic Church is the largest of the Eastern Catholic churches (accounting for more than a quarter of all such Catholics).[6] More importantly, in the former USSR, its very existence generates friction related to "multiple belongings."[7]

---

5. In addition to the works cited in footnote 1, the following can be helpful: Mahieu and Naumescu, *Churches In-Between*. And for those needing a very basic introduction, see Faulk, *101 Questions and Answers*, and Petras, *Eastern Catholic Churches in America*.

6. The following is an outline history of the Ukrainian Greco-Catholic Church adapted from Galadza, "Eastern Catholic Christianity," 294–95:

In 1596, the Metropolitan of Kiev (Kyiv) and most of his suffragans renewed union with Rome at the Synod of Brest (in present-day Belarus). (A previous primate of the Church, Isidore, had supported the Union of Florence [1439].) The Metropolia of Kiev was entirely within the Polish-Lithuanian Commonwealth, and as the latter's support—and size—waned, so did the "Uniate" Church. Ukrainian Cossacks, followed by the tsarist government, consistently opposed the union in favor of Orthodoxy.

By the end of the nineteenth century, the Church was restricted to the Austro-Hungarian realm, having been banned in the Russian Empire. Owing in part to the benign treatment of Greco-Catholics by the Habsburgs (who provided, for example, university education for the clergy), a sincere commitment to Catholicism developed, reaching its height in the twentieth century.

During the interwar period, Ukrainian Greco-Catholics maintained their life in Polish-dominated western Ukraine. In eastern Ukraine, Soviet control after the Bolshevik Revolution led to the deaths of millions. Between 1939 and 1941, the Soviets extended their rule to western Ukraine, Greco-Catholicism's heartland. Thus, when the Germans invaded western Ukraine in June 1941, they were initially welcomed as "liberators."

When the Soviets again took control of western Ukraine after World War II and declared the Greco-Catholic Church absorbed by the Orthodox Patriarchate of Moscow (at the Pseudo-Synod of Lviv, 1946), most Greco-Catholics retained their commitment to Rome (frequently clandestinely) and reemerged in 1989 as communism collapsed. This forced an announcement by Mikhail Gorbachev, during a visit to Rome on December 1, 1989, of the Greco-Catholic Church's decriminalization.

During the Soviet period, the most contentious issue was the Vatican's willingness to sacrifice this Church in the interests of dialogue with Moscow. Today, this is no longer the case, though the Vatican's refusal to recognize a Ukrainian Catholic patriarchate, championed by a former primate, Cardinal Josyf Slipyj, after his release from eighteen years in Siberia in 1963, is partially a remnant of this policy, previously called *Ostpolitik*. Other Orthodox churches also oppose the creation of a Ukrainian Catholic patriarchate, viewing it as an endorsement of "Uniatism," that is, the attempt to bring Orthodox jurisdictions into Roman obedience piecemeal.

In North America, Ukrainian Greco-Catholics have four dioceses, or eparchies, as they are called in Byzantine terminology. In Canada, they have five.

7. For a superb presentation of today's religious landscape in Ukraine, see the special issue of the journal *Religion, State & Society* 38:3 (2010). Two works that deserve attention as contemporary Ukrainian Catholic ecclesiological reflections are Marynovych,

Symbolic of this is that, for more than twenty years Russian Orthodox patriarchs rebuffed invitations to meet with the pope primarily because Rome refuses to return to its previous policy of *Ostpolitik*.[8] The policy had the Vatican sacrificing the Ukrainian "Uniates" in the interests of rapprochement with Moscow. Thus, as recently as April 2013, shortly after the new pope's election, the Moscow Patriarchate's head of external relations, Metropolitan Hilarion Alfeyev, stated the following about Pope Francis and the UGCC. He expressed hope that the new pope "will continue the policy of rapprochement with the Orthodox Church and will not support what he [Metropolitan Hilarion] calls the expansion of the Ukrainian Greek Catholics." He said that "the union is the most painful topic in the Orthodox-Catholic dialogue, in relations between the Orthodox and the Catholics. If the pope will support the union, then, of course, it will bring no good."[9]

Needless to say, the issues between Moscow and the Greco-Catholic Church are tied directly to nationality, and Patriarch Kirill's new campaign to globally gather and guide the *russkiy mir* ("the Russian world"), especially in Ukraine, entrenches the tendency to favor ethnic blood over baptismal water.[10] Of course, the tendency runs both ways,[11] though Ukraine, it should be noted, has never ruled Russia.

Before proceeding, a comment about "method" and "correlations with other disciplines." It will become readily apparent that my paper makes no

---

Українська Ідея і Християнство [The Ukrainian Idea and Christianity], and *Dymyd*, Херсонеське таїнство свободи [The Chersonesus Mystery of Freedom].

8. For an overview of this policy, see Hebblethwaite, "From *Ostpolitik* to *Europapolitik*." There is also the hefty tome edited by Ramet, *Catholicism and Politics*. Probably indicative of the unseemly nature of this policy in relation to the Greco-Catholics is the fact that the first-person account by one of *Ostpolitik*'s main protagonists, Cardinal Agostino Casaroli, entirely avoids discussing the Greco-Catholics and the USSR. See Casaroli, *Martyrdom of Patience*. The full title should actually read, "*Several* Communist Countries." Had Casaroli dealt with the Greco-Catholic Church in Ukraine, for example, he would have had to discuss the Vatican's plans to entirely abandon that Church in the interests of "rapprochement" with Moscow.

9. *The Economist*, "The New Pope."

10. For a sense of the kind of discourse surrounding "ruskii mir," see Russkiy Mir Foundation Press Service, "Patriarch Kirill."

11. In reaction to the rhetoric of *russkiy mir*, some leaders of the UGCC in Ukraine had begun proposing an *ukrainskyi svit* ("Ukrainian world"). Fortunately, it has not gained momentum. See "Не біймося 'русского міра,' будуймо український світ" ("The Head of the Ukrainian Greco-Catholic Church, Sviatoslav Shevchuk: 'Let's Not Be Afraid of the "Russian World": Let's Build a Ukrainian World'") at https://rozmova.wordpress.com/2012/09/17/ne-biimosya-shevchuk/. Note, incidentally, that the present lecture was delivered and edited before Russia's invasion of Ukraine. The ideology of *russkiy mir* has inflamed the Kremlin's aggression. One can only admire the Ukrainians' ability to avoid the temptation of "ideological retaliation."

pretensions to being anything more than elemental theological reflection and an entry-level presentation of the problematic. Elsewhere I have engaged in more systematic biblical analysis of some of the issues discussed here.[12] However, being a liturgist, and not a religious sociologist or ecclesiologist, I hope I can be forgiven my limited scope. My only consolation is that so little is known about Eastern Catholicism in Western countries that a less sophisticated presentation will probably be welcome.

Incidentally, however, theologically and methodologically I feel a kinship with the work of Michael Budde[13] and Dorian Llywelyn.[14] While the two might not usually be classed as allies, in typically antinomic Eastern manner, I feel compelled to synthesize elements of their approaches in "both/and" fashion. Benedict XVI stated in 2006 that one's nationality is to be "inserted, relativized, and also carefully located in the great unity of the Catholic communion."[15] Budde masterfully relativizes, while Llywelyn skillfully "inserts" and "locates" (though also relativizing). In any case, my paper will hopefully amplify their insights with additional material.

The Catholic Difference

The first of three questions posed to the speakers by the organizers of this conference was this: "What difference does being a Catholic Christian make in a world of powerful institutions and processes that shape identities, loyalties, and allegiances?"

The short answer is, "all the difference in the world." The long *question* is, how Catholic is the Ukrainian Greco-Catholic Church? First, the answer. The latter is colored by my perception that "powerful institutions and processes" is intended to describe generally negative phenomena. In any case, this is how I understand the question. There is no reason, however, why this should always be so. In recent years, powerful institutions that care nothing for "the Church" have performed an immense service to Catholicism by exposing horrific abuse when some of the Church's own leaders preferred a less ethical course.[16] And previously, it was "powerful institutions and processes"—also of a secular bent—that compelled the Church to eventually embrace, for example, democracy.[17] More directly related to the

---

12. Galadza, "Structure of Eastern Churches," 373–86.
13. Budde, *The Borders of Baptism*.
14. Llywelyn, *Toward a Catholic Theology*.
15. Cited in Allen, "Europe's Christian Roots."
16. Among the multitude of books that have partly done the Church's penitential work for her are France, *Our Fathers*.
17. For a study that reads like a novel, see Bokenkotter, *Church and Revolution*.

question of nationalism, secularizing nationalists have sometimes shown more solicitude for their impoverished co-nationals than self-professed Christians.[18] Hopefully, these three examples will help demonstrate that I am not interested in promoting Catholic triumphalism, even though some of my formulations below may create that impression.

With those caveats in mind, I turn to my answer. Catholicism, and more particularly Roman Catholicism (as opposed to Eastern Catholicism), has achieved a transnational identity, loyalty, and allegiance among its members that can only be the envy of any person of goodwill. Of course, I am speaking of the present, not the past. Consequently, today, in spite of some glaring exceptions (e.g., the Rwandan genocide), it is the Roman Catholic Church that uniquely models humanity renewed. Roman Catholicism's imposing transnational identity puts into relief the nationalism that dominates many Eastern churches. Especially when compared with Eastern Christianity's penchant for ethno-dogmatism (more on this term below), the ability of Catholic blacks and Koreans, Hispanics and Hungarians, Russians and Rwandans to gather for worship and regularly collaborate in ecclesial institutions—without anyone even *being allowed* to ask, "What are *you* doing here?"—is almost miraculous. Certainly it is the Roman Catholic Church that regularly—and systemically—actualizes Acts 2:8–12. And it does so not partitively, with each group *allegedly* "sharing *koinonia*" while, in fact, remaining isolated and even antagonistic. Rather, it does so organically and consistently.

Several other positive examples are apropos. A Roman Catholic bishop will not publicly bestow a certificate of merit on a prominent pro-abortion politician simply because of the politician's association with his "ethnic Church."[19] A racist Roman Catholic layperson will not be preferred by the bishop for a seat on a parish council over an unprejudiced—and truly devout—parishioner only because the racist possesses strong "ethnic credentials." A Roman Catholic diocese will not tolerate the official promotion of

---

18. An example that is particularly apropos in the context of a discussion of Ukrainian Catholicism is the anticlerical social democrat of nationalist bent, Ivan Franko (d. 1916). He and some of his collaborators were far more solicitous for the impoverished Greco-Catholic peasantry and proletariat than certain Church leaders. This has earned his portrait a place of honor in many UGCC church halls, even though his relationship with the Church was at best ambiguous and he died without the "last rites," a paramount symbol in its day.

19. Greek Orthodox Archdiocese of America, "Leadership 100 12th Annual Conference." See also a Greek Orthodox priest's letter of concern regarding his Church's attitude toward Senator Sarbanes: Bell, "Open Letter to His Eminence Archbishop Demetrios."

parochial folkdance ensembles in parishes where catechesis for these same youth is neglected.

The first example is specific to Eastern Orthodoxy, but the next two can be typical of Eastern Catholicism. And before continuing, allow me to note that if my discourse seems all too concrete, this is intentional. Near-surrealistic discussions of "Eucharistic ecclesiology" and "sobornicity" pervade Eastern Christian theological literature,[20] when some Eastern Christian communities seem incapable of accepting the most basic tenets of Eph 2:16–19,[21] Rev 14:6,[22] and Gal 3:28.[23]

In sum, an Eastern Catholic (and hopefully, an Eastern Orthodox) who has traveled worldwide marvels at the ability of the Roman Catholic Church to makes its faithful "members of a community broader than the largest nation-state, more pluralistic than any culture in the world, more deeply rooted in the lives of the poor and marginalized than any revolutionary movement, more capable of exemplifying the notion of 'E pluribus unum' than any empire past, present, or future."[24]

Catholicism's Embrace of Nationalism

This brings me to the "long question": how Catholic is the Ukrainian Greco-Catholic Church? It also leads to the *second* question posed by the conference organizers: "Has Catholicism's embrace of nationalism and other powerful forms of political/cultural identity limited, inhibited, or thwarted

---

20. Among the countless Eastern Orthodox articles presenting a proper approach to ethnicity/nationality and Church are the following: Lossky, "Catholic Consciousness," 183–94; Harakas, "Living the Orthodox Christian Faith," 153–58; Buciora, "Ecclesiology and National Identity," 29–38; Krivocheine, "Catholicity and the Structures of the Church," 41–52; and Karmiris, "Nationalism in the Orthodox Church," 171–84. The arguments are theologically flawless and cogent—even inspiring. Their implementation, however, is nowhere in sight.

21. "[. . . that he] might reconcile us both to God in one body through the cross, thereby killing the hostility. And he came and preached peace to you who were far off and peace to those who were near. For through him we both have access in one Spirit to the Father. So then you are no longer strangers and aliens, but you are fellow citizens with the saints and members of the household of God" (ESV).

22. "Then I saw another angel flying directly overhead, with an eternal gospel to proclaim to those who dwell on earth, to every nation and tribe and language and people" (ESV).

23. "There is neither Jew nor Greek, there is neither slave nor free, there is no male and female, for you are all one in Christ Jesus" (ESV).

24. Budde, *Borders of Baptism*, 4.

the call of the Gospel to form communities of discipleship across human borders and divisions?"

Before proceeding, I should clarify a dimension of the term "Catholic" within our context and provide some reflection on the term "nationalism." With regard to the former, a basic problem since the Union of Brest (1596 AD) is that the "Uniate" Church has often been considered less than Catholic because its liturgical, spiritual, and canonical traditions are not Latin.[25] This is ironic, and in one sense insulting, as thousands of Ukrainians suffered martyrdom and exile between 1944 and 1989 only because of their Catholicism—their unwillingness to break with Rome.[26] And suspicions regarding the UGCC's Catholic identity endure because of its married clergy.[27]

In the context of our present discussion, these points warrant attention, as in the past some of the promoters of an otherwise proper Catholic universalism (transnationalism) could also be aggressive advocates of ecclesial uniformity. In other words, they argued for the curbing of the Eastern Catholics' liturgical, spiritual, and canonical particularities.[28] This provoked antipathy for otherwise healthy universalism, as the latter made no room for legitimate particularity.[29] During the interwar period, for example, Greco-Catholics in Pilsudski's Poland—more specifically, Galicia—could be denied government employment or promotion for refusing to switch to the Latin Rite. The government drove the campaign. This is because a "change of Rite" had the net effect of making a Ukrainian into a Pole. One can imagine the aversion to "Catholicism" that could ensue. Thus, even the adoption of the

---

25. See Pospishil, *Ex Occidente Lex*.

26. This is not to deny that among the additional reasons for deporting these believers was their support of Ukrainian sovereignty. But certainly in the case of many of these confessors and martyrs, this (entirely legitimate) political dimension—that is, their political engagement—was secondary or even entirely negligible.

27. The following superb study exposes some aspects of this prejudice: Petrà, *Due Carismi*.

28. Vatican II, incidentally, introduced the possibility of *theological* distinctiveness as well (*LG* 23), but the Ukrainian Catholics' low theological output means that there has been little to "curb"—with one significant exception. In 2008, the Vatican's Congregation for the Doctrine of the Faith intervened at the Ukrainian Catholic University in Lviv to curtail momentum among Greco-Catholic theologians in Ukraine for concrete action to foster ecumenical understanding with all the Orthodox of Ukraine—including the Moscow Patriarchate. As the editorial cited below indicates, it seems that Rome is committed to ecumenical dialogue with the Russian Orthodox, provided that Rome controls it, and that the dialogue builds bridges to the Kremlin rather than among Ukrainians and Russians in "provinces" like Ukraine. See Galadza, "Rome's Congregation for the Doctrine of the Faith and Ukrainian Ecumenism."

29. Llywelyn draws attention to this in reference to developments *within* Roman Catholicism (*Toward a Catholic Theology*, 287).

Gregorian calendar—three hundred and fifty years after its promulgation—could be denounced by some Greco-Catholics as "Polonization."

As just noted, the confusion of healthy universalism with illegitimate uniformity means that some Eastern Catholics have come to suspect the former. The challenge, then, is to cultivate a *transnational* identity while simultaneously fostering ecclesial particularity (that is, theological, liturgical, spiritual, and canonical distinctiveness).

To understand why many Eastern Catholics have been slow to meet this challenge one must recall that, while Vatican II provided the conceptual means for melding missional universalism and ecclesial particularity, the Council's shift in thinking was an unexpected and extrinsic importation for many Eastern Catholics—among them, the Ukrainians.[30] Unlike the Latin Church, where a biblical, catechetical, ecumenical, and liturgical movement had prepared at least some leaders for the Council's new vision, right up until the 1960s Ukrainian Catholics were often censured for attempting to move in the direction eventually adopted by Vatican II. In addition to cutting off Eastern Catholics from their Eastern Orthodox roots—in particular, an appreciation for the genius of their authentic liturgy—Rome also forbade them from engaging in missionary work. Before Vatican II, an Eastern Catholic hoping to undertake such work had to adopt the Latin Rite.[31]

All of this has left its mark. Thus, in the absence of other criteria for ecclesial distinctiveness, Ukrainian Catholics frequently fall back on ethnicity. In the West, this is particularly burdensome. This is because it is precisely to Western countries that Ukrainian nationalists emigrated after World War II. (One of the tragic ironies of history is that the communists, who would have gladly assimilated into any Western nation, won the war and got to stay in the country for which the nationalists pined.) As it stands, it is this nationalism[32]—in part—that prevents the Ukrainian Catholics from collaborating with their Byzantine Ruthenian and Melkite coreligionists in

---

30. For a discussion of this, see Galadza, "Reception of the Second Vatican Council," 312–39. Incidentally, unlike the Ukrainians, the Melkites were far better prepared for the Council. Unfortunately, there is no room here to discuss why.

31. A frequently overlooked fact is that Archbishop Andrei Sheptytsky (1865–1944), a confessor of the faith, was never made a cardinal even though his predecessors *and* successors were. His protoecumenism, for example, anticipated Vatican II, and so among the accusations against this most Catholic of hierarchs during the last two decades of his life was "schismophilia." And in the context of our discussion, it is particularly apropos to note that his promotion of legitimate Ukrainian political aspirations also made him unpopular with Catholic authorities opposed to such goals. See Galadza, *Work of Andrei Sheptytsky*, 359–62.

32. Obviously, in this case I understand nationalism as an "undue exaltation of the feelings of piety toward one's own people." Pius XI, *Caritate Christi compulsi*, 4.

the West to forge the kind of fellowship that would help those committed first and foremost to the gospel to find much-needed mutual inspiration and support.[33] At a time when countercultural Catholicism will be facing tougher opposition, Ukrainians, Ruthenians, and Melkites—not to mention Romanians, Italo-Albanese, Hungarians, and others of the Byzantine tradition—should be able to bond rather than separate. Michael Budde's stress on solidarity applies here in a particular—intra-territorial—way.[34]

Incidentally, in the United States, the Ruthenians and Ukrainians were, in fact, one church until 1924. And if the Vatican today were interested in these churches' missional universalism, it would compel them to reintegrate their jurisdictions.[35] The argument that they themselves do not want this is moot. The Vatican has ignored their wishes before. It has not shied away, for example, from forcing them to adopt mandatory celibacy, even though the imposition was—and remains—unpopular. In any case, the continued separation of these communities sometimes perpetuates a deleterious *cultural* Catholicism[36] and, in the case of some Ukrainian Catholics, an ethno-dogmatism.

I introduced this term earlier and should now explain why I prefer it to the term "nationalist" when discussing Eastern churches in Western "diasporas." The term avoids the oddity of describing individuals who are thousands of miles and possibly two or three generations removed from "the nation." Thus, it brings greater conceptual clarity to a very "imaginary" realm.[37]

Ethno-dogmatism construes the retention and promotion of ethnic languages, folklore, ancestral homeland commitment—and the requisite financial obligations—as absolutes. Thus, a Ukrainian Catholic of this bent may forego Sunday Eucharist if the service is not in Ukrainian (even though

---

33. For reflection along these lines, see Pulcini, "Byzantine Catholic Ecclesiology," 5–22, and the more modest proposal in Bouyer, *Church of God*, 449.

34. Budde, *Borders of Baptism*, 24–42. But Budde's otherwise insightful and inspiring reflection is marred by his naïve evaluation of Adrian Pabst's estimation of Patriarch Kirill's "drive to gain greater independence from the Russian state" (ibid., 42).

35. It should be noted that many Ukrainian Catholics would gladly "integrate" their ecclesial structures with the Ruthenians' (that is, absorb the latter) provided the Ruthenians would be willing to accept the nomenclature "Ukrainian." This, of course, is an unreasonable—and unnecessary—demand. But the problem could easily be solved if both churches simply returned to the name "Greco-Catholic"—without any qualifiers.

36. Of course, I am using the term here to refer to a superficial attachment to Catholicism as a cultural and ancestral artifact, not Catholicism's commitment to, and absorption of, culture.

37. On nation and nationalism as constructions, see the classic by Anderson, *Imagined Communities*.

he/she is a native speaker of the other language—e.g., English). He or she will complain to church authorities about the cancelation of a folk festival on parish grounds but will undermine the parish's pro-life activities (if any such exist). He or she will passionately support the Church in Ukraine, with significant financial contributions, but simultaneously ignore, or even undermine, efforts to (re)evangelize the local (North American) community.

Within the world of ethno-dogmatism, terms such as "assimilation" and "unity" metastasize perversely. Ethnosocial assimilation becomes an evil to be avoided at all costs, yet spiritual assimilation goes unrecognized. Unity with all members of the ethnic group is highly prized, yet fellowship with committed Christians of a church who are not of the designated ethnic background is spurned.

Having conceptually fine-tuned one aspect of nationalism—as it relates to our concerns—let me now turn to the *abuse* of the term by those who have little understanding or concern for *collective* rights, as well as the dangers of globalization, "massification," and/or imperialism.[38]

If my discussion of ethno-dogmatism focused on "the diaspora," my discussion of nationalism per se takes us back to Ukraine. It may appear to contradict some of my previous formulations, but the logic should be evident. Occasionally, one hears criticisms of nationalist tendencies within the Greco-Catholic Church in Ukraine.[39] My experience working there for almost a quarter of a century compels me to insist that, in general, the UGCC in the former USSR is the wrong place to be looking for Ukrainian nationalism.[40] As noted above, many nationalists emigrated to the West,

---

38. In this case, a healthy "nationalism"—which I personally would not even describe as such, since it is more akin to a patriotism committed to political and social subsidiarity—is a movement seeking to "attain and maintain the identity, unity, and autonomy of a social group, some of whose members deem it to constitute an actual or potential nation." A. Smith, *National Identity*, 73.

39. See Senyk, "Victim to Nationalism," 167–87; and my response, Galadza, "Response to Sophia Senyk," 125–42. Senyk then replied to my article: "Response to a Response," 143–48. I do not believe that her response addressed my criticisms, but I am willing to concede bias. I am emboldened in my assessment, however, by the fact that Senyk's next article—a more substantial piece—was refuted by an Irish-American. Senyk's article is "The Ukrainian Greek Catholic Church Today," 317–32. The response is by Keleher, "Response to Sophia Senyk," 289–306. Incidentally, in my response to Senyk, my reference to "an outsider's *inside* view" relates to the fact that, unlike Senyk, I had actually worked in Ukraine for extensive periods of time beginning in 1990. In fact, 1999–2000 saw my entire family and me take up residence there. This, of course, can be irrelevant as regards objectivity. It did, however, provide extensive opportunities for observation.

40. This is not to suggest that nationalism will not increase in the UGCC in Ukraine in the future, but the present leadership and the majority of clergy do not espouse the ideology. An important source of official statements by the UGCC in Ukraine that

and it is not entirely facetious to suggest that there are probably more of them in New York and Toronto than Kyiv and Lviv. As for the nationalists who remained in Ukraine, most of them spent years in Siberia and returned home after Krushchev's "secret speech" of 1956 with a purity of heart born of unimaginable suffering. (Some of them are singularly noble indeed.) Paradoxically, then, the Church stands a far better chance of developing its universalism in Ukraine than in most Western countries. This is because Greco-Catholics there have no need for a surrogate nation-state. They live in a real one—thoroughly flawed as it may be.

As noted above, the accusation of "nationalism" is nonetheless occasionally hurled at Greco-Catholics in Ukraine. This usually occurs when Greco-Catholics (1) defend the use of the Ukrainian language—*in Ukraine* where a recent, previous prime minister (Mykola Azarov), for example, refused to learn Ukrainian; (2) show preference for the Ukrainian Orthodox Church of the Kyivan Patriarchate rather than that of the Moscow Patriarchate (which also favors Russification); and (3) occasionally participate in unveilings of memorials to Stepan Bandera, the World War II nationalist leader assassinated by the Soviets in 1959. This last issue is the most problematic, and while I certainly have no devotion to the man, one should hardly be surprised that Greco-Catholic clergy participate in such unveilings given the fact that (*a*) Bandera spent much of the war incarcerated by the Nazis at Sachsenhausen, (*b*) his two brothers died at Auschwitz, and (*c*) he was *the* Soviets' preferred target of denunciation—not to mention that it is common for one group's "freedom fighter" to be another's "terrorist." Again, the point is not to present an apologia. But as with any issue related to World War II in Eastern Europe, the question is entangled in conflicting interpretations and myths. However, I cannot insist enough that collectively the Church in Ukraine has never done anything to honor Bandera. And the UGCC is very consistent—and effective—in avoiding support for any one political group. In fact, the UGCC honors all those—be they nationalists or communists—who defended innocent life.[41]

---

deserves its own study but that, in any case, would confirm my assertions about the UGCC's approach to nationality is Kovalenko, *Соціяльно зорієнтовані документи УГКЦ* [Documents of the UGCC Related to Social Questions].

41. See, for example, the activities of the UGCC's Justice and Peace Commission in bringing together veterans of the Soviet Red Army and the Ukrainian Insurgent Army at http://www.dyhdzvin.org/index.php/zvernennia-ta-poslannia/2-uncategorised/9-uhkts-spryiaie-prymyrenniu-uchasnykiv-druhoi-svitovoi-viiny. Incidentally, it should be obvious that I part company with Michael Budde regarding pacifism, even though I would strongly support condemnations of American military "interventions" during the last fifty years.

Another nuance is apropos. I would suggest that, in the interests of bringing about healing (not justifications or rationalizations, but healing), one must always acknowledge the distinction between the nationalism of the oppressed and that of the oppressors. The latter frequently evolves into imperialism or an *übermensch* chauvinism. The former, on the other hand, is essentially defensive. Of course, it is the immoral excesses—and divisiveness—of such "defense" that require us to condemn even defensive nationalism. But in the case of the Ukrainians, we are dealing with a nation traumatized for eight hundred years. Whatever else one might think of Samuel Huntington's "clash" paradigm, he is certainly correct in noting how Ukraine is a fault line.[42] Or, to invoke another modern analyst's imagery, Ukraine is at the center of the twentieth century's "Bloodlands."[43] The struggles of the indigenous population have almost always been about survival, not conquest.[44] Since the thirteenth century, the territory has been subjected to a constant brain drain—and brain annihilation. And among the things that did not grow in this war zone was national consciousness. Frequently dubbed a "non-historic nation," it was not until 1929 that the Organization of Ukrainian Nationalists was even created.[45]

This heightens the importance of distinguishing between nationalism and patriotism. And in response to the questions "can a true Christian be a 'patriot'?"—and "how patriotic?"—the simple answer is, "it depends." It depends on what the "patria" is up to. Peoples who have experienced shifting borders—and statelessness in particular—understand this instinctively. Thus, when the "patria" does good, Christians associate with it.[46] When not, they continue to pray for it "so that by their [i.e., the government's] tranquility, we [Christians] may pass our life in quiet and calm, in all piety and purity."[47] This is "code," a way of asking God to keep evil governments and invaders "off the backs" of the Church.

---

42. Huntington, *Clash of Civilizations*. See the map on 159.

43. Snyder, *Bloodlands*.

44. Among the myriad of books describing this are Conquest, *Harvest of Sorrow*, and Berkhoff, *Harvest of Despair*.

45. On this, see Motyl, *Turn to the Right*, and Armstrong, *Ukrainian Nationalism*. See also Krawchenko, *Social Change and National Consciousness*. These older studies treat the evolution of Ukrainian nationalism during its formative phases. Naturally, there is a vast body of literature on national consciousness in Ukraine that has appeared since the demise of the USSR, but I must leave the readers to research these on their own.

46. I think that a "surplus of meaning" derived from Phil 4:8 might be invoked to support this.

47. "Anaphora of Saint Basil the Great," 296.

And then there is the question of a narrative's context and how this impacts valuations. I was delighted to read Dorian Llywelyn's critique of the Moscow Patriarchate's 2009 exhortation to the nations of Russia, Ukraine, and Belarus with its reference to "the unity of Holy Russia as the most precious possession of our Church and peoples . . . our most cherished treasure."[48] Llywelyn writes, "[This] was not only an assertion by the Moscow Patriarchate of ecclesiastical primacy over Ukraine and Belarus, but also a less-than-subtle expression of support for Russian dominance in the region."[49] Ironically, just twenty-five years ago, Llywelyn's critique would have been branded "nationalist"—an "insensitive endorsement of discord"—or even a promotion of the arms race! But his—and others'—recognition of the downtrodden's wounds will go a lot further in fostering future harmony than impositions of "imagined unities." Reconciliation, in this case between Russians and Ukrainians, will be aided by truth, not avoidance. (The proliferation of "Truth and Justice" commissions throughout the world seems to support this.) And this will, of course, require truth on the part of the Ukrainians, not just Russians.

Celebrating Diversity while Rejecting Parochial Priorities

I now turn to the final question posed by the conference organizers: "How can the Church respect and celebrate the diversity of its members—many nations, cultures, and communities—while maintaining a coherent witness to the Kingdom of God that is not undermined by more parochial ideologies or priorities?"

As regards diversity, at stake is more than a desirable "supplement" to ecclesial identity. There is a moral imperative to opposing monoculture—even if the effort risks becoming another end in itself. One must recall Solzhenitsyn's observation that, at Pentecost, witnesses heard the kerygma in their own tongue, rather than some miraculous, pneumatic Esperanto.[50]

More recently, Cardinal Bergoglio, now Pope Francis, asserted, "The globalization that makes everything uniform is essentially imperialist and instrumentally liberal, but it is not human. In the end, it is a way to enslave nations . . . we must preserve the diversity in the harmonious unity of humanity."[51] Incidentally, I have seen stunning elements of indigenous cul-

---

48. Cited in Llywelyn, *Toward a Catholic Theology*, 9–10.

49. Llywelyn, *Toward a Catholic Theology*, 10.

50. I have not been able to locate the reference to Solzhenitsyn's expression, but I know that he made the statement sometime in the 1970s or 1980s.

51. Bergoglio and Skorka, *On Heaven and Earth*, 158. Similarly, the noted Orthodox

ture eliminated in Ukraine during the past twenty-five years, not because of Russian domination—now in abeyance—but because new economic forces "inspired" it. The celebration and respect of cultural diversity, then, requires a preparatory pedagogy that would valorize an *ascetical* stance toward "the economy."

This is even more urgent in the West, where consumerism has become a religion, and (cheap) entertainment its liturgy. The commodification of art, time, sex, and health challenges any community aspiring to live *kath' olon* (according to the fullness, or wholeness—the Greek sense of "catholic"). We Catholics in the West are woefully impervious to the corrosive *spiritual* effects of unbridled capitalism, and we are not likely to receive much pastoral guidance on the topic. (Pastors and bishops need to pay bills; any hint of "socialism," even if it is simply the gospel inculturated to contemporary economic realities, is bound to "alienate benefactors.")

Another issue related to the respect of diversity concerns a point mentioned above (i.e., ecclesial latinization) but needs to be analyzed more globally. Having lauded the Roman Catholic Church for its near miraculous ability to integrate every "nation and tribe, language and people," I should note that this applies to Roman Catholicism qua *Latin* Rite Catholicism. But as regards Roman Catholicism qua Catholicism (that is, the Catholicism that includes Eastern Catholics), we find the scandalous situation of otherwise inspiring Roman Catholic missionaries working in countries like Ethiopia, where they sometimes treat the indigenous *Eastern* Catholic Church with outright contempt. Even though the Latin Rite missionaries are in full communion with this Church, the *koinonia* leaves something to be desired. Derision—or at least, willful ignorance—frequently characterizes the members of the *Ritus praestantior*.[52] This demonstrates that even the most universal of churches can retain elements of "parochial ideologies and priorities." Prior to Vatican II, the situation was far worse. But residue remains.

As regards the "Western diasporas" and the obligation of Eastern Catholics themselves to overcome such ideologies and priorities, it would seem that the creation of "particular" fellowships or associations ("brotherhoods") in otherwise unified Eucharistic communities would be the key.[53]

---

theologian John Zizioulas writes, "Culture cannot be a monolithically universal phenomenon without some kind of demonic imposition of one culture over the rest of culture" (*Being as Communion*, 258).

52. I say this on the basis of personal experience in Ethiopia. Fortunately, other Roman Catholic missionaries are very supportive of indigenous Eastern Catholic traditions, but they are not the majority.

53. Zizioulas suggests something along these lines: *Being as Communion*, 255–56.

This would enable them to continue "respecting and celebrating ethnic diversity." Thus, a parish could bring together Melkites, Ruthenians, and Ukrainians (and other Catholics of the same Rite) for joint Eucharists, where the language employed would be one that most members of the assembly use (e.g., English), with the inclusion of some parts in ancestral languages. The chants employed would also reflect the assembly's diverse composition.[54] However, in order to maintain and foster legitimate ethnic diversity, members of the parish would be encouraged to coalesce around fellowships that would gather *after* services to cultivate the riches of their own linguistic, and other ancestral, treasures. This could actually provide an enrichment that paradoxically would benefit the ethno-dogmatists. Ukrainian Americans would be sensitized to the suffering of Lebanese Christians, and Melkites would learn about the needs of Christians in the former USSR. Of course, I am fully cognizant that this proposal is thoroughly "unrealistic," but so is much of the gospel.

In the West, this need to support *immigrant* communities in their *social acclimation*, while combatting *spiritual assimilation*, cannot be overemphasized. Demographers remind us that the only North American churches maintaining or increasing their numbers are those with significant immigrant populations.[55] Thus, ignoring them is not only un-Christian; it is foolish. However, allowing subsequent, that is, third- and fourth-generation descendants of immigrant Eastern Catholics to be lost to the faith by not responding to their new (more universal) needs and mentality once they have acclimated (or assimilated) is to neglect an even greater evangelical imperative.

Conclusion

Let me conclude with two theological points. In discussions of the relationship between nation and Church, it is common to invoke one or even all three of the following theological mysteries: the Trinity, the Incarnation, and grace. These are deployed as "root metaphors." Invoking them provides a splendid means to "take every thought captive for Christ" (2 Cor 10:5). But may I remind this predominantly Western Christian audience[56] that in Western theology, "Trinity," "hypostatic union," and "grace" are considered

---

54. In Eastern Christianity, distinctive chant traditions carry an importance almost analogous to, and sometimes equal to, liturgical language.

55. Bibby, *Beyond the Gods and Back*, 190–93.

56. Such was the composition of the audience at the conference where this paper was delivered.

the uniquely great mysteries of the faith. To complicate matters even more, Greek patristic approaches to these mysteries can be quite different from Augustinian or Thomistic ones. Consequently, not only will the mystical nature of these metaphors always create problems for those hoping to invoke them in discussions of nation and Church, but even cataphatically, one can end up affirming different truths depending on whether one believes, for example, that nature is inherently graced or that grace builds on nature. (As an Eastern Catholic, I believe both, but that complicates matters even more.) Consequently, it seems that far more caution—and nuancing—is required whenever we inject these metaphors into our analysis. Llywelyn's ability, then, to deploy these metaphors effectively—without mystification—deserves recognition.

Finally, to bring us back to the "borders of baptism" and "the borderland," Ukraine, I believe that the theological foundations of our discussions are impoverished whenever we forget that baptism was not "founded" (even if we want to say "instituted") when Christ told his disciples to pronounce a formula and immerse people in water (Matt 28:19). It was founded when blood and water poured from His side (John 19:34). Thus, the way to ensure that baptismal water becomes thicker than ethno-national blood is to extol those who were not only baptized in water, but also—or especially—in blood. In the Gulag, Russian Orthodox and Ukrainian Catholics—not to mention people of various other nationalities and faiths—frequently enjoyed a *koinonia* of which most of us can only dream.

Similarly, but on the other side of the East-West fault line, in Nazi death camps, Eucharistic Blood could also dissolve ethnic *Blut*. A Ukrainian Greco-Catholic priest, jailed at Majdanek and eventually killed there for sheltering Jews, wrote the following to his wife and six children:

> I understand that you are trying to get me released. But I beg you not to do this. Yesterday they killed fifty people. If I am not here, who will help them to get through these sufferings? . . .
>
> I thank God for His goodness to me. Apart from heaven, this is the one place where I wish to remain. Here we are all equal: Poles, Jews, Ukrainians, Russians, Latvians, and Estonians. Of all these here, I am the only priest. I cannot even imagine how it would be here without me. Here I see God, who is the same for all of us, regardless of our religious distinctions. Perhaps our Churches are different, but the same great and Almighty God rules over us all. When I celebrate the Divine Liturgy, they all join in prayer. . . .
>
> They die in different ways, and I help them to cross over this little bridge into eternity. Is this not a blessing? Isn't this the

greatest crown that God could have placed upon my head? It is indeed. I thank God a thousand times a day for sending me here. I do not ask him for anything else. Do not worry, and do not lose faith at what I share. Instead, rejoice with me.

Pray for those who created this concentration camp and this system. They are the only ones who need prayers. May God have mercy upon them.[57]

Initially, I thought of adding a commentary. That would be an exercise in unintended banality. I will only say then that the Ukrainian Greco-Catholic Church has made this priest, Fr. Emilian Kovch, its patron of priests. But the hope symbolized by this act comes at a very high price—the price of blood. Fortunately, the ultimate Witness's Blood is given to us as *sweet* Wine—along with Bread—and these become the medicine of immortality.[58] It is this "prescription," and it alone, that constitutes the cure for all of us tempted to strive for "immortality" through ethnic blood and belonging.

---

57. Quoted in Gudziak, "'Besides Heaven.'"
58. Ignatius of Antioch, *Letter to the Ephesians* 20.

9

Baptismal and Ethnocultural Community: A Case Study of Greek Orthodoxy[1]

PANTELIS KALAITZIDIS

Christianity has appeared in history not as a new religion but as a new sort of community, that is, a Eucharistic and eschatological community. If since its beginning this community did acknowledge the Eucharist as the constitutive sacrament and the very core of the church's identity, assuming at the same time the moral, social, and even political consequences that derive from this new experience, it has always considered Baptism to be the sacrament of initiation through which one might enter the Christian community, the sacrament which offered spiritual birth or rebirth to the faithful as well as membership in the Christian community. In fact, through the sacrament of Holy Baptism, the church was not only seeking the regeneration and rebirth of humans out of water and the Spirit, but also the formation of a new humanity according not to the natural rules and the worldly spirit, but the way set out by Jesus Christ and his gospel which is bringing "good news of great joy for all the people" (Luke 2:10 NRSV).

In this paper, I will first focus on the multiple and radical consequences that stem from the spiritual birth of the faithful through their participation in the baptismal and Eucharistic community regarding the issues of belonging and identities. I will then turn to the Greek and the wider Orthodox context and consider the relationship between baptismal and ethnocultural community, as well as baptismal and ethnocultural identity. Additionally, I will explore to what extent the Byzantine "symphonia" and, later, the

1. This paper is partly based on my previous writings:"Church and Nation in Eschatological Perspective," 339–73; "La relation de l'Église à la culture," 7–25; "Orthodoxy and Hellenism," especially 368–79; and, with Nikolaos Asproulis, "Greek Religious Nationalism," 201–21.

nationalized Orthodoxy played an important role in the fusion of the two identities, and if they do coexist harmoniously or not. I have to clarify here that I examine the Greek Orthodox case as a paradigm insofar as the same or analogous phenomena can be found in the majority of Orthodox churches or traditional Orthodox countries. In the last section ("In Place of a Conclusion"), an attempt will be made to raise the crucial issues that these matters entail for Greek and wider Eastern Orthodoxy.

Baptismal Community

What characterizes the Christian community is that it is constituted not on the basis of racial, ethnic, social, or political criteria—in other words, on any biological or even cultural foundation—but on the spiritual basis initiated by Baptism and fulfilled in the Eucharist. We have to be reminded here that Baptism is not so much about deliverance from original sin, nor about individual salvation and questions related to the issue of the sacrament's validity; it is rather an act of the catholic church, embracing the whole of the ecclesial body, with social and cosmic dimensions insofar as it signifies the beginning of Christian life and the ecclesiological being, and leads to the creation of a new community, the Christian community, and a new humanity, the Christlike humanity.[2]

As the eminent Orthodox theologian of the Russian diaspora Fr. Alexander Schmemann[3] (perhaps the most important Orthodox liturgical scholar of the twentieth century) points out, through Baptism we are reborn out "of water and the Spirit," and our rebirth constitutes a great gift of the Holy Spirit toward our personal Pentecost, which lays the way open toward the church, toward the kingdom of Heaven. We are baptized in order to become active members of the body of Christ and enrich our special gifts within the church, and this membership finds its fulfillment and expression through Eucharist. Some people's miscomprehension of the connection between other sacraments and the Divine Eucharist is due to the fact that they have been influenced by another type of theological perspective. According to them, the Eucharist is nothing more than just a sacrament among the others, one that functions as a "vector of grace" and aims at the worshipper's individual sanctification. In this perspective, the connection between Eucharist and the other sacraments is lost, while Eucharist itself is no longer considered the sacrament *par excellence*, in which the church is revealed and fulfilled as the body of Christ, the Temple of the Holy Spirit, and the

---

2. See Schmemann, *For the Life of the World*, 67–68.
3. Schmemann, *Of Water and the Spirit*, 115ff.

realization of God's kingdom within this world. Their misunderstanding comes from the distorted Western legalistic medieval theology which, for many centuries, has formed contemporary theological perception of the Eucharist (even in the Orthodox context), seeing the latter as a simple issue of "transubstantiation" of bread and wine into the body and blood of Christ, excluding, therefore, any other possibility and dimension of this sacrament. We should not be surprised, then, that we do not in fact share the same understanding with the Fathers concerning the link between Eucharist and the other sacraments.

According to Schmemann's analysis,[4] within the true Orthodox tradition, we find a totally different view. The *metabole*—the changing of bread and wine into the body and blood of Christ—is viewed as the crowning point and the climax of the whole Eucharistic liturgy, whose meaning is that it constitutes the realization of the church as a new creation, redeemed as the Body of Christ, reconciled with God, and blessed by the Holy Spirit. In this perspective, the Eucharist is revealed as the self-evident and necessary fulfillment of Baptism. If Baptism integrates us within the church, then by necessity, the entrance to the church also involves entrance to the Eucharist, and consequently, participation in the Eucharist which is viewed as Baptism's fulfillment (to the extent that Eucharist is considered the sacrament *par excellence* of the church) and the church's ultimate being and essence. The best way to understand all of this, according to Schmemann's analysis (which is based on the Orthodox *ordo* of Baptism), is to follow the newly baptized as they enter the church in procession. The deeper theological meaning of this liturgical *ordo* of entrance to the church is that the newly baptized are not seeking individual salvation or piety, but to join the body of Christ and to set out with the other believers to participate in the Eucharistic celebration. In the words of Fr. Schmemann,

> Indeed their entrance is first of all the act of joining the gathered community, the *Church* in the first and most literal sense of the Greek word ἐκκλησία, which means assembly, gathering. Their first experience of the Church is not that of an abstraction or idea but that of a real and concrete unity of persons who, because each one of them is united to Christ, are united to one another, constitute one family, one body, one fellowship. The Eucharist, before it is or can be anything else, is thus *gathering* or, better to say, the Church *herself* as unity in Christ. And this gathering is *sacramental* because it reveals, makes visible and "real," the invisible unity in Christ, His presence among those

---

4. Ibid., 117–18.

who believe in Him and in Him love one another; and also because this unity is truly *new unity*, the overcoming by Christ of "this world," whose evil is precisely alienation from God and therefore disunity, fragmentation, enmity, separation.

This new unity, as the gathering that they have joined reveals to the newly baptized, is not limited to people alone. Having left the world behind the doors of the church, they find the same world, but purified, transfigured, filled again with divine beauty and meaning—the very icon of the kingdom of God. It is not a gathering of "escapees" from the world, bitterly enjoying their escape, feeding their hate of the world.[5]

Through Baptism and Chrismation we thus enter and through the Eucharist we fulfill the ecclesiological hypostasis and existence, the new life in Christ in which all previous forms of being are overcome or even left behind, and all kinds of worldly bounds (biological but also cultural/spiritual) are relativized. In the words of Fr. Georges Florovsky, probably the most preeminent Orthodox theologian of the twentieth century,

In Holy Christening the one to be enlightened leaves "this world" and forsakes its vanity, as if freeing himself and stepping out of the natural order of things; from the order of "flesh and blood" one enters an order of grace. All inherited ties and all ties of blood are severed. But man is not left solitary or alone. For according to the expression of the Apostle "by one Spirit are we all baptized," neither Scythians nor Barbarians—and this nation does not spring through a relationship of blood but through freedom into one body. The whole meaning of Holy Christening consists in the fact that it is a mysterious acceptance into the Church, into the City of God, into the Kingdom of Grace.[6]

It has been established that Eastern Orthodoxy's identity and existence, which is identified with the notions of "body" and "communion" commonly shared by the eschatological and Eucharistic community of the faithful, brings about a deep social dimension. As Florovsky characteristically remarks, following on this point the ancient patristic tradition, Eastern and Western alike, in its entirety:

Christianity from the beginning existed as a corporate reality, as a community. To be Christian meant just to belong to the community. Nobody could be Christian by himself, as an isolated individual, but only together with "the brethren," in a

5. Ibid., 118.
6. Florovsky, "On the Veneration of Saints," 201–2.

"togetherness" with them. *Unus Christianus nullus Christianus* [one Christian—no Christian]. Personal conviction or even a rule of life still do not make one a Christian. Christian existence presumes and implies an incorporation, a membership in the community. This must be qualified at once: in the *Apostolic* community.[7]

The first Christians chose to use the Greek political term *ecclesia* (a term already used in the Septuagint Old Testament text to translate the Hebrew *qahal*) in order to define their identity, their understanding of charismatic co-belonging, and the social, communal, and "corporate" character of Christian existence. This is why Christianity, according again to Florovsky,

> is fundamentally a social religion . . . Christianity is not primarily a doctrine or a discipline that individuals might adopt for their personal use and guidance. Christianity is exactly a community, i.e., the Church . . . The whole fabric of Christian existence is social and corporate. All Christian sacraments are intrinsically "social sacraments," i.e., sacraments of incorporation. Christian worship is also a corporate worship, "*publica et communis oratio*" in the phrase of St Cyprian. To build up the Church of Christ means, therefore, to build up a new society and, by implication, to rebuild human society on a new basis . . . The early Church was not just a voluntary association for "religious" purposes. It was rather the New Society, even the New Humanity, a *polis* or *politeuma*, the true City of God, in the process of construction.[8]

During the second generation after the Pentecost, which is marked by Saint Paul's decisive contribution, the church reached highly global and ecumenical levels. It was an all-inclusive church where all people—Jews and Gentiles, Greeks and barbarians, circumcised and uncircumcised, abiding or not by the law, slaves and free, men and women—were equally welcome, as Paul indefatigably repeats.[9] If, for Paul, the participation in a nation or in a linguistic-racial community characterizes and accompanies our nature and our historical course,[10] those characteristics are "relativized" and retreat in the perspective of faith and salvation.[11] Thus, participation in the church event goes beyond every natural bond (blood, race, language, social class,

7. Florovsky, "The Church," 59.
8. Florovsky, "Social Problem," 131–32.
9. See Col 3:10–11. Cf. Gal 3:26–29; 1 Cor 12:12–13.
10. See among others Rom 11:1; 2 Cor 11:22; Phil 3:5.
11. Rom 10:12–13.

etc.), making the formation of the Christian community an action overcoming nation and class. Physical definitions no longer constitute an important factor. Instead, they are replaced by the charismatic formation of the body of Christ through Baptism, leading to the fulfillment of the eschatological sacrament of unity (to which common participation testifies) bearing all evident social consequences, in the Eucharistic event.[12] The church is a spiritual genus, the new Israel, the "Israel in Spirit."

This new community of Christians was indeed affected by the fact that they belonged to this "new society," or even yet "new humanity." They perceived themselves as an entirely distinct nation—the new Israel, the new people of God, *the third race*, neither Jews nor Greeks. Aristides, the apologist, states that Christians "trace their origin from the Lord Jesus Christ,"[13] while according to Saint Basil, "all believers in Christ are one people; all Christ's people, although He is hailed from many regions, are one Church."[14] Fr. Georges Florovsky, from his perspective, points out that "there is, after Christ, but one 'nation,' the Christian nation, *genus Christianum* . . . i.e., precisely the Church, the only people of God, and no other national description can claim any further Scriptural warrant: national differences belong to the order of nature and are irrelevant in the order of grace."[15]

Consequently, common faith in Jesus Christ is what provides the solid foundation of this race of Christians, and not racial or ethnic criteria. There are no predetermined differentiating criteria that are based on birth in the flesh. Instead, what is of utmost importance is the unity being granted by the spiritual rebirth in Christ through Baptism and Eucharist, and the fidelity to the commandments of the gospel. This newly formed community's mission is to become an all-inclusive one, embracing all humanity, all nations, in complete accordance with the concluding words of the Gospel of Matthew: "Go therefore and make disciples of all nations, baptizing them in the name of the Father and of the Son and of the Holy Spirit" (Matt 28:19 NRSV). This is the same understanding we witness being expressed in the Eucharistic anaphora of the Divine Liturgy of the Apostle Mark, when the celebrant prays, "O good Lord, remember in Thy good mercy the Holy and only Catholic and Apostolic Church throughout the whole world, and all Thy people, and all the sheep of this fold."[16]

---

12. 1 Cor 10:16–17.

13. Aristides, *Apology* 15:1. Cf. Florovsky, "Antinomies of Christian History," 131, and Florovsky, "Le corps du Christ vivant," 55–57.

14. Basil, *Epistle 161*, 1, PG 32, 629 B.

15. Florovsky, "Revelation and Interpretation," 35.

16. "Divine Liturgy of the Holy Apostle and Evangelist Mark," *Ante-Nicene Fathers* 7:555. Cf. also the Divine Liturgy from the *Apostolic Constitutions*, Book 8: "Let us pray

Within the earliest Christian communities, a sense that the Eucharist constituted a gathering of those who were scattered, a union of those who had previously been separated, and a form of participation in the supper of the kingdom, was prevalent. As the *Didache* (a Christian text from the second century AD with a strong eschatological connotation) notes, characteristically, in its chapter on the Eucharist, "Even as this broken bread was scattered over the hills, and was gathered together and became into one, so gather together your holy church out of every people and every land and every city and street and house, and make one living catholic church."[17] The Sacramentary of Serapion of Thmuis (a liturgical *euchologion* of the fourth century) repeats and extends the *Didache* as follows: "And as this bread was scattered upon the mountains and having been gathered together became one, so gather together your holy church out of every people and every land and every city and street and house, and make one living Catholic Church."[18] Therefore, we can conclude that *Eucharist, catholicity, and universality* are what shape the identity of the church and outline the sense of self-consciousness that was an eminent characteristic of the early Christian communities.

Taking all of the above into consideration, the church is seen as a spiritual homeland, a spiritual genus, in which all divisions based on nature (race, language, culture, genus, gender, social class) are surpassed and the mystery of unity in Christ and the fellowship of the previously divided humanity unfold.[19] The church constitutes a new people—a new nation, a new belonging—which is not identified with any other people, race, earthly nation, or worldly belonging. This can be seen if we become aware of what are its main characteristics. These are certainly not blood ties or subjection to the natural state of affairs but the voluntary personal response to the call of God and the free participation in the Body of Christ and the life of grace.[20]

In order to understand the above analysis we have to take seriously into account the eschatological dimension, that is, the active expectation of the kingdom of God, and the way of life that derives from it. It is well

---

for the Holy Catholic and Apostolic Church which is spread from one end of the earth to the other" (*Ante-Nicene Fathers* 7:485).

17. *Didache* 9.4 (Lightfoot and Harmer, 261). Cf. also 10.5. For an eschatological interpretation of the "fraction" and the unity of the Church, cf. J. Taylor, "Fraction du pain," 284 ff.

18. Sacramentary of Serapion, in Bradshaw, *Eucharistic Origins*, 118.

19. John 11:52. Cf. John 10:16; 1 John 2:2.

20. I am glad to notice that this Orthodox understanding of baptismal community, inspired by the tradition and theology of the undivided church, meets many of the questions and concerns of Michael L. Budde's work, *The Borders of Baptism*.

known that eschatology is the fundamental constituent of primitive Christianity. It provides the solid foundation to Christians' paradoxical stance within the world which is summarized in the biblical "in the world, but not of the world"—in other words, a permanent tension between history and eschatology, the "already" and the "not yet." According to this perspective, which is of profound importance for our discussion, the believer could be considered an "alien" and an "exile" in this world (Cf. 1 Pet 2:11). He refuses to be situated within the world or rejects being identified with the here and now because, even though he lives in the world, he is not of the world: "but our citizenship is in heaven" (Phil 3:20 NRSV); "For here we have no lasting city, but we are looking for the city that is to come" (Heb 13:14 NRSV). The believer does not despise the world, although he refuses to identify his life and mission in it with the forms and powers of the present age. While his faith can be described under the perspective of cosmic/worldly dimensions, he refuses to identify it with one existing in the world. Without disdaining history, he refuses to confine his purpose within the limits of history. History provides the context in which he lives, yet he refuses to be absorbed, or even assimilated, by it. While Christianity is primarily historical, it nevertheless aspires to point toward another reality—the kingdom of God—which is metahistorical, yet has already begun to influence and illuminate the historical present, just as the eschaton is continually (although paradoxically) breaking into history.

Certainly, since the Resurrection and Pentecost, a foretaste and glimmer of the coming kingdom has been provided in the Eucharist; however, the completeness of the new life will be revealed to us in the eschaton, at the end of history, when corruption and death are definitively abolished.[21] The Christian, therefore, leads his life between these two ultimate points—the Resurrection and the eschaton—finding himself in the state of "in between," a state that leads neither to a flat rejection of the world nor to a firm acceptance of it in its present form. It is a state affecting all his choices and values: everything is assessed based on the eschaton perspective. The Christian's whole life is evaluated in the light of the anticipated new world and oriented toward it. The present time assumes both its identity and hypostasis, its meaning and its purpose, from this new world.[22]

In light of the above analysis, we can understand why Florovsky so characteristically stressed that Christians had their own polis, their own

---

21. Vassiliadis, *Lex Orandi*, 110 [in Greek]. Cf. Florovsky, "Le corps du Christ vivant," 23–24.

22. Cullmann, *Christ and Time*, xix–xxi; Agourides, "Hope of the Orthodox Christian," 101–3 [in Greek].

"order of life," "another system of allegiance."²³ One can observe that from the beginning, Christianity was perceived as a particularly conscientious community, a new kingdom, a holy nation, and a chosen people.²⁴ Once again according to Florovsky, "the church was conceived as an independent and self-supporting social order, as a new social dimension, a peculiar *systema patridos*, as Origen put it. Early Christians felt themselves, in the last resort, quite outside of the existing social order, simply because for them the church itself was an 'order,' an extraterritorial 'colony of Heaven' on earth."²⁵

A classic Christian text from the end of the second century AD, the *Epistle to Diognetus*, with strong eschatological overtones, seems to further affirm this analysis. It places an added emphasis on this notion of being a foreigner which stressed Christians' paradoxical position within the world. This, of course, hardly leaves any room for them to be preoccupied with questions of ethnic identity. We read,

> For Christians are not distinguished from the rest of humanity by country, language, or custom. For nowhere do they live in cities of their own, nor do they speak some unusual dialect, nor do they practice an eccentric life-style . . . But while they live in both Greek and barbarian cities, as each one's lot was cast, and follow the local customs in dress and food and other aspects of life, at the same time they demonstrate the remarkable and admittedly unusual character of their own citizenship. They live *in their own countries, but only as aliens*; they participate in everything as citizens, and endure everything as foreigners. *Every foreign country is their fatherland, and every fatherland is foreign.* They marry like everyone else, and have children; but they do not expose their offspring. They share their food but not their wives. They are "in the flesh," but they do not live "according to the flesh." *They live on earth, but their citizenship is in heaven.* They obey the established laws; indeed in their private lives they transcend the laws.²⁶

Christianity, then, displays what could be described as a unique eschatological anarchism—an estrangement from every form of natural bond (such as language, customs, culture, marriage, family, homeland, ethnicity, law, etc.) deriving from eschatological ideas and aspirations. That is the new

---

23. Cf. Florovsky, "Christianity and Civilization," 126.
24. Cf. Florovsky, "Social Problem," 131.
25. Ibid., 132.
26. *Epistle to Diognetus*, 5:1–3, 4–10 (Lightfoot and Harmer, 541). My emphases.

life in Christ, which has already begun and is expected to be completed at the eschaton.

Could we, therefore, realize the necessity of relativizing the concepts of nation and earthly homeland, of worldly identities and allegiances? If the church constitutes a spiritual genus as well as a spiritual homeland, can it, at the same time, revert to the "shadow of the law" and, in servitude to nature, be identified with a nation, serving the objectives and goals of the earthly, worldly homeland? Even if we consider these goals legitimate, can they serve as the core of the ecclesial *kerygma*, replacing and marginalizing the most essential and primary elements of the church—above all, the eschatological dimension? Perhaps such an eschatological dimension somehow abates and relativizes an otherwise legitimate patriotism—the interest in nations and homelands according to the flesh—precisely due to the fact that eschatology provides a solid foundation to another measure of evaluation. After all, isn't this the spirit of what St. Gregory of Nazianzus maintained with such astonishing boldness and clarity?

> My friend, every one that is of high mind has one Country, the Heavenly Jerusalem, in which we store up our Citizenship . . . And these earthly countries and families are the playthings of this our temporary life and scene. For our country is whatever each may have first occupied, either as tyrant, or in misfortune; and in this we are all alike strangers and pilgrims, however much we may play with names.[27]

Additionally, in his work *To the Holy Hieromartyr Cyprian*, Gregory of Nazianzus, in praising martyrdom, echoes the church's eschatological conscience, relativizing the earthly homeland as well as other worldly values. He even goes so far as to assure us that "there is one country for those of lofty character, the Jerusalem of the mind, not these earthly nations set apart in their little borders with their many changing inhabitants."[28] The same church father, in his *Panegyric on Caesarius*, mentions and elaborates once again on the Pauline theology of unity and its eschatological realization in Christ's Resurrection, in which he clarifies that there is no room for any form of distinction. He even goes so far as to delineate distinctions based on gender, nation, or social class as "badges of the flesh" that mar the image and likeness of God in man. Regarding our topic, Gregory observes,

---

27. Gregory of Nazianzus, *Against the Arians*, PG 36, 229, *Nicene and Post-Nicene Fathers* 7:332.

28. Gregory of Nazianzus, *Oration* 24, PG 35, 1188 AB (Vinson, 152).

> This is the purpose of the great mystery for us. This is the purpose for us of God, Who for us was made man and became poor, to raise our flesh, and recover His image, and remodel man, that we might all be made one in Christ, who was perfectly made in all of us all that He Himself is, that we might no longer be male and female, barbarian, Scythian, bond or free (which are badges of the flesh), but might bear in ourselves only the stamp of God, by Whom and for Whom we were made, and have so far received our form and model from Him, that we are recognized by it alone.[29]

This ecclesial perspective on the relationship between church and nation, ecclesial and ethnocultural identity (even if quite often it has been forgotten or distorted) cannot be described as a dead letter in the Orthodox tradition, because it has survived in the prophetic voices of each era. One such prophetic voice, a twentieth-century witness to the church's conscience, was the Serbian theologian Fr. Justin Popovich, who briefly described the aforementioned patristic tradition in his own theological language. He wrote the following, which is significant for the topic at hand:

> The Church is ecumenical, catholic, God-human, ageless, and it is therefore a blasphemy—an unpardonable blasphemy against Christ and against the Holy Ghost—to turn the Church into a national institution, to narrow her down to petty, transient, time-bound aspirations and ways of doing things. Her purpose is beyond nationality, ecumenical, all-embracing: to unite all men in Christ, all without exception to nation or race or social strata. "There is neither Jew nor Greek, there is neither slave nor free, there is neither male nor female: for you are all one in Christ Jesus" (Gal 3:28), because "Christ is all, and in all." The means and methods of this all-human, God-human union of all in Christ have been provided by the Church, through the holy sacraments and in her God-human works (ascetic exertions, virtues). And so it is: in the sacrament of the Holy Eucharist the ways of Christ and the means of uniting all people are composed and defined and integrated. Through this mystery, man is made organically one with Christ and with all the faithful.[30]

---

29. Gregory of Nazianzus, *Panegyric on His Brother*, PG 35, 785 C, *Nicene and Post-Nicene Fathers* 7:237.

30. Popovich, "Inward Mission," 23–24.

Vladimir Lossky,[31] the great Russian theologian of the diaspora and historian of Western medieval philosophy, expresses the same sensitivity in his views on the subject. Lossky writes,

> No differences of created nature—sex, race, social class, language, or culture—can affect the unity of the Church; no divisive reality can enter into the bosom of *Catholica*. Therefore it is necessary to regard the expression "national Church"—so often used in our day—as erroneous and even heretical, according to the terms of the condemnation of phyletism pronounced by the Council of Constantinople in 1872. There is no Church of the Jews or of the Greeks, of the Barbarians or of the Scythians, just as there is no Church of slaves or of free men, of men or of women. There is only the one and total Christ, the celestial Head of the new creation which is being realized here below, the Head to which the members of the one Body are intimately linked. At this point, any private consciousness which could link us with any ethnic or political, social or cultural group must disappear, in order to make way for consciousness "as a whole" (*kath' olon*), a consciousness greater than the consciousness which links us to humanity at large. In fact, our unity in Christ is not only the primordial unity of the human race, which has only one origin, but the final realization of this unity of human nature, which "is recapitulated" by the last Adam—*o esxatos Adam*. This eschatological reality is not some kind of ideal "beyond" but the very condition of the existence of the Church, without which the Church would not be a sacramental organism: her sacraments would have only a figurative sense, instead of being a real participation in the incorruptible life of the Body of Christ.[32]

The words of the Metropolitan of Diokleia Kallistos (Ware), however, should be especially noted and attract our attention. As an eminent patristic scholar at Oxford University as well as a bishop of the Ecumenical Patriarchate in Great Britain, his words are of great importance within the context of the Orthodox diaspora and especially within Western Orthodoxy. If we pay attention to them, all of us who were born Orthodox will be reminded of what is ecclesiastically and theologically self-evident for someone who consciously made the choice to be Orthodox:

---

31. It is worth noting that it was Lossky who nurtured generations of non-Orthodox and made Orthodoxy known in Europe and America with his book *The Mystical Theology of the Eastern Church*.

32. Lossky, *Image and Likeness*, 184–85.

> While respecting national identity, we should not forget that the Church is, in its essence, One and Catholic. The basic element in the structure of the Church on earth is not the nation, but the local *synaxis*, the gathering around the bishop each Sunday for the celebration of the holy Eucharist. And this Eucharistic gathering is supposed to unite all Christians in a given place, regardless of their national origin. According to the holy canons, the bishop is responsible not for an ethnic group, but for a particular region. The Church as a Eucharistic community is not organized on a national basis, but on a local basis. Therefore, the national element ought to serve the Church, not enslave it.[33]

Even the Synaxis ("Assembly") of the Primates of the Orthodox Church at the Phanar (Nativity 2000), which is considered to be the higher instance of today's Orthodoxy regardless of the prevalent alienation that has been observed in the Orthodox world, is persistent in highlighting this eschatological vision of unity which enables us to overcome every type of discrimination:

> When gathered in the Holy Eucharist, the Church realizes and reveals to the world and to history the incorporation of all in Christ, the transcendence of every discrimination and contrast, a communion of love wherein "there is neither male nor female, neither Greek nor Jew, circumcised or uncircumcised, barbarian or Scythian, slave or free" (Col 3:11 and Gal 3:28). In this way, it presents an image of the Kingdom of God, but at the same time also an image of ideal human society, and the foretaste of the victory of life over death, of incorruption over corruption, and love over hatred.[34]

Having read the above analysis, one would not be out of context to ask the following, in regard to the topic of this paper dealing with a case study of Greek Orthodoxy: to what extent is the church in Greece today concerned with the above theological analysis (as in the case of every Orthodox Church in traditionally Orthodox countries) and, finally, why is the relationship of Orthodoxy with the modern Greek identity and the Greek nation so emphatically stressed? And if things are as described regarding the relationship of the church with the nation and the ethnocultural identity, then how should one explain the fact that the so-called Orthodox are known for their intense nationalism and messianic tendencies of national exclusivity?

33. Ware, "L'unité dans la diversité," 14.
34. "Message of the Primates of the Orthodox Church," §5.

The Byzantine Model of "Symphonia," the Nationalized Orthodoxy, and the Fusion of Baptismal/Ecclesial with the Ethnocultural Identity

> Because, to put it very simply, Baptism is absent from our life. It is, to be sure, still accepted by all as a self-evident necessity. It is not opposed, not even questioned. It is performed all the time in our churches. It is, in other terms, "taken for granted." Yet, in spite of all this, I dare to affirm that in a very real sense it is absent, and this "absence" is at the root of many tragedies of the Church today.[35]

Due to the almost universal application of the infant baptism practice (from the end of the fourth until the late sixth century), and the establishment of Christianity as the state religion of the Roman/Byzantine Empire by Emperor Theodosius (380), many things were changed regarding not only the understanding and interpretation of Baptism (as well as the sacramental liturgical *praxis* and the overall Christian life), but also the church's formation itself. The prerequisite preparation period before Baptism, which sometimes lasted up to three years, had begun to become obsolete. Catechesis, which had been functioning as a form of initiation into the truths and experiences of new life in Christ, was eventually replaced by some form of mechanistic automation that makes the godfather and godmother of the infant responsible for his/her Christian awareness. However, we are all aware that this is scarcely the case, and at the same time, it is quite dubious whether the godparent herself has received any form of Christian "education," or even if she has ever participated in any kind of church or sacramental life. Furthermore, the institutionalization of infant baptism as a commonly followed practice deprived the new members of the church community of the fundamental option to make their own personal, mature, conscious, and aware decision to belong to a new community and undertake a new way of life, bearing every respective ethical and social consequence this decision might have brought along. As a result, even the church's members found it hard to distinguish the biological birth (which is natural and self-evident) from the spiritual birth or rebirth, which constitutes a seal of the Holy Spirit's gift. This gift is bestowed in and through baptism of the new member. Such a gift presupposes a form of spiritual preparation, and above all, a denial of the old world and a rejection of Satan's works. Through Baptism we enter a new order of grace, transcending the order of nature and mortal biological bonds. However, one could argue that the most important consequence of

---

35. Schmemann, *Of Water and the Spirit*, 16.

the universal application of infant baptism and of the official recognition of Christianity as the empire's religion was the gradual transformation of the church from a baptismal community (in other words, a spiritual and charismatic community that transcends every form of biological or sociocultural bound) into an ethnocultural community with predefined "rules of entrance." The most important of these rules is that, in order to enter this community, one should have been born (in flesh) within it or have the privilege of "hereditary succession," or at best, be an active participant in a common culture or a common religious and cultural legacy.

As far as the Greek case is concerned, and in addition to what has so far been mentioned, we should take into consideration the disastrous consequences deriving from the persistent denial on the part of certain conservative and fundamentalist circles of the Greek Orthodox Church's use of liturgical translations. Such translations would facilitate the congregation's active participation in the liturgy, especially in the sacraments and the Eucharist. Certainly, Baptism is not an exception. This means that, because the faithful are not fully aware of the profound theological meaning of the blessings, they usually attend a secularized ceremony—in some sense, a form of magical ceremony—in which the highest point would be the time of name-giving. In this context, it would be completely irrelevant to even mention the terms "baptismal community" or "baptismal theology," since even the sacrament of Baptism itself—the first and foremost fundamental presupposition for anyone to enter the life and actions of that new community—remains completely incomprehensible and misinterpreted. In this perspective, the whole theological meaning and nature of Baptism remains an issue limited exclusively to theologians or liturgical scholars. It is not a surprise then that the baptismal community has been replaced by what could be considered to be the closest alternative to human beings' natural order or "biological hypostasis," that is, by an ethnocultural understanding of the church event—an understanding of faith in terms of patrimony, identity, and culture—since ignorance and absence of genuine participation in the church's life leave no room for any serious discussion of people's "ecclesial hypostasis." Besides, as we have already argued elsewhere,[36] the basic reasons that led to a rejection of the liturgical texts' translation were primarily ethnocultural and not theological. It is a rejection that comes as a stark contrast to the Orthodox Church's theological awareness, tradition, and missionary practices, by actually integrating into them a foreign element, that of the Western medieval "sacred languages" doctrine.

---

36. Kalaitzidis, *Orthodoxy and Modern Greek Identity*, 96–110 [in Greek].

Fr. Alexander Schmemann's critical remarks regarding an individualistic and formalistic understanding of Baptism also apply in the case of Greek Orthodoxy. This deformed conception of Baptism still prevails among many Orthodox today, which in practice annuls any impact of baptismal theology on people's lives, or any visibility of Baptism's effects on society and the dominant worldview.

> Finally, having ceased to feed Christian piety, Baptism obviously has lost its power to shape our Christian worldview, i.e., our basic attitudes, motivations and decisions. There exists today no Christian "philosophy of life" which would embrace the totality of our existence, family as well as profession, history as well as society, ethics as well as action. There is simply no difference between the "values" and "ideals" accepted inside the Christian community and those accepted outside of it. A Christian today may be a "parishioner in good standing" while living by standards and philosophies of life having nothing to do with, if not openly opposed to, the Christian faith.
>
> A Christian of the past knew not only intellectually but with his entire being that through Baptism he was placed into a radically new relationship with all aspects of life and with the "world" itself—that he received, along with his faith, a radically new understanding of life. Baptism for him was the starting point and also the foundation of a Christian "philosophy of life," of a permanent sense of direction guiding him firmly throughout his entire existence, supplying answers to all questions, solving all problems.
>
> This foundation is still here with us. Baptism is performed. But it has ceased to be comprehended as the door leading into a new life and as the power to fight for this new life's preservation and growth in us.[37]

What lies beneath the problems raised above is, in fact, the oblivion of the eschatological consciousness and vision of the church, the loss of the dialectical tension between eschatology and history, the church and the world, and—to recall the well-known scheme of Fr. Georges Florovsky—the desert and the empire. In other words, what happened over time is a gradual slide from the realm of the ecclesiological hypostasis to the ethnocultural one, from the ecclesial to the imperial and secular belonging. All these elements are integral parts of what we may call "culturalistic slide,"[38] that is,

---

37. Schmemann, *Of Water and the Spirit*, 9–10.

38. See Kalaitzidis, "La relation de l'Eglise à la culture," especially 15–24. Cf. Papathomas, "*Culturalisme ecclésiastique*," 61–67; for the same paper, cf. *Episkepsis* 41:711 (March 31, 2010) 20–25.

the long-existing problematic (in the Orthodox context) relationship of the ethnocultural to the ecclesial, and the understanding of the faith and the ecclesial event in terms of culture, identity, and ancestral heritage; and eventually the replacement of the theological by the ethnocultural criteria, and of the history of salvation by the history of the national revival.[39]

The first step toward this slide, and therefore a permanent confusion between religious and secular/ethnocultural belongings, can be traced back to the secularized political eschatology of Byzantium and its claim for the incarnation of the kingdom of God on earth. Another integral part of this process is the politico-religious model of "symphonia"—the Byzantine political ideal referring to mutual cooperation between church and state for the sake of the people, who are simultaneously members of the church and subjects of the empire—which was partly adopted later by the Balkan national states. However, the culmination of this long process of the recession of the ecclesial identity (obtained through Baptism and Eucharist) and the ascendance of the ethnocultural one (granted by natural birth and participation in an ethnic community) has to be related to the nineteenth-century emergence of the principle of nationalities, and the consequent phenomenon of "national Orthodoxy," that is, the identification of Orthodoxy with every single "Orthodox" nation or state, and the understanding of the church in national terms. Despite the fact that an abysmal gap separates Byzantine "symphonia" and the secularized political eschatology of Byzantium from nationalized Orthodoxy—insofar as the former was operating in the framework of a supranational, multiethnic empire and the latter was associated with the splintering of Byzantine and Ottoman *ecumene*, and the emergence of the Balkan national states—there are, nonetheless, common features uniting these two distinctive models.

We are now aware, after the work of many respected historians and theologians (Francis Dvornick, Steven Runciman, Gerhard Podskalsky, Hans-Georg Beck, Hélène Ahrweiler, Georges Florovsky, Savas Agourides), that the Byzantines saw their state and societal structures as the realization of the kingdom of God on earth. Runciman states this quite explicitly at the outset of his classic study, *The Byzantine Theocracy*, which he describes as an effort to give an "account of an Empire whose constitution . . . was based on a clear religious conviction: that it was the earthly copy of the Kingdom of Heaven."[40] In this not only political but also theological ideal, the emperor stood "in the place of Christ," and his kingdom was a reflection

---

39. For an extensive analysis of the last idea, see Kalaitzidis, "Temptation of Judas," especially 368–73.

40. Runciman, *Byzantine Theocracy*, 1.

of its heavenly counterpart. As Greek professor Savas Agourides notes, "The Byzantine state, particularly from the Justinian era forward, following as it does along the lines of Jewish apocalyptic literature... sees itself as the final actualization of Christian hope, as the eschatological prelude to the kingdom of God."[41] According to this viewpoint, we are clearly facing a deeply particular form of "realized eschatology" (one that can be described as political or secular) which seems oblivious of the tension between the "already" and the "not yet"—that is, between the first and the second coming of Christ, his resurrection and the expectation of our own resurrection along with the recapitulation of history, which will signal our personal incorruptibility and the end of death's dominion. Christians are "aliens and exiles" (1 Pet 2:11), continuously moving toward the eschaton, in accordance with the biblical injunction to be "in the world, but not of the world." Our loss, as Orthodox Christians, could be once again described as a disorientation from our focus toward the anticipated new world, from which the present takes its identity and hypostasis, its meaning and its purpose.

Therefore, realized eschatology and identification of the true and genuine faith with Byzantium, tsarist Russia, or with one of the Balkan monarchies exists in reality as a constant temptation, one that historical Orthodoxy faces to the extent that it annuls the paradoxical dialectics between history and eschatology as well as the eschatological expectation of the kingdom of God and the openness of history itself.

This capitulation—or conciliation, in the best of cases—of the church to the empire, and the identification of the faith community with the wider society, had many other serious effects for the topic under discussion: the emphasis on faith as that which is passed down from generation to generation and embraces entire peoples and nations; the addiction to spiritual self-sufficiency and the *ex officio* way of thinking under the influence of stereotypes of race and nation; the praise of our ancestors and the homeland, and, as a result of the above shift, the neglect, even the abolition of the element of innovation and personal choice that Christianity brought at its beginning. Meanwhile, the scornful way in which great theologians and Fathers of the church, such as St. Gregory of Nyssa,[42] spoke of praising the achievements and virtues of one's ancestors has been forgotten. We neglect the fact that the main criticism the opponents of Christianity expressed in the first centuries (Celsus, Porphyry) was that Christianity was abolishing the ancestral traditions.[43]

41. Agourides, "Religious Eschatology and State Ideology," 53.

42. See, for example, Gregory of Nyssa, *Ejusdem De vita Beati Gregorii*, PG 46, 896 C.

43. See the observations made by Papathanasiou, "Postmodern Revival of Polytheism," especially 6 [in Greek].

We Orthodox remain so spellbound and trapped in the premodern, medieval, or romantic communitarian model that we seem to have forgotten that acceptance of the gospel message and inclusion in the body of the church cannot be understood on the basis of collectives—such as that of a people, a nation, a language, a culture, etc.—but on the basis of a completely personal act, free of every kind of biological, cultural, or ethnic predetermination. That is why the personal call made by God through Jesus Christ for the evangelization, encounter, and relationship with him (as well as the answer to this call, which is also personal) is the new constituent introduced by the ecclesial way of life. Many of the gospel stories are not only purely personal events and choices—not mediated by any kind of group or community, or any religious, national, linguistic, cultural, or class collectivities; in fact, they are quite often directed *against* particular communities/collectivities, or violate any borders and limits that might have been set by these communities. However, these choices do not lead to a private religiosity or an individual version of faith and salvation.[44]

Additionally, we Orthodox (primarily of the traditionally "Orthodox" countries) have become increasingly identified with our national churches and local traditions. Orthodoxy has been combined, in our mentality, with our individual national narratives (the "Great Idea," nationalism, etc.) to an extensive degree, and we have interwoven faith with customs. All these have led to our losing the fundamental awareness of catholicity and universality, thus reducing Orthodoxy to the realm of custom, ancestral heritage, and ethnic-cultural identity.

Remaining self-content, we Orthodox refer to—or perhaps even boast about—Byzantism, Hellenicity, and Greek uniqueness, Holy Russia, the third Rome and the Slavophile movement, the Serbian people as the servant people of God, the Latin features of Romanian Orthodoxy, the particularity of Antiochian Christianity and Arabness, etc. This comes as a stark contrast to a well-established trend in other Christian—or, more broadly, religious—traditions in which there is an urge toward inculturation. Yet, in the case of the Orthodox peoples, with their well-known, firmly established bonds (even to the point of identification in some cases) between church and nation, as well as between church and local traditions, what seems to be of outmost importance, as well as need, is a disengagement from these particular cultures and local traditions (deculturation), a reordering of priorities vis-à-vis the theological and cultural criteria, ecclesial/baptismal and

---

44. For a more extensive analysis, see Kalaitzidis, *Orthodox Christianity and Modernity*, 64–67 (in Greek; English translation by Elizabeth Theokritoff, St. Vladimir's Seminary Press).

ethnocultural community—a new form of balance between the local and the universal, the particular and the catholic.

It is clear that the vast majority of us Orthodox have replaced the ecclesial sense of belonging with an ethnocultural or societal one. We have identified the communitarian structures and authoritarian models of a patriarchal society with what is considered the golden age of the church and "Christian" civilization. Mainly, that is why we continue being, among other things, so negative toward modernity, human rights, or any attempt to raise women's place inside the church. In this regard, Enlightenment, modernity, and secularization, which marked the end of religiously organized societies (but not necessarily the end of the quest for the true God or the thirst for genuinely spiritual life), could be beneficial for the Orthodox Church, to the extent that they may help it adapt to the new situation, address the issues of today's pluralistic postmodern societies, and free itself from the burdens of the so-called traditional "Christian" societies. Under some conditions, they could even help Orthodox Christians rediscover the dialectical tension between the church and the world, eschatology and history, the baptismal/Eucharistic community and the ethnocultural community. Quoting His Eminence, Metropolitan John D. Zizioulas of Pergamon,

> The Orthodox Church, however, particularly after the fall of Byzantium, was in danger of confusing the Church with the world. During this time, the bishops of the Orthodox Church undertook purely secular—and even sometimes political—roles, such as ethnarch and leader of the struggle for peoples' (national) liberation. The result is that today in countries such as Greece, the bishop is viewed as an official person, to such a degree even that as soon as the government does something which slights the clergy or takes away some of their secular authority, one can see an immediate reaction which betrays deep theological confusion. This example shows how important it is for Orthodoxy today to develop its own theological criteria, so that it can determine what is related to the structure of the Church as an eschatological community and what is related to the Church as a community that belongs to the world.[45]

However, returning to the topic of baptismal and ethnocultural communities in the wider context of the relationship between Orthodoxy and Hellenism in contemporary Greece, an important question being raised that urgently seeks an answer could be summarized as follows: How and why did a church and a people with a universalistic tradition and mission reach

---

45. Zizioulas, "Déplacement de la perspective eschatologique," 99.

such a point? Which are the historical or wider cultural factors that led to the permanent confusion between baptismal and ethnocultural community, between ecclesial and ethnocultural identity? To all these questions I will try to offer some answers in the rest of my paper.

The Complex and Controversial Historical Relationship between Orthodoxy and Hellenism, Church and Nation

For centuries, Hellenism—and Greek-speaking Orthodoxy along with it—has been experiencing several changes in its history that can be described as both extreme and excruciating. The most significant of these is that Hellenism has now been marginalized in regard to history, diminished to the simple provincial power that is modern Greece after having constituted, for centuries, the focal point of history, political and economic power, literature, art, and culture—after the conquest of Constantinople by the Franks in 1204, the Frankish rule that followed, the fall of Byzantium to the Ottoman Turks in 1453, and finally the Asia Minor Catastrophe and the compulsory population exchange with Turkey in 1922–23. Hellenism ceased to be the center of the world, and Greece, following its liberation from the Turks, has deteriorated into a small, unstable Balkan country on the edge of Europe, which has existed and survived only with the help and assistance of the Great Powers of each era. This picture has changed during recent years after Greece's accession to the European Union's institutions and the Eurozone. However, the successive oversights and disastrous mistakes of the Greek governments have plunged the country into an unprecedented financial crisis and have caused the Greeks, once again, to live under the burden of feeling humiliated. Greek people, in responding to such feelings, resort to their common practice: touting the accomplishments and virtues of their glorious ancestors—primarily the ancient Greeks, but also, for those who are closest to the church, the Byzantines. This last point, however, is a stance that has characterized Hellenism for many decades now, if not centuries: Greeks exist and function in the world, based primarily on the accomplishments of the past rather than on anything they can display as an achievement or a reality of the present. They feel that this invocation of the past compensates for the lack of a constructive present. This attitude is directly connected with the founding myth of modern Hellenism, which pervades their collective imagination, foreign policy, education, as well as their overall understanding of history.

The Greeks, and the Orthodox in general, were inseparably identified with Byzantium, a sense that led them to feel that the fall of the empire in

1453 inflicted an incurable wound upon them. From that date onward, the Greeks have felt as if they have somehow been orphaned and handicapped, with a sense that they have been deprived of something that history ought to give back; they are thus waiting for this restoration and their vindication within history. The greatest challenge for Hellenism around the world—for all of Orthodoxy as well—is to surmount this historical trauma, to right itself and clarify what its mission should be in today's world without bearing the usual reference to ancient Greece or Byzantium. Yet Orthodoxy, both Greek-speaking and non-Greek-speaking (although to different extents), derives its legitimacy as well as all of its points of reference (i.e., the source of its liturgical tradition, the rhetorical forms of its *kerygma*, and the theology of the Fathers and the Councils) from Byzantium. Many Greek clergymen and theologians, as well as Greeks who do not have any particular relationship with the church, regard all of these as part of an unbroken continuum. The establishment of this continuum is considered to have begun with Jesus's meeting with the Greeks and the so-called election of the Greeks as the new chosen people of God (see John 12:20–23)—bearing all kinds of attendant racial criteria and historical anachronisms. Trying to rationalize this continuum, they begin by stating that the books of the New Testament were written originally in Greek; move on to the use of Greek philosophical categories in patristic theology and the decisions of the Ecumenical Councils, as well as the "Greek" character of Orthodox worship; and conclude with Hellenism's unique role in the Divine Economy (due to all of the above). They also point toward some special honor and primacy entailed in that role, as well as the prominent role that modern Hellenism rightfully holds within Orthodoxy due to both its historical accomplishments and the innumerable martyrs it has offered in more recent times during its fight "for God and country." These battles are above all connected with Greek Orthodoxy's period of rule by ethnarchs under the Ottomans and then its rule by the nation. A brief retrospect of the historical events can help us better understand this paradoxical situation.

The gradual slide of the Orthodox Church, from being the church of the multiethnic Byzantine Empire to becoming the ark of Hellenism and an elemental component of modern Greek identity, occurred in moments of exceptional historical urgency and need (viz., the Turkish occupation), when it laid aside its main mission and began concentrating on saving the Greek nation from destruction—saving its language, existence, and political representation. During that phase, the church (mainly the Ecumenical Patriarchate of Constantinople), being the only Christian institution that had survived the Ottoman conquest, undertook the responsibility to fill the political void, representing all the Orthodox people before the Muslim sultan, trying to save the language and the tradition of the Orthodox people while at the same time rescuing them from the Islamization forced upon them. It was perhaps the first time that the church, so clearly and distinctively, was forced to become involved in matters that did not fall under its sphere of jurisdiction, such as the salvation of the race, the language, and the national identity. It did so because its people, its flock, and its very existence were in danger of becoming extinct.

However, the church is paying an unbearable price for forgetting its eschatological dimension and perspective and its supranational mission, which is actually creating distortions in its ecclesiological structure and its Eucharistic formation—confusing at the same time the national element with the religious one and becoming "the power and the authority of this era," getting involved in procedures of ethnogenesis and national competitions. This heavy price is also closely connected with the alteration of its ecclesial identity, its full nationalization, the abandonment of its universality for the sake of some ethnic identity and particularism of Modern Hellenism, the adoption of a secularized eschatology that directly refers to the resurrection of the nation instead of the Cross and the Resurrection of Jesus Christ. Finally, due to all of the aforementioned changes both in its orientation and priorities, the church also pays for its relationship to the nation by being clenched into a defensive stance, steadily tied to the past—a social, cultural, and ideological anachronism, a conservatism that is constantly facing the temptation to turn back time and is entrenched in fundamentalism and anti-Westernism. To put it simply, the church displays an inability to participate in the modern world. By "provisionally" undertaking this role, the church in Greece eventually abandoned its primary spiritual, theological, and ecumenical mission, evolving into a form of aberration that is difficult to give up, even today, despite the establishment of the modern Greek state (1830, 1832), its territorial completion (1947), and its full entrance into European Community institutions (1981) and the core of the financial and numismatic union and the Eurozone (2000).

Now that the state has been firmly established and historical circumstances are completely different than they were at the end of the Byzantine Empire and the first centuries of the Ottoman occupation, many Greek theologians maintain that the time has come for them, on behalf of and for the church and theology, to call into question the identification of the church with the nation, of Orthodoxy with the modern Greek identity.[46]

46. As an example of the new attitude of the younger generation of Greek theologians toward the relationship of church and nation, cf. the special issue (79, 2001) of the leading theological journal *Synaxi*, with the characteristic title "Church and Nation: Ties and Shackles."

The most serious and urgent issue still unresolved—which is preserved by the aberration that does not want to end—is what I have otherwise characterized as the replacement of the history of salvation by the history of the national revival.[47] This replacement has crystallized a latent tendency within the Greek population, which identified the ecclesiastical with the national. The church assumed this range of political and secular responsibilities after the fall of Byzantium. It displayed such an absolute involvement and identification with national issues and patriotic ideals (while at the same time lacking eschatological self-consciousness and pure, authentic Orthodox theological criteria) that it finally became identified with the nation, and the ecclesial was considered as identical to the national identity and national life.

In the conventional ecclesiastical rhetoric, however, the events of the history of divine economy not only form a vision of unity beyond ethnicity and of transcending the consequences of sin, but are also symbolically connected and emotionally loaded with events from Greek national history. Thus, one can observe a significant shift, a slide in meaning, from the history of salvation or the history of the divine economy to the history of national revival. Therefore, we see that there is no feast of the church that is not somehow connected with patriotic symbolism or to some great national event: the Annunciation of the Mother of God with the feast of the 1821 Greek revolution (March 25),[48] and the Resurrection of Christ with the resurrection of the Greek nation after four hundred years of slavery; the Dormition of the Mother of God with the celebration of the armed forces; the Exaltation of the Holy Cross with the anniversary of the Asia Minor Catastrophe in 1922; the feast of the Holy Protection (*Aghia Skepi*) with the anniversary of the resistance against the Italians and the Nazis on October 28, 1940; the feast of the Archangels Michael and Gabriel with the celebration of the air force; St. Barbara with the artillery, St. Artemios with the police force, and so on. I stop here because the list seems endless.[49]

In the context of this particular religious nationalism, worshipping Christ and overcoming all forms of division and fragmentation are replaced by national adoration and a sort of sanctified national egoism. The eschatological suspense of the final victory over evil and the inclusive unity in Christ is overshadowed by the worship of "our heroic and glorified ancestors" and the sanctification of a patriotic folklore. Christians' consciousness

---

47. See Kalaitzidis, "The Temptation of Judas."

48. The anniversary of the Greek national revolution of 1821 against the enslavement to the Ottoman Turks.

49. Cf. Kalaitzidis, "Temptation of Judas," 370.

as being the new nation and the church's consciousness as the new spiritual homeland have been forgotten and racked by the exaltation of nationalisms, eliminating the differences between national and Christian identity, church and nation, Orthodoxy and Hellenism, spiritual life and patriotism, between personal/spiritual decisions (which are expressed in our personal commitment to the church) and inherited succession (which is expressed by the phrase "we are Orthodox, because we are Greeks").

Today, 190 years after the Greek Revolution of 1821, the church in Greece seems unable to be delivered from its identification with the nation; it seems unable to separate its work, teaching, preaching, and mission in general from the course of the nation; and it seems unable to realize that the boundaries of baptism, the boundaries of church, are no longer identified with national boundaries. And whenever the Greek state heads toward a policy that will adapt to the new international reality and moves in a direction that could lead to its formal separation from the church, the latter protests by pointing to the past as well as to the significant contribution it has made to the "struggles of the nation." In this way, it manages to sustain its codependence and absolute relationship to it. And while the Greek state—as a result of the broader realignment of globalization and multiculturalism—gradually *de*-nationalizes, the church *re*-nationalizes even more, displaying an inclination to feeling unsafe and uncertain if deprived of its special relationship with the state and its absolute relationship with the nation.

Thus, religious nationalism and phyletism seem to be the most prominent problems that the Orthodox Church—and especially Orthodox ecclesiology—has faced since the fall of Byzantium (1453), a decisive historical event that initiated an introverted period. More importantly, at the time and in the context of a multinational pluralistic postmodern society, Orthodoxy seems to reduce the theological and spiritual resources of the patristic and Eucharistic tradition to an "identities" rhetoric and an outdated religious tribalism which stands in stark contrast to the gospel's call for supraracial, even supranational, identities and communities. Many Eastern countries' insistence on seeing Orthodoxy as part of their national identity and culture, which has been and still is related to their customs and traditional folklore, undermines any other serious attempt to successfully confront the challenges that the contemporary world poses to Orthodoxy. Thus, Orthodoxy is confined in traditionalism, fundamentalism, social anachronism, or even reactionism. It is trapped in premodernity statuses after having adopted the authoritarian structures of patriarchal society.

In Place of a Conclusion

In light of what was presented and analyzed above, one could claim that this whole ideology constructed around "Greek Orthodoxy"—as well as its corresponding narratives and mythologies of Holy Russia, "Third Rome," the Slavophile movement, the medieval Christian kingdom of Serbia, the idea of the Serbian people as the servant people of God, the Latin character of Romanian Orthodoxy, the Antiochian uniqueness and Arabhood, the Latin character of Romanian Orthodoxy, etc.—is nothing but a means of intensifying the historical and cultural conditioning of Orthodoxy, its collective cultural narcissism and intellectual self-sufficiency. At the same time, they function as a means of promoting a metaphysical essentialist view of an ethnocultural identity that is not receptive to change over time and within history, and that has come to be equated with the identity of the church. I think that what lies beneath all of the problems and difficulties that Orthodoxy is currently facing is the inversion of the paradoxical and antinomic relationship between eschatology and history, or the obliviousness of the biblical "in the world, but not of the world, for the sake of the world." Orthodoxy has been commonly described as being defined by the eschatological vision of the church. Nevertheless, a more attentive approach to the issue will reveal that, without being completely stripped of its eschatological nature, Orthodoxy is to a large extent shaped by history. To be more precise, what has come to shape today's Orthodoxy are the historical experiences and wounds of its peoples, as they can be traced especially in its social conservatism or even anachronism as well as in the phenomena of ecclesiastical culturalism and religious nationalism.

The time has come for Orthodoxy to close the "parenthesis" opened in 1453 with the fall of Byzantium and return to its main and fundamental mission, which is the evangelization and transfiguration of the world, the preaching of the coming kingdom of God for the salvation and restoration of the whole creation. A renewed and fresh theological reflection should be aware that the church constitutes a route to the eschaton and not a return to the glorious and painful story of Byzantium, the "Christian Empire," or the heroic period of the Turkish occupation. If the church wants to address the modern world and its people in order to preach the gospel of the kingdom—and not what can be described as the bygone world of yesterday—it is urgent that it move beyond its ethnocentric discourse, to abandon any dream of a return to Byzantine theocracy, or any other antimodern romantic version of "Christian society." Theocracy and neo-nationalism, which are presumably nothing but secularized forms of eschatology, constitute the permanent historical temptation of Orthodoxy, and they cannot, for any reason, continue to form the Orthodox Church's political and social vision. In response to the modern person's thirst for life, the Orthodox Church can and ought to offer its own proposal, using its "words of eternal life" (cf. John 6:68), and not a continuous appeal to the past and its own achievements in the struggles and conflicts of the nation. For that reason, the adoption of an ecumenical ecclesiastical discourse, which will have freed itself from continuous references to the nation and to the schemes of the Constantinian era, is not just a demand for genuineness, authenticity, and faithfulness to the Orthodox Tradition. It is also an absolutely fundamental and imperative prerequisite, an inviolate condition that will help the church adjust to the century in which we live and avoid finding a convenient and safe shelter in the past. To this end, I consider that reflecting on the difference between baptismal and ethnocultural community, as well as baptismal and ethnocultural identity, is an absolutely necessary first step toward a theological hermeneutic and an eschatological fulfillment of history.

10

African Cases and Theological Reflections

AGBONKHIANMEGHE E. OROBATOR, SJ

Introduction: Heirs to Multiple Identities

The premise of this essay is simple: in Africa, the religious person by necessity operates between multiple religious polarities that shape his or her identity. In other words, religious identity is not a matter of simple affiliation or adherence, practice of beliefs, or profession of faith. Rather, it involves a complex combination of factors, intersection of processes, and overlapping points of reference. Thus, for example, to be Catholic is to define one's self always in relation to a multiplicity of faith traditions and denominations. The bonds of allegiance to a single pole can be stronger or weaker depending on one's immediate circumstances and interests. Specifically, this means that Catholic identity is incarnated at multiple levels or loci of religious practice. The space and experience of one's identity are almost always heterogeneous or loosely circumscribed. Devotees of various different faiths or traditions navigate and traverse these borders at will. Catholic enclaves are rare; rarer still are Catholic ghettos. This situation produces an economy of identities that allows for flexibility and fluidity in delineating the borders of religious belief, practice, and allegiance. To understand how religious identity is formed and how it functions in Africa, it is important to pay attention to the dynamics of this economy of identities.

This essay analyzes the question of incarnated religious identities at three levels. The first level explores the wider context of religious growth, affiliation, and allegiances that has produced a variety of religious identities in Africa, while the second examines instances where the mix of religious identities produces pathological consequences. The third level, which concludes this essay, advances the argument that an inclusive understanding of baptism—that is, as a Eucharistic experience—offers an effective means for overcoming the challenges and clashes of religious identities in Africa and elsewhere.

Economy of Identities

Overload of Identities

The first noticeable consequence of the overlay of religious identities manifests as an overload of religious identities. The religious African is a bearer of multiple religious heritages. In addition to indigenous tradition, Christianity and Islam form part of African religious traditions. Many people are accustomed to thinking of Christianity as a foreign import. In reality, some of the oldest traditions of Christianity are found in Africa, dating back to the fourth century of the Common Era. Notable examples include Coptic Christianity in Egypt and Orthodox Christianity in Ethiopia. Islam came later (seventh century), but it too has become an indispensable fabric of Africa's religious tradition. Each tradition has a significant demographic representation and presence on the continent. Unsurprisingly, "Christianity and Islam are now the two largest religions in Africa."[1] There is yet a second consequence, namely, competition.

In light of the preceding point about the overload of multiple religious identities, the space within which a person defines his or her particular identity is marked by intense competition among a variety of religious faiths and traditions. The list would include Islam, Protestantism, Pentecostalism, African Instituted Churches, and African Religion. In this context, to form identity is to negotiate a series of border points across a vast religious landscape. The following are obvious examples of contentious religious border crossings or the lack thereof in Africa.

Christianity v. African Religion

A first set of tensions pits Christianity against African Religion. Numerically speaking, Christianity has thrived at the expense of African Religion. The significant growth of Christianity on the continent has no parallel in African Religion. However, to think in such linear terms is to ignore the

---

1. Pew Forum, *Tolerance and Tension*.

nature of African Religion. Religious practices and traditions in Africa are steeped in orality, embedded in cultural codes, and devoid of obsessive preoccupation with doctrinal rectitude, orthodoxy of belief, and proselytism. In reality, what we call religion "is a late-comer to the scholarly discourse about Africa, and is still noticeably absent in most popular descriptions of African cultures."[2] Religion resembles or forms a cultural substratum on which—as I have mentioned earlier—a multiplicity of identities have been superimposed. Thus, in Africa, Christianity or Islam cannot simply be understood as something planted on the virgin forest of religious primitiveness. African religious consciousness is anything but a tabula rasa. Like a dormant volcano, this religious substratum erupts repeatedly into the consciousness and beliefs of the imported religions. Thus, the lava of African Religion runs deep in shaping the constantly rising profiles and identities of Christians and Muslims alike.

The ascendency of Christianity and Islam in sub-Saharan Africa over the last one hundred years may have weakened the practice of African Religion, but, it should be said, it has not eradicated completely the influence of indigenous African religious beliefs, practices, and rituals.[3] These beliefs, practices, and rituals form the context wherein Christianity and Islam attempt to construct new and complex identities in Africa.

Christianity v. Islam

A second kind of tension exists between Christianity and Islam. In the public sphere, there is deep tension and intense antagonism between Christianity and Islam. Evidence and instances of mutual suspicion and ignorance of each other's traditions abound, resulting in violent confrontations, especially in places where Moslems constitute or claim to constitute the majority. This tension is not primarily defined by the struggle for the soul of the African. Nor is it even about theological polemics on the nature of religion or opposing doctrines of God. On the contrary, it seems quite prosaic: it is about religion as a means of gaining and retaining political power and legal ascendancy, accessing and controlling natural resources, and acquiring economic gains. Examples of this tension include historical and ongoing crises in Nigeria, Côte d'Ivoire, Tanzania, Kenya, Central African Republic, and Mali, where fringe but lethal groups seek to impose religious restrictions on political practice and police social behavior via strict Islamic penal code or Sharia. To quote Emeritus Pope Benedict XVI, we are witnessing in Africa

2. Ray, *African Religions*, xi.
3. See Pew Forum, *Tolerance and Tension*, 33–35.

the rise and intensification of "religious fundamentalism, combined with political and economic interests," and linked to an international network of extremist and militant organizations: "Groups who follow various religious creeds are spreading throughout the continent of Africa: they do so in God's name, but following a logic that is opposed to divine logic, that is, teaching and practicing not love and respect for freedom, but intolerance and violence."[4]

Christianity v. Christianity

Sub-Saharan Africa is awash with myriad traditions and denominations of Christianity, among which is Catholicism.

> The majority of Christians in sub-Saharan Africa are Protestant (57 percent), as broadly defined in this report; this includes members of African Independent Churches and Anglicans. About one in three Christians in the region (34 percent) are Catholic. Orthodox Christians account for about 8 percent of the region's Christians, and other Christians make up the remaining 1 percent.[5]

There is an intra-Christian tension that pits various denominations of Christianity and Christian traditions against one another. In this context, the overarching dynamic is intense competition for souls. The place where this tension is most visible is the media, especially television and the Internet, which offer Christian churches not only a platform to ply their trade but also subtly to discredit their competitors—that is, other Christian churches—in order to recruit followers. In this hodgepodge of denominationalism, Catholicism has stood out for its commitment to social evangelism, that is, a focus on service institutions such as health, education, development, and social justice based on Catholic social tradition.

If African Catholicism, as elsewhere, favors the path of social justice and prophetic denunciation of structural ills, African Pentecostals and Evangelicals prefer the route of "the prosperity gospel" and emphasize "that prayer and effort can translate into material gain."[6] The priority of the prosperity gospel is not simply to establish the preeminence of God over Mammon; rather, it is a recognition of the theological import of material resources and how they are to be valued, acquired, and protected for the per-

---

4. Benedict XVI, "Homily at Opening of Second Special Assembly for Africa."
5. Pew Forum, *Global Christianity*.
6. Allen, *Future Church*, 438; Gifford, *African Christianity*, 39–40.

sonal benefit of professing Christians.[7] Such is the appeal of this "prosperity gospel" that a constant preoccupation of African Catholicism and Orthodox Christianity is the fear of losing ground and members to well-heeled and technologically sophisticated Pentecostal and Evangelical groups, who have perfected the trade of marketing the gospel for the consumption of juvenile and upwardly mobile populations in Africa.

Received Identities

To quote a veteran American missionary of several years in Africa,

> The [African] Catholic Church does remind one of the pre-Vatican II Church—sometimes I call it the Irish Church transplanted to parts of Africa. It is a young, growing, searching church and the faith needs to be tested and deepened. It is a heavily sacramental church, sacraments and sacramentals. And it is a positive, enthusiastic, warm, welcoming church. Its problems are problems often due to growth and youthfulness—not to lack of energy or good will. If that is a remnant of the past, I am happy to live with it. Progress may be slow, and not always in the straight direction. But as the proverb reminds us "you gather a bundle of firewood stick by stick."[8]

An important theme that runs through the foregoing analysis is the idea that the African Christian is a bearer of an identity not his or her own. Roman Catholicism in Africa is no different; it is the fruit of diverse missionary expeditions of varying degrees of success and failure by the Portuguese, French, Italians, Belgians, Dutch, and Irish. Not a few religious congregations owe their foundation and *raison d'etre* to the missionary rush of the eighteenth through the twentieth centuries. The more famous ones are the Sisters of St. Joseph of Cluny, Society of St. Patrick, Millhill Congregation, the Congregation of the Holy Ghost, Missionary Sisters of Our Lady of Africa, Our Lady of Apostles, Medical Missionaries of Mary, and the Society of African Missions, not forgetting the ill-fated missions of the Society of Jesus (Jesuits) in Ethiopia in quest of the mythical Christian king, Prester John.

Catholic missionary expeditions were largely successful thanks to an army of religious congregations that established schools, clinics, dispensaries, and hospitals, and to a heavy investment in primary evangelization conducted by pioneering missionaries and a cohort of dedicated catechists.

---

7. Katongole, *Sacrifice of Africa*, 50.
8. Schineller, "African Christianity in the Twenty-First Century."

Millions of Africans were baptized with amazing rapidity to swell the ranks of the Catholic Church. To be a baptized Catholic was to receive an identity that connected the initiate to a worldwide network of Catholicism.

The Borders of Baptism: "Blood Is Thicker than Water..."

Pathologies of Identities

Speaking at the first African Synod in 1994, the late Bishop Obiefuna of the Awka Diocese in Nigeria made the following intervention:

> The Church is indeed a family. Its boundaries extend beyond the clan and the tribe. The typical African even if he or she be a Catholic does not consider that. Indeed the African Christian with his exaggerated ethnicism finds it difficult to accept the truth that the man or woman in India who is a Christian is much more a brother or sister than the non-Christian brother or sister in the natural family (Gal 5:10). This mentality is so pervading that the saying goes among the Africans that when it comes to the crunch, it is not the Christian concept of the Church as a family which prevails but rather the adage that "blood is thicker than water." And by water here one can presumably include the waters of baptism through which one is born into the family of the Church. Blood relationship is more important even for the African who has become a Christian.[9]

This frank admission by the bishop shows that *natural* ties developed through family, clan, and ethnic affiliations flow deeper and stronger than the waters of baptism. In other words, the prioritization of blood ties subordinates Christianity to pathologies of tribal loyalties and clan-based identities. These relationships take precedence over Christian values and obligations.

At issue here is the tension between kin-centered identity and faith-based identity—the former epitomized in ethnicity and tribalism, the latter in baptism. The question, then, is "whether and to what extent Christian faith is supposed to bypass, negate, or affirm the claims any culture has on the loyalty of its people."[10] Baptism may confer a new identity and secure membership in a family of God, the church, but the operative family is founded on clan and tribal affiliation and obligation. In this context, identity and belonging surface more intensely and affectively in and through the family

---

9. Obiefuna, Intervention delivered at First Special Assembly for Africa.
10. Hillman, *Toward an African Christianity*, 29.

and clan. The loyalty or identity created by the sacramental conferment of baptism hardly matches this clan identity in strength and intensity. Hence it is through loyalty to this primary affiliation that the relative strength or weakness of each level or kind of identity is to be measured and assessed in regard to multiple and overlapping identities, including religious identity.

On the evidence of the state of contemporary African Catholicism, it may be wishful thinking to assert that "their Christian identity must be primary—before state, before markets, before tribe, even before (biological) family."[11] Michael Budde puts it simply: "'Being a Christian' is one's primary and formative loyalty."[12] Sadly, examples drawn from real-life situations consistently invalidate this claim. During the Rwandan genocide in 1994, the waters of baptism did not protect the victims of this catastrophe that served as a tragic illustration of how the waters of baptism are easily polluted by the blood of tribalism and how Christianity fails to make a visible and lasting difference in Africa.[13] I would argue that a further process is needed to strengthen the bond of baptism in the context of intensely significant natural ties. In this regard, an excursus relating the identity debate to nationalism in Africa would be useful.

Nationalism and Catholicism

In the context where blood ties and family obligations override baptismal alliance, it is hard to imagine a specifically Catholic construction or imagination of nationalism in Africa. Unlike in the West, nationalism strictly construed "may have minimal importance in Africa."[14] There are countries that count large Catholic majorities, like Rwanda, Burundi, and the Democractic Republic of the Congo (DRC). Yet the demographic preponderance

---

11. Carney, "Waters of Baptism," 22. In this regard, some nuancing is needed of Michael Budde's claim regarding the "irrelevance of Christianity as a category having any purchase on human loyalties or obligations" ("Pledging Allegiance," 214).

12. Budde, *Borders of Baptism*, 3.

13. Carney, "Waters of Baptism," 9–30; see Katongole, *Sacrifice of Africa*, 47–50, 74–78. I believe that Carney pushes the argument too far when he insists that "to some extent the Church that baptized and educated those who committed atrocities against fellow humanity, bears at least a measure of responsibility for their actions" (18). How is this responsibility to be measured? In the likely event of a positive outcome, does the church also take credit? We should refrain from a precipitated and sweeping assignment of moral responsibility without paying attention to the intentionality that underlies every moral action. Besides, assigning moral responsibility can provide an alibi or excuse for those directly responsible for the heinous crimes committed in a place like Rwanda.

14. Gifford, *African Christianity*, 34.

of Catholicism does not translate into a nationalist fervent that determines social values and shapes political attitudes. Oftentimes what is paraded as nationalism is nothing more than a glorified tribalism motivated by parochial intent and founded on ethnic agenda. As Paul Gifford correctly notes, "Catholicism was generally just one among many competing denominations, entering the continent about the same time and on roughly the same footing . . . So in Black Africa Catholicism simply was not what it was in Latin America, and could not play the same role. Generally, in Africa, Catholicism has been an example of voluntarism, in exactly the same way as the Baptist, Lutheran, and Pentecostal churches."[15] Although Gifford's point need not be contested, it is too summary and sweeping to offer a framework of interpretation of the incursion of African Catholicism into the national sphere.

When, on occasion, debate erupts around constitutional changes relating to moral issues like abortion, contraception, capital punishment, and gay relationships, the Catholic leadership rarely commands the support of Catholics as a voting bloc, let alone a significant authority to influence political leaders and legislative and judicial institutions. Yet, there are identifiable indicators of how Catholicism and its unique identity engage the national consciousness to maintain a zone of influence, even if this is symbolic and largely sacramental.[16] Three quick examples include the national celebration of Catholic religious feasts, the influence of Catholic leadership on national issues, and the enduring legacy of Catholic-educated political leaders:

1. The Solemnity of the Assumption on August 15 is a public holiday in eleven African countries (Burundi, Cameroon, Central African Republic, Republic of the Congo, Côte d'Ivoire, Republic of Guinea, Madagascar, Mauritius, Rwanda, Senegal, and Togo), while All Saints' Day on November 1 is celebrated nationally in fifteen African countries (Benin, Burkina Faso, Burundi, Cape Verde, Central African Republic, Chad, Côte d'Ivoire, Gabon, Guinea, Madagascar, Mauritius, Rwanda, Senegal, Seychelles, and Togo).

2. As mentioned above, the hallmark of Catholicism in Africa is the network of church-run education and health care institutions across the

---

15. Ibid., 35.

16. Emmanuel Katongole has identified three paradigms of relationship between church and state: political, pastoral, and pious. It is important to avoid treating them as mutually exclusive categories. A close look at the history of the mission of the Roman Catholic Church in Africa belies any strict demarcation—all three categories interrelate dynamically, with one's gaining ascendancy or prominence depending on place, context, and time. Katongole, "A Different World Right Here," 153–84. See Carney, "Waters of Baptism," 11–16.

continent. In regard to education, this has meant that several African leaders are products of Catholic schools. Their level of allegiance to Catholic morality and social teaching may be queried and the public display of their Catholic identity suspect, but their identification with Catholic background and influence remains unmistakable.[17] It could be argued that, so far, the influence of Catholicism on nationalism in Africa via Catholic-educated leaders has produced mixed results: DRC's late dictator, Mobutu Sese Seko, was legendary for his religious devotion and close links to the Roman Catholic hierarchy of his country; President Robert Mugabe of Zimbabwe oftentimes embarrasses the Jesuits by claiming to be the quintessential specimen of discipline, service, and moral probity inculcated through Jesuit education (notice his prominence at the liturgy of installation of Pope Francis!); former President Julius Nyerere of Tanzania has been declared a "Servant of God," an important step toward possible beatification and canonization; and Kenya, in April 2013, elected an openly practicing Catholic president, Uhuru Kenyatta, to succeed former President Mwai Kibaki, also a practicing Roman Catholic. One of these leaders won the praise of the African Catholic hierarchy at the second African Synod in 2009: "It is heartening that the cause of the beatification of Julius Nyerere of Tanzania is already on course. Africa needs saints in high political office: saintly politicians . . ."[18] The Synod also recognized the shortcomings of Catholic politicians and leaders and reserved unflattering remarks for them: "Many Catholics in high office have fallen woefully short in their performance in office. The Synod calls on such people to repent, or quit the public arena and stop causing havoc to the people and giving the Catholic Church a bad name."[19]

3. There are examples of significant interventions in national politics by high-ranking African ecclesial leaders. In at least five countries (Benin, Gabon, Togo, DRC, and Congo), African Catholic bishops served as chair of Sovereign National Conferences during the protracted democratization process in several sub-Saharan African countries in the 1990s. That was the summit of Catholicism's impact on processes and institutions that have shaped African sociopolitical identities. The notable religious figures

---

17. There is evidence to show that, in some instances, missionary commitment to the education of an African elite stemmed from ulterior political motive and considerations. In the words of one high-ranking ecclesiastic in colonial Africa, "The question is whether the ruling elite will be for us or against us; whether the important places in native society will be in Catholic or in non-Catholic hands; whether the Church will have through education and its formation of youth the preponderant influence in Rwanda." Quoted in Carney, "Beyond Tribalism," 181.

18. Second Special Assembly for Africa, "Message to the People of God," par. 23.

19. Ibid.

include the late Bishop Ernest Nkombo in Congo-Brazzaville and Archbishop (now Cardinal) Laurent Mosengwo Pasinya in the DRC.[20] More recently, a Roman Catholic priest, Fr. Appolinaire Mulohongo Malumalu, served as chair of the Independent Electoral Commission in the DRC. In related instances, such as in Madagascar and Kenya, the Catholic Church has offered to mediate between opposing political parties or groups.

Conclusion: Baptism Without Borders

In describing the context of the formation and functioning of religious identity in Africa, I have employed terms such as *competition* and *tension*. While it is true that Christianity in general and Catholicism in particular do not "carry the weight of centuries of history and tradition"[21] in Africa, navigating the contours of this competition and the challenges of this tension appears a much more daunting task. Oftentimes, this experience results in a plurality of religious identities that have been pejoratively labeled "religious double-mindedness" and "faith schizophrenia," to quote two African churchmen, Nigerian theologian Enyi Ben Udoh and South African prelate Desmond Tutu. Their point is that Africans struggle to integrate their religious identities and, therefore, are neither fully Christian nor solely practitioners of African Religion. As I have demonstrated in this essay, the origin of this amorphous religious identity is the context and pattern of religious affiliation incarnated in overlapping and shifting platforms of beliefs, practices, and allegiances. When mixed with pull factors of tribal cultural loyalties and obligations, it produces a complexity and plurality of identities and belongings.[22] Baptism offers one means for negotiation and fixing the borders of religious identity but a very limited one at that simply because, for many Africans, blood is thicker than water.

Although theologians facilely characterize the phenomenon of multiple religious identities as a schizophrenic crisis of identity, a critical analysis could allow for a more positive valuation. To find oneself part of multiple and overlapping religious and cultural communities of identity and belonging calls for a high degree of religious competence and astuteness. The African is not the subject of divided loyalty; he or she holds a diffused loyalty

20. Gifford, *African Christianity*, 21.

21. Allen, *Future Church*, 434.

22. I am avoiding the question of whether ethnic identities are primordial or whether they are created and modified as circumstances and contexts dictate for political intents and purposes. See Carney, "Beyond Tribalism," 192–94; Katongole, *Sacrifice of Africa*, 74–78.

or identity.²³ He or she is able to hold in tension—and operate effectively in—competing and overlapping religious spaces. Specifically, for a baptized African Christian—Catholic, Protestant, Pentecostal, African Instituted (Independent) Churches (AIC), or Orthodox—baptism does not necessarily impose impenetrable borders. On the contrary, it opens up borders. Catholic identity is not shaped in isolation from but in relation to other religious or faith identities, the contours of which are rigid when they need to be and fluid when the need arises. In this context, a Christianity without borders may yet be the most authentic manifestation and embodiment of the unity of Christ effected in baptism and sustained by the Eucharist.

In this line of thinking, I have deliberately connected baptism and Eucharist. Very often baptism in presented as a vertical reality, that is, "a transforming encounter with the living person of Christ."²⁴ The result is the "formation of a *spiritual* identity," as an interior reality of "the inner spiritual transformation of the individual."²⁵ This represents the classic Protestant view prevalent in contemporary Pentecostalism. While I do not dispute the centrality of a personal encounter with Christ for fixing religious identity, the stress that evangelical Pentecostalism puts on the individuality of this encounter evacuates the equally significant horizontal dimension including social, ethical, and political implications, which represents the Catholic view. If, as Emmanuel Katongole argues convincingly, Christianity births an alternative constructive imagination at once social, cultural, ethical, and political, the mechanism for actualizing this imagination in the face of pathological identities and loyalties cannot be supplied solely by baptismal ablution. Alone baptism cannot withstand the tsunami of multiple and competing identities. I hold the position that Eucharist underlines the specifically horizontal dimension of Christian identity. Hence baptism *and* Eucharist play a mutually reinforcing role.²⁶

The adage "blood is thicker than water" serves as reminder of an exaggerated emphasis on baptism as a single act of conferring identity on an individual Christian. As I mentioned above, it is insufficient to presume

---

23. On this note, I differ from the position held by theologians such as Kwame Bediako and Emmanuel Katongole, who devote much analysis to diagnosing the failure of Christianity to have a significant social impact on Africa. It is much less the failure of Christianity than the resistance and resilience of primary social and cultural allegiances and loyalties. Focusing on how Christianity has been or should be understood is a futile exercise. We need to ask the question, how has Christianity misunderstood and taken for granted its local context? Cf. Kantogole, *Sacrifice of Africa*, 40–50.

24. John Paul II, *Ecclesia in Africa*, par. 57.

25. Katongole, *Sacrifice of Africa*, 34.

26. Carney, "Waters of Baptism," 21.

that the "borders of baptism" offer a stronger base for developing loyalties and identities that embody the ideals of the kingdom of God, however we define this reality.[27] It helps to conceive of baptism as a process leading to the formation of a community. It is this community that confers identity, not the act itself in isolation. The consolidation of this community is symbolized and actualized by a "blood feast"—the Eucharist. To partake in this feast is to recognize oneself as an integral member of, and to enter into solidarity with, the global Body of Christ.

Finally, therefore, I also hold the position that in the specifically African understanding of ritual—in this case, the Eucharist—Catholicism can prove effective in generating new identities and loyalties capable of attenuating and replacing existing pathologies of tribalism. However, for this to happen, a new understanding of the Eucharist is required: "Eucharist is indeed a spirituality that includes everything."[28] For all who are gathered into the Body of Christ through baptism, the shared Eucharistic meal is the seal of a new identity of solidarity, mutuality, and inclusivity. Significantly, belonging is sealed not solely by water, but by blood (see 1 John 5:6). Thus, as Budde rightly affirms, if baptism means leaving "old identities and allegiances behind,"[29] Eucharist means a "celebration of our identity as God's children."[30] Thus, the trajectory of identity progresses from isolation and individuality to relationality and community. The concomitant reality is a new community characterized by its universality and ability to operate at the interstices of the local and the global. In practical terms, identity is not simply a by-product or end product of baptismal experience; it is the catalyst for, or production of, a new identity constructed and developed in the Eucharistic context. Whether we name this reality an embodiment of "ecclesial solidarity" (Michael Budde), the "Body of Christ" (Paul), "Eucharistic community" (several theologians), or simply "the Church" makes no difference. The baptismal community is a Eucharistic community. Those who eat together do not eat one another.

---

27. For a fuller description of "the kingdom of God" in this context, see Budde, *Borders of Baptism*, 23.
28. Kantongole, *Sacrifice of Africa*, 186.
29. Budde, *Borders of Baptism*, 5.
30. Kantongole, *Sacrifice of Africa*, 185.

11

Cases and Controversies from Africa

EUNICE KARANJA KAMAARA

Introduction

Long before colonialism and the attendant Christian missionary activity on the "Dark Continent," well before Africa was named, the people who occupied this mass of land had a rich religious experience with a holistic worldview. Christianity especially disrupted this worldview, often demanding that individuals discard their thought forms, beliefs, and practices before they could become Christians. Consequently, the postcolonial period in Africa has been characterized by an identity crisis, often with desire and attempts to undo the colonial impact. The central question continues to be this: What does it mean to be a Christian (in this context, Catholic) and to be African at the same time? In spite of continued appreciation that religion exists within culture, tension exists between being Catholic and being African. In this paper, I seek to highlight and theologically reflect on a specific case in Africa and the controversies that arise from it. First, I endeavor to provide an understanding of the terms "Catholicity" and "incarnated identities." Second, I present the complexity of the African context with emphasis on the traditional African worldview, the postcolonial experience, and the modern worldview as the background against which Catholicity in Africa may be understood. Third, I present the case of the Reformed Catholic Church in Kenya out of which various controversies in Africa emerge. Finally, I raise questions without necessarily answering them as a way of sharing and inviting theological reflections on Catholicity and incarnated identities not just in Africa but the world over.

Catholicism, Catholic Identity, and Incarnated Identities

In the spirit of ecumenism and inclusivity, I appreciate that there are multiple meanings of "Catholicism" and the related term "Catholicity." For some, Catholicity may not be used interchangeably with Catholicism because reducing the Catholic faith to an "ism" is unacceptable. For example, according to Anthony J. Kelly, CSsR, using the word *Catholicism* to refer to the Catholic faith "gives the impression, like all 'isms,' of an ideology, of a closed system of principles and positions."[1] In the context of this presentation, Catholicity—derived from the word *Catholic*—is used interchangeably with Catholicism with particular reference to the Catholic Church, the oldest institution in Western history. It refers to the beliefs of the Catholic Church, which may be summed up as beliefs in the saving mystery of God's will of love for all humanity through Christ. The values of faith, hope, and love are seen as not only fundamental but also universal, that is, accessible to all regardless of time and space.

In broader terms, Catholicity refers to the universality of not just humanity, be they Christian or not, but of all creation, under Christ, the Word through which all things were created (John 1:1) and in Christ through whom all creation holds together (Col 1:17). In relation to human persons, the term presupposes inclusivity of all into an unlimited domain of the One United Holy Church whose defining characteristic is faith in Christ. In essence, therefore, every human person is a member of this one Church regardless of whether (s)he is Christian or not. Indeed, one need not be a Christian to fall within the grace of God, for Christ came not to be served but to serve all (Matt 20:28). Thus, all creation is one and owes its origin and destiny to a single source.

The concept of Catholicity presupposes that there are universal standards of right and wrong behavior in any human act. This is accurate, for there are basic ethical values common to all cultures and religions. These common values may be considered universal. However, these values are understood, expressed, and lived differently depending on cultural contexts. Hence, to be ethical does not only require clear understanding of universal values but also, of necessity, deep understanding of the specific real-life situations within which these universal values apply. Indeed, while Catholic values and principles are constant, cultural and religious contexts differ from time to time and from place to place.

Therefore, I emphasize that Catholicity does not imply sameness for, or homogeneity of humankind, less still sameness of creation—creation is

---

1. Kelly, "Catholic Identity," 3.

diverse. There can never be anything like homogeneity in human history, within which the Catholic faith operates. To be Catholic is to uphold these values regardless of the different ways in which these may be understood, interpreted, expressed, and lived. Anthony J. Kelly puts it more eloquently:

> Mere planetary universality in aspiration or effect is not what the Catholic identity is about... If all things are made in Christ and for him, and if in him all things hold together (cf. Col 1:15–18), there is a wholeness, a 'catholicity' that is not the homogenization of a system or a universal product or design, but that of the personal love of Christ for each and every one.[2]

Catholicity presupposes a shared identity of humans in their origin in God affirmed by faith in the Risen Christ but lived in specific cultural contexts.

Further, Catholicity does not refer to a constant reality since reality—especially human reality—is dynamic. Christ Incarnate is the central Christian mystery and dogma that God became human and dwelt upon earth (John 1:1). Clearly, the Catholic faith may be understood as a movement within history in that its foundation may be linked to a specific place and time in history: Jesus became human and was therefore born at a specific place and time as all humans are. Moreover, the growth and development of the faith has been experienced through specific historical contexts. Therefore, to be Catholic is to be born into the limitless domain of God's love, but it is also to be born into a specific geographic and sociocultural context. The different contexts within which individual Catholics are born and grow account for incarnated identities and explain the diversity and dynamism resulting from different understandings, interpretations, expressions, and living of the Catholic faith.

Given the limitations of human experience in spite of their Catholicity, various tensions often exist within an individual as (s)he seeks to be Catholic, especially in specific cultural contexts. H. Richard Niebuhr describes the tensions caused by Catholic identity and incarnated identities as "the double wrestle of the church with its Lord and with the cultural society with which it lives in symbiosis."[3]

In this paper, I seek to bring out the African Catholic identity problem by presenting the complexity of the cultural contexts within which Catholics in Africa operate. Using a specific case and controversies that have threatened to break the unity of the Catholic Church, I argue that these tensions are merely expressions of the contradictions of human experience and need not be seen as threats to Catholicity. In so doing, I hope to raise controversy

---

2. Ibid., 4.
3. Niebuhr, *Christ and Culture*, xi.

on the identity of an African Catholic by posing questions without necessarily answering them.

The Complexity of the African Cultural Context

Africa has never been a homogenous unity from any perspective. Culturally, there are hundreds of ethnic communities on the continent, each with its own language and its own political, social, and economic organization, not to mention the many products of many years of groups interacting with other ethnic groups from within and outside Africa throughout the history of migrations and conquests. Suffice to mention some African languages to bring home the point about the waxing and waning of identities in Africa. The Kiswahili language, spoken across many African countries, is commonly referred to as an African language and is taught in many institutes of African languages. Yet, it is not an indigenous African language but a product of the fusion of the cultures of East African coastal peoples with those of Arabs. Other examples include pidgin in Nigeria and the emerging Sheng in Kenya, which are products of African languages' interaction with English. At the same time, some indigenous languages of Africa are almost extinct, having been assimilated by more dominant indigenous languages. For example, in Eastern Africa, the Olusuba dialect has been absorbed by Dholuo.[4]

At the dawn of the twenty-first century, Africa is at a crossroads: the indigenous African worldview and the modern global worldview govern the people's way of thinking and acting. Thus, the peoples' interpretation of what it means to be Catholic is intricately related to these two worldviews, with all their complexities. While the modern and indigenous worldviews are often contradictory, they do not operate in binary forms. Often, the two are so intricately integrated into a total whole that it is difficult to distinguish one from the other.

The postcolonial experience that characterizes nearly all African countries is an interlude that serves to complicate immensely the African context. For many postcolonial theorists,[5] colonialism has had so adverse and long-lasting an impact on the African continent that the contemporary situation cannot be understood without reference to the process. For example, according to Crawford Young, "Overall colonial legacy casts its shadow over the emergent African state system to a degree unique among

---

4. Kembo-Sure, *Literacy, Language, and Liberty*.
5. See Leys, *Underdevelopment in Kenya*; Mamdani, *Citizen and Subject*; and C. Young, "Heritage of Colonialism."

the major world regions."⁶ A brief description of each of these worldviews and of the interlude presents the backdrop against which Catholicity and incarnated identities in Africa may be understood.

The Indigenous African Worldview

In this context, "indigenous African" (herein used interchangeably with "traditional African") refers to the African way of life as practiced before colonialism and the attendant nineteenth-century missionary Christianity. While African peoples are diverse, common principles guide their worldview. This is perhaps true not only in African but also in all traditional societies. While I appreciate the dynamism of all cultures, including the African way of life before external influences, I contend that change in precolonial Africa was moderate and did not affect the worldview in terms of the basic values governing life. New knowledge leading to new attitudes and practices characterize all human life but just as globalization may be understood as an age-old practice, it is only with the rapid and significant changes of the current information age that the phenomenon has been clearly observed and a term developed to refer to it. Today, it is not common to find the practice of indigenous ways of life as practiced in precolonial times, but many of the values that governed this worldview continue to hold among many individuals and groups. This explains why many scholars of African indigenous life appropriately refer to it in the present form. Consistent with my argument that the contemporary African cultural context is complex, I too refer to African indigenous religion as a living religion.

The indigenous African worldview is guided by the ultimate questions of human existence: the questions of ultimate origin, ultimate purpose, and ultimate destiny. It is formulated and passed on from generation to generation through a lifelong system of socialization using oral traditions like stories, proverbs, and songs as well as lived experience. For want of time and space, I will present the main values of the African worldview, namely theocentrism, anthropocentrism, and communitarianism, all of which integrate into a holistic worldview.

Indigenous societies in Africa are characterized by a theocentric worldview founded on the acknowledgment of God as the ultimate designer, creator, sustainer, purpose, and destiny of everything in the created order. Hence, there is no dichotomy between what is sacred and what is secular, as every element of the created order (including all inanimate things, such as stones and mountains) is considered sacred. Traditional Africans, therefore,

6. Young, "Heritage of Colonialism," 24.

do not distinguish between religion and culture. As J. S. Mbiti observes, traditional Africans do not know how to live without religion; for them, to live is to be religious.[7]

The indigenous African worldview is also anthropocentric in that the human person is recognized as the center of creation and God's steward under whom responsible management of the rest of the created elements directly lies. Thus, human life is considered most sacred, and every human activity in every aspect of life is considered a religious activity. The earth is acknowledged and respected as host and it nourishes all creation. Given the central role of humanity in God's creation, human procreation (and more specifically, perpetuation of lineage) is considered fundamental to human life. Sex is considered sacred and as having mysterious power that must be guided and guarded for human prosperity. To die without children is most unfortunate. But traditional Africans appreciate that procreation needs to be socialized into the values and ways of the tribe. Thus, sex outside marriage is condemned, and marriage is highly exalted and compulsory for all. A man or woman who remains unmarried after a certain age is scorned. The purpose of marriage is first and foremost for procreation with emphasis on a large progeny. To ensure a large progeny, there are various institutions across various African communities. For example, polygamy (both polygyny and polyandry) and levirate marriages (commonly referred to as wife inheritance) are common and highly valued in nearly all African societies. The functional value of the former is to ensure many children, while the latter ensures that the dead continue to procreate through their close relatives.

Central to the African indigenous worldview are relationships. Hence, according to African spirituality the ultimate purpose of life is relationships: relationships between Creator and created, and among the created. As designer, author, purpose, and destiny of the created, the Creator determines relationships between the Creator and created, as well as among the created. Therefore, in order for the created to understand how to relate with the Creator and among themselves, the created need to know the will of God—more or less, it is similar to needing manuals to effectively operate products of human creativity such as radios, computers, and mobile phones. For traditional Africans, the will of God is expressed in nature and is easily understood by human persons who seek to understand it in humility and truth. Unhealthy relationships are identified as all relationships that lead to antilife situations, while healthy relationships are found in all activities that promote life. At the risk of glorifying the past, I dare say that this worldview served the communities well and ensured that unity, justice, and peace

---

7. Mbiti, *African Religions and Philosophy*, 4.

prevailed within each of the autonomous states, and individual rights were respected in the context of community.

The ultimate destiny of life is God, who ensures perpetuation of life through healthy relationships from one generation to another through birth and rebirths. God maintains the cycle of life as human persons and all other creation transit from one stage in life to another: from prebirth to birth to ancestorhood through death. All creation is designed to work together in unity and rhythm: when healthy relationships flourish among all creation, life is promoted for all creation, and all creation rejoices together. When there are unhealthy relationships, life is threatened and all creation suffers together. Life is therefore understood as a unitary whole in which individual elements of creation are understood as interdependent parts of the whole creation, hence the concept of ethical community. This is the *Utu* ethos, which recognizes human life as the highest value and healthy relationships among creation as the goal of life.

A systematic process of formulating and passing on this education exists basically in the form of rites of passage from prebirth to ancestorhood. In recognition of the difficulties of youth as a stage in human development that is characterized by identity and sexual crises, the rite of passage from initiation from childhood to adulthood marks one of the major levels of education. This rite is an elaborate process of intensive education with special emphasis on

1. the importance of maintaining the right relationships with the Creator and among the created;
2. the centrality of humans in God's reign and of the earth as host and mother of all created elements;
3. the concept and practice of rights and responsibilities with clear indication that all actions have consequences;
4. the dignity of all human persons in the context of family and community and the need for self-esteem and self-worth.

Chris Nwaka Egbulem identifies seven values or "pillars of African life" that constitute the essence or core of African spirituality:

1. belief in the active presence of the creator God in the world;
2. a unified sense of reality;
3. identification of life as the ultimate gift from the Creator;
4. emphasis on the family and community as the place to be born, live, and die;

5. belief in the active role of ancestors;
6. reliance on oral tradition; and
7. a sense of the sacredness of nature and environment.[8]

This effectively summarizes the African worldview.

The Colonial Interlude

The scramble for Africa and the consequent partitioning of the continent in the colonization process, and the attendant process of civilizing and Christianizing the African native, significantly disrupted the traditional African worldview. The famous Berlin Conference (1884–85), which came up with the policy of effective occupation as a strategy toward the peaceful partitioning of the "Dark Continent," marked the beginning of a new era of globalization, after slavery and slave trade. This decision made in Berlin—many miles away from Africa, with no representation of Africans—provides the background to the current situation in Africa. In order for European governments to effectively occupy specific regions and, therefore, acquire them as protectorates, they needed numbers. Since their home populations could not suffice, many governments supported individuals and individual organizations interested in Christian missions in going out to "evangelize" the "Dark Continent." In this way, governments killed two birds with one stone: they achieved effective occupation as well as agents of pacification for colonization.

Christianity's disruption of the traditional African worldview, among other agents of colonization, led to various forms of alienation. Merely for purposes of clarity we discuss the various forms of alienation separately, although in reality these are heavily interrelated.

Alienation from Land

It is no secret that the cross served to prepare for the flag and, as the colonists scrambled for land and political control, the missionaries too scrambled for souls as well as for land on which to build facilities for civilizing the bodies in which the souls live: churches, schools, hospitals, and other agents of alienation. This explains why—to both the Church and the colonists—the Mau Mau fighting for land and freedom were not freedom fighters but "rebels" and "terrorists" whom the missionaries derogatorily referred to as *acenji*

---

8. Egbulem, "African Spirituality," 17–21.

(pagans) as opposed to the collaborators who were *athomi* (Christians equated to "readers"). It is on record that, by 1960, thirty-four hundred European farmers—most of them professing Christians—were settled on 7.5 million acres of prime agricultural land, with about two hundred and fifty thousand African men contributing thirty-six million Kenya pounds out of the total marketed output of forty-two million pounds, which accounts for about 78 percent.[9] Besides, whole clans were displaced to give space to church missions. For example, the land on which the Kikuyu Mission Station stands (with the famous Church of the Torch, the Presbyterian Church of East Africa Kikuyu Hospital, Thogoto Teachers College, the Alliance High Schools, and the newly built Presbyterian University) is authentically the ancestral land of *Mbari ya Waiyaki* (the Waiyaki clan) from which I descend. Since the displacement, the Waiyaki clan is largely dispersed throughout various parts of the country with little or no land to call their own.

Worse than the scramble for physical colonies by the Church is the rivalry that accompanied this scramble. Different missions and Christian denominations colonized certain regions as their "mission fields," sometimes barring other missionaries from operating in the area, while in other situations hatred and intolerance characterized the relationship between the different missions. In all these missionary areas, the trend in the institutional setting was the same: school, hospital, and training colleges alongside the churches led to regional imbalances in development, a factor that pitted all tribes against the Kikuyu. The Kikuyu's region, the Central Province, is ahead of many other regions in terms of infrastructure, primarily because of its location near Nairobi, the center of missionary and colonial activity.

By independence, Kenyans (especially Kenyan Christians) had lost the traditional values of communalism and relationships, which hold respect for the earth and all creation.

Alienation from the African Way of Life (Culture and Religion)

The traditional African way of life, which integrates culture and religion, is closely related to land, because the earth is held as sacred and is considered the host and sustainer of humanity with all of its beliefs and practices (culture). Hence, to alienate an African from land is to alienate the African from religion and culture, because some beliefs and practices have no meaning and, therefore, no value outside ancestral land. This, for example, explains why many Africans such as the Luo of western Kenya insist on burying their dead in their ancestral homeland even when it puts economic strain on the

---

9. Sandbrook, *Proletariats and African Capitalism*, 4.

family; the value of burying a person on his ancestral land outweighs the economic cost. Hence, in displacing Africans from their land, the missionaries and colonists alienated them from their religion and culture.

Further, the missionaries condemned all African beliefs and practices as either evil and primitive or backward, and in their place imposed European beliefs and practices disguised as Christian. Of course, the Africans resisted this as much as they could, and this necessitated enforcement of the new culture. In other missionary settings, Africans were enticed with goods and services such as free education and health care to abandon their religion and culture. Consistently, education served to alienate individuals physically, ideologically, and spiritually from the family and community. To be converted to Christianity meant to give up one's whole way of life: dressing, thinking, talking, worshipping, dancing, eating, and relating. Communitarianism was adversely affected as the ideas of individual salvation, individual education, and individual human rights were introduced and emphasized.

Adulteration of Education

The missionaries condemned the systematic form of lifelong education. Specifically, all initiation rites were condemned as evil and/or primitive, and in their place, they introduced a formal system of education that revolved around the schooling of individuals. The task of imparting education was largely left in the hands of missionaries. Since it has different objectives, this formal system of education also has different values from the traditional system. While the traditional system integrates an individual into his community's holistic way of life, formal education was designed to alienate the individual from his/her community and prepare him/her to serve the colonial government in the new political and economic structures. As Wa Thiong'o puts it, formal education is colonizing in that it propagates cultural imperialism: indeed, this medium of formal education in Africa demands knowledge of another people's language and undermines one's own language.[10] To date, many schools in Kenya are Christian-based and will punish their students if they speak in their mother tongue. While traditional education emphasized relationships as the purpose of life, formal education emphasizes individual goals such as self-fulfillment and self-realization.

The impact of this is seen in various injustices such as corruption and poor distribution of resources manifested in regional imbalances and the large gap between the rich and the poor, which in turns breeds poverty, conflict, and violence in society.

10. Wa Thiong'o, Preface to *Decolonizing the Mind*.

Alienation from Self

The sum total of all forms of alienation is alienation from the self. Africans are so alienated from themselves that many of them, collectively and individually, do not have self-value and self-esteem, especially in relation to non-Africans. While many Africans are not conscious of this alienation, it is clearly manifested in attitudes and practices. Collectively, this is manifested in the fact that, in spite of forty or more years of political independence, many African countries continue to operate with the colonial mindset, which is manifested in our continued use of a colonial system of education with colonial curriculum, constitutions, and lifestyle.

In place of traditional African communalism within which the African way of life is lived, Christianity emphasized individual salvation, thereby alienating individuals from their families and communities. Perhaps the worst form of this alienation is expressed when priests withdraw from community to live secluded lives. The impact of this alienation was the development of dual cultural and religious identity, which leaves many Africans with serious inconsistencies, confusion, and brokenness. As Wa Thiong'o observes in the preface to his book *Decolonizing the Mind*,

> The present predicaments of Africa are often not a matter of personal choice: they arise from an historical situation. Their solutions are not so much a matter of personal decision as that of fundamental social transformation of the structures of our societies starting with a real break with imperialism and its internal ruling allies. Imperialism and its comprador alliances in Africa can never develop the continent.[11]

The continued identity crisis is part of the subject addressed here in this conference, under the theme "Multiple Belongings and Transnational Processes of Catholic Formation."

The Modern Worldview

If the modern worldview has any common values, they are the values of competition and profit for the individual. This breeds materialism, individualism, and consumerism, and Africans have been sucked into this worldview. This is evident in that nearly all Africans will use their positions of leadership to acquire huge tracts of land and other material resources in the model of missionary and colonial activity. The higher the positions of

---

11. Ibid.

leadership, the more resources they acquire. For example, given the enormous power wielded by the Office of the President over the first fifty years of independent Kenya, it is no wonder that the three individual families owning the largest piece of land in Kenya are the families of the current and former presidents of Kenya, all families who claim to be Christian.

Leadership in Africa is therefore interpreted in relation to material things, such that a leader is expected to have many material things, not necessarily for sharing with others but for personal use. Consistently, leadership is interpreted as an opportunity to acquire more of these materials, again not necessarily for communal use but for personal use.

Such a perverted worldview is endorsed by a system of schooling that makes no reference to human service to other persons or to other elements of the created order. Instead, the focus is on how much the individual can acquire for the self even at the expense of human life. Such a situation is characterized by—among other injustices—corruption, greed, selfishness, violence, and irresponsible behavior in all aspects of life. Suffice to note that the entertainment mass media is consistent in terms of propounding values of individualism, materialism, and consumerism commonly manifested in irresponsible sexual behavior and violence as opposed to the values of family, sacredness of sex, dignity of human persons, and sacredness of the earth.

The modern system of education, as mentioned earlier, is geared toward self-fulfillment and self-realization/actualization, which is measured by material acquisition and consumerism at the level of individual. Hence, success is measured by individual acquisition of such material objects as land, cars, houses, clothes, and furniture, among others, for individual consumption.

Tragically, the postcolonial situation with the brokenness associated with various forms of alienation drives Africans to seek satisfaction in materialism and consumerism, but because they have an African worldview in their unconscious or conscious minds, they find no satisfaction in these. The result is escalating violence among Africans and with those with whom they associate.

The Identity of an African Catholic

Against the postcolonial context in Africa, alienation (especially in relation to alienation of the self) and the question of African identity continue to occupy the minds of many Africans. But this is not unique to Africans: other postcolonial communities such as those in the Caribbean face the same challenges.¹² It is common knowledge that it is impossible for any human person to completely give up his/her way of life in favor of another. This implies that Africans did not quite fully give up their way of thinking and acting. For many of them, they continue with the traditional way even as they seek to engage the modern worldview.

It may seem easy to understand who is a Catholic even though this may be complicated, too. As has already been mentioned, in the narrow sense of the word, any person who believes in the saving grace of Jesus Christ is Catholic. But in earlier history, the Roman Catholic Church maintained that there is no salvation outside of it, thus limiting the term "Catholic Church" to the former. Thankfully, this position has consistently shifted to the present post-Vatican II times when other faiths have been theologically reevaluated with understanding and respect. Who are Africans and what does Catholicity call them to be in view of traditional values, with all the challenges and realities of the modern world?

Despite more than fifty years of reflection on African identity, it is still not so easy to respond to the question, who is an African Christian? In all spheres of life, Africans continue to be significantly informed by their traditional worldview and, as the modern worldview creeps in, to feel nostalgic about their lost African beliefs and practices. Many scholars (for example, Luke Fashole and Laurenti Magesa[13]) have written on the desire and attempts by African Christians "to incarnate Christianity in local culture," but these works have not sorted out the question of the African Christian's identity. According to Okolo, "Africans strongly desire to be fully Africans and fully Christians: is this possible? It depends upon the essence of 'Africanness' and that of Christianity, neither of which is easy to determine or define."[14] My contention is that the question of African identity can never be resolved, because there is no reality such as "an African," even if we think cosmetically in terms of color or descent; what we have are fluid, ever-changing African identities. But this discussion is outside the realm of this paper. For now, I limit myself to discussing and understanding cases and controversies from Africa. Toward this objective, I critically analyze the case of the Reformed Catholic Church in the contemporary Church in Africa through two controversies as they relate to the search for African identity: 1) the anti-celibacy controversy, and 2) the exercise of the gifts of the Holy Spirit. To this I now turn.

---

12. See, for example, Hall, "Negotiating Caribbean Identities," 3–14.

13. See Fashole, "What Is African Christian Theology?," 383–88, and Magesa, *Anatomy of Inculturation.*

14. Okolo, "The African Experience of Christian Values," 173–86.

The Case of the Reformed Catholic Church in Africa

One of the fastest growing groups of Catholics is those clergy who are opposed to the Catholic Church's mandatory rule of celibacy. They go by many names. In Kenya, for example, they are referred to as the Reformed Catholic Church, the Catholic Diocese of One Spirit in Kenya, the Ecumenical Reformed Catholic Church, the Restored Universal Apostolic Church, and the Ecumenical Catholic Church of Christ, among others. In this context, we will refer to all of these as the Reformed Catholic Church (RCC).

Without a doubt, the establishment and growth of the RCC in Africa is one of the major issues throughout history that the global Roman Catholic Church has had to address. While the RCC or the ideals for which it stands are not limited to the African continent, and while in Africa the movement may be traced to earlier times, it is the particular case of Emmanuel Milingo of Zambia that brought this movement to the fore. Emanuel Milingo was the Roman Catholic bishop of the Archdiocese of Lusaka, since his consecration by Pope Paul VI in 1969, when he was only thirty-nine years old.

Drawing from his rich African heritage, Milingo believed in the African central value of relationships. For him, as for his ancestors, all phenomena could be explained from the point of view of relationships: healthy relationships among creation (including spirits) result in fortune, while unhealthy relationships lead to misfortune. Thus, for him, spiritual healing (and more specifically, exorcism) is critical to human well-being. Therefore, even as a Catholic clergy, Milingo practiced this with applause from African traditionalists and Christian theologians alike. Milingo became popular throughout Zambia, as well as the central, southern, and eastern regions of Africa. His ordination provided him an opportunity to popularize, against Vatican expectations, his practice of exorcism and healing. On a number of occasions—but to no avail—the pope invited Milingo to the Vatican to attempt to have him reflect on his conduct, repent, and return to the fold.

The climax of Milingo's disobedience to the Vatican came in 2001 when he, at seventy-one, married Maria Sung under the Family Federation for World Peace and Unification (FFWPU). Led by the Korean Reverend Sun Myung Moon, the FFWPU is a socioreligious global movement whose mission is to bring all humanity to unity and peace. Many people wondered how Milingo, a Catholic bishop, could marry at that age and what exactly he was seeking. But only non-Africans could ask the question. For Africans, Milingo had finally heeded the call of his ancestors to perpetuate his lineage.

What followed, barely five years after Milingo's marriage to Maria, was open defiance by many African priests to the Catholic celibacy rule. In 2006, Milingo established the Married Priests Now! movement to advocate for allowing and accepting married Catholic priests. In July 2006, Milingo officiated weddings of priests in Latin America. As expected, the Catholic Church hierarchy resorted to excommunicating him according to the dictates of Canon 292 of the Code of Canon Law. In October 2007, Milingo was stripped of his clerical state. This meant that he lost all of his rights and privileges as a Roman Catholic priest and could thereafter not serve as a clergy in any ministry of the Church. This meant that he no longer had authority to join people in the Sacrament of Holy Matrimony or to ordain anyone into the Sacrament of priesthood. Any marriage or ordination that was officiated by Milingo after October 2007 would be null and void and, therefore, not recognized by the Church. The Church claims to do this to protect the faithful.

What is amazing is that, while the Vatican thought it was dishonoring Milingo by stripping him of his clerical status, the controversial former archbishop's popularity rose among Africans to unimaginable levels. It would seem that Milingo was connecting with Africans in a very direct way. Despite being stripped of his clerical duties by Rome, he was sought out by many African priests for blessings to start breakaway churches from the Roman Catholic one. For example, in June 24, 2009, Milingo conferred episcopal ordination on Fr. Daniel W. Kasomo in Nairobi, Kenya. Kasomo is a bishop of the Married Priests Now! movement in Kenya and a senior lecturer in the Department of Religion, Theology, and Philosophy at Maseno University, a public university in Kenya. He holds a doctorate in religious studies and is the author of many books, including *Understanding Human Sexuality*. Following this in Kenya was the case of Godfrey Silvester Shiundu, a former Roman Catholic priest whose publicity makes him the face of the Reformed Church in Kenya. Suspended from the Roman Catholic Church's ministry in 2004 for marrying a former nun, Shiundu is well known in Kenya for this controversial marriage, which was covered by the Kenyan print and electronic media and the talk all over the country throughout the year.

In August 2010, Milingo was named Patriarch for Southern Africa by the Ecumenical Catholic Apostolic Church of Peace. In southern Africa, this title of patriarch is reserved for persons of great honor. Since 2009, Milingo has ordained and consecrated many married deacons, priests, and bishops throughout Africa; one of the latest was in April 2011, when he consecrated Fr. Peter Njogu Kubutu as a bishop of the Restored Universal Apostolic Church. But what are the controversies surrounding the RCC in Africa? In the following section, I discuss the controversy raised by the RCC in Africa on the celibacy rule.

Controversy: The Value of Progeny in Africa and the Catholic Anti-celibacy Rule

Different worldviews and, therefore, different values exist among Africans, and occasionally, an individual is caught between two contradictory worldviews. As discussed above, central to the African worldview are relationships, with human life having the greatest value. Actually, the perpetuation of human life through marriage has intrinsic value and is expected of all human persons. To date, it would seem that the ultimate value of any human being as understood, expressed, and lived in Africa is to perpetuate lineage.

Alongside this, Africans have a great sense of togetherness, of communion, of family. The single major purpose for one's life is to increase progeny. As has already been noted, to die without children is the worst that can happen to an individual. Well after colonialism, these practices prevail even among highly educated individuals and, in many instances, continue to mark prestige and honor.

For more than a thousand years, the Roman Catholic Church has taught that celibacy is required of its clergy. This puts Africans in awkward situations as they seek to perpetuate their lineage as expected by their cultures and, at the same time, be in public Catholic Church ministry. This leads to immense tensions between being African and being Roman Catholic.

For some African priests, the solution to these tensions lies in living double lives—of a celibate priest and of an African who values progeny and community living and is, therefore, secretly married. According to Fr. John Karimi, who joined the RCC after fifteen years in the mainline Catholic Church, "Ninety-seven percent of priests live a hypocritical life. They should be allowed to maintain their sex life."[15] He was speaking in an interview with the Catholic Information Service for Africa (CISA).[16] It would seem that some priests use the prevalence of "hypocrisy" as justification for calling for the abolition of this law. But does the prevalence of an act make it right?

Adherents of the RCC argue that celibacy should not be mandatory, because it is not a divine law. In 1 Cor 7, Paul praises celibacy as a better state for public Christian ministers compared to "burning in desire" or to marriage. For Paul, a celibate minister can devote more attention to providing service than if married. But he did not prohibit marriage among public Christian ministers. Indeed, in his first letter to Timothy, he states that a church elder must be the husband of one wife (1 Tim 3:2).

---

15. Catholic News Agency, "Anti-celibacy Sects."
16. Free Republic, "Anti-celibacy Sect."

Could the breaking of the anti-celibacy rule be mere lack of discipline? Another argument, for example, by Fr. Karimi of the Ecumenical Catholic Church of Christ is that the anti-celibacy rule is not only unacceptable in Africa but also in all other parts of the world, because sex is a basic human need—sex is indispensable. Consequently, along with Fr. Karimi, many of the priests in the Reformed Catholic Church wonder, why does the Catholic Church insist on such an unnatural practice as celibacy when its entire morality is based on natural law?

For many African priests, celibacy is one of the Roman Catholic Church's archaic laws. But one would also wonder why some priests (African, in this context) committed themselves to celibate lives in the first place. Some of them would argue that they were naïve when they committed themselves to the vow. But in that case, shouldn't priests voluntarily leave the priesthood rather than insist on remaining priests when they have broken the rule of celibacy? But it would seem that some commit themselves to celibacy when they have no intention of maintaining it. For example, by the time of his ordination in 1992, Kasomo had a steady girlfriend with a child.[17] But why do priests breaking away from the Catholic Church insist on having the name "Catholic" or "universal" or "ecumenical" in the name of the new church that they create? Responding to the ordinations of more priests into the RCC by Godfrey Shiundu, the bishop of the Catholic Diocese of Kitale, Maurice Crowley argued that this is a new sect and should drop its use of the name "Catholic."[18] But perhaps the priests are right in insisting on the name "Catholic"—as far as they are concerned, all persons are welcome and, indeed, belong to the Church by grace regardless of their various statuses. If they were to make their churches exclusive, they would fall into the same evil of which they accuse the mainline Catholic Church. Characteristic of all of these churches is that they insist on the universal character of the Church, accept all the rites of the Catholic Church, and are opposed only to Church structure and the celibacy rule.

It would seem that some Catholics are torn between African traditional values and those of the Catholic Church. But this contradiction is not unique to Catholic priests. In many situations, Africans will adhere to indigenous values and to modern values at the same time without thinking of it as contradiction. Joyce Nyairo, for example, graphically analyzes Kenyan obituaries to show how relatives of the dead

> go to great lengths to establish the lines of perpetuation. Sometimes they invoke the names of long-dead ancestors with whom

17. Odalo, "Rebel Priests Await Milingo Visit."
18. *Standard Digital News*, "Celibacy Debate Back."

the deceased may have had little if any credible contact, thereby linking "personal immortality" with "collective immortality"... And as a rule they underline continuity with a roll-call of living relations, some of whom are only very remotely related to the deceased but who must get a mention within this space as part of a cultural project that emphasizes kinship and shared responsibilities over individual exploits. This state is achieved precisely on account of lineage for as Mbiti states "unless a person has close relatives to remember him when he has physically died, then he is nobody and simply vanishes out of human existence like a flame when it is extinguished."[19]

Yet, as Nyairo illustrates, these indigenous values of communitarianism and lineage perpetuation are punctuated by the display of materialism. She observes,

> The significance of a person's life is often debated through a description of the perceived successes of his/her off-spring. If you want to know what struggles over recognition are taking place in the Kenyan socio-economic sphere a useful place to look is at the obituary pages... Today Eng., Arch., Geol., and Adv., establish new social protocols and urge a reframing of the society's measures of modern success so that educational qualifications are seen as markers of a sustained acquisition of modernity's socio-economic props. When these titles precede the names of one's off-spring, the consensus that the obituary is inviting from readers is that the deceased has led a successful life and left a legacy that should be envied by all. And wherever any of these titles apply to the deceased person, once again the appropriate unanimity being sought through the obituary is that his/hers has been a life well lived.[20]

Further, even as individuals and individual families mock death as they celebrate the lines of biological perpetuation in line with indigenous African values, however remote, there is another marker of success "read in the presence and the extent of a family's global networks. Whenever a family can name a transnational relative—so-and-so of the U.S. or UK or Botswana or South Africa—the point is not simply to locate the individual correctly but also to display the family's long extensive association in the networks of modernity." Such are the contradictions of African identity; even within one person, we can only speak of multiple African identities.

19. Nyairo, "'Modify,'" 139.
20. Ibid., 140. The abbreviations Eng., Arch., Geol., and Adv. stand for engineer, architect, geologist, and advocate, respectively.

Conclusions: The Tensions Continue

Many years after Vatican II, many years after the African Synod, and many years after the pope declared that Christ is African, tensions persists and the question remains, what does it mean to be African and Catholic? There are various perspectives on the tensions between culture and Christianity. For some, the Catholic hierarchy based in Rome does not understand the realities of specific sociocultural contexts and, therefore, does not see the need to address the issues. For others, Catholic Christians are docile and unnecessarily waiting for Rome to effect necessary changes.

My perspective is that this tension will not be resolved soon, because the nature of the Church as a universal but incarnated reality calls for these contradictions. Even if African priests were to be allowed to marry, they would perhaps seek to be allowed to be polygamous. If they are allowed polygamy, they will ask to inherit wives or to have their wives inherited after they die. Indeed, it is these incarnated identities that allow for one to be a Christian: if humans had no incarnated identities, why would they need salvation? Without the need for salvation, why would Jesus become human? Contradiction is at the center of every human by the very nature of his/her being—the rational, the physical, and the spiritual being are almost always in tension. Indeed, human nature is itself contradictory such that human life is a constant struggle to harmonize these contradictions.

To add "Catholic" to African identities is to add to an already complex whole. Tension will remain "till thy kingdom come," for, as observed in Vatican II, this is a mystery: "when Christ presents to his Father an eternal and universal kingdom . . . Here on earth the kingdom is mysteriously present; when the Lord comes, it will enter into perfection."[21] Suffice to close with the following observation by Hall: "Identity is not in the past to be found, but in the future to be constructed."[22]

---

21. *Gaudium et Spes*, par. 39, 983.
22. Hall, "Negotiating Caribbean Identities," 3–14.

12

Poverty, Injustice, and Plurality: A Complex Question for Catholics in Latin America

MARIA CLARA LUCCHETTI BINGEMER

I wouldn't call it a coincidence that I am writing this text at the exact moment that Pope Francis—previously, Cardinal Jorge Mario Bergoglio, archbishop of Buenos Aires, Argentina—is beginning his pontificate. His first words and gestures won the world over with their simplicity and affability. It was a good beginning for the Catholics all over the world, still shocked with Pope Benedict XVI's resignation and all of the scandals that became known as a result.

I would like to start with some of the words he used when presenting himself as bishop of Rome for the first time, from St. Peter's balcony: "My fellow cardinals had as a task to give a bishop to Rome. And they went to search for him at the end of the world." With this radical expression—"the end of the world"—he was obviously referring to his homeland, Argentina, but I am sure it was not only a geographical remark. The situation of his country, of his continent, was certainly present in his words as well.

In this text, I want to reflect on the challenge of being a Catholic "at the end of the world," in a place where wealth, culture, and progress have not arrived in the same proportion as elsewhere, in the so-called First World. The countries of Latin America are bursting with potential—especially mine, Brazil, which has dominated the headlines for hosting World Youth Day this year and preparing to host, in the next few years, the World Cup and the Olympic games. Yet, in spite of all of this promising potential, in most of the Latin American world, poverty, injustice, and a precarious future are still central issues.

And theology is not a stranger to these social, economic, and political questions—particularly, Catholic theology, considering that most Latin American people on our continent are still Catholic, despite other religions' growth trends in recent times. These trends are mostly Protestant: Pentecostals, among the new ones, and religions of the African matrix among the older ones, according to the 2010 census.[1] Being a Catholic in Latin America and thinking about this Catholic identity is surely a process not exempt from novelties and complexities at this precise moment in the continent's history.

A Multicultural Reality

In Latin American society, the modernization process has come with a foreign face rather than an indigenous one as has been the case in Europe and North America. The colonization movement—in which the three major traditions that form Brazil's cultural backdrop (Portuguese, African, and indigenous) have come together—is, then, not free from complexity or problematic aspects. These cultures also blended in different ways, such that Brazil and the Caribbean countries have a greater incidence of African religions, very different from other Latin American cultures that developed in the wake of Spanish colonization.[2] This has led, in turn, to the fact that the Brazilian and Caribbean cultural and symbolic universes exist together and are simultaneously premodern, modern, and postmodern.[3] As a result, Brazilian and Caribbean cultures and religiosity have suffered the impact of the modernization crisis in a very specific and unique way.

Brazilian and Caribbean religious identities today have been greatly influenced by several factors: differences between urban and rural areas, the syncretism proper to cultures that were born already marked by miscegenation, and the inadequacy of many of the modern theoretical paradigms to deal with this unique synthesis. Although the other countries, those born from Spanish colonization, did not have the same cultural cradle, elements of mixed cultures also have impacted religion there. For instance, in the

---

1. In 2012, the Catedra Carlo Maria Martini of the Pontifical Catholic University of Rio de Janeiro (PUC-Rio) organized a seminar with scholars and representatives of various religions in Brazil. The fruit of this seminar will appear as a collective book edited by PUC-Rio Press.

2. See Freyre and Santa Rosa Júnior, *Casa grande e senzala*, and Holanda, *Roots of Brazil*.

3. See the book published by the Brazilian Bishops' Conference, *Para onde vai a cultura brasileira?*, and especially Azevedo, *Dinâmicas atuais da cultura brasileira*, 15–47.

Andean countries, like Peru and Bolivia, and in Mexico, the indigenous culture is still a very present influence on the way that Catholic faith is lived and celebrated. However, Latin America remains a continent with a majority of Catholics, and Catholicism continues to hold an important place in the whole of Latin American religious culture.

The religious plurality in which Latin American Roman Catholicism grew and developed has given it an extremely rich and significant identity. The Catholic Church there, "at the end of the world," has always had to confront challenges and questions that have given it a quite different configuration from the Church in other latitudes. The plurality of distinct African, indigenous, and European identities living side by side with the Roman Catholic faith has obliged the Church to search constantly—in a dynamic process—for its identity, which is the very heart of its cultural and religious shape. Catholics living in South America have always had to search for a different synthesis, uniquely their own, at each step and each moment. Herein lies a good part of the secret—that is, the capacity of Latin American Catholicism to find new and original answers to the challenges of the times (economic, social, or cultural) and to open spaces and paths to dialogue with the different religions and cultures that reside alongside it.

Initially, the Catholic faith appeared with the European conquest's colonial movement and was itself also a conqueror.[4] The result was, on the one hand, a distance created between the people and their understanding of the sacred, and, on the other hand, overhasty attempts at syncretism, which proved to be neither very conscious nor very consistent.[5] As an example, in countries like Brazil, "the singing of the saints was not always in harmony with the dance of the orixás."[6]

Over four centuries, Europeans uprooted millions of Africans from their homeland and established them mostly in Brazil, Venezuela, Colombia, Cuba, the Dominican Republic, and also the English and French Caribbean. Bound in slavery in the Americas, the half of them who survived the transatlantic trip suffered a process of "deculturation" that left them, almost exclusively, with their religion as a means of affirming their past, history, and traditions.[7] Sometimes, the resulting forms of syncretism hid the Afri-

---

4. See Frisotti, *Passos no diálogo*, and also the issue of "Consciência negra" in *Revista Humanidades* 47 (December 1999).

5. Regarding the concept of syncretism or "mix of cultures and religions," see Soares, *Sincretismo e inculturação*.

6. "Orixá" is the name given to the saints and divinities of Afro-Brazilian religions.

7. In terms of the dialogue among religions and the inculturation of faith, some points should be clarified: "deculturation" is the loss of a people's own values and meanings; "enculturation" is a socialization into the ethnic-mythic nucleus and elements of

can protest against oppression more than it preserved the original "corpus" of beliefs. Even so, an Afro-Black "diaspora" culture emerged, expressed in a new family—the *familia de Santo* (saintly family, meaning the religious community)—united in the search of the "*axé*," the vital force, which was created and made visible in diverse religions' forms of expression.

The Africans brought by the Portuguese to work as slaves in Brazil faced the obligation of being baptized into, and adopting, the colonizer's religion. They pretended to accept this religion while giving the names of Catholic divinities or saints to their own "orixás." Something similar happened in the Caribbean countries, where the practice of Catholicism sometimes coincided with the practice of Santería.[8] This strategy of resistance allowed the Africans to maintain relatively peaceful relationships with the whites without actually adopting their religions. Instead, they continued to practice their own under the guise of Catholicism.

This miscegenation of races and multiple religious belongings converged with the social injustice created by slavery and impacted both the indigenous and Africans. Slavery had many different faces throughout Latin American countries: in Brazil, white landlords sometimes procreated with female African slaves, resulting in more miscegenation, while in countries like Mexico and Peru, the indigenous could insert themselves into society and function within it, racial characteristics notwithstanding. Slavery has always been an extremely negative seal, present since the beginning of Latin American history. It resulted in the exclusion of citizens from rights as basic as food, health, and education, creating a situation of poverty and misery that some countries still experience today.

The number of people living in poverty in Latin America and the Caribbean has dropped to its lowest level in three decades due to higher wages and more jobs.[9] However, despite lower poverty levels overall, 167 million people in the region are still considered poor. That is one million fewer than in 2011, or about 29 percent of the region's population. Of those, sixty-six million remain stuck in extreme poverty. And that is, more or less,

---

the civilization of the original culture; "acculturation" is the asymmetric integration, or adaptation, between cultures (which transforms the otherness into a differentiated type of sameness, in folklore); and "inculturation" is the manner in which people re-create their lifestyle, starting from the dialogue of faith with another culture and religion. We follow the definitions and concepts accepted by Suess (see his "Inculturação, desafios, caminhos, metas"), which will be more appropriate as this theme is reanalyzed, a task I will take up later, based on Torres Queiruga (and his concept of "inreligionization") and Basarab Nicolescu (and his perspective of transcultural dialogue).

8. See the excellent work of Espin del Prado, "Evangelización y religiones negras."

9. This is according to a 2012 report issued by the U. N. Economic Commission for Latin America and the Caribbean. See Associated Press, "Poverty in Latin America."

one-third of the whole population. The most recent statistics for eighteen countries indicate that, on average, the richest 10 percent of Latin America's population receives 32 percent of the total income, while the poorest 40 percent receives 15 percent of the total income, making it one of the most unequal regions in the world. Women and children are especially vulnerable to poverty in Latin America. Underage minors make up 51 percent of those living in extreme poverty.[10]

The deep and ongoing poverty experienced by so many in Latin America and the Caribbean has challenged the continent's Christian churches, especially the predominant Catholic Church; the Catholic Church responded with the Second Vatican Council in the 1960s, which brought with it a new face for Latin American Catholicism and a turning point in the way the Catholic faith was lived south of the Rio Grande.

The 1970s, 1980s, and 1990s: A Catholicism of the Poor

The Second Vatican Council concluded in 1965. It left behind a good deal of enthusiasm and hope as well as less positive feelings. In the Latin American air, we could taste and smell a new spring. The whole world received what the Latin American church was experiencing in terms of this new way of being church: a church in dialogue with the world and with earthly things.[11]

For the Catholic Church in Latin America, it was the beginning of a new era. The Church ached to be a "source" church and not only a "reflex" church, the latter of which merely replicated—uncreatively—Europe's situation in a very different cultural context. That was the spirit with which Latin American bishops convoked the conference of Medellín in 1968.

The event in Medellín, Colombia, gathered all of the continent's bishops together with theologians and pastoral ministers. And still today, Medellín is a pivotal moment in the history of Latin American Catholicism. Medellín was an event created by the Spirit of God who renewed this part of the planet, calling attention to the centrality of justice, which is the essence of the gospel message and of the Church's mission. With that, Medellín introduced Latin America, and the whole world, to a new way of being church: a church of service, committed to justice and to finding a new place in the margins of history, a place where the poor were clamoring for liberation. The conference's concluding document said, "This continues to be the time of the word, but has also become, with dramatic urgency, the time of

---

10. Associated Press, "Poverty in Latin America."
11. See *Gaudium et Spes*.

action."[12] The Latin American church, inspired by the Spirit, understood that it was time to act in favor of those whose destinies were oppressed and diminished by poverty.

In Medellín—three years after Vatican II—Latin American bishops stated that they no longer wanted to be a church that "reflected" guidelines and priorities issued from afar, but one that was a *source* of new thought emerging from the Latin American context.[13] The Medellín bishops, in their conclusion, highlighted three major points: (1) to connect the preaching of the gospel with the practice of justice, (2) to consider the mysteries of revelation from the perspective of the poor, and (3) to inaugurate a new way of being a church, by gathering lay people from the poorest parts of the continent to interpret the Bible in a transformative way.[14]

In 1979, the Latin American Conference of Bishops (CELAM) in Puebla, Mexico, reaffirmed those three points, officially instituting a system of grassroots groups called Basic Ecclesial Communities, preferentially ministering to, and existing for, the poor. This new theology was dubbed "liberation theology."[15] In 2007, the Fifth Conference of Latin American bishops met in Aparecida, Brazil, and brought attention to the importance of ministering to the poor. In the opening speech, Pope Benedict XVI reconfirmed this option as an evangelical one, no longer to be discussed in terms of validity, for it is already implicit in the christological faith in God, who became poor for us in order to enrich us with his poverty.[16]

The poor are the center of Christian life, essential in Gustavo Gutiérrez's definition of liberation theology, "a critical reflection on praxis."[17] Gutiérrez affirms nevertheless that liberation theology neither starts nor departs from a simple critical analysis of reality, but instead from a mystical experience: a deep encounter with the Lord in the face of the poor.[18] From here, a system and discourse are developed: to see, judge, and act.[19] In

12. Latin American Episcopal Council, *Medellín: conclusiones*, introduction.

13. See the reflection of the great Brazilian philosopher Henrique C. de Lima Vaz, "Igreja-reflexo vs. Igreja-fonte."

14. See Latin American Episcopal Council, *Medellín: conclusiones*. See also the comments and reflections following Medellín—for instance, Brighenti, "A opção pelos pobres."

15. See Boff, "A originalidade historica de Medellin."

16. See Benedict XVI, "Address at the Inaugural Session [Aparecida]."

17. See Gutiérrez, *A Theology of Liberation*.

18. See ibid.

19. This method had been systematized by the lay movement Catholic Action (*Action Catholique*), which originated in France and was very strong in Latin America in the 1950s and 1960s. It helped Christians who engaged socially in the search for a critical understanding of reality and commitment with transformative action.

an oppressive context, there can be no theology without social analysis (to see), which must then be tied to the Scriptures (to judge). The transformative stage (to act) will then emerge, inspire, and guide the commitment and political positions of Christians.[20] This theology was not meant to remain only in books and academic courses, but instead to relate back to the poor and help put into action their actual liberation process. Liberation theology sought to build a new society by struggling alongside the poor and making them the subjects of their own history.[21]

It is worth saying that this idea was not invented by liberation theology. For twenty centuries of church history, the poor have occupied the center of attention for Christian social teaching. The poor, the saints, and the mystics were—for the church fathers—subjects of a privileged form of love.[22] The novelty here is that the Catholic Church in Latin America inaugurated a movement within the Church, which had a strong social and political impact on the configuration of the continent's society. It was not an individual task, the attention to the poor, but a commitment from the whole Church. To confirm that, it is worth remembering that after the Second Vatican Council, in 1968, the Church moved toward greater secularization; Pope John XXIII defined the Church as the Church of the poor.[23]

The Option for the Poor: The Heart of a Reformed Theology

The preferential option for the poor is not a recent invention but one of the basic principles of the Catholic social teaching tradition.[24] It is present in the Church's canon law, which states that "the Christian faithful are obliged to promote social justice and, mindful of the precept of the Lord, to assist the

---

20. The method of this theology is inductive and not deductive. Rather than revelation and ecclesial tradition, for theological interpretations applied to life, it departs from realities of poverty and exclusion, and the commitment to liberation, to do a theological reflection and invite transformative action of this same reality. It brings also a critique of modern theology and its pretension to universality, considering it Eurocentric and unconnected to the reality of poor and peripheral countries.

21. See Leonardo and Clodovis Boff, "A Concise History of Liberation Theology."

22. See the works of Ambrosius, Chrysostomus, etc.

23. The phrase "Church of the poor" was first used by Pope John XXIII in his inaugural address to the Fathers of the Vatican Council in 1962.

24. For instance, Leo XIII in *Rerum Novarum*, Pius XI in *Quadragesimo Anno*, and John XXIII in *Mater et Magistra* and *Pacem in Terris*—and, before them, the Fathers of the Church. See, for instance, Saint Ambrose: "You are not making a gift of your possessions to the poor person. You are handing over to him what is his. For what has been given in common for the use of all, you have arrogated to yourself. The world is given to all, and not only to the rich."

poor from their own resources."[25] What Vatican II did was to call the faithful back to the origins of their faith and to live it fully in commitment to justice and charity. The phrase "option for the poor" was first used in 1968, in a letter to the Jesuits of Latin America from Fr. Pedro Arrupe, SJ, then the superior general of the Society of Jesus.[26] The Peruvian priest Gustavo Gutiérrez further developed the concrete consequences of this option as a theological principle in his landmark book, *A Theology of Liberation*.

In fact, liberation theology was never a purely academic practice, but it was also an ecclesial one meant to help the Church develop a clearer goal to serve the poor.[27] Liberation theologians were simply trying to return to the source, the core of the gospel: blessed are the poor.[28] Conversion implies and includes not only "helping" the poor with charitable handouts but also a willingness to live like them, to experience—even to a limited extent—what they endure. It implies participating in, and "empathizing" with, their suffering and condition and then, from within, helping the poor become artisans of their own history and destiny. As Gutiérrez states,

> When it is lived in authentic imitation of Christ, the witness of poverty does not alienate us from the world at all . . . Only through concrete acts of love and solidarity can we effectively realize our encounter with the poor and the exploited and, through them, with Jesus Christ. To give to them is to say yes to Christ.[29]

Many questions arose from this change made by the Latin American church, which built its new methodology to be closer to the poor. Groups of Catholics formed who tried different models of "following" Christ by following the poor. However, other groups—middle-class Catholics, for example—rejected the idea of becoming poor as the only way to live their faith and complained that their Church was neglecting them. That was when Clodovis Boff, one of the most prominent liberation theologians, came up with a typology that helped broach an understanding of what it meant to share the life of the poor, making the option for the poor preferential (but not exclusive), while respecting one's state of life, work, and familial commitments. Boff stated that every Christian must commit to the option for

---

25. Catholic Church, *Code of Canon Law*, 222 §2.

26. This letter, now known as "Carta de Río," was addressed to the Jesuits of Latin America.

27. See Brighenti, "A opção pelos pobres."

28. See Matt 5, Luke 6, etc.

29. Gutiérrez, *A Theology of Liberation*.

the poor, because this is the only way to truly follow Jesus Christ.[30] Early fathers of the Church—such as Irenaeus,[31] Chrysostomus,[32] Ambrose,[33] and others—repeat this idea in different but also radical ways. Life circumstances can be, and often are, diverse. However, this mandate for all Christians also has diverse nuances when put into practice. For example, one can opt for the poor with a *conversion of interests*. A person can, on the one hand, hold a respectable position among peers and the public, and on the other hand redirect skills, capabilities, and efforts toward the needs of the poor to help and empower them, thus ensuring a social impact and making systems more just and society more fair.

One can also opt for the poor by *alternating* one's social standing with theirs. That is the case of many Christians, both religious and lay people, who work for a living during the week but on the weekend help in a poor neighborhood. Those who teach at a university can spend holidays living among the poor, giving classes, building houses, or providing free medical or dental consultations and services. To some extent, they share in the living conditions of those who are poor, if only for a certain number of hours, days, or weeks.

A third way of living the option for the poor is through *incarnation*: cutting ties with a previous life—including comfort, privacy, time, and money—and going out to share entirely in the life of the poor. There have been many people—lay, monks, and clergy—who have done this and continue to do so still.[34] As Gustavo Gutiérrez writes with strength and prophetic passion,

> Love of neighbor is an essential component of Christian life. But as long as I apply that term only to the people who cross my path and come asking me for help, my world will remain pretty much the same. Individual almsgiving and social reformism is a type of love that never leaves its own front porch . . . But the existence of the poor . . . is not neutral on the political level or innocent of ethical implications. Poor people are by-products of the system under which we live and for which we are responsible . . . That is

---

30. Boff and Pixley, *Opção pelos pobres*.

31. "The glory of God is a human being 'fully alive'" (*Against Heresies*, Book 4, 20:7).

32. "Not to enable the poor to share in our goods is to steal from them and deprive them of life. The goods we possess are not ours, but theirs" (*On Wealth and Poverty* 2, 5, PG 48, 992).

33. "The rich man who gives to the poor does not bestow alms but pays a debt."

34. See, for instance, those nuns who live in the poorest parts of the Amazon, or with the indigenous in the Bolivian altiplano, or in favelas in large Latin American cities, etc.

why the poverty of the poor is not a summons to alleviate their plight with acts of generosity but rather a compelling obligation to fashion an entirely different social order.[35]

The option for the poor, liberation theology, and Basic Ecclesial Communities were ways of being conscious Catholics until the mid-1980s. Then, a movement of restoration began within the Church, and it spread also (and primarily) to Latin America. Many theologians were silenced or punished. Publications underwent censorship. The publication of the Theology and Liberation Series, envisioned as having fifty volumes, was interrupted.

Two Vatican documents, *Libertatis Conscientia* and *Libertatis Nuntius*, written by the Congregaton for the Doctrine of the Faith, presided over by Cardinal Joseph Ratzinger, future Pope Benedict XVI, included very critical statements about liberation theology. *Libertatis Nuntius* pointed to three motivating factors that led to liberation theology: (1) the impatience and desire for efficiency of some Christians, who, having lost confidence in any other method, adopted a Marxist analysis; (2) those Christians thought that an intolerable situation demanded an efficient action that could no longer be postponed, and an efficient action supposed a scientific analysis of the structural causes of misery. Marxism would be the instrument for such an analysis, and it needed to be applied to Latin America's situation; (3) a totalizing concept that imposed its logic and brought liberation theologies to accept numerous positions that were incompatible with the Christian vision of the human being. The ideological core, taken from Marxism and serving as the point of reference, exercises the role of determining principle.

After these two documents, liberation theology and the organizations within the Church related to the privilege of the poor began to face a difficult period. In 1989, with the fall of the Berlin Wall, a dark depression settled upon Catholic activists in Latin America. Nevertheless, what happened then was that those groups started to discover other areas of focus for pastoral interest, work, and resistance.

Liberation theology extended its range of interests beyond economic injustices and social struggles. Issues such as ecology, gender, racism, and ethnicity also entered its agenda. Although less numerous, Basic Ecclesial Communities continued to exist, and the popular reading of the Bible, according to Carlos Mesters' method, continued to be a strong influence and inspiration.[36]

35. Gutiérrez, "Liberation Praxis and Christian Faith," 8.

36. Carlos Mesters is a Carmelite priest from the Netherlands who has a PhD in biblical studies from the Pontifical Bible Institute in Jerusalem. During his time in Brazil, he has worked on a method for a popular reading of the Bible based on the Catholic Action method (to see; to judge; to act): *fato da vida* (reality); *texto iluminador* (biblical text); *ação transformadora* (transformative action).

In the 1990s, interreligious dialogue began to capture the attention and efforts of liberation theologians. Given that Latin America—as we saw, from the beginning of its history—was a very plural continent in terms of ethnicity, culture, and religion, Catholic theology discovered that it was impossible to elaborate its reflection without a deep, sincere, and fruitful dialogue with other religious traditions. And that dialogue bore very good fruit for the Latin American church.

Nonetheless, it is undeniable that Latin American Catholicism was then facing a significant change. This change coincided with movements within the Church that shaped the moment in which we live now, in the second decade of the new millennium: the new Catholic movements that were so strongly present in the Aparecida document and the growth of Pentecostal Protestantism.

The Census of 2010: The Decline of Catholicism

In absolute numbers, the number of Catholics worldwide has quadrupled in a century. In 1910, there were 291 million; today, there are 1.1 billion. Not all parts of the world, however, show an expansion. Europe, seat of the Holy See, and North America are home today to only 32 percent of the world's Catholics—less than a third. The fact is that Catholicism is less Eurocentric and more global than ever. Two-thirds of the Church's faithful are now in Latin America, Africa, and Asia. In Latin America, from 1910 to 2010, the total number of Catholics increased from 70 million to 425 million, or 45 percent of the global total. In Asia, the number rose from 14 million to 131 million.

The largest explosion, however, occurred in Africa. In 1910, the African continent was home to about 1 million faithful (1 percent of the world total). Today, there are 171 million (16 percent). The data also point to an important change in the ranking of the countries with the largest Catholic populations. In 1910, the top-ranking country was France, with 40 million Catholics, followed by Italy with 35 million. Brazil was third with 21 million, compared to 16 million in Germany and 14 million in Mexico.

By 2010, however, Brazil had established itself as the largest Catholic country in the world, with 126 million faithful (although the percentage of Catholics within the Brazilian population itself fell from 96 to 65 percent). Mexico takes "second place" with 96 million Catholics, followed by the Philippines and the United States, each with 75 million. And for the first time, an African country has entered the "top ten": the Democratic Republic of Congo is home to 31 million Catholics.

The 2007 Aparecida document acknowledges the challenges that are happening throughout the world and throughout our continent. There are several significant changes underway that accompany this global shift of Catholicism: (1) religious pluralism and the loss of historic Christianity's hegemony; (2) the need for ecumenical dialogue and macroecumenism; (3) the spiraling poverty and injustice present on the Latin American continent, which have only increased over the decades (it is scandalous that, on the continent of hope—the largest Catholic continent in the world—a full one-third of the population lives below the poverty line); and (4) a change in how the Church's standards and guidelines are received—namely, the personal synthesis that many Catholics undertake insofar as their personal morality or lifestyle does not always match up with formal Church teaching. And yet these Catholics still feel that they are part of the Church. In other words, there are new forms of believing and evangelizing that are constantly unfolding and need to be studied carefully.

While the Latin American continent is still home to 39 percent of the world's total Catholic population, this percentage is dropping. At the beginning of the last century, Catholics made up 90 percent of the Latin American population—in 2010, the number was down to 72 percent. Brazil in 1940 was 95 percent Catholic; even though it ranks as the country with the most followers in the world today, it has been losing millions.

The Aparecida document points to shadows of excessive secularization in most segments of the Church, such as the religious life, and it points to the need to overcome this state of affairs. It also points to the exodus of Catholics to the Pentecostal faith and other evangelical religions, resulting in significant losses for the Church. Along with this has come the decline in priestly vocations, the shrinking number of faithful, etc. The document calls on Catholics to dispel these shadows and to promote such particular strengths as the parish, the diocese, the new movements, and the family, the first agent of evangelization (although it is a family that, in my view, no longer corresponds to the plurality of family forms that exist among Latin American Catholics). The solutions that the Aparecida document presents to dispel the shadows that persist in the Christian life of the continent are, in my view, still timid and somewhat problematic. As an example, I cite the problem of many Catholic communities that are unable to participate in the Eucharist on Sunday because there is no clergy available in their location. They are thus deprived of that which is the central mystery of Catholicism.

Some recent studies contend that this crisis of Catholicism is, in fact, a process of *detraditionalization*. The argument is that there is a process of transformation of Catholic culture, which has inhibited the transmission of Catholicism by tradition.[37] The reflections I have presented here about Catholicism in Brazil could also be applied, more broadly speaking, to most other Latin American countries. For instance, it could be said that in most Latin American countries, the continual decline in the number of Catholics should be interpreted as part of a much larger cultural process that transcends the Catholic Church's capacity to control or influence the loss of members, the action of new religious agents, or the success of other churches and groups that attract and congregate them.[38]

Catholicism continues to lose faithful at a rapid pace. Between 1990 and 2000, the disaffiliation process had grown very much within Catholicism, as is demonstrated by the study of Paulo Fernando Carneiro de Andrade of the Department of Theology at the Pontifical Catholic University of Rio de Janeiro.[39] In the decade 2000–2010, it kept the same pace. Over the course of these two decades, the Catholic population of Brazil has fallen by nearly 19.2 percent. If, in 1970, Catholics still comprised 91.7 percent of our population, now that percentage is down to 64.6. This process of disaffiliation has been accompanied by rapid growth in the evangelical sector: from 5.8 percent of the Brazilian population in 1970 to 22.2 percent in 2010. It has only been in recent decades that the country has gained more evangelicals: 13.2 percent of the population. One should take into account that the number who became evangelicals in this twenty-year period is even greater, since part of this group is comprised of those who are always in transit from one religion to another—for example, from Catholicism to Pentecostalism to no religion—or converts from Pentecostalism to Catholicism, according to a 2002 survey by CERIS.[40]

Even if the continent is the largest reserve of Catholics of the world, the fact is that Latin American Catholicism is in an accelerated process of losing members. And, obviously, the Vatican is concerned and thinking about ways to reverse this trend. For William Cook, professor of history at SUNY, the changes initiated by Ratzinger—most especially his resignation—symbolize a more global church facing the drop in the number of believers in Europe, while Africa and Latin America have a greater number of Catholics. In twenty-five more years, only one in five Catholics will be

---

37. See Steil and Toniol, "O catolicismo e a igreja católica no Brasil."
38. Ibid.
39. See Andrade, "As religiões no Brasil," 93–98.
40. CERIS (Centro de Estudos da Religião e Investigações Sociais) is a branch of the Brazilian Bishops' Conference that studies and publishes statistics related to the Catholic Church and other religions in the country.

white and non-Hispanic, according to Cook. "Benedict XVI recognizes that the world has changed and he is forcing the papacy to recognize that."[41]

Conclusion: What Can We Expect for Latin America from the New Pope?

The joyous announcement of having a new pope was a great surprise for many, and the name announced—Jorge Mario Bergoglio—was not the one expected. When Francis arrived at the balcony overlooking St. Peter's Square, with a cheerful and joyful voice, he said, "Good evening," and also, before giving the blessing to the crowd, asked for prayers and blessings for himself. With this, all over the world, there was a feeling of a new beginning, a new paschal time.

Ever since that moment, the new pope's simplicity and modest style have captivated everyone. His words are sealed with a central concern—the poor—and all of us who have heard him have discovered how much we have missed hearing these words from the pope's lips.

Coming from the Southern Hemisphere, from "the end of the world," where poverty and injustice destroy human lives, Francis does not forget—or allow others to forget—whom the Church he oversees must serve. In addition, his faith proclaims that those whom the world considers the least and the last are—and truly must be—the most dear and preferred by God. Therefore, they must be the first and preferential option of Christ's Church.

The Argentinean pope magnetizes attention and radiates contagious strength and joy. His first few gestures slowly revealed his character and style: refusing to use official cars and luxurious clothes; coming down from the altar to embrace a sick person during his inauguration ceremony; washing and kissing the feet of a Muslim woman during Holy Thursday Mass.

Francis speaks as he acts, and his words reflect the figure with whom he wanted to identify by the name he adopted: Francis of Assisi, the "poverello," who loved poverty as a bride and served the poor as his dearest friends. It was this same Francis who heard from the crucified Christ of San Damiano the loving demand, "Francis, rebuild my Church."

Catholics all over the world, and specifically in Latin America, feel a great deal of hope with the start of Francis's pontificate. They can sense once again the joy of Vatican II in the air through his words and actions that center on ecumenism and interreligious dialogue, ecclesial collegiality, and liturgical reformation.

---

41. Louriero, "Bento XVI mudou a ideia do que é ser papa."

However, perhaps one of the most beautiful surprises, which touches the very heart of the Latin American church, will be to see the poor return as a central concern of the Church. "How much I would like a Church that is poor and for the poor!" the Pope said during an audience, using the words of John XXIII.

Coming from the end of the world, from those latitudes where inequity and oppression are present on such a large scale, Francis is conscientious and calls such injustice by its name: social sin.[42] We can expect, then, that during his pontificate the Latin American church will recover its proper means of doing theology. That includes all the questions of the poor and victims as primordial content and method in order to be able to pronounce a qualified word about reality.[43]

This is an exciting—and very hopeful—moment in history to be a Catholic in the Southern Hemisphere.

---

42. See his words at Aparecida in Allen, "CELAM Update": "The unjust distribution of goods continues, creating a situation of social sin which cries out to heaven and limits the possibilities for a fuller life for many of our brothers."

43. Everyone who followed his words and actions at World Youth Day 2013 in Rio de Janeiro could see how eager he was to be close to the simple, the poorest; he entered some homes in poor areas, praying with the people, even though they were from other religious backgrounds.

13

A Crown of Counterrevolutionary Thorns? Mexico's Consecration to the Sacred Heart: January 6, 1914[1]

MATTHEW BUTLER

Almost one hundred years hence, the consecration of the Mexican nation to the Sacred Heart of Jesus on January 6, 1914, remains a controversial moment in the religious history of the Mexican Revolution. In good measure, this is because this national vow of consecration—with its simultaneous enthronement of the Sacred Heart as "Christ the King" (*Jesucristo Rey*)—has too often been viewed as a semiofficial festival, the aim of which was to solemnize the military dictatorship of General Victoriano Huerta (1913–14). Because of this allegedly "counterrevolutionary" character, the 1914 consecration is frequently cited as an important factor in the genesis of revolutionary anticlericalism circa 1914–15.[2] Catholic historians of a

---

1. Leonor Correa Etchegaray, Ben Fallaw, Yves Solís, José Alberto Moreno Chávez, Valentina Torres Septién, and Ed Wright-Rios kindly commented on a previous draft of this paper. I would also like to thank the organizers of World Catholicism Week ("The Borders of Baptism: Multiple Belongings and Transnational Processes of Catholic Formation," DePaul University, April 14–19, 2013) for their invitation to participate.

2. For Michael Meyer, who absolves Huerta of many other charges, "the most convincing suggestion" of a Huerta-Church alliance is to be found in the 1914 ceremonies (*Huerta*, 168–69). Jean Meyer avers that the Constitutionalist revolutionaries saw the consecration as "the worst of all insults," for in their eyes it contained "proof positive of the alliance between the saber and the aspergillum [sprinkler] and of the Church's collusion in the usurpation" (*La cristiada*, 91–93). Knight, *Mexican Revolution*, argues that large sectors of the clergy celebrated the Huerta coup (2:1–2), even though Huerta was no clerical instrument (2:5, 99); the supposed link between *huertismo* and clericalism, Knight continues, as expressed in the consecration, to a great extent explains the anticlerical outbursts of 1914 and later (2:203–9). This claim, we might add, simply takes Constitutionalist rhetoric at face value. The problem, of course, is how to separate

conservative bent, it is true, fan the flames of the polemic by interpreting the consecration not merely as the proclamation of Christ's social kingdom by the Church but as an act of state submission to the Church, one that was supposedly condoned by Huerta himself. That is to say, no less than prorevolutionary historians, the Catholic right exaggerates the statist character of the coronation by painting Huerta—like some Huichol García Moreno—as the architect of a confessional state that was gifted to the Church through the Sacred Heart ceremony.[3]

Given the consecration's supposed importance to the political history of *huertismo*, however, it is surprising that the *huertista* political class shows such scant interest in it. The consecration is not mentioned by any important political actors of the time in their memoirs: not by Nemesio García Naranjo or Querido Moheno—both of them members of the notorious congressional *cuadrilátero* and Huerta's cabinet; not by Toribio Esquivel Obregón, for a time Huerta's treasury secretary, and not by the pious Federico Gamboa; it is not even mentioned in the memoirs of Doctor Urrutia, military surgeon and, as interior minister, the regime's political fixer with responsibility for religious affairs.[4] The consecration is also absent from the memoirs, considered apocryphal, of Huerta himself;[5] and we find no mention in the diaries and travelogues of the most prominent foreign observers—O'Shaughnessey, Bell, and Leander de Bekker.[6] On the contrary, the most controversial religious question of the day seems to have been the political dispute that followed Huerta's appointment as minister of public education, without prior congressional approval, of the Tlaxcalan Catholic deputy Eduardo Tamariz; failing that, it was Huerta's much-derided declaration to Congress, made

---

empirical evidence of political clericalism from the accusers' own political considerations and ideological predispositions, and to see how far such claims derive from demonstrable fact or from the character of Constitutionalism. As Knight shows, for example, the Constitutionalists also accused the Zapatistas and Villistas of clericalism (2:213, 288 respectively), which suggests that anticlericalism functioned as an identity marker or cultural-political trait of the movement. Knight synthesizes these lines of analysis in "The Mentality and *Modus Operandus* of Revolutionary Anticlericalism."

3. See Barquín y Ruiz, *Cristo, Rey de México*, 125–75; Rius Facius, *De don Porfirio a Plutarco*, 7–54.

4. García Naranjo, *Memorias*, vol. 7; Moheno, *Mi actuación política*; Esquivel Obregón, *Mi labor en servicio de México*; Gamboa, *Mi diario*, vol. 6; Urrutia's memoir is reproduced in Ross, "Victoriano Huerta visto por su compadre," and see also Urrutia Martínez, *Aureliano Urrutia*.

5. Huerta, *Memorias de Victoriano Huerta*.

6. O'Shaughnessy, *Intimate Pages*; Bell, *Political Shame of Mexico*; De Bekker, *The Plot against Mexico*; and *De como vino Huerta*.

in his 1913 presidential address, that he stood before the nation as well as God.[7]

Returning to our theme, Huerta attended neither the national consecration to the Sacred Heart on January 6, 1914, nor the public homage to Christ the King celebrated on January 11; on the latter day, in fact, he went to the theater to watch a pro-Huerta revue—written in poor taste, according to Taracena—called *1913*.[8]

In more general terms, Huerta's relationship to the Catholic clergy was more opportunistic than intimate in accordance with his personal brand of religiosity, which was "semi-religious and semi-superstitious," in Moheno's words.[9] At the end of the *decena trágica*, for example—the ten-day battle in Mexico City that culminated in Huerta's usurpation and the execution of President Madero in February 1913—Huerta exacted a loan of twenty thousand pesos from Archbishop Mora y del Río, so as to feed his troops and prevent an orgy of looting.[10] Two months later, Huerta wrote to Mora to recommend the parish priest of Papalotla for a more substantial living in Mexico City; that is the only direct communication between the general and the archbishop that exists in the archive of the Archdiocese of Mexico.[11] On other occasions, Huerta kissed Archbishop Orozco y Jiménez's episcopal

---

7. García Naranjo, *Memorias*, 7:139–45, 357; *De como vino Huerta*, 324–34.

8. Taracena, *La verdadera revolución mexicana*, 134–37.

9. Moheno, *Mi actuación política*, 113–14. See also O'Shaughnessy, *Intimate Pages*, 280–81, for the most detailed religious portrait of Huerta: "[Huerta] probably does not 'love Jesus,' neither would he have called for hymns with 'more Jesus' in them had he been at Sunday-school. His true attitude was doubtless uncertainty . . . as to the essence and shape of the hereafter, mingled with an uneasy feeling that he ought to propitiate whatever gods there be by burnt or other offerings. That he recognized the value of the Catholic Church to the Indian, that it clothed in actual form the visions of the Indian race, that he had some instinctive, not theological, knowledge of its supreme and vital uses in government, also as an element of prosperity and happiness, I have no doubt. He knew, too, that society cannot exist without inequality of fortune, and that this inequality is impossible to support without religion. His enemies, and those of the Church, said he desired to maintain the Catholic Party to further his own ends. The Catholic Party on the contrary found that the Huerta cymbals, when struck, were apt to give back a faint and uncertain sound. He was in his usual position, on both horns of the dilemma. In the night that shrouds his birth, one cannot know if he were baptized in the faith, but he was married in the faith; he had his children baptized in the faith. As the world knows, he died in the faith. To him the Church was as integral a part of Mexico as her seasons, her rainfall, and her droughts. He was mostly respectful and conciliatory to the ministers of religion, doubtless recognizing the Church as one of the few available rocks on which to build his state; that he was completely uninterested (except politically) by dogma, I also do not doubt."

10. Ruiz y Flores, *Recuerdo de Recuerdos*, 66.

11. Huerta to Mora y del Río, Mexico City, April 17, 1913.

ring and then berated him because his diocesan leadership made life difficult for Jalisco's state governor (and fellow Catholic) José López Portillo y Rojas.[12] In late January 1914, indeed, Huerta dragged Orozco y Jiménez all the way to Mexico City and accused him of allowing the Guadalajara faithful to violate the Reform Laws during the procession in honor of Christ the King, which suggests a clear distance between the regime's political objectives and those of the Church.[13]

In sum, it is necessary to detach the consecration ceremony from too close an association with the political history (or historiography) of the Huerta dictatorship; at the very least, it must be stressed that the enthronement of the Sacred Heart as King of Kings, while partly political in nature, was not overtly, or even significantly, *huertista* in character. Above all, we must understand the consecration—a Catholic pageant without precedent in Mexico—more in terms of its own political context and devotional history,[14] and as a significant national and transnational moment.[15] In this sense, the consecration can be seen first as an attempt by the Mexican church to recuperate, in a radically different political context, the public and social space that had been lost with the Liberal Reform of the mid-nineteenth century and not entirely recovered during the long decades of the *Porfiriato* (1876–1911). At the same time, the consecration needs to be understood in light of the universal Church's response to modernity, given that its key objective was the expiation of the national "sin" of official *laïcité* via the Catholicization of the social order and the propagation of Catholic orthodoxy—but not the blessing of an illegitimate neo-Porfirian regime. From this perspective, and as we shall see when tracking the experience of the coronation in various Mexican dioceses, the coronation of the Sacred Heart of Jesus symbolized a Catholic-style modernity that was to be implanted across the Catholic world, not just in Huerta's Mexico. In a word, the consecration ceremony formed part of a project and an ideology that was more epochal than conjunctural.

12. García Naranjo, *Memorias*, 7:357–64.

13. Taracena, *La verdadera revolución mexicana*, 138.

14. It is curious, moreover, that the scholarly literature on Huerta is so silent on religious questions, except when rehearsing the claim of ecclesiastical complicity in the usurpation of February 1913. See, for example, Delgado, *Aspecto agrario*; Mancisidor, "El huertismo," 34–51; Sherman and Greenleaf, *Victoriano Huerta*; Arenas Guzmán, *El régimen del general Huerta*; Langle Ramírez, *El militarismo de Victoriano Huerta*; Tuñón Pablos, *Huerta y el movimiento obrero*; MacGregor, "Una Perspectiva del Régimen Huertista"; Ramírez Rancaño, "La república castrense de Victoriano Huerta," 167–213.

15. Transnational studies of revolutionary-era Mexican Catholicism are only just beginning. See, for instance, Young, "*Cristero* Diaspora," 271–300; Edwards, *Roman Virtues*.

Put another way, the ceremonies of 1914 formed a belated part of Mexico's devotional revolution[16] of the late nineteenth and early twentieth centuries, which has been so well studied for Archbishop Gillow's Oaxaca by Edward Wright-Rios.[17] As much in Mexico City as in Oaxaca, the coronation of images with pontifical insignia was a key part of the consolidation of a "modern" Catholic culture that was meant to buttress the Church against the secular state. The first fruits of this process were meant to include the professionalization of the clergy in a context of bureaucratic (and hierarchical) centralization involving both the Mexican bishops and Rome; the fomenting of a lay piety that was heavily sacramental in character; and the incorporation of the lay faithful in regimented pious/canonical associations such as the Apostleship of Prayer and Mexican Nocturnal Adoration. As Wright-Rios well argues, the main Porfirian coronation ceremonies (those of the Virgin of Guadalupe in 1895, or the Virgin of Solitude in Oaxaca in 1909) represented the symbolic culmination of this change, in that they visually marked the new influence that Rome exercised over national churches in a mutual bid to resist the advances of the liberal state. No matter how much the popular character of these ceremonial coronations was also stressed, however, at bottom the aim was to resignify local devotions and mobilize the faithful that sustained them in accordance with a new spirit of Catholic intransigence. That is, the aim was to link local devotions with modern religious practices, a mass "spirit of association," and a renovated line of clerical command. It is this sense of pious rebooting that gives rise to Wright-Rios's comparative critique of Mexico vis à vis nineteenth-century Europe: unlike their counterparts in Europe, the Mexican bishops wished to mobilize their pious legions and meet secularism head on but without encouraging any corresponding reports of divine revelation on Mexican soil. By gambling on the enduring spiritual appeal of old colonial icons, Wright-Rios argues, the Mexican bishops broke the strong dialectical association between the social and political stresses of modernization and the consolation of imminent theophany, an association that had underwritten a powerful sense of religious expectation in parts of Catholic Europe. In the end, the Mexican bishops piloted a Marianism that was partially modernized in the fashion of modern European devotions.[18]

16. I borrow the term from Emmet Larkin's classic thesis on the transformation of nineteenth-century Irish Catholicism, "The Devotional Revolution," 625–52.

17. Wright-Rios, *Revolutions in Mexican Catholicism*.

18. For the 1895 coronation of the Guadalupe, for example, a Lourdesian, French-style model was tried, right down to the modernizing of the mountaintop shrine as a sort of grotto and (very controversially) the alleged airbrushing of the Guadalupe image. The Guadalupe was reconceptualized on clerical lines, in sum, as a symbol

Since it was more a question of adding new and Eurocentric brios to old colonial devotions, without injecting a necessary infusion of modern grace, the coronations typically produced "quasi-devotions," short-lived recalibrations that marshaled popular spirituality and placed it at the service of a reformist ecclesiastical project with centralizing tendencies.[19] As such, many of the Mexican coronations enjoyed only brief success: popular pilgrimages were steered by clergy and now ended in sacramental clinics; the landscape surrounding the shrines was Europeanized, and the vestments of the icons grew more regal; yet, in many cases, once the churches had filled for that dramatic moment when an imported filigree coronet would be placed atop the head of an old saint, the intended synthesis of indigenous piety, modern Catholic practice, and resurgent ecclesiastical majesty collapsed. At least in indigenous areas, the Porfirian coronations created rather parallel religious meanings, or, more precisely, gave rise to a constant negotiation between official and popular Catholicisms within a common Marian repertoire, rather than a simple clash between traditional and modern Catholics.[20]

---

of militant anti-secularism, "Mexico's Mary Immaculate," as opposed to a symbol of providential *mestizaje*: the participation of lay and indigenous Catholics, meanwhile, was minimized or made passive. See Wright-Rios, *Revolutions in Mexican Catholicism*, 73–97, especially 85–87; Brading, *Mexican Phoenix*, 288–310; Adame Goddard, "Significado de la coronación," 187–98; Ceballos Ramírez, "Siglo XIX y guadalupanismo," 317–32; and Traslosheros, "Señora de la historia," 105–30. The European roots of the Mexican coronations are discussed by Tapia Méndez, *José Antonio Plancarte y Labastida*, 75, 119–23, 152, 158, 197–200, 202–10, 215–58, 293–96, who shows that Mexico's coronation boom—of which the Michoacán priest José Antonio Plancarte y Labastida was the real architect—was inspired by various Mexican and European sources. These included the ceremonial canonization of San Felipe de Jesús, Mexico's first saint, which Plancarte himself witnessed in Rome in 1862; the enthusiastic reports of his nephew (and also priest), Father Miguel Plancarte Garibay, who in 1885 witnessed the coronation of the Madonna della Strada image in Roma; a chance meeting in 1884 with the English priest Kenel Vanham, who proposed to build a church of universal expiation in London; the earlier project of the Italian aristocrat Lorenzo Boturini, who launched a 1738 petition calling for the coronation of the Virgin of Guadalupe; and a suggestion made by Pelagio Antonio de Lábastida y Dávalos, Plancarte's uncle and protector as well as archbishop of Mexico, to the effect that the 1880s' coronation of Our Lady of Hope (a syncretic icon venerated in Jacona, Michoacán) be repeated in the case of the Guadalupe. Tapia Méndez's assertions, it can be observed, are written with an eye to conveying saintly humility in that they tend to describe Plancarte y Labastida merely as the coronations' executor, when in fact he was the driving force behind them. On this point, see also the short biography by Treviño, *Antonio Plancarte y Labastida*, 87–99, 111–35, and the article by Bautista García, "Dos momentos en la historia de un culto," 11–43, on the first Mexican coronation at Jacona.

19. Wright-Rios, *Revolutions in Mexican Catholicism*, 36.
20 Ibid., 7.

The great exception to this rule—and with this we return to the central theme of the paper—came with the cycle of devotional events that was organized across Mexico in January 1914: the consecration of all Mexico to the Sacred Heart of Jesus, on January 6, 1914; the coronation of the Sacred Heart as Christ the King, in the second and concluding part of the consecration ceremony of January 6; and finally, the extension of this cycle from the symbolic into the public sphere by means of a public demonstration convened on January 11 in honor of Christ's social kingship (*la realeza social de Cristo*). The controversy surrounding this ceremonial cycle gave rise, in part, to the black legend of clerical *huertismo*. In fact, the coronation represents a somewhat unique case, in the context of revolutionary Mexico, of the highly successful assimilation of a very recent and Eurocentric devotion of obvious clerical manufacture, the connotations of which were also militantly anti-secular.[21] That success was palpable in the ceremonies and marches that occurred in many parts of Mexico in 1914; in the violence that occurred in the name of Christ the King from 1926; and in the mass pilgrimages that took place in Mexico City and elsewhere on the feast of Christ the King, especially during the worst years of religious persecution and armed Catholic resistance to the regime (1926–29).[22]

The Consecration-Coronation of 1914

In Mexico, devotion to the Sacred Heart of Jesus—symbolizing divine love as well as a divine reproach to predilect Catholic nations that violate historic pacts with God—had colonial origins, although it only truly flowered in the course of the nineteenth century. This was due, in part, to the efforts of the besieged Pius IX, who incorporated the feast of the Sacred Heart into the liturgy at mid-century and conceived of the devotion as the Church's last hope in the face of the advancing tide of secular liberalism. Henceforth, the cult was central to the development of modern-style Catholicism and came to be seen as symbolic of the Church's rejection of the laicist tendency.

---

21. The Christ the King ceremony, it should be said, rested on much more solid institutional grassroots foundations: it was built, among other things, on the patient work conducted by laity and priests in previous decades to promote sacramental organizations such as the Vela Perpetua and the Adoración Nocturna Mexicana, as well as devotion to the Sacred Heart. See, for instance, Chowning, "The Catholic Church and the Ladies of the Vela Perpetua," 197–237; Butler, "Transplanting the Eucharistic Seed," 53–90; and Moreno Chávez, "Devoción y cultura católica," 165–258.

22. On the Christ the King devotion, see Torres Septién and Solís, "De Cerro a Montaña Santa," 113–54; Torres Septién, "Guanajuato y la resistencia católica," 83–119; and Butler, "Trouble Afoot?," 149–66.

Pope Leo XIII was another devotee; it was Leo who consecrated the world to the Sacred Heart in his encyclical *Sacrum Annum* (1899).[23] By this time, according to Miguel Rodríguez's interesting study, the devotion had undergone an important transculturation in Latin America, by which it shed its legitimist, counterrevolutionary (and originally French) connotations as a referent for monarchical restoration. Instead, and following the national consecrations performed in Ecuador (1873) and Colombia (1902), the Sacred Heart became strongly associated in Latin America with Catholic-style republicanism: reparation for the damage caused by secular states' turning away from God would now be made by *the people*, not through the person of the monarch.[24] For the same reason, the act of consecration was realized through a series of concentric circles—family, diocese, Church, *pueblo*— that were collectively constitutive of a Catholicized national identity.[25] In Mexico, by contrast, the Reform Laws and the state's lay character thwarted the realization of any national consecration to the Sacred Heart, which perhaps explains why the much-desired national oath took the politically irresistible shape of a Marian coronation.[26]

If the political moment at which coronations were enacted clearly mattered, so, too, did their moment of inception. Here it is important to stress that the decision to consecrate Mexico to the Sacred Heart reflected a long-held aspiration and was not born in the Huerta dictatorship but long before. In fact, even the immediate antecedents for the 1914 ceremony went back at least three years, precisely to May 1911. That is to say, the coronation was

23. The historiography on the devotion in Mexico is now growing. See Rodríguez, "El Sagrado Corazón de Jesús," 147–68; Correa Etchegaray, "El rescate de una devoción jesuítica," 369–80; Arenal Fenocchio, "Una devoción mariana francesa en México," 161–94; Moreno Chávez, "Devoción política" (unpublished ms.).

24. On France, see Jonas, *Tragic Tale of Claire Ferchaud* and *France and the Cult of the Sacred Heart*. On Latin America, see Williams, "The Making of Ecuador's *Pueblo Católico*," 207–29, and Londoño-Vega, *Religion, Culture, and Society in Colombia*, 153–57.

25. Rodríguez, "El Sagrado Corazón de Jesús," 157–58. The anti-secular aspect of the devotion provoked a strong reaction in many countries. In France, during the First World War, efforts by the Catholic hierarchy to attribute a theological as well as teleological significance to the war as a divine punishment for the post-1789 rupture in France's obeisance to the Sacred Heart outraged the government; when similar ideas were revived in the peasant visions of Claire Ferchaud, and a campaign demanding a national consecration to the Sacred Heart in 1915 began, the regime reacted badly. In Peru, according to Jeffrey Klaiber, the formation of the American Popular Revolutionary Alliance (APRA) was initially a "protest" against attempts to install the Sacred Heart as the national patron in 1923, because of which the consecration ceremony was postponed until 1954. Jonas, *Tragic Tale of Claire Ferchaud*; Klaiber, *Religion and Revolution in Peru*, 115–38.

26. Rodríguez, "El Sagrado Corazón de Jesús," 158–60.

first mooted in the month of greatest revolutionary optimism, which saw Porfirio Díaz depart for exile and also, at the behest of Francisco Madero, the foundation of the National Catholic Party (PCN). From this perspective, the consecration represents an early response by democratic Catholics and their allies in the Mexican episcopate to the post-Porfirian political climate and, more specifically, to Francisco Madero's call for political pluralism, not nostalgia for Porfirian dictatorship. It also shows a willingness to reclaim, via the social and political mobilization of the laity, as much as possible of the civil and social space that the Church had forfeited in previous decades. Lastly, as we shall see, the coronation reflected the episcopate's fears that a democratic system built without a Catholic counterweight would mean Mexico's certain return to political anarchy, bloodshed, and the total abandonment of Catholic values.[27]

27. Theoretically, following Bernardo Barranco, we might define this project as one of "radical intransigence" as opposed to other ("integral" or "moralistic") kinds of intransigence, given its overtly political aspect (the PCN). "It is understood," Barranco writes, "that a central characteristic of the social-Christian position is its rejection and combating of the modern world. On the basis of Thomist theology—which correctly formulates the connection between the 'natural' and the 'supernatural'—the new state of things proper to modernity (the appearance of an autonomous realm of scientific enquiry, of modern secular states, etc.) is 'accepted' as a field of action for the Church: fundamentally, it is a question of crystalizing the new society. This position denotes a certain pessimism before the world. The preferred way of carrying out this Christianization is through confessional institutions—in the field of education and culture, in economic and political activities—which become newly 'religious' spaces for Catholics and Christianization's advance party in the midst of a secularized society. This presupposes the use of 'power' in ecclesiastical tasks and the participation of solidly trained lay people. Directly with reference to the modern state, the state's 'laïc' character (church-state separation) is accepted so long as the exercise of the Church's mission is guaranteed through certain kinds of juridical recognition. From this it follows that this ideology may imply, in certain circumstances, a reserved attitude towards modern states, and even, should occasion arise, a combative attitude . . . We may therefore affirm that this spirit of neo-Christendom implies at some level a mysticism of reconquest concerning the Church's recovery, at the very least and seen from a position of *realpolitik*, of some basic rights 'in order to carry out its mission.' The 'laïc' (i.e., a-religious) category that has been attributed to States is recognized. The demand, therefore, is that the Church simply be given sufficient juridical space so as to act in all ambits of civil society. Without demanding the prerogatives of an 'official religion' of state, the Church fights for the right to maintain religious schools, for recognition of its juridical personality by the state, and for the civic and political rights of the clergy, etc." Barranco distinguishes this position, which clearly describes the formulation of the PCN and bodies such as the Association of Mexican Catholic Youth (ACJM), from merely "integral intransigence," which rests on a "relative separation" of the political and religious fields, and in which "ecclesiastical society" does not intervene directly in the political field, but only indirectly. Barranco, "Posiciones políticas," 39–70, especially 60–64.

The key actor in promoting the Mexican consecration was Leopoldo Ruiz y Flores, then archbishop of Linares (Monterrey).[28] It was Ruiz y Flores, for instance, who in 1911 suggested that the episcopate renew *at the national level* the act of consecration of the Mexican *Church* to the Sacred Heart, a ceremony that had been celebrated in Rome in 1899 by the Mexican prelates attending the Latin American Plenary Council. Clearly, then, the 1899 consecration was an elitist, even cosmopolitan affair. Meanwhile, Ruiz y Flores proposed the date of October 12, 1911, for the national consecration, which coincided with the anniversary of the Marian coronation of 1895. The episcopate, we might add, endorsed Ruiz y Flores's suggestion almost unanimously, following the dissemination of his proposal in episcopal circulars dated May 23 and June 30, 1911.[29]

Probably an event not too unlike that of 1895 was considered at first, to conclude with a great act of public worship led by the episcopate in Mexico City. Only times had changed. Some episcopal voices, indeed, sound almost prophetic in retrospect: the consecration could wait, said the bishop of Zamora—the militant social Catholic, José Othón Núñez—"while public order is restored, and so that suspicious souls do not attribute other ends to a general meeting of the bishops";[30] the bishop of Veracruz called for similar prudence,[31] while his counterpart in Tamaulipas, while approving of a series of local consecrations, opposed the idea of a collective, national consecration:

> Because I am assailed by the fear that if we the episcopate, in whole or in significant part, were to meet in the Capital in the current circumstances, this would give liberal elements as well as the impious and scandalous newspapers cause to make

---

28. Later of Morelia (1912–42) and also, from 1929 to 1942, Apostolic Delegate. See Ruiz y Flores, *Recuerdo de Recuerdos*.

29. AHAM, c. 91/exp. 30, letters to Mora y del Río, all 1911, from the bishops of: Saltillo (Paris, August 11); Tehuantepec (Tehuantepec, July 19); Chihuahua (Chihuahua, July 12); Yucatán (signed by the vicar general, Merida, n/d); Chiapas (San Cristóbal, June 23 and 27); Sonora (Lerdo, July 17, and Hermosillo, June 5); Cuernavaca (Cuernavaca, July 8); Tamaulipas (Ciudad Victoria, July 10); Zamora (Zamora, July 14); Tepic (Tepic, May 30, and Tala, July 14); Durango (Lerdo, July 11); León (León, June 2 and July 13); Chilapa (Chilapa, June 4 and July 11); Colima (Colima, May 30 and July 7); Michoacán (all signed by the vicar general, Morelia, May 31 and July 1); Aguascalientes (Aguascalientes, July 8); Querétaro (Querétaro, July 9); Veracruz (Jalapa, May 30 and July 10); Zacatecas (Zacatecas, May 29 and July 8); Guadalajara (Guadalajara, July 11); Durango (Durango, June 6); Puebla (Puebla, May 28); Tulancingo (Tulancingo, May 29).

30. AHAM, c. 91/exp. 30, Othón Núñez to Mora y del Río, Zamora, May 29.

31. AHAM, c. 91/exp. 30, bishop of Veracruz to Mora y del Río, Jalapa, May 30.

comments disfavorable to the Episcopate, and might even occasion some kind of insulting demonstration against us; for while these [elements] have ignored us during the revolution, our enemies' instincts might be reawakened by [the consecration], and they might even try to turn the current government against the Episcopate.[32]

More clairvoyant still was the archbishop of Guadalajara, José de Jesús Ortíz:

> Concerning the presence in this city [Mexico] of all the Prelates of the Republic, I consider that to be highly dangerous in these moments of political excitation and with the National Catholic Party so recently founded, because our enemies would not cease to impute political motives to such a meeting in order to provoke suspicions about us and perhaps even to renew religious persecution. At the very least, they would demand strict implementation of the Reform Laws, which would fit well with the revolutionary program, and without our being able to count on the dissimulation and the benevolent, conciliatory spirit of the illustrious General Díaz, who until today has been our only defense after God.

The safest course was to organize simultaneous local consecrations throughout México, because then, Ortíz affirmed, "we would all be united in the same thoughts and prayers, but without exposing ourselves to the dangers that the collective presence of the Bishops in the capital would entail."[33] Thus, we can see that prominent members of the episcopate, particularly so-called liberal prelates that had made their peace with the Porfirian regime, feared that Madero's victory would unleash a new Jacobin frenzy against the Church, particularly if the episcopate were implicated in Catholic politics. It is interesting to observe that these bishops so greatly feared the possible consequences of a collective reunion for all that they endorsed the idea of a consecration ceremony. In the end, a collective meeting of the episcopate in Mexico City was averted; nonetheless, the episcopate's more intransigent faction won out in alliance with the social Catholics and democrats of the PCN, given that the 1914 ceremony did not merely consecrate the Mexican Church to the Sacred Heart but proclaimed Christ's social kingship.[34]

---

32. AHAM, c. 91/exp. 30, bishop of Tamaulipas to Mora y del Río, Ciudad Victoria, May 31.

33. AHAM, c. 91/exp. 30, de Jesús Ortíz to Mora y del Río, Guadalajara, May 29.

34. Ruiz y Flores himself conspicuously identified with the democratic goals of the PCN, to the extent that he preached to the Party in Morelia cathedral and reminded

At a semantic level, similar ambiguities were apparent in the episcopate's 1911 correspondence to Ruiz y Flores. We can see, for instance, how frequently the bishops conflated the terms "Mexico," "nation," and "Republic." Indeed, some prelates seem to have understood that Ruiz y Flores was proposing to consecrate the *Mexican Republic* to the Sacred Heart, not the sum total of Mexican Catholics. The bishop of Sonora, for example, applauded the imminent "consecration of *all the Republic* to the Most Sacred Heart of Jesus"; the bishop of Colima admired the "proposed *consecration of Mexico* to the Sacred Heart of Jesus"; Morelia's vicar general, Lorenzo Olaciregui, looked forward to the "consecration of *all the Mexican nation* to the Sacred Heart of Jesus"; and the bishop of Tulancingo anticipated a ceremony that would "consecrate . . . the *Entire Nation* to the Sacred Heart of Jesus."[35] Ruiz y Flores, for his part, was delighted by the "warm reception [*buena acogida*] that the idea of a Consecration of *all the Republic* to the Sacred Heart ha[d] received" among his brother bishops, though he accepted that it was necessary to organize the celebrations at the diocesan level, "so as not to convene a significant number of prelates in Mexico City," and also to delay the holding of the ceremony somewhat in light of the ongoing political instability of summer 1911. So that the significance of a national consecration was not lost, however, "and so as to set a tone of collectivity and union," Ruiz y Flores suggested that the bishops publish a collective pastoral "explaining what the consecration is and using the occasion to stress that the Church expects no salvation except from its Savior."[36] From a consecration to the Sacred Heart that would be "national" in the sense that it would be performed by all of the nation's bishops, collectively or individually, some prelates advanced, almost imperceptibly, to the idea of consecrating *the Republic itself*; that is, to an expression of Christ's social imperium, which was anyway latent in the Sacred Heart devotion.

When the consecration project was once again considered by the episcopate, in mid-1912, the idea of renovating the 1899 consecration of the Mexican Church in the *Republic* was firmly fixed. The second element just discussed—re-Catholicization of the social order—was also given more prominence and was expressed in the idea of a liturgical *coronation* as well as a simple consecration ceremony. This innovation also originated in

---

the faithful of their Pauline obligation to shun revolts against President Madero. See, for example, Ruiz y Flores, "Instrucción Pastoral sobre los Deberes de los Católicos en Política."

35. AHAM, c. 91/exp. 30, Valdespino to Mora y del Río, Lerdo, July 17; bishop of Colima to Mora y del Río, Colima, July 9; Olaciregui to Mora y del Río, Morelia, July 1; bishop of Tulancingo to Mora y del Río, Tulancingo, May 29. My emphasis.

36. AHAM, c. 91/exp. 30, Ruiz y Flores to Mora y del Río, Monterrey, June 7.

Michoacán, according to Ruiz y Flores, who writes in his memoir that the idea came to him as a result of discussions with lay Catholics in Morelia for whom he acted as spiritual director.[37] By June 12, 1912, Ruiz y Flores could count on the support of Archbishop Mora y del Río, concerning "the idea of renovating the Consecration of the world to the Sacred Heart and of a liturgical coronation." Again, Mora y del Río told Ruiz y Flores to put the matter to the other archbishops, for approval in turn by the bishops.[38]

Unfortunately, we do not know exactly when Ruiz y Flores's proposal received the episcopate's definitive approval: however, on March 19, 1913—a few weeks after Madero's downfall—the episcopate published the collective pastoral that had been promised since June 1911 and in which the bishops presented their decision to consecrate the Mexican Republic to the Sacred Heart and, at the same time, "to proclaim the kingdom of the Sacred Heart of Jesus in Mexico." These acts of worship, it was stated, had "germinated in many pious hearts," and for that reason, the bishops believed that they were doing no more than giving form to a general feeling among the Catholic people.[39] It was not for another eight months, however, that Ruiz y Flores was able to travel to Rome and present the project to Pius X in person.[40] In a papal brief dated November 12, 1913, Pius X approved the Mexican hierarchy's plan to consecrate the Mexican Republic to "the Divine Heart, immor-

---

37. "Several years previously, a pious soul that I directed had asked me to promote the proclamation of Jesus Christ as King of the Nations, starting with Mexico, and [proposed] that the best way to achieve this would be by crowning in every church the image of the Sacred Heart of Jesus, placing at the image's feet the inscription 'Christ the King.' I studied the matter, consulted with all the bishops, and once all were in agreement concerning such a petition, I resolved to travel to Rome by joining a pilgrimage that had been organized by the Señor Archbishop of Puebla, D. Ramón Ibarra ... His Holiness Pius X received the proposal benignly, telling me that he would write a letter to the Mexican bishops granting what we had asked for Christ the King, but [stating] that the crown and scepter must be placed at the feet of the image and not on the image's head or in its hands, because only in this way was the idea of Christ the King of kings and Lord of those that govern [*Señor de los que mandan*] expressed. I received this letter and immediately returned to Mexico. The day of January 6, 1914, was appointed for the ceremony, which was celebrated with great solemnity throughout the country." Ruiz y Flores, *Recuerdo de recuerdos*, 65–66. Ruiz y Flores's claim, we might note, is furiously disputed by Catholic historians of the right, who are indignant at the suggestion that the prelate who signed the armistice (*arreglos*) ending the Cristero rebellion in 1929 should also take credit for founding the Christ the King devotion. See Barquín y Ruiz, *Cristo, Rey de México*, 125–28.

38. AHAM, c. 46/exp. 37, Ruiz y Flores to Mora y del Río; AHAM, c. 46/exp. 37, Mora y del Río to the archbishops.

39. Barquín y Ruiz, *Cristo, Rey de México*, 126.

40. Ruiz y Flores made the journey as part of a pilgrimage organized by Archbishop Ramón Ibarra of Puebla.

tal King of the ages," in accordance with the encyclical *Annum Sacrum*. He also approved the Mexicans' plan "to decorate images of Jesus Christ's Heart with the insignia of royalty," meaning a crown and scepter, so as to give the event greater solemnity still and to illustrate its transcendental importance to the Mexican people. Crucially, however, Pius insisted that such worldly regalia (signs of "kingly majesty") be placed *at the feet* of the image of the Sacred Heart, since the only divine crown was composed of thorns and "vanquished crowns of jewels in splendor" as easily as it surpassed kingly scepters in power. Lastly, Pius expressed his deep concern about the revolution in Mexico (the "grave disorders") and articulated his sincere hope that "from this Heart may pour forth for you, Venerable Brothers, and for your entire Nation that is so rudely agitated by incessant discord, the grace of which you have need for eternal salvation and that peace which your fellow citizens desire with indescribable anxiety and with one voice, as the endless source of all goodness."[41]

Thus we see how the consecration project, if European in inspiration, slowly was transformed, becoming both Mexicanized and Romanized in a process of collaboration involving Mexican clergy, Mexican laity, and ultimately, the pope himself.[42] In particular, we can observe the development of a Sacred Heart/*Cristo Rey* religious couplet, which fused, on the one hand, the reproachful and sentimental tone of the Sacred Heart devotion and, on the other, a new element of masculine triumphalism, whose attributes were those of conquest and imperium over earthly powers. In sum, a devotional metamorphosis—from veneration of the Sacred Heart to vassalage to *Cristo Rey*, expressed in the joint consecration/coronation ritual—had already begun when news of Pius's endorsement was received in Mexico in the form of a telegram, sent from Rome by Archbishop Ibarra of Puebla in mid-November 1913.[43] By this time, and as a clear reflection of the rising influence of intransigent prelates like Mora y del Río and Ruiz y Flores, the Sacred Heart project had evolved from a plan for an internal commemoration to an increasingly open reaffirmation of the Church's role as rector of Mexican society.[44]

---

41. Pius X, "A Nuestros Venerables Hermanos," AHAM c. 91/exp. 57. Pius's brief can also be read in Rius Facius, *De don Porfirio a Plutarco*, 47, and Barquín y Ruiz, *Cristo, Rey de México*, 129.

42. Here, we should recall Christian, *Visionaries*, 399: sacralization as a process in which the Church seeks to channel religious enthusiasm by shaping memory.

43. As noted in AHAM, c. 91/exp. 62.

44. O'Dogherty Madrazo, "El ascenso de una jerarquía eclesial intransigente," 179–98.

On November 30, the corresponding episcopal edict was published. This document underscored the healing character of the consecration ceremony. "The prelates of this Mexican Nation," it ran, "filled with sorrow on seeing the conflictive circumstances through which the Fatherland passes, because of the war that for more than three years has sown desolation and misfortune," now invoked the words of Leo XIII, particularly his affirmation that the sores afflicting modern society would disappear "*when every tongue confesses that Jesus Christ is in glory with God the Father.*" To this end, the episcopate had sought permission from Rome for the making of a solemn vow to Christ the King, "Most August King of all the Nations." Once again, the idea that Mexico's sufferings derived from the country's violation of an historic contract with God was emphasized: the faithful must beseech the Sacred Heart "to exert precious influence over the Celestial Father, so that He deigns to view us with merciful eyes, forgiving our many sins and returning our benighted Fatherland to the path of wellbeing and happiness." To this end, a triduum in the presence of the Blessed Sacrament and a general communion were scheduled for the three days leading up to the consecration on January 6, 1914; during this preparatory cycle, meanwhile, priests would sermonize the faithful, reminding them "that the only remedy for our many evils is the Kingdom of Jesus Christ, and that, for so long as His Most Sacred Heart does not reign among us, it is inevitable that numerous calamities will afflict us." On January 6 would come the national consecration, using an oath written by Leo XIII; then, in a separate coronation ceremony, a crown and scepter would be placed at the feet of the Sacred Heart, as symbols of Mexico's submission to God and the Church.[45] As we shall see, this devotional cycle would be further widened to incorporate a public homage to *Cristo Rey* five days after.

The social and anti-secular character of the festival now became more prominent elsewhere. In some of the pastoral letters published in the provinces, for example—and particularly in the one published in Guadalajara (Jalisco) on December 18—a much more strident interpretation of the coronation ceremony was given. What was still presented in Mexico City as being fundamentally a penitential act was presented in Jalisco—where the National Catholic Party held power[46]—not merely as a collective plea to "disarm the vengeful hand [*brazo justiciero*] of God" but very obviously as "the public proclamation of the Social Kingdom of Jesus Christ." Moreover, the new and socially militant archbishop of Guadalajara, Francisco Orozco

---

45. "Edicto Diocesano sobre la Solemne Consagración," 303–6.

46. O'Dogherty Madrazo, *De urnas y sotanas*; *II Jornada Académica Iglesia-Revolución Mexicana*.

y Jiménez, chose to stress the mystical-social meaning of the coronation date (Epiphany). In the words of this young prelate,

> By crowning Him as He ought to be crowned, and by offering Him a scepter symbolizing His dominion over societies and individuals, over Kings and their subjects, as much in the emporia of civilization as in small villages, from all corners there will be raised a great hymn of praise, love, and exculpation [*desagravio*] to the Heart of Jesus, which is so troubled by our iniquities ... By professing faith and practicing charity on the day of our acts of worship to the Most Sacred Heart of Jesus, we shall be stirred by that powerful mystery that the Church teaches on the date providentially chosen for the solemn Consecration: the Epiphany of Our Lord Jesus Christ. On that day, Our Savior is presented to the world dressed anew [*revestido*] with the royal authority of Supreme Monarch and receives the deepest adoration; gentility, represented by three great personages, comes to the feet of Jesus Christ; science, the Arts, and all of human magnificence come forward to make to Christ a vow of vassalage.[47]

Perhaps the most striking reading of the ceremony came from the pen of a Mexican Jesuit, J. R. Carrión, in an article published in *El Mensajero del Corazón de Jesús*, official organ of the Apostleship of Prayer (ADO). Carrión affirmed that the consecration, celebrated "in the midst of the tremendous anguish of the present, offered the best hope for the salvation of the Fatherland"; indeed, it was impossible that the Sacred Heart would allow any nation to perish if, like Nineveh, it repented of its public rejection of Christ.[48] Beyond the symbolic renovation of a pact linking a nation in revolutionary turmoil and an ever-merciful God, however, Carrión emphasized that the ceremony's full meaning was to be found in the rejection of the laicist principle and in the proclamation of the social kingdom of Christ in Mexico:

> Because, and note this well, [the consecration] is not and cannot be a mere ceremony, performance, or external and material act, no matter how grandiose and beautiful: Oh no! It is, in itself, an idea, or more properly a proclamation; even more than this, it is a tribute from the heart of a whole people which, martyred and laid low by horrible bitterness, and in the face of near universal apostasy among other nations, suddenly rises up, magnificent

---

47. *Segunda carta pastoral del Ilmo. y Revmo. Sr. Dr. y Mtro. D. Francisco Orozco y Jiménez*.

48. Carrión, "La renovación solemne," 12–18. In the same publication, the papal brief of November 12, 1913, was reproduced both in Latin and in Spanish (23–27). The article can also be read in Barquín and Ruiz, *Cristo, Rey de México*, 130–33.

and believing; lifts its eyes to the heavens, and pierces the loving and trusting Divine Heart with its gaze; amid the frightful blasts of fratricidal cannon and the cowardly blasphemies of the rabble and the impious, [this people] rushes through the countryside, the cities, the home, and the churches, calling on children, mothers, virgins, and priests, in a word, on all its sons; when all are congregated at the feet of its altars, as the best proclamation of faith and hope, and in firm contrast to the Jews in Jerusalem, it deposits a crown and scepter at the feet of the Divine Heart of Jesus and clamors before the world and heaven: *Volumus hunc regem*, this is our King, the only King that we desire . . . Save us, a thousand times, save us![49]

In sum, it was insufficient for Mexicans to offer Christ "their whole being from a corner of the church or in the intimacy of the home." Now that other nations boasted of their emancipation from God, Mexico had to be "the people of the Renovation," an example of divine sovereignty "for all men and all peoples, [a sovereignty] synthesized in a crown and scepter, deposited at the feet of the Sacred Heart, King of Kings . . . only King of [Mexico's] heart and of her history!"[50] The "history" that Carrión invoked, of course, was one of divine predilection for Mexico, as announced in the apparition of the Guadalupe in 1531. This legacy had been spurned, post-colony, by secularizing liberals like Juárez, prompting Mexico's moral decline and a descent into Aztec barbarism in the revolution.

Now the aim was to renovate this primordial pact, but through the Sacred Heart. Indeed, said Carrión, since 1689—year of Margaret Mary Alacoque's prophetic visions of the Sacred Heart in France—"the Divine Heart of Jesus has been urging Mexico, the *pueblo* of his Mother, to come to Him, to be her Guide along all paths, her Consoler in all misadventures, and her omnipotent Defender against all foes." Now that the moment had arrived, "all Mexicans, as if soldiers with one Captain," should kneel down at the feet of the Sacred Heart, surrendering their own hearts, and proclaim in the name of their Fatherland, "*Esto Rex Noster!* . . . Be our King!"[51] In this way the consecration was inserted into a teleological—here meaning a providential—reading of Mexican history, as the fulfillment of the first Guadalupan revelation. In order to retie the thread of divine election that liberals had severed, however, it was the Sacred Heart that was invoked. Only now the traditional image of a passively wounded Christ, flaming heart lacerated by

49. Carrión, "La renovación solemne," 13.
50. Ibid., 13–14.
51. Ibid., 18.

the arrows thrown by ingrate nations, was being transformed and given a multifaceted quality: along with the usual image of the Sacred Heart, a conquering, quasi-military image of Christ as King/Captain was advanced for the edification of the faithful.[52]

The process was, therefore, a dynamic one. From the Porfirian-style proposal for an exculpatory consecration within the precincts of the Church there had developed, by 1914, the idea for a national coronation whose goal was the reconquest of public social space and the inauguration of the social kingdom of Christ the King. This dynamism demonstrates how quickly the Church in Mexico sought to make a transition from the sociopolitical quietism of the Porfirian dictatorship and to broaden the liberties enjoyed by Catholics, for all that the excesses of the Mexican Revolution were still to be deplored. It is true that the public enactment of this Catholic project of penitence followed by social restoration coincided fatally with the years of the Huerta government; but it had been coming since 1911, since the heyday of *maderismo*. The consecration should therefore be understood not as a neo-Porfirian relic but, like the National Catholic Party that did much to promote it, as part of a Catholic social and political project that had been welling up in the final years of the Porfiriato. Now, with the Revolution's experiment in democracy and the ascendancy of both socially minded prelates and politically committed Catholics, that project was finally set free. The ceremonies of January 1914 should be seen as an integral part of the development of a combative Church that wanted to turn its back on the compromises of the Porfirian years.

The Ceremony: From Sacred Heart to Christ the King

In comparison with the coronation of 1895, that of 1914 was quite decentralized and involved a much higher degree of popular participation. This was achieved through the enactment of collective vows, public pilgrimages and street marches, Eucharistic processions, the singing of specially composed canticles, flag ceremonies, collections for Sacred Heart statues and royal insignia, and prayer sessions. In Mexico City's cathedral, it must be admitted, something of the elitism of 1895 persisted in the 1914 celebration, but this was perhaps the least representative of all the celebrations even if it was the most commented upon. It must be recalled, though, that for the vast majority of Mexican Catholics the consecration was experienced as a local, diocesan or parochial, event. Unlike most Porfirian coronations, for

---

52. We should note that, in Mexican Spanish, *capitán* denotes military chieftain, not just an officer's rank.

instance, devotion to the Sacred Heart was not centralized in any particular location; nor was there one great ceremony or image, but hundreds in every diocese as well as thousands across Mexico. As we have suggested, the 1914 ceremonies at one level reinforced the hierarchical principle, as the liturgical standardization implied. But at the same time, the devotional cycle was designed to create horizontal lines of religious-political solidarity, tending toward the construction of a Catholic *pueblo* that was conscious of its civic and political rights and more militant when it came to demanding that they be recognized or exercised more fully.[53]

In Mexico City's cathedral, the consecration was a very disciplined affair. The evening before, instructions were published explaining to the faithful through which doors they must enter and exit the cathedral in order to witness the ceremony. Specific points were reserved for certain religious corporations: pious associations, Catholic guilds, the *cabildo* (chapter), the parish clergy. Catholic businesses were exhorted to close their doors for the duration of the ceremony and Catholic families to adorn the facades of their homes with placards and banners.[54] The cathedral's internal walls were bedecked with velvet curtains and hangings, and the statues garlanded with flowers; four large candles draped with ribbons flickered in the crossing, one each to represent Rome, the Mexican Republic, Spain (Mexico's spiritual benefactor), and France (home of the modern Sacred Heart devotion).[55] The ceremony was performed before thousands of faithful, *El País* commented, who participated "without distinctions of class" and made a collective homage "to the Almighty, so as to ask Him devoutly for peace and tranquility in our Fatherland." At nine o'clock, a bell rang to signal the beginning of the ceremony. Archbishop Mora then gave a blessing and proceeded to the celebration of a pontifical Mass. During the offertory, the Sacred Heart's Honor Guard—which comprised some of the cream of *capitalino* society— and other religious associations presented their offerings of gold, incense, and myrrh. At the same time, a procession of Catholic women presented the archbishop with the ceremonial crown; a procession of Catholic men made a presentation of the scepter. After these offerings were made, a sermon was delivered by canon Gerardo Herrera, who preached on the following question: "Are you King?" ("*¿Eres tú Rey?*"). Finally, Archbishop Mora processed up to the image of the Sacred Heart of Jesus, "on his knees placed the crown

---

53. I have explored this popular dimension elsewhere. See Butler, "La coronación del Sagrado Corazón," 24–68.

54. "La Solemne Coronación al S. Corazón de Jesús: Indicaciones," *El País*.

55. "La Solemne Coronación del S. Corazón de Jesús: Se Efectuará en la Catedral de Méjico," *El País*.

and scepter at the Lord's feet," and recited the oath of consecration to *vivas*, applause, and the ringing of bells:

> Sweetest Jesus, Redeemer of the human lineage: we are here, humbly prostrated before your altar. We are yours; we desire to be yours; and so that we may be more closely united with you, today each one of us consecrates his heart to your Most Sacred Heart. Many have never known you; many, despising your commandments, rejected you. Show mercy, Oh most kind Jesus, to all of these and draw them to your Sacred Heart. Be Lord, not only to those faithful who have never left your side but to those prodigal sons that abandoned you; make them return soon to their paternal home, so that they do not perish of hunger and poverty. Be King to those that error has tricked and discord driven away, and lead them back to the door of truth and to the unity of the faith, so that before long we shall be a single flock with one shepherd. Be, lastly, King to those that still follow in the path of superstition and idolatry, and hurry to bring them out of the darkness in which they languish and into the light of the Kingdom of God. Grant, Lord, certain liberty and security to your Church; allow peace and tranquility to reign in the world, and may one voice be heard everywhere. Praise be given to the Sacred Heart of Jesus, source and origin of our wellbeing; to Him glory and honor, forever and ever.[56]

Once again, it must be stressed that public references to discord, fratricide, and peace only acquired their full significance when linked to a Catholic social project that was articulated freely following the collapse of the Díaz regime and the sacred teleological history of election, transgression, and redemption as just outlined. We might note, for instance, the reference to the prodigal son (indeed, familial language was a constant in Catholic discourse); likewise, the prayers for Church liberty, which, following the *maderista* interlude, were less immediately partisan than they were a call for the re-Christianization of Mexican society under Church auspices. We need to exercise care when considering the homilies delivered during the coronation ceremony, however, because many surviving newspaper reports—for instance, those of *El País*, a Catholic newspaper that was censored heavily by the Huerta regime—tend to efface this social and historical vision. On the contrary, it is usually stressed that the ceremony was simply a protest against the violence of the Mexican Revolution, rather than one premised on calls for renewed social Catholicization. "The most interesting part," commented

---

56. "Se Efectuó la Solemne Consagración," *El País*. For further details, see Barquín y Ruiz, *Cristo, Rey de México*, 135.

El País when reviewing the sermon preached by canon Herrera in Mexico City's cathedral,

> was [Herrera's] reference to the very critical situation through which we are currently passing, especially [concerning] the fratricidal revolt that stalks our countryside, shedding the blood of brothers who do not wish to hear the voice of conscience commanding them to follow the path that Jesus Christ set out for us here on earth. To finish, the orator called upon the faithful to kneel down, and taking advantage of the tribute that was being offered to the Sacred Heart of Jesus, to plead for peace in the Republic.

In other major sees, the format and homiletic tone were quite similar to that followed in the metropolitan cathedral. In San Luis Potosí, canon Jiménez delivered an impressive piece of religious oratory, according to *El País*:

> He painted in broad brushstrokes the influence that religious faith exercises in the life of prosperous peoples; he waxed lyrical about the beautiful Gospel theme: "Your reign is a reign for all ages, your dominion for all generations";[57] and he ended by making fervent vows for the peace and prosperity of the Republic, inciting all those present to march always together, whatever their political creed, "with their gaze fixed on God, who is supreme truth, and who, in His white tunic, made of all possible whiteness, will vanquish all evil passions and see them bow in submission before the sanctuary of His law."[58]

In Puebla's cathedral, canon Díaz Calderón delivered "a brilliant piece, demonstrating with irrefutable arguments the right of Jesus Christ to receive the public and private adoration of all men and all nations: *Ego constitutus sum Rex super omnes gentes.*"[59] In Guadalajara, however, the *chantre*, Miguel Silva, placed much greater emphasis on the anti-secular character of the Sacred Heart devotion. Beyond making pacifist allusions, he denounced the de-Catholicization of public life as the cause of revolutionary violence, and in so doing illuminated much more clearly the deeper historical-theological backdrop of the 1914 ceremonials, rather than any merely conjunctural significance. On ascending to the pulpit, Silva made clear that it was nine-

---

57. Psalm 145 ("Tu reino es de todos los siglos, y tu imperio se extiende a toda generación").

58. "La Solemne Coronación del Sagrado Corazón de Jesús en este C.," *El País*.

59. "Grandioso, Imponente, y Sublime Fué el Acto," *La Nación*; "Con Gran Solemnidad Se Consagró la C.," *El País*.

teenth-century liberalism, Juárez not Madero, that had created the infernal machine that had spread terror across the land since 1910. According to *El País*, this "eloquent sacred orator" spoke movingly, and above all

> made allusions to how this unfortunate nation had lived in better times and to the accumulation of great misfortunes that have come to form the weave of its painful history ever since our forefathers distanced themselves from the life-giving principles of Christianity, before they fell into the official atheism that is the cause of our greatest tragedies. He ended by making the tenderest pleas to the Sacred Heart of Jesus, recalling the inspired phrases of His ecstatic lover, Blessèd Margaret [Mary Alacoque], and begging for an end to the terrible fratricidal struggle, which at this very moment is sinking its claws into the very entrails of our beloved Fatherland.[60]

The Demonstrations of January 11, 1914

As we have seen, the ceremonies celebrated in Mexico on the Epiphany of 1914 tended rhetorically toward the organization of a repentant, thus conscious, Catholic people, pledged to the Sacred Heart of Jesus as a prerequisite for peace and a sign of reparation; and, simultaneously, toward the symbolic expression of a Catholic project of social reconquest, to be carried out in the name of Christ the King. From an act of individual and internal contrition came forth a collective vow and, finally, the theoretical recovery of the social terrain once occupied by the Church. The final third of the 1914 cycle, although it was not envisaged at the start, represented an attempt to enact the ideology of Christ the King in practice, by translating the devotion to the public, indeed civic, sphere in provocative fashion. In this way, the consecration process would be realized in a series of concentric sites, until it embraced the whole of Mexican society and the Mexican nation: home, church, village square, and city street.

On the one hand, this change marked the extension of the idea of the social Kingdom of Christ to a concrete social context. On the other hand, it signaled an important and new lay intervention, given that the idea of a public homage to Christ the King was apparently born among the most active lay Catholic circles in Mexico City. It is also true, however, that this lay contribution was developed (and indeed was authorized), because it coincided in spirit with the social project driven by the more socially militant

60. "Las Solemnidades de la Consagración," *El País*.

prelates; it was not as autonomous as some Catholic writers contend. It was the public homage, finally, that did most to contribute to the consecration's "black legend," since it was this event that also permitted various Porfirian Catholics, some of them political reactionaries associated with *huertismo*, to associate themselves with the consecration alongside the social Catholics mentioned previously. These *porfiristas* did not merely seek to reaffirm the social and political rights of Mexican Catholics but to associate the revindication of those rights with the defense of the Huerta regime. At the same time the Huerta regime conducted a none-too-subtle but in some ways effective attempt to appropriate the public homage, which was to take place in Mexico City on January 11, 1914. Nonetheless, the central thrust of the event was opposed to this and indeed obeyed a political logic that was always more Catholic than *huertista*.

It must be stressed from the outset that this initiative, too, emerged from the ranks of what was then the Catholic vanguard in Mexico. According to Barquín y Ruiz, the executive committee of the Center of Mexican Catholic Students—a social organization whose ecclesiastical assistant was a Belgian Jesuit, Bernardo Bergoënd—formulated the project for a national homage to Christ the King in December 1913 and presented it to Archbishop Mora y del Río in an audience that same month.[61] In an obvious sign of ecclesiastical favor, a communication was sent at Mora's behest to the group on January 1, 1914, inviting the students to participate in the main ceremony of January 6 by forming a commission to present the offerings of gold, incense, and myrrh.[62] In a pastoral letter published two days later, Mora officially extended the religious cycle that otherwise would culminate on January 6 by authorizing a "public demonstration [*manifestación*] . . . in honor of Christ the King" for January 11, 1914. He did so, he added, in response to the petitions that he had received from "various Catholics." In this way, Mora assimilated the militancy of leading lay Catholics into the official celebrations and made their petition his own; he seemed not to fear the consequences of this action since he ended by commending the plan to both the archdiocesan clergy and the generality of the faithful, all of whom were encouraged to second "such a beautiful initiative."[63]

On January 6, *La Nación*—the PCN's official newspaper, which by this time was facing intimidation from the Huerta regime and being accused of promoting opposition to the government—published its own invitation

---

61. Barquín y Ruiz, *Cristo, Rey de México*, 139–41, and Barquín y Ruiz, *Bernardo Bergoënd, S.J.*, 62–79. The Center, a male spin-off of the Asociación de Damas Católicas Mexicanas, was founded in Mexico City on February 2, 1913.

62. Barquín y Ruiz, *Cristo, Rey de México*, 133–34.

63. AHAM, c. 70/exp. 8.

to the demonstration using the provocative biblical title "No Peace for the Wicked" (*No hay paz para el impío*).⁶⁴ In the context of the mass militarization latterly organized by the Huerta regime, *La Nación* now adopted a visibly critical line and stressed that field-based solutions to the problems of social violence were useless unless Mexico's historic link to the supernatural was restored:

> It may be possible to restore material peace to the nation through the deployment of Mausers, machine guns, high-caliber guns, and the largest contingents of the Army. But we have seen already that such peace, imposed by force, is not enough; an organic peace is required, a peace of the spirit, the fruit of morality and justice, which emanate from God, Prince of Peace. Peace imposed by force is easily disturbed and is not recovered except at the cost of bloodshed and extermination . . . We have seen too much cruel and desperate struggle, and the desired peace seems ever further from us; the bonfires of fratricidal hatred blaze more violently every day and in their fury threaten to devour us. The impious wished to cast God out of our Fatherland, and upon it have rained evils without end, in fulfillment of the divine oracle: "There is no peace for the wicked." For these evils to cease, we must turn again to God, restitute the throne that we seized from Him in our ingratitude, and repair our national apostasy with an act of national reparation and homage. For these reasons you are invited to convene at a civil demonstration . . . in which we hope men of all social classes will take part, to the unanimous cry of "Christ lives! Christ reigns! Christ governs!"⁶⁵

We might note, in passing, that the Catholic Republic was clearly as gendered as the liberals': indeed, the Christ the King devotion urged a masculinization of Catholic piety in tandem with a Catholic political awakening. It was the devotional arm of a campaign in which Mexican men would re-Catholicize the Republic via agencies such as the PCN and civic organizations like the Mexican Association of Catholic Youth.⁶⁶ It was at this point, however, that the Huerta government, as well as the most reactionary elements of the PCN (the Elguero brothers, Eduardo Tamariz, the *licenciados* Juan, Leopoldo, and José Villela) attempted to make political capital out of the Christ the King demonstration. For a start, the bureaucratic issue of a permit for the demonstration was politicized. The militant social Catholic

---

64. Isa 57:21.
65. Ríus Facius, *De don Porfirio a Plutarco*, 49; Barquín y Ruiz, *Cristo, Rey de México*, 144.
66. Espinosa, "'Restoring Christian Social Order,'" 451–74.

and journalist Eduardo Correa did not understand *why* it was necessary to seek a permit from the Interior Ministry and was furious when one was sought, since it tagged the demonstration to the regime. In Correa's view the move was unnecessary, "since there was no law whatsoever prohibiting [the demonstration], given that it was not a political meeting . . . still less an act of public worship [*culto público*], for although the participants were Catholics, they were not to carry standards or insignia, but to convene in a place agreed beforehand and march united to church." Finally, Correa argues, permission was granted by the governor of the Federal District, General Ramón Corona, in consultation with Huerta, who "at once understood that he might take advantage of the happening, ingratiating himself with the faithful and using the event for ulterior ends."[67] Conservative Catholic writers, in contrast, stress complicity between Catholic militants and Huerta, not official manipulation. According to Barquín y Ruiz, *La Nación* made known the gratitude of the leaders of the Center of Mexican Catholic Students to Huerta, who granted them permission to hold the demonstration in person; according to Barquín y Ruiz, the students also left their interview with Huerta contented, since the general immediately endorsed their petition and gave orders to governor Corona not to impede in any way the holding of the demonstration.[68] Either way, on January 9, the invitation to the civic demonstration, now "in honor of *Christ the King*," was published in the official columns of *El País* and made known more generally.[69]

The organization of the demonstration was also marked by political interference or naïvety. According to the organizers, the demonstrators were to gather at the statue of Charles IV (an equestrian bronze located in downtown Mexico City), and from there march in procession to the cathedral. First would go a squadron of mounted police, then the members of the Center of Catholic Students led by Pedro Durán and the other directors,

---

67. Correa, *El Partido Católico Nacional*, 181, provides the only firsthand account that I know of. Correa stresses that the permit was a simple police measure, which it probably was, albeit one that was subsequently used by the regime for propaganda purposes. This may also be true, but it is unlikely that the meeting could have gone ahead without a license of some kind. Catholics would have well understood that holding a para-religious event without a license would have invited all kinds of criticism, from the regime as well as liberals anxious to see violations of the Reform Laws.

68. Barquín y Ruiz, *Cristo, Rey de México*, 160–62. I have not found any corroboration for the allegedly warm meeting between Huerta and the members of the Center of Mexican Catholic Students. As we have seen, however, such a meeting would contradict the critical, anti-militaristic tone of the consecration and also belies the fact that by early 1914 the regime was treating the National Catholic Party with contempt and, increasingly, aggression.

69. Barquín y Ruiz, *Bernardo Bergöend*, 73–74.

Luis Beltrán y Mendoza,[70] Rafael Capetillo,[71] and Jorge Prieto Laurens;[72] next

70. Member of the Association of Mexican Catholic Youth (ACJM) and from 1932 president of Acción Católica Mexicana (ACM). Later a *panista*. See Barranco, "Posiciones políticas," 64, and Aspe Armella, *La formación social y política*, 69, 167.

71. Lawyer and founder member of the Liga Nacional Defensora de la Libertad Religiosa (LNDLR) in 1925.

72 *Potosino* lawyer (b. 1895) and by turns a *maderista, zapatista, acejotaemero*, and founder of the Partido Nacional Cooperatista (1917), a pro-Catholic party and indirect successor to the PCN that was highly influential in the early 1920s. Prieto Laurens's loathing of the Huerta government, we might note, was such that he launched an abortive rebellion aganst the regime in Xochimilco in April 1913, for which he was imprisoned for two months; only a timely *amparo* prevented the regime carrying out his execution. In April 1914, while still on parole for rebellion, Prieto Laurens was advised to flee Mexico City again, because the Huerta regime was seeking to apprehend him as a "dangerous enemy." At this time, Prieto Laurens was both a political revolutionary (in the sense of his willingness to use force to overthrow stubborn dictatorships and install a democracy) and a committed social Catholic, which shows that in the early 1910s it was possible to see these value systems as mutually reinforcing. Indeed, Prieto Laurens's revolutionary attitude, particularly his hatred of authoritarian and pseudoscientific government, was deeply imbued by social Catholicism. In 1910, he and other Catholic students in the Escuela Nacional Preparatoria, among them his friends Luis and Eduardo Beltrán y Mendoza and José Pedro Durán, founded the Sociedad Filosófica Católica de Estudiantes, which later developed as a PCN affiliate, the Liga Nacional de Estudiantes Católicos. In 1913, under the influence of "a friend and great spiritual guide," the Jesuit priest, Carlos M. Heredia, this radical group founded the Centro de Estudiantes Católicos as a counterweight to the YMCA in Mexico City. In its study sessions, the group was instructed by "priests as wise and eloquent as Father Méndez Medina and others who initiated us in the study of Catholic Social Doctrine, analyzing the famous encyclical *Rerum Novarum*." It was from this group, finally, and under the influence of a third Jesuit, Bernard Bergoënd, that the Mexican Association of Catholic Youth (ACJM) sprang forth in the autumn of 1913. As Prieto Laurens recounts in his memoirs, these were oppositional, countercultural groups—not reactionary legions— deployed at the service of Díaz or Huerta: "We were an insignificant handful of young students that . . . in 1911 felt sufficient preoccupation and the need to form a group, as Catholics, in order to confront the atmosphere of the time, which was heavy with the false philosophical theories of Auguste Compte's materialistic Positivism, imported into our country by thinkers and educators who formed a distinguished group headed by Gabino Barreda, Porfirio Parra, Justo Sierra, Agustín Aragón, and Antonio Caso. And so as to challenge the Jacobin liberals that predominated in political circles, from where they imposed their rebellious ideas [on Mexico], adulterating and obscuring historical truth . . . [C]ongregated in the Sociedad Filosófica Católica de Estudiantes, under the direction of a noble, humble, and wise priest, R[everend] F[ather] Vicente M. Zaragoza, we began to immerse ourselves in the study of Thomist philosophy and the knowledge of Catholic apologetics, in order to confront the enemies of God and the Church. First we hurried to form the Liga Nacional de Estudiantes Católicos, which fought as a kind of vanguard for the shortlived and courageous National Catholic Party. Later we formed the Centro de Estudiantes Católicos de México, where we began the organizing and preparatory work that would result in the foundation of the ACJM, an organism of greater size and scope, thanks to what might be called a providential

would come men's pious associations, the Knights of Columbus, and finally, corporate groups divided along rough class lines: professionals, industrialists, shopkeepers, bureaucrats, workers. In the cathedral, Archbishop Mora would receive the procession while reciting the Creed from the altar.[73] On the day itself, however, sympathizers with the regime tried to place known *huertistas* at the head of the Catholic rank and file. Democratic Catholics in the PCN—again, the testimony is Correa's—watched in horror as such reactionaries infiltrated the march.[74] By the end, Correa himself even doubted the wisdom of holding a street protest to actualize the social Kingdom of Christ, even though the event was also intended as a pray-in to ask for the termination of civil war.[75]

The organizers endeavored to stress the event's nonpartisan character. The Center urged all participants to wear national (tricolor) insignia but "to abstain from carrying religious insignia, or portraits of political figures" and prohibited marchers from "making any kind of cries alluding to religion or

---

occurrence: a change in the Ecclesiastical Assistant of the Centro de Estudiantes Católicos de México, resulting from the fact that our unforgettable friend and counsellor, R. P. Carlos M. Heredia S.J., was obliged to leave Mexico City, being replaced by the no less well remembered and beloved spiritual director R. P. Bernard Bergoend S.J. This last priest was the inspiration and the soul of the ACJM, to me falling the honor and good fortune of translating a small book or pamphlet titled: *Association Catholique de la Jeunesse Française*, that Father Bergoend placed in my hands so that it would serve as the model and basis for the statutes of the ACJM ... With great affection I recall the names of that fine group of young Catholic students that was ready to fight for God and the Fatherland, this being the legend of the Centro and later the ACJM! *Luis B. Beltrán y Mendoza and his brother Eduardo, José Pedro Durán and his brother Alfonso, Bernardo Fernández y Grajales, René Capistrán Garza, Julio Jiménez Rueda, Enrique Loaiza, Luis Barquera, José Mendoza, Guillermo Rodríguez de Solar, José Valdés Rubio, Manuel Cordero Sevilla, Marciano Villaseñor, Gonzalo Suárez Escalante, Miguel y Francisco Orozco,* and others whose names escape me ... All were from or belonged to the student middle class but we were concerned for the lot of all young people in Mexico: peasants, workers, employees, public as well as private. We founded Círculos de Estudios among the working class, and we went into the workshops and factories of the most populous Parishes." Prieto Laurens, *Cincuenta años de política mexicana*, 9–33. See also Prieto Laurens, *Anécdotas históricas*, 9–32, for Prieto Laurens's April 1914 flight from Mexico City. Frustratingly, Prieto Laurens does not describe his participation (as secretary) in the 1914 ceremonies in either of his political memoirs. On the PNC, whose electoral success and congressional majority in both houses propped up the Obregón government in its early years (1920–22), allowing the *caudillo* to break free of his own Liberal Constitutionalist Party (PLC) while subsequently providing the popular bases in western and eastern Mexico that were mobilized during the *delahuertista* rebellion, see Valenzuela, "Entre el poder y la fe," 199–220.

73. "En Honor a Cristo Rey," *El País*.
74. Correa, *El Partido Católico*, 80.
75. Ibid., 181.

politics."⁷⁶ The invitations to the "civic demonstration" that were sent from the archbishop's palace reiterated these instructions and repeated that this was to be "an act [that] has no political character but simply has as its objective the offering of *a solemn national tribute* to Jesus Christ imploring Him to grant us peace."⁷⁷ In *La Nación*, letters written by various prelates endorsing the National Homage to Christ the King were published, among them letters from the (arch)bishops of Mexico, Aguascalientes, Guadalajara, León, Zacatecas, Zamora, Morelia, Puebla, and Oaxaca. The more cautious prelates, like Ruiz y Flores of Morelia, did not go so far as to second what the organizers called the "Holy Crusade" to reconstitute Mexico's public and spiritual life ("return to God or perish") but limited themselves to endorsing Archbishop Mora y del Río's approval.⁷⁸ On January 9, the Vatican's approval, written by Cardinal Merry del Val, arrived in response to a telegram sent by Mora on the previous day.⁷⁹ In sum, the demonstration could not have been more "official," but from a strictly Catholic perspective only.

Some ten thousand Catholics of all social classes joined the demonstration, according to *El País*, offering "the most latent and sincere proof that the Mexican people unanimously acclaim [*Cristo Rey*] as their God before the entire world, challenging the reproaches of the impious." It had been years since Mexico City witnessed a similar religious event. As it turned out, Pedro Durán and the other organizers were preceded not merely by the mounted police but by the band of the Silesian College, and joined at the head of the march by the *ingeniero* Rafael de la Mora, "a prominent member of the Catholic Party and deputy to the Congress of the Union," as well as another group of "distinguished Catholic gentlemen, among whom we noted these *señores, licenciado* Eduardo Tamariz, doctor Eduardo Limón, *licenciado* Ramón Rivero, Manuel Amor, *licendiado* Francisco Elguero, José Ortíz Monasterio, Estanislao Suárez, Manuel de la Peza, Rafael Manterola, José Watson, Emanuel Amor, Angel Sandoval, Francisco Manzano, Alejandro Traslosheros, Benjamín Anguiano, Francisco Arce, and others." Again, we see that press coverage stressed the presence of members of the political elite as opposed to the more democratic strain of Mexican social Catholicism.

76. "Centro de Estudiantes," *El País*.

77. AHAM, c. 90/exp. 35, Capetillo to Guillén, Mexico City, January 8. Original emphasis.

78. "Página que La Nación Bondadosamente Destina," *La Nación*. Ríus Facius, *De don Porfirio a Plutarco*, 50; Barquín y Ruiz, *Cristo, Rey de México*, 149–50.

79. Ríus Facius, *De don Porfirio a Plutarco*, 51. See also Barquín y Ruiz, *Bernardo Bergöend*, 75, and Barquín y Ruiz, *Cristo, Rey de México*, 153.

As the marchers processed down the Paseo de la Reforma to the sound of applause and bell-ringing, flowers rained down from balconies. There was such a concentration of people in the *zócalo* that many had to climb trees or clamber onto the railings surrounding the cathedral in order to witness the ceremony. In the cathedral itself, the religious associations deposited their flags at the feet of an image of the Sacred Heart as the ceremony began: first came the Creed, then a sermon preached by a young Jesuit, Eduardo Peza, on the theme of Christ the King's inevitable triumph over those "modern ideas that struggle to deny the unlimited power of the Almighty over all the things of the earth." Finally, Archbishop Mora y del Río held aloft a monstrance and blessed those present.[80] According to Correa, who was there at the time,

> In the interior of the Cathedral there was attendance at a religious act that was among the most exciting of any that I have seen. Given the union of two sentiments, the religious and the patriotic, our hearts felt overwhelmed and filled with such enthusiasm that in the sacred precinct there erupted cries of *¡viva!* to God, the [Sacred] Heart of Jesus, Christ the King, the Virgin of Guadalupe, and the reigning Pontiff . . . When joy reached the point of delirium and applause crashed like thunder in the cathedral vaults; and when at the feet of the sculpture of Jesus there fell a shower of roses and every breast cried out proclaiming Him as Sovereign; somebody, sent with perverse intentions, gave one *¡viva!* to General Huerta and another to the army, cries that were drowned out by voices of angry protest, proclaiming that here only God was to be so acclaimed.[81]

Archbishop Mora y del Río, in the course of the religious ceremony, also heard one *viva* in honor of Huerta, though he assumed that this was simply a reference to the government's decision to authorize the procession. That, at least, is what the archbishop claimed in a bitter correspondence with *El Heraldo de Cuba* in September 1914.[82] Unhappily, though, it was this

---

80. "La Manifestación de Ayer," *El País*. Correa's memoir rehearses two aspects of Peza's sermon consistent with our argument concerning the ceremony's dual meaning: on the one hand, Peza delivered "a patriotic oration filled with fire, in celebration of the fact that the march, notwithstanding its character as a silent procession, signified the reconquest of the streets and the recognition of the social sovereignty of Jesus Christ in our Fatherland, held captive in the sin of apostasy." On the other, he "appealed to the mercy of He who died on Calvary that there be peace in Mexico." *El Partido Católico*, 182.

81. Correa, *El Partido Católico*, 180.

82. On reaching Cuba in mid-1914, Mora y del Río was accused by *El Heraldo de Cuba* of being "one of the most resolved supporters" of *huertismo*, and of tolerating

aspect of the event—"that government machination," as Correa had it—and Peza's sermon, which was reported as a series of "anathemas against the rebel movement and . . . eulogies to the dictator," that prevailed in the official press, where "the demonstration was described as being . . . organized by the National Catholic Party and frankly governmental in character."[83] The damage, especially the impression that the ceremony was a political event designed to throw holy water over the Huerta dictatorship, was done. According to Correa, who saw things clearly, the tribute to Christ the King was so stained by partisanship that it became "a transcendental fact in the hatred of the rebellion of the North for the clergy and the [National Catholic] Party; better said, it has been the pretext for fluttering the flag of religious persecution."[84]

Conclusion

And yet, the 1914 ceremony was *not* a *huertista* pageant, notwithstanding the political clumsiness with which it was organized, at least in its final phase. Unlike the Marian coronations of the Porfiriato, it was not an officially pontifical event, performed in the pope's name; no miraculous, stereotypically "feminine" devotional style was disseminated in its wake, as with some Marian coronations; and, in contrast to earlier coronations, no luxurious coronet was commissioned from the finest jeweler in Paris. Moreover, this was not an attempt to neutralize or appropriate a popular indigenous devotion, as occurred with the first coronation of Michoacán's Virgin of the Root (rebaptized the Virgin of Hope) in 1886, and even the Guadalupan coronation of 1895. Nor, finally, was this an unconfident attempt to fan the flames of a smoldering colonial devotion, as Plancarte y Labastida did when consecrating the Church of National Expiation to San Felipe de Jesús

---

in his cathedral "the sacrilege, for he must have considered it so, of giving *vivas* to Huerta, an incident unprecedented in the history of Mexico." In reply, Mora y del Río denied absolutely that he had lent moral or economic support to Huerta or allowed the cathedral to be a site for huertista propaganda. This, he wrote, was "a pack of lies, with what little truth it contains distorted." The only truth it contained was that "in the demonstration of January 11 . . . a *viva* was given to Gen. Huerta *for having allowed the demonstration*, but the person who made this cry was immediately brought to order, because the demonstration was only to be a homage to the Sacred Heart of Jesus, King of Kings, and of all who govern." This text can be read in AHAM, c. 90/exp. 26, Mora y del Río to *El Heraldo de Cuba*, Havana, September 24, and in Sánchez, *Episodios eclesiásticos de México*, 447–48.

83. Correa, *El Partido Católico*, 182–83.

84. Ibid., 180.

in 1897.[85] Rather, the 1914 consecration/coronation belonged to another Church entering another period: in terms of devotional style, it represented an important moment of change, in that it marked the transition from a loving and reproachful religious lexicon associated historically with the Sacred Heart to the concept of a triumphant, severe, regal Christ. This model was linked, in turn, to the vision of a militant Catholic *pueblo*, re-created in symbolic fashion in the devotional cycle of 1914, and to a concrete national project of a Catholicized social order, a project that would be achieved through the electoral success of a National Catholic Party. In the final analysis, the consecration was the public face of a broad project of Catholic regeneration that was kept under wraps during the Porfiriato, with its particular theology, iconography, and sociology. Except as an imposture, it was not an act of conjunctural collusion with the Huerta government. The regime had little to do with the ceremony, and in some ways appeared to have regarded it as a potential threat, not a blessing. This was not so surprising, perhaps, given that the meaning of the ceremony was the re-Catholicization of Mexican society in the context of an open democratic system, one in which Catholics would be able to participate politically for the first time since 1867.

Lastly, it is in the coronation of the Sacred Heart of Jesus that we find the roots of Mexico's devotion to Christ the King, in whose name thousands of Catholics challenged the revolutionary government in the Cristero Rebellion of 1926–29. Here, it is important to stress again that, in religious terms, this evidently powerful devotion was simply devotion to the Sacred Heart enthroned as King and social sovereign of Mexico.[86] The Christ the King devotion thus shows us how a clearly imported European devotion, of Jesuit and French origin, could very quickly become understood as a *Mexican* phenomenon, particularly when it corresponded to urgent religious needs and to a sense of profound social and spiritual crisis. From 1914 to 1926, conditions in Mexico favored such a process of interiorization. The violence and depredations of the Revolution, which by 1914 were already being felt around Mexico City, set the ceremony in credibly sharp—even eschatological—relief and illustrated in supremely concrete fashion the intellectual meaning of the festival. When the punishment was itself so real, it became easier to imagine the ceremony as the end point of an historic process of spiritual rupture, divine punishment, and restoration. Subsequent events merely reinforced this interpretation, as far as many Catholics

85. See note 17.

86. In 1921, for instance, plans to build a monument to Christ the King were still sometimes conflated with plans to build a monumental tribute to the Sacred Heart of Jesus. See AHAM, c. 79/exp. 21, *Carta pastoral colectiva con ocasión del Monumento Nacional*.

in Mexico were concerned. Thus, the Christ the King devotion soon acquired an intense religious significance that was largely lacking in the case of some of the other images that were crowned by the Mexican Church in this period. Because of its emphasis on penitence and struggle, the devotion offered scope for martyrdom and self-sacrifice, particularly in the context of the fierce religious persecution that Mexico endured in the 1920s. By this time, the Christ the King devotion had put down roots deep enough to move thousands of Catholics to offer armed resistance to the revolutionary state, and gave them a powerful ideological means to encode and legitimize such resistance. At the same time, a quarter of a million Catholics from the Archdiocese of Mexico alone would take part in the annual October pilgrimage to Tepeyac, celebrated in honor of Christ the King, as a protest against revolutionary religious persecution. Vast numbers offered passive resistance to the Mexican government through attendance at underground Mass, their prayers, and the reading of Cristero propaganda.

14

Kenotic Identities: Political Self-Emptying and Redefined Belongings

BRADEN P. ANDERSON

The theme of the conference from which this volume emerges was "Catholicity and Incarnated Identities." Incarnation calls us to the person of Jesus Christ, the "enfleshment" of the Second Person of the Trinity, who, for the sake of God's love for us, became one of us in order to save us. It is a mark of ecclesial discussion these days to speak of Christian discipleship as properly "incarnational," the implication being that we seek to be fully fledged embodiments of Christ in our world, especially in solidarity with the oppressed. This is a good thing. Of course, we must remember that, according to the model of Christ himself, incarnation requires *kenosis*. Any embodiment of God in the world—whether in the person of Jesus, in the lives of individual disciples, or in Christ's body, the church—necessarily entails self-emptying, dispossession, letting go. Yet, as the present volume attests, we face constantly the opposite temptations: to hold onto, to grasp, to secure ourselves and our identities.

    Nationalism is a specific form of grasping that has marked the church for centuries, a collective securing of political identity that aims at lesser ends that it claims to be ultimate, and uses means often opposed to those of Christ to realize those ends. It is a phenomenon that is particularly important to the discussions in this book because it distorts Christian theopolitics. Theopolitics, at its root, is the understanding that all salvation narratives (i.e., stories that convey how we are saved from threat) entail a politics, an outworking in community. But theopolitics also understands that all political communities presume some sort of salvation narrative. What "Christian" nationalism does is intertwine the biblical story of salvation with a given people's history and myth to create a new story whose communal embodiment, the nation, affects our salvation and that of the whole earth.

In light of that, I would like to do several things here. First, we need to be sure we know what we are talking about when we use the term "nationalism," because our inability to define it properly allows us as Christians to escape culpability for its ongoing development and propagation. We therefore need to understand what it is and how it operates, and then to understand its relation to the Christian faith. Second, given the Catholic context of the present volume, I will examine a few items published by the United States Conference of Catholic Bishops (USCCB) on what they refer to as "faithful citizenship" and, within that context, look at the bishops' collective response to perceived threats to religious liberties. I believe such an examination will indicate to what extent some of our political actions as Christians are shaped, however unwittingly, by a nationalist theopolitics. Third, I will offer a few brief thoughts about how our identities are reordered by a biblical theopolitics, and how our relationships with various communities of belonging are reconfigured by our primary allegiance to the gospel of the reign of God in Jesus Christ. Let us begin, though, by understanding the phenomenon of nationalism better.

Nationalism and the Authentication of National Identity

According to Canadian theologian Gregory Baum, there is a dearth of systematic reflection on nationalism from Catholic theological or ethical perspectives. Despite a rich tradition of Catholic social teaching, very little has been said regarding the phenomenon of nationalism, its theological implications, or the nuances of how Christians and the Church as a whole ought to evaluate it.[1] There is a history of the Catholic Church either directly supporting or resisting specific nationalist movements,[2] and a few encyclicals, such as *Christi Matri* (1966) and *Populorum Progressio* (1967), mention it in passing, but there is precious little by way of recent rigorous ecclesiastical reflection.

Protestant theology has been more attentive to nationalism in the past few decades, but even there the picture is incomplete. Recent ecumenical documents have arisen in response to various situations of ethnic and national conflict in Latin America, South Asia, and Eastern Europe, attempting to assess the deeper issues that give rise to such violence.[3] These works con-

   1. Baum, *Nationalism, Religion, and Ethics*, 5.
   2. Ibid., 5–7.
   3. See the Colombo Statement, published as "Ethnicity and Nationalism," 225–31;

ceive of ethnicity and cultural diversity as good creations by God, helping humanity to flourish and in no way necessitating exclusivity or aggression. Here, nationalism is perceived as an extreme and disordered form of a more proper and affirming national identity, the latter being inherently healthy and even God-given; superiority and exceptionalism are perversions of this, so nationalism is really a problem of degree. Churches should contribute to the appropriate development of human culture and national identity, but they too often succumb to nationalist tendencies, tying themselves too closely to the nations in which they reside and echoing their opinions and practices. Churches should rather be the site of ethnic and national reconciliation, of unity animated by fruits of the Spirit.

These Protestant documents are helpful in that they affirm ethnic and cultural diversity as part of human flourishing and in no way is such diversity a threat to Christian unity; this diversity enriches rather than detracts from the whole Body of Christ. They also rightly note how identity in Christ and his church relativizes all other differences and divisions, precluding the identification of God's kingdom with any particular earthly nation or ethnic group, and fostering human reconciliation by virtue of the Christian salvation narrative and its attendant practices. They are unafraid to cite ecclesial complicity with nationalism and nationalist violence, as churches tie themselves to the nation-state for their own survival, and they note how the church must critically examine itself in light of Scripture and tradition, allowing its propensity toward national division to be challenged and corrected.

Yet these documents remain problematic in ways that shed light on the discussion to follow. They treat human culture as a monolithic package and an unqualified good, with no acknowledgment that some cultural content—particularly elements of national identity—can be rooted in theological distortion. Such distortion often arises from the church's misreading of its own theological tradition, which can lead directly to the very exceptionalism these documents eschew. There is, in fact, too little attention to the theology involved in the churches' moves to tie themselves to particular nations, so no critique of the distorted theology is available. Tied to an anemic ecclesiology that is robbed of eschatological significance (the church as

---

the World Council of Churches Commission on Faith and Order, "Ethnic Identity, National Identity, and the Search for Unity"; and Hüffmeier, *Church, People, State, Nation*. Of these, the last is by far the most thoroughgoing with regard to understanding the nature of the phenomena at work, though it ultimately fails to adequately define nationalism (contenting itself with an imprecise "national awareness") and presents in response to nationalism what one critic indicts as an anemic ecclesiology. See Van der Borght, "Uniting Europe," 113.

harbinger of the kingdom of God irrupting into and transforming the world through Jesus Christ), this results in a failure of imagination, specifically, a failure of *theopolitical* imagination. As we will see, these problems plague U.S. Catholic documents as well.

It would seem, then, that an adequate ecclesial response to nationalism requires an accurate understanding of the phenomenon itself. Let us first understand precisely what is meant by "nation." A nation is not merely an ethnic or cultural people group, though ethnicity (biological or cultural) is absolutely necessary. Rather, a nation is a people group that has also developed a measure of distinct public culture and law[4] and believes itself to possess political self-determination over a particular geographic territory. This is different from "state," which is the principal political unit in a defined territory.[5] Enthusiasm for one's culture or ethnicity alone, then, is not nationalism and can actually be, if properly ordered, a source of beauty to the human community and the church. This is not the problem at hand. Indeed, even in disordered form, where ethnic or cultural exclusivity can be abusive and lead to violence, it is not nationalism per se. And neither is patriotism, since patriotism has to do with love of state rather than with love of nation.[6] Thus, nationalism cannot merely be a disordered form of a more proper patriotism. This is not merely a question of semantics: if nation and state are distinct from one another, then the purveyors of nationalism may not be state actors, and may be found emerging from and operating within other contexts, including communities of faith.

So, to put the matter succinctly, *nationalism is not a problem of degree, but of type.* Historical and social-scientific research suggests that, rather than being an excessive outworking of national identity, nationalism is in fact the very process leading to national identity in the first place, and of propagating that identity amongst a given people group. This can be orchestrated either by state or non-state actors, depending on the context. But, as political scientist Lowell Barrington points out, nationalism is also the process of pursuing political rights and power, up to and including territorial autonomy, usually in the form of a state.[7] According to Barrington, among the questions nationalist elites address in these processes is "who belongs

---

4. A. Smith, *Cultural Foundations of Nations*, 19.

5. Barrington, "'Nation' and 'Nationalism,'" 712–13. Incidentally, this distinction indicates why the use of "nation-state" is no longer as appropriate or helpful as it used to be, since it designates the tight identification of a national (people-group) boundary with the political borders of a state, a situation that is becoming harder and harder to find.

6. Ibid., 714.

7. Ibid.

to the nation?" and "what territory does it claim?"⁸ However, an additional question—one that is often more central in certain contexts—is the following: What is the nation's purpose in the world? What is its *raison d'être*? In already established states, such as the U.S., pursuing the political power to definitively answer this question can take the form of campaigns for cultural renewal, where advocates of a particular vision of the nation perceive threats in competing visions and seek to have their own institutionalized in politics and culture. We will discuss the notion of threat below, but suffice it here to say that claims as to the origin, purpose, and mission of the nation comprise the central process of nationalism: authentication.

According to nationalism scholar Anthony D. Smith, who coined the term, *authentication* is the process wherein nationalist elites determine what constitutes the "true" nation. The nationalist acts as a sort of archaeologist, "rediscovering" the people's ethnic/cultural past and, in particular, identifying a golden age, which, when reconstructed, becomes the standard for critiquing the present community and inspiring its correction. The golden age is the "canon of authenticity and creativity for latter-day nationalists."⁹ It is the period narrated by nationalist leaders when "the community was great and glorious in political and military terms, or when it was wealthy and prosperous, or at its most creative in intellectual and artistic, or religious and spiritual terms."¹⁰ And most importantly, it is the point in the narrated life of the people from which they have since declined, and to which they must now return with fervor. To be compelling and effective, this entire "ethno-history" must be authenticated, determined to be both distinctive and indigenous relative to that people's origins and achievements. Finally, the authenticated narrative is reappropriated by nationalist elites, who encourage their people to take ownership of that story as their own, to seek the institutionalization of their national vision in government and society, and to purify culture of any foreign and competing elements.¹¹ National identity is thus the product of "the maintenance and continual reinterpretation of the pattern of values, symbols, memories, myths, and traditions that form the distinctive heritage of the nation, and the identification of individuals with that heritage and its pattern."¹²

Given that many nationalist narratives portray national purpose as transcendent, even divinely ordained or given, the appropriation of faith

---

8. Barrington, "Nationalism & Independence," 10–11.
9. Smith, *Nation in History*, 67.
10. Smith, *Cultural Foundations*, 44.
11. Smith, "Formation of National Identity," 149.
12. Smith, *Chosen Peoples*, 25.

traditions is frequently a central component in the authentication process. For Smith, religion is uniquely effective in inspiring the passionate commitments people make to their national identities. Nationalism, which he describes as a "religion of the people," becomes best understood as a type of "church," where the process of authenticating the true nation amounts to the pursuit of national holiness and salvation. The nationalist movement binds the people together through a form of liturgical practice, proclamation, and teaching; it becomes "a form of culture and a type of belief-system whose object is the nation conceived as a sacred communion."[13]

The nation is required to stand apart and follow a special course that is a function of divine promise, and thereby to play a singular role in "the moral economy of global salvation." The people accept this unique identity voluntarily, and in so doing "become God's elect, saved and privileged through their obedience to His will and their identification with His plan."[14] Such holiness revolves around the people's reconstructed ethno-history, which becomes the "sacred foundation" of the nation.

According to Smith, in narrating these sacred foundations, "the nationalist belief-system draws much of its content from *key elements of traditional religions, duly sifted and reinterpreted.*"[15] Note, then, the significance of nationalism for theology and religious studies: in projects attempting to recover elements of religious heritage in order to authenticate national identity, nationalists *selectively appropriate and reinterpret* traditional theological elements. As Smith and other nationalism scholars note, this move often distorts those traditional theologies for the sake of what amounts in the end to alternative salvation narratives. Therefore, in many cases, nationalism and the identity it produces lie in considerable tension with, if not outright opposition to, the traditional theologies upon which they rely. This is why nationalism is such an important question for us, and it raises key questions: What is going on when such nationalism arises from within the church? What in the Christian Scriptures or tradition directs the present church to reorient itself toward the perpetuation of any particular nation over another? What occurs *theologically* to allow Christians to propagate a national vision rooted in an intertwining of Christian and American salvation narratives? These are the questions I wish to keep foremost in mind as we turn to the writings of the U.S. Catholic bishops.

---

13. Ibid., 17–18.
14. Ibid., 47–49.
15. Ibid., 42. Emphasis added.

USCCB on "Faithful Citizenship" and Religious Liberties

In my book *Chosen Nation: Scripture, Theopolitics, and the Project of National Identity*,[16] I examine the nationalism propagated by the American Christian Right (CR) as well as by select academic theologians. In these works (especially those of the CR), nationalism is relatively easy to track, as Christian Right elites publicly and explicitly propagate narratives consisting of a syncretism of Christian and American themes. For these authors, America is in many ways a New Israel, the people chosen by Providence to be the definitive harbinger of the kingdom of God on earth, mainly by means of militaristic democracy and market capitalism. Yet, America has fallen away from this election, refusing to acknowledge its God-given role or the God who gave it. As such, we must recapture the vision of chosen America in faithfulness to its God and institutionalize that vision governmentally and culturally, lest we be judged by that God and relegated to historical irrelevance.

Most writings by the U.S. Conference of Catholic Bishops do not display such explicit nationalistic themes, but there are elements that give me pause as a theologian working in this area. These are elements that raise questions of identity and mission, of perceived threat and the means of our political discipleship and salvation, and as such, I believe they call for careful scrutiny.

"Faithful Citizenship"

In 2011, the bishops published *Forming Consciences for Faithful Citizenship*.[17] The cover image of this statement is that of a cross set against a waving banner of stars and stripes. It is an ambiguous image, suggesting anything from a simple notion of Christian discipleship in the American context to a union of flag and cross, or even, as the eye travels left to right, the cross proceeding from the stars and stripes. I do not doubt that the bishops have in mind the first—a simple reminder of our lived context—but I mention this because such ambiguity pervades the document as a whole.

In its introduction, *Forming Consciences* states, "We are members of a community of faith with a long tradition of teaching and action on human life and dignity, marriage and family, justice and peace, care for creation, and the common good." It also states in the next sentence, "As Americans, we are also blessed with religious liberty which safeguards our right to

---

16. Anderson, *Chosen Nation*.
17. United States Conference of Catholic Bishops (USCCB), *Forming Consciences*.

bring our principles and moral convictions into this public arena."[18] Here, we have the two main identities at play in this document, which, as the document progresses, are worked out in terms of political sensibilities and policy orientations. One is a moral community rooted in a particular faith, and the other is the public political community in which that moral community seeks to remain an active participant. But two questions emerge as the text goes on: What precisely is the faith in which this moral community is grounded? And which identity is at work, and where, when discerning political discipleship in our context?

Let me address the second question first. In Part I of the document, which is a statement of the bishops' general reflections on Catholic teaching and political life, we find the following phrases: "As a nation, we share many blessings and strengths"; "We are a nation founded on 'life, liberty, and the pursuit of happiness'"; "We are a country pledged to pursue 'liberty and justice for all'"; "We are a nation of immigrants"; "We are a society built on the strength of our families"; "We are a powerful nation in a violent world." Yet, intermixed with these phrases, and without any explicit distinction, is the statement, "We are called to be peacemakers in a nation at war."[19] It seems there are different "we's" at work here—two quite distinct identities and communities of belonging—yet the bishops make no attempt to distinguish them. They are conflated, and the bishops seem quite comfortable with that conflation.

This would be but a minor quibble if it were not for the utter ambiguity with which this document treats the Christian faith, and therefore Christian mission and identity. There is clear mention of the Catholic moral community here, over which the bishops assert authority as leaders and teachers. They clearly demarcate and explicitly address moral teachings for the formation of the individual Catholic's conscience. What seems absent, though, is a clear identification *of* and *with* the theology—the salvation narrative—that ostensibly gives rise to those teachings. The bishops claim a "primary responsibility to hand on the Church's moral and social teaching," particularly within the American political context, but there is no mention of the *theological* content from which such teachings are derived. For whatever reason, the relevant teachings are assumed rather than taught. This is an ironic oversight given the reminder in the document's own notes that "ignorance of Christ and his Gospel . . . can be at the source of errors of judgment in moral conduct."[20]

18. Ibid., v.
19. Ibid., 1.
20. Ibid., 31 n. 2.

While *Forming Consciences* is ostensibly catechetical in nature, it seems the content has more to do with cultivating an American political identity than an ecclesial one. The document states that the "obligation to teach about moral values that should shape our lives, including our public lives, is central to the mission given to the Church by Jesus Christ."[21] It calls "responsible citizenship" a virtue, political participation an obligation "rooted in our baptismal commitment to follow Jesus Christ."[22] It grounds the formation of conscience in a study of Scripture and Church teaching, and it reminds readers that Catholic moral judgment must be consistent with the gospel.[23] Yet, at no point does the document delve into the content of the gospel, delineate the mission Jesus gave us, explore the significance of baptism for reorienting political identity, or explicitly address what Scripture has to say about the radically alternative *and political* nature of *ekklesia*. Such content and context is all but ignored here. Identity and politics in American and ecclesial contexts are blurred, with little to no distinction offered between the two, little to no imagination of how the two might lie in potentially considerable tension.

This ambiguity is abundant as well in the images chosen for the document. The title page preceding the main body of text displays an iconic photograph of a field with a peaceful farm in the background, and in the foreground, a woman—perhaps a child—walking through the field with an American flag streaming behind her. The only words on the page are "faithful citizenship." Even where the text discusses the importance of the Eucharist as a public form of worship before a watching world, the closest image is not that of the Lord's Table or its elements but that of a voting booth. While there is one photo of people praying in church pews, the overall impression is that of a merely cultural faith, a nostalgically melded image of "Christian America," with little to no awareness of the radical nature of the gospel to which the document claims to be beholden.

Why such a conspicuous absence of theological content? Is theology merely taken for granted, assuming congregations already sufficiently understand it? Given laments I have heard about congregational ignorance of theology from Catholic clergy and laity alike, I seriously doubt it. Is it because the bishops are deliberately dismissive of Christian theological content here out of concern for intelligibility and acceptance of their statement? I'm not sure that makes sense either in light of a document directed not at American society in general but at Catholic congregations. I think it is much more likely that these bishops, at least in their capacity as a conference

21. Ibid., 3.
22. Ibid., 4.
23. Ibid., 7.

addressing political discipleship, are already formed according to a decidedly American, culturally Christian theopolitics. In light of that formation, they act here, however inadvertently, as nationalist elites, espousing a particular vision of proper national identity.

As opposed to explicit "nationalisms by commission," those blatantly syncretized narratives formulated and propagated by the Christian Right or even the Christian Left, *Forming Consciences* is a sort of "nationalism by *omission*," a narrative distorted by the *absence* of theological content in favor of explicit commitments to America and to our patriotic duties as its citizens. It is an account of one community, the church, whose salvation narrative seems to entail the church's safeguarding of the culture and political institutions of our properly *political* community, America. The statement selectively appropriates the Christian salvation narrative by using terms like "mission" and "baptismal commitment" to refer to "responsible citizenship" and political participation, not in any sense of transnational ecclesiality, but rather in the specifically American context. This selective appropriation leaves out the biblical roots of church identity and mission, which I will address in the final part of this chapter.

As stated in its introduction, the purpose of the document is to "form . . . consciences," to "contribute to civil and respectful public dialogue," and to shape voting preferences for the upcoming election in light of Catholic teaching.[24] Together, these goals constitute "political responsibility" for Catholics in the American context. What is interesting here is the degree to which these ends are defined by the terms of the American identity and politics, rather than the mission of the church to make *of all nations* disciples to the new reality of *basileia*, the kingship of God. The apparent goal of the document is to produce proper American citizens, rather than theopolitically engaged Christian disciples. And the bishops seem to forget, as theologian William Cavanaugh has amply demonstrated, that forming consciences alone falls a bit short when it is bodies that are beholden to the state.[25] In short, *Forming Consciences* strongly suggests a vision of America as the political outworking of Catholic moral teaching, rather than a vision of the church stemming from the considerably more radical gospel of the reign of God in Jesus Christ.

Make no mistake: I find many of the policy prescriptions in the document to be rightly argued and admirable in their commitments, particularly those having to do with immigration, care for and solidarity with the poor, and, so far as the statement goes, a commitment to peace. These are helpful teachings. Yet there seems to be little specific theological grounding for

24. Ibid., v.
25. See, for example, Cavanaugh's *Myth of Religious Violence*.

them; that is left for the individual reader to interpret as she or he will. So I am left wondering: of what are we to be faithful citizens? Of the United States, with all that faithful citizenship to this country implies—including its obsessions with national security and market expansion—or are we citizens of heaven (Phil 3:20), pilgrims and aliens in this land, with allegiance to another sovereign altogether and a solidarity with fellow pilgrims around the world that is more real, more "solid," than any earthly national identity? It is difficult to answer that question when the content of the faith goes unexplored, reduced in large part to mere morality.

Fighting for "Religious Liberty"

The *Forming Consciences* statement is a general introduction to theopolitical identity as the U.S. Catholic bishops conceive of it. As I have said, it is a form of nationalism by omission, where the refusal to explore the potentially subversive claims of the Christian gospel results in a distorted theopolitical narrative. Statements by the bishops on the subject of religious liberty, however, are more explicit in their interweaving of identities. For example, the bishops' official "Statement on Religious Liberty" begins as follows:

> We are Catholics. We are Americans. We are proud to be both, grateful for the gift of faith which is ours as Christian disciples, and grateful for the gift of liberty which is ours as American citizens. To be Catholic and American should mean not having to choose one over the other. Our allegiances are distinct, but they need not be contradictory, and should instead be complementary.[26]

Note here the explicit claim that Christian identity and national identity *necessarily* go hand in hand; they should never require a choice between them, because they are never in conflict, at least when each is true to its own vision or nature. This assumes, of course, that the Christian and American *narratives* are inherently complementary, that in their fundamental claims, commitments, practices, and conceptions of divine will and human flourishing, they say pretty much identical things. That the church calls the incarnated, crucified, and risen Jesus "Lord," whereas America merely cites an unnamed, amorphous Creator as inspiration for its version of freedom, seems to suggest otherwise. Indeed, that America's very birth required Christians to kill other Christians—clearly a deliberate choice between church and nation—is one point of many that are conspicuously absent.

---

26. USCCB, "Our First, Most Cherished Liberty," 1.

With this conflation of identities in mind, we see throughout much of the rest of the statement another attempt, more explicit this time, at *authentication*, that process of narrating the content of the "true" American nation and our responsibility for its endurance. This narrative begins with the arrival of Catholic and Protestant settlers to Maryland in 1634, who lived together peacefully and gave rise to the 1649 "Toleration Act," the "first law in our nation's history to protect the individual's right to freedom of conscience."[27] But toleration ended with the Church of England's establishment of religion in the colony a few decades later, prompting discrimination against Catholics. The account goes from there straight into a discussion of the U.S. Founding Fathers, highlighting the roles of Madison, Jefferson, and Washington, the latter of whom is quoted approvingly as saying, "The establishment of Civil and Religious Liberty was the Motive that induced me to the field of battle."[28] This gave rise to religious freedom as the first of the Bill of Rights. As the statement goes on to say,

> That is our American heritage, our most cherished freedom. It is the first freedom because if we are not free in our conscience and our practice of religion, all other freedoms are fragile. If citizens are not free in their own consciences, how can they be free in relation to others, or to the state? If our obligations and duties to God are impeded, or even worse, contradicted by the government, then we can no longer claim to be a land of the free, and a beacon of hope for the world.[29]

Note the interesting claims in this quotation. Freedom begins in the conscience, again implying a compartmentalization of body and soul. The position of the conscience then determines our position vis-à-vis our communities of belonging; the inward and private governs the outward and public. Most importantly, our "obligations and duties to God," to the mission we are called to in Christ, can be impeded by the state: faithfulness to the gospel therefore *depends upon* American political arrangements. The statement assumes that "we," as American citizens—the "we" does not seem to refer to the audience first and foremost as disciples of Christ—must be able to fulfill our nation's divine mission, because the world is depending upon us to do so.

But not all Americans subscribe to this story, and this fact prompts alarm in the discourse of American Christian nationalists. Let us first

---

27. This account is taken from "Our First, Most Cherished Liberty," 5.

28. Ibid., 6. Again, an ironic statement considering the "field of battle" required Christians to kill other Christians for the sake of religious liberty.

29. Ibid., 7.

understand what is at play here theoretically. An inevitable, if not essential, feature of nationalism as a process leading to national identity is the notion of *threat*. To begin with, identity is relational—it defines and redefines "self" and "other"—and thus, "nationalism does not simply 'express' a preexistent identity: it 'constitutes' one."[30] This is important in two respects: (1) there is no "self" without the "other," and (2) in agreement with nationalism scholarship, nationalism is not merely the "acting out" of identity; it is just as much the creation thereof. Of course, marking oneself and an "other" is not necessarily to be threatened by the other; it can be just as much about respecting the identity and distinctiveness of the other and of oneself. However, as the work of Anthony Marx has demonstrated, nationalism almost always entails the identification of the other as a threat to self and to one's own nation, and that threat thus becomes a means by which to cohere one's own nation.[31]

Add to this the insights of David Campbell, who argues within the different, though related, context of foreign policy that the "inability of the state project of security to succeed is the guarantor of the state's continued success as an impelling identity. The constant articulation of danger through foreign policy is thus not a threat to a state's identity or existence: *it is its condition of possibility*."[32] It is no great stretch to assume the same is true of nations and cultural groups, and particularly of nationalist movements and discourse. The articulation of threat as a "condition of possibility" for existence is clear in that it produces unity in the face of danger, as well as a crystallization (and continuous *re*-crystallization) of all aspects of identity and purpose. National identity is created, ennobled, and revitalized in the face of threat, and that threat is necessary for the nationalist movement to continue and to justify its own existence. Of course, such threat may not be in the form of an external force impinging upon the existence of the nation from without. Rather, threat may be perceived within the nation itself, particularly in terms of disputes over the very *meaning* of the nation. One can never assume a nation's sense of purpose to be monolithic; multiple visions of national identity can be at play in a given context, in which case one finds a struggle between competing narratives.[33] Such competition characterizes much of the debate in what we would call the "culture wars" in the U.S. Hence, our own "Christian" nationalisms, which are typically engaged in a contest over the meaning of "America's story."[34]

30. Ignatieff, "Nationalism and the Narcissism," 92.
31. See Marx, *Faith in Nation*.
32. Campbell, *Writing Security*, 12–13. Emphasis added.
33. Brass, *Ethnicity and Nationalism*, 20.
34. Heinz, "Clashing Symbols," 155.

This type of struggle is precisely the context for much of the USCCB's stated concerns about religious liberty. According to an October 2012 homily by Baltimore Archbishop William Lori, posted alongside the "Statement on Religious Liberty" on the USCCB Web site, "life and liberty have been under assault by an overarching godless secularism" that seeks to marginalize the faith and the faithful in America.[35] This assault works itself out most recently in the form of policies that legalize abortion and issue mandates to Catholic health care institutions and other employers requiring funding for abortifacients and other measures that violate Catholic teaching. The proper response, says Lori, is to return to the intent of the Founding Fathers, fidelity to which is interwoven in his homily with prayers to "Mary our Mother, the Seal of Wisdom, so that we might have the wisdom we need to defend God's gifts of life and liberty." Lori goes on to argue that faith requires a public outworking; it cannot remain private. Therefore, "we must robustly engage in the political process by voting with a properly formed conscience and by continually letting our elected officials know that we expect them to protect the God-given rights of life and liberty."

The point here is not that Lori's policy concerns have no merit, or that the bishops' appeals for religious liberty in the U.S. and around the world as a public good are not worthwhile. Indeed, various influences in Western culture do seek to do precisely as they say, namely, to further privatize faith and to demand that public policy be shaped and formed a-religiously, a position whose proponents do not recognize is itself inherently theological. No, the important point here is that the bishops have crafted a nationalist narrative, a selectively reinterpreted interweaving of Christian theology with American history and myth. It is a vision of an America that, from its settlement through its founding, was inherently hospitable to active and public Christian faith in various forms, and consequently, to their claim that Christian identity and American identity are, by their very nature, partners.[36] The bishops perceive threats to that narrative now in government policy and culture, so they attempt to propagate both narrative and perceived threat among their congregations for the sake of calling those congregations to rise and struggle for political rights and power, for institutionalization of the bishops' vision of the American nation. This is apparently, for these bishops, the only conceivable *political* response, the way in which Catholic

---

35. Lori, "Homily for Rosary Pilgrimage."

36. As opposed to *Forming Consciences*, there are marked similarities between Lori's discourse and that of the American Christian Right, which narrates an explicitly syncretized narrative of theology and history/myth, in part to institutionalize privilege and protection for that narrative and its proponents. See Anderson, *Chosen Nation*, ch. 6.

Christians work out their faith in public. And this process is, by definition, the process of nationalism.

Letting Go of Nationalist Narratives

Is the nationalist narrative—selectively appropriating various theological themes as it finds them useful—our story as the church? Is nationalism's struggle for rights and power the struggle of Christ's disciples in America? I have trouble squaring affirmative responses to those questions with the actual content of the Christian salvation narrative.

The story that claims Christians is one in which God chooses a people without hope, without much at all in the way of identity, and establishes them from the ground up as a nation—Israel—whose entire reason for being lies in its alternative mission to be a witness to and embodiment of God's salvific reign. And the way they do this is precisely by *not* following the ways of the nations: power politics, national security, and social stratification for the sake of empowering a national security apparatus. This nation is to be holy, set apart for God's special use, a priestly nation whose mediation of God's grace to the world manifests itself in a distinctly alternative theopolitics. It fails to do so, at least for a time, because out of its own collective anxieties, it adopts the politics of the nations, and thus its mission—leading to the salvation of the world—is undermined. So, it is sent a savior, one in whom all the nations, to whom Israel was supposed to minister, would be blessed. This savior, the incarnation of both Israel and of the God who called Israel into existence, is the Jesus of the gospels. And it is he who commands us in Matthew 28 to make of the nations disciples to his lordship (Matt 28:19), citizens of the kingdom of God over which Christ reigns, and which even Christ himself will one day submit to the Father.[37]

But what does this mean for Christians sociopolitically? Theopolitically? First Peter tells us that we—the *ekklesia*—are rooted in the nation Israel and its mission. It calls *us* to be set apart, to mediate grace, and to declare God's praises. This *ekklesia* is the community of disciples of Jesus, who, as Douglas Harink explains, "enacts in his concrete historical life and death, within the concrete historical conditions of his time, an *alternative sociopolitical messianic life*," calling his disciples to follow in those steps "as their baptismal share in his own being and act as the incarnate Word, crucified, risen, exalted, coming again in glory."[38] This means that the church in

---

37. See Lohfink, *Does God Need the Church?*, as well as Anderson, *Chosen Nation*, chs. 4 and 5.

38. See Harink, *1 & 2 Peter*, 20. Emphasis in the original.

no way requires the methods of conventional politics in order to be faithful to its mission. Rather, all that we need has already been provided, and not on the battlefield or in the halls of politics, but on the cross. Our impetus for faithful action is found not in a declaration or a constitution, but in an empty tomb.

First Peter also calls Christ's disciples "scattered," "dispersed," "exiles." We are a pilgrim people, a fully fledged community transcending the various societies in which we reside. We are on a journey whose only certainties are its ultimate end, and persecution—perhaps even martyrdom—along the way.[39] We do not secure ourselves as the nations do, because we follow the One who was Israel as Israel was meant to be, whose victory—and therefore our salvation—lay in insecurity without anxiety, in letting go and in giving up what he could have rightfully claimed.

Indeed, Philippians 2 tells us that the Second Person of the Trinity did not consider his right to divine glory and power something to continue to grasp in light of the need at hand, namely, the salvation of creation. Instead, he humbled himself, accepted unjustified scandal, and made himself utterly vulnerable to the powers of the day. Christ subjected his politics to theirs, and he absorbed their violence without returning it. As we find in Colossians 1–2, it is precisely this cross that reordered those powers, that broke their sovereignty; it is precisely his submission that resulted in his triumph. In light of this core theological truth, I think we would be justified in responding to the U.S. Catholic bishops that we Christians need to stop trying to secure ourselves. That is not our mission. That is not our story.

Our story reconfigures Christians' relationships to all other communities of belonging. We may be American citizens, but we have more in common with fellow Christians in Ecuador, Iran, or China than we do with fellow Americans who do not call Jesus "Lord." We engage our communities and our nations for the sake of our neighbor's good (even if to our own detriment), with an eye toward the interests of the marginalized and oppressed, and not for our own so-called rights. We must remember that the church does not live primarily in the context of earthly nations and states and their attendant politics of security. Rather, our national and international systems exist, in all their complexity and messiness, within the context of the cosmic salvation and reign of Christ, of which the church—not America—is harbinger in our worship, service, and our solidarity with one another and the "least of these." That is our story, the kenotic identity that turns our eye away from ourselves, and in so doing makes us, the church, more faithfully incarnational.

---

39. Wall and Lemcio, *New Testament as Canon*, 202.

15

Is Catholicism a Religion? Catholicism and Nationalism in America[1]

WILLIAM T. CAVANAUGH

In October 2005, Stephen Kobasa, a teacher with twenty-five years of service in Catholic schools, was fired from Kolbe Cathedral High School in Bridgeport, Connecticut, where he had taught for six years. He was fired for refusing to display the American flag permanently in his classroom. Just before he was fired, Kobasa wrote a letter to the bishop of Bridgeport, explaining that to display the flag "would be to act against my conscience as a believing Roman Catholic Christian. My teaching can never take its legitimacy from any symbol except the Cross of Christ. To elevate any national emblem to that level would be for me to ignore the fundamental call of Jesus to compassion without boundaries."[2] Kobasa added that the threat of dismissal being leveled against him "creates the unmistakable impression that national loyalty is being valued over faithful obedience to the Gospel."[3] After he was fired, Kobasa said, "Everything in the Gospel rejects what flags stand for: boundaries, hatreds, creation of enemies. For a Catholic Christian school that holds up the crucifix as a symbol of God's love, the flag can only be a contradiction. The Church can only function with its prophetic voice by standing outside the state."[4] The irony of this happening at a school

---

1. Much of the last six pages of this chapter are taken more or less verbatim from an article I published in *Pro Ecclesia* titled "Are We Free Not to Be a Religion? The Ambivalence of Religious Freedom" (*Pro Ecclesia* 23 [2014] 7–21). That article has been included in my recently published book, *Field Hospital: The Church's Engagement with a Wounded World* (Grand Rapids: Eerdmans, 2016).

2. Rothschild, "Catholic High School Teacher Forced Out over Flag."

3. Ibid.

4. Ibid.

named after St. Maximilian Kolbe was apparently lost on those in charge. Kolbe was a Franciscan priest who gave himself up to be starved to death at Auschwitz in place of another man, a simultaneous act of obedience to God and defiance of National Socialism.

What the school supervisor and bishop had in mind in firing a faithful Catholic man with a family to support in the middle of the semester was never made public; Kobasa himself never received a reply to his letter asking for their reasons. One of the most remarkable aspects of the entire episode is that no one among those responsible for firing Stephen Kobasa seems to have put forth an argument for displaying the American flag in a Catholic school classroom. All inquiries after the fact were directed to the statement on the Diocese website, which read, "The Diocese of Bridgeport has long believed that the American flag is an important fixture in its Catholic School classrooms"[5]—without giving any indication as to why.

The irony here is that the Diocese's response, or lack thereof, confirms the point of Stephen Kobasa's protest: there is an aura of unspeakability, untouchability, obedience, allegiance, transcendence surrounding the American flag that threatens to rival our loyalty to God. The Diocese treated the flag like something sacred, while firing Kobasa for saying so. The flag is revered as sacred: one must honor it, pledge allegiance to it, never let it touch the ground, ritually fold it, cremate or bury rather than discard it, and, above all, be willing to kill and die for it. And yet, as with a totem surrounded by taboos, one must never acknowledge that it is really sacred.

The bishop who confirmed the firing of Stephen Kobasa would of course deny that the flag or the nation is a sacred object. The bishop would no doubt acknowledge the Catholic Church's teaching on idolatry and even its warnings about idolatry and the nation-state. Pope Pius XI wrote that nationalistic attempts to monopolize the education of the young spring from "an ideology which clearly resolves itself into a true, a real pagan worship of the state—a Statolatry which is not less in contrast with the natural rights of the family than it is in contradiction to the supernatural rights of the Church."[6] In its section on idolatry, the Catechism makes clear that "idolatry not only refers to false pagan worship. It remains a constant temptation to faith." The Catechism continues, "Man commits idolatry whenever he honors and reveres a creature in place of God" and includes "the state" in a list of examples.[7] Elsewhere, the Catechism warns against the "idolatry

---

5. Ibid.
6. Pius XI, *Non abbiamo bisogno*, §44.
7. *Catechism of the Catholic Church*, §2113.

of the nation."[8] Kobasa's bishop could affirm all these teachings but simply claim that they do not apply in this case; all that is required is a healthy respect for the nation and its flag, not reverence or worship.

Idolatry is usually a matter of degree. It is rare that someone actually bows down to a golden calf or claims to worship Jupiter; it is most often the case that earthly things that are not God—money, for example—take on an inordinate importance in a person's life, a temptation present to all of us. The difference between respect and reverence, then, is an important distinction to maintain in one's spiritual life, but it can also have an ideological function, which keeps us from recognizing idolatry when it occurs. The distinction can be used to draw a sharp line when in fact none exists. When we are in danger of committing idolatry, we can simply claim that we value and respect a particular earthly good but do not cross the line into reverence.

In a Supreme Court case on the legality of an amendment against "desecration" of the flag, Justice William Rehnquist recognized that the flag is set apart from other ordinary objects, but stopped just short of acknowledging idolatry. "The flag is not simply another 'idea' or 'point of view' competing for recognition in the marketplace of ideas. Millions and millions of Americans regard it with an almost mystical reverence regardless of what sort of social, political, or philosophical beliefs they may have."[9] Here the word "almost" is crucial, because it maintains a line between a proper respect for the flag and a "mystical reverence" that most people would find conceptually objectionable if presented in those terms, either because of a secularist demand that religious matters be kept out of public life or because of Judeo-Christian scruples about idolatry. In their important book on blood sacrifice and the nation, Carolyn Marvin and David Ingle ask why the ostensible line between national symbols and "religion" is scrupulously upheld:

> If nationalism is religious, why do we deny it? Because what is obligatory for group members must be separated, as holy things are, from what is contestable. To concede that nationalism is a religion is to expose it to challenge, to make it just the same as sectarian religion. By explicitly denying that our national symbols and duties are sacred, we shield them from competition with sectarian symbols. In so doing, we embrace the ancient command not to speak the sacred, ineffable name of god. The god is inexpressible, unsayable, unknowable, beyond language. But that god may not be refused when it calls for sacrifice.[10]

8. *Catechism of the Catholic Church*, §57.

9. Justice William Rehnquist, *Texas v. Johnson*, 401 US 397, quoted in Marvin and Ingle, *Blood Sacrifice and the Nation*, 30.

10. Marvin and Ingle, "Blood Sacrifice and the Nation," 770.

What I propose to do in this essay is to question this line between nationalism and religion. In particular, I will reflect on nationalism and Catholicism as religions. I want to examine what it means to deny that nationalism is a religion and affirm that Catholicism is a religion. Both the denial and affirmation, I will argue, are problematic. On the one hand, denying that nationalism is a religion keeps us from seeing the idolatrous tendencies in our reverence for the nation and national symbols. On the other hand, affirming that Catholicism is a religion has a tendency to marginalize it from the public sphere, making it an essentially private set of beliefs and behaviors that, as private, cannot conflict with allegiance to the nation. I will argue that we should not too hastily downplay that conflict.

Religious and Secular

When we use the terms "religious" and "secular" in everyday speech, we usually assume that the meaning is clear. Religions are things like Christianity and Islam and Judaism and Hinduism where a God or gods are explicitly worshipped. Everything else is labeled "secular," which basically means "not religion." In this category, we would usually place things like nationalism, because no one thinks that nations are gods; nations refer to groups of people who occupy certain lands, and so on, all mundane realities, as important as they might be. People sometimes use the word "religion" to describe mundane activities, as in "I read the morning paper religiously" or "Baseball is my religion," but we usually understand that those types of meanings are merely metaphorical: no one really believes that Derek Jeter is a god with superhuman powers, despite the occasional use of that kind of language. Religion is generally understood to refer to things that are not mundane but that belong to another, supernatural, realm.

When the Romans used the term *religio*, however—the origin of our term "religion"—they used it to describe mundane realities as well as things that referred to the gods. To say *religio mihi est*—"it is religion to me"— was to say that something was a serious and binding obligation to me. This might refer to one's oblations to a god, but it might equally refer to one's civic obligations to one's fellow citizens.[11] Augustine writes in the *City of God* that

> The word "religion" [*religio*] would seem, to be sure, to signify more particularly the "cult" offered to God, rather than "cult" in general; and that is why our translators have used it to render the Greek word *thrêskeia*. However, in Latin usage (and by that

11. W. Smith, *Meaning and End of Religion*, 19–21.

I do not mean in the speech of the illiterate, but even in the language of the highly educated) "religion" [*religio*] is something which is displayed in human relationships, in the family (in the narrower and the wider sense) and between friends; and so the use of the word does not avoid ambiguity when the worship of God is in question. We have no right to affirm with confidence that "religion" is confined to the worship of God, since it seems that this word has been detached from its normal meaning, in which it refers to an attitude of respect in relations between a man and his neighbor.[12]

Brent Nongbri's recent survey of the different meanings of *religio* in Roman usage—scruples, rules, worship practices, etc.—is less sure than Augustine that there is one "normal meaning" of the term, but is equally sure that the term cannot be restricted to usages having to do with gods. Nongbri comments, "What I show here is only that the word had a variety of meanings in antiquity and that none of those corresponds to the modern notion of religion or delineates 'religious' from 'secular.'"[13] The term *religio* appears only thirteen times in the Latin Vulgate version of the Bible used for more than a thousand years in Christendom. In the New Testament, it is used for the Greek *thrēskeia*, but in the Old Testament, it is generally used to translate the Hebrew *ḥuqqah* (statute or enactment).[14] In the Middle Ages, the term came to be used very differently from how either the pagan Romans or the Christian translators of the Bible used it: it was used almost exclusively for clergy bound to a rule, first applied to monastic life and subsequently to mendicant orders. The religious/secular distinction was the distinction between priests who belonged to orders like the Benedictines or Franciscans and priests who belonged to a diocese. It meant nothing like what we mean today when we distinguish religious from secular.

So, where did our common use of "religious" and "secular" come from? It arose, not coincidentally, at the same time that modern sovereign states, which would become nation-states, arose in Europe in the sixteenth and seventeenth centuries.[15] One of the things that marked the ascension of the modern state was the transfer of various powers from the Church to the state: the ecclesiastical court system was shut down and jurisdiction given exclusively to the state, Church appointments were increasingly put under state control, taxation was made the exclusive prerogative of the state,

---

12. Augustine, *City of God*, X.1 (Bettenson, 373).

13. Nongbri, *Before Religion*, 26.

14. Ibid., 31.

15. I cover this history in much greater detail in chs. 2 and 3 of my book *The Myth of Religious Violence*.

and so on. The first uses of the term "secularization" referred to the transfer of material goods from ecclesiastical control to state control.[16] Church and state were not separated; it was rather that the new dominance of the state over the Church was expressed and justified in terms of the Church being in charge of a distinct area of life called "religion," which essentially dealt with beliefs and the relationship of the individual to God. The state would be in charge of mundane activities such as politics and economics, which came to be called "secular." Religion, over which the Church had control, was viewed by rulers as an essential support to their attempts to create obedient and orderly citizens, but Church leaders were not to meddle in "secular" affairs. The Church became a support for nationalism precisely as it lost power to the state.

We must be clear that nationalism is not something that was imposed on Christians from without; the architects of the state and of nationalism in the West were overwhelmingly Christians, members of the Church. The contest between ecclesiastical and civil authorities was an intra-Church affair. It is not something "they" did to "us."[17] As Brad Anderson has emphasized, nationalism often built on Christian theological concepts.[18] The mystical body of Christ, for example, was a ready concept of mystical union that was easily absorbed by nationalist sentiment, as Ernst Kantorowicz[19] and Sheldon Wolin[20] have shown. The lines between sacred and profane are really quite blurry. What the religious/secular dichotomy allows, however, is for Christians to draw an imaginary line between loyalties to God and Church on the one hand and loyalties to the nation-state on the other. In an age when earthly power was being transferred from the Church to the nation-state, the religious/secular dichotomy allowed one conceptually to separate one's "religious" duties from one's "secular" duties, even though the

16. Wartburg, "Saeculum, séculariser," 11:44–46, quoted in Bremmer, "Secularization," 433.

17. In his book *Chosen Nation*, Brad Anderson has rightly taken me to task for underemphasizing this point; Anderson, *Chosen Nation*, 12–13. I agree with Anderson that nationalism is not simply imposed upon Christian people by governing elites, but is in some respects, or at least becomes, a popular movement. Anderson chides me for overemphasizing the role of the state, but Anderson misunderstands "state" as equivalent to "government." When I argue that the state comes before the nation, I do not mean that governing authorities invented and imposed nationalism, but rather that the borders of the territorially sovereign state—a very different arrangement than the overlapping and porous loyalties of medieval Christendom—were necessary before the people gathered within such sharply defined borders could begin to think of themselves as belonging to a nation.

18. Anderson, *Chosen Nation*, passim.

19. Kantorowicz, *The King's Two Bodies*.

20. Wolin, *Politics and Vision*, 86–92, 121.

"secular" nation was taking on the aura of the sacred, for which people were required to lay down their lives. The religious/secular dichotomy, in other words, allowed Christians to live in both worlds, without seeing their loyalty unto death to the new nation as fundamentally in conflict with their loyalty to Jesus Christ and his body, the Church.

Timothy Fitzgerald has traced the earliest uses in English of this type of religious/secular dichotomy to the seventeenth-century William Penn and John Locke, two important foundational figures for the United States.[21] For Locke, the dichotomy was essential to the reduction of the Church's influence to the interior life, so that the state would be free to exercise its power over exterior goods. As Locke writes, "All the life and power of true religion consist in the inward and full persuasion of the mind."[22] "The end of a religious society," Locke continues, "is the public worship of God and, by means thereof, the acquisition of eternal life. All discipline ought therefore to tend to that end, and all ecclesiastical laws to be thereunto confined. Nothing ought nor can be transacted in this society relating to the possession of civil and worldly goods. No force is here to be made use of upon any occasion whatsoever. For force belongs wholly to the civil magistrate, and the possession of all outward goods is subject to his jurisdiction."[23] The religious/secular divide, construed in this way, would in the modern era come to be seen as transhistorical and transcultural—that is, as a feature of human life in all times and places, and not simply a contingent European institutional arrangement of the modern era. One of the reasons for telling the history of the concepts of religion and secular is to remind us that it has a history and is not simply part of the way things are.

We have come to accept the notion that one's loyalty to the nation-state is a "secular" phenomenon, and one's adherence to Catholicism (or Hinduism or Judaism, etc.) is a "religion." It is a formulation that seems to conform to our institutional arrangements. And furthermore, it seems to protect us from the taint of idolatry. Loyalty to the nation is not a religion, we say, and so the things of God are kept separate from the things of Caesar, and one can be dutiful to both without contradiction.

Is Nationalism a Religion?

There are, nevertheless, scholars who claim that nationalism *is* a religion. Carolyn Marvin writes, "Nationalism is the most powerful religion in the

21. Fitzgerald, *Discourse on Civility and Barbarity*, 20–22, 231–99.
22. Locke, *Letter Concerning Toleration*, 18.
23. Ibid., 22–23.

United States, and perhaps in many other countries."[24] Mark Juergensmeyer claims, "Secular nationalism, like religion, embraces what one scholar calls 'a doctrine of destiny.' One can take this way of looking at secular nationalism a step further and state flatly, as did one author writing in 1960, that secular nationalism *is* 'a religion.'"[25] The author in question is Carlton Hayes, whose 1960 book was titled *Nationalism: A Religion*. According to Hayes, the flag occupies the same central place in official ritual that the Eucharistic host previously held.

> Nationalism's chief symbol of faith and central object of worship is the flag, and curious liturgical forms have been devised for "saluting" the flag, for "dipping" the flag, for "lowering" the flag, and for "hoisting" the flag . . . In America young people are ranged in serried rows and required to recite daily, with hierophantic voice and ritualistic gesture, the mystical formula: "I pledge allegiance to our flag and to the country for which it stands, one nation, indivisible, with liberty and justice for all." Everywhere, in all solemn feasts and fasts of nationalism, the flag is in evidence, and with it that other sacred thing, the national anthem.[26]

The author of the Pledge of Allegiance, Francis Bellamy, himself said that the pledge was meant to sink in with schoolchildren through ritual repetition, and added, "It is the same way with the catechism, or the Lord's Prayer."[27] For such reasons, sociologist Robert Bellah identified "an elaborate and well-institutionalized civil religion in America" that "has its own seriousness and integrity and requires the same care in understanding that any other religion does."[28]

Scholars who argue in this vein are obviously using a different definition of religion than the one to which we have become accustomed. Their use of "religion" is closer to the Roman use of *religio*, in which the difference between something being *religio* and something not being *religio* is a matter of the degree of obligation involved, not a matter of the subject matter having to do with gods or not. It is not so much about what a person claims to believe, but about how a person behaves. It is about the function, not the content, of a person's loyalties. This type of approach, often called "functionalist," is associated with Émile Durkheim, for whom "a religion is a unified

24. Marvin and Ingle, "Blood Sacrifice and the Nation," 767.
25. Juergensmeyer, *New Cold War?*, 15.
26. Hayes, *Essays on Nationalism*, 107–8.
27. Bellamy, quoted in O'Leary, *To Die For*, 178.
28. Bellah, "Civil Religion in America," 21.

system of beliefs and practices relative to sacred things."[29] For Durkheim, *anything* can be considered sacred by a given society. What matters is not content but function, how a thing or set of practices operates within a given society. Certain things are set aside as sacred in any society as a means of symbolizing and reinforcing communal solidarity; the sacred is a society's worship of itself. Durkheim writes, "Religious force is the feeling the collectivity inspires in its members, but projected outside and objectified by the minds that feel it. It becomes objectified by being anchored in an object which then becomes sacred, but any object can play this role."[30] In a Christian society, the national flag might be associated with Godliness, but for Durkheim the association or not with a god is not the crucial point. What does matter is that the flag is a sacred object in American society—perhaps the one object most universally revered as sacred—and is thus an object of "religious" veneration.[31]

Why adopt this approach to religion instead of the conventional modern religious/secular divide? Because it is more helpful in describing how people actually behave, and because it corresponds more closely to the Bible's approach. The Bible is saturated with the critique of idolatry. And as the Catechism recognizes, idolatry in the Bible is not at all limited to the explicit worship of false gods. As Moshe Halbertal and Avishai Margalit show, idolatry in the Bible is not usually a matter of error, mistaking what is not God for God, but of betrayal, becoming devoted to other things.[32] This is why the Bible's primary metaphors for idolatry are adultery and treason. The Israelites are continually whoring after other nations, or replacing the kingship of God with mere human kings. Isaiah accuses the Israelites of idolatry not for worshiping Egyptian gods but for asking the Egyptians for military help instead of relying on God. "Woe to those going down to Egypt for help, who put their trust in horses, who rely on the quantity of chariots, and on great strength of cavalrymen, but do not look to the Holy One of Israel" (Isa 31:1). In this passage, Isaiah goes on to link this turning away from God with the idolatrous reliance on what is created instead of the Creator: "The Egyptian is human, not divine, his horses are flesh, not spirit" (31:3). Here, idolatry is not fundamentally a matter of mistaking material things for God, nor of consciously attributing God's attributes—immortality, omnipresence, omnipotence, etc.—to an earthly king. The key question is one

---

29. Durkheim, *Elementary Forms of Religious Life*, 46.
30. Ibid., 174.
31. Durkheim addresses flags as sacred objects; see ibid., 154, 165, and 174.
32. Halbertal and Margalit, *Idolatry*, 108–9.

of trust. In similar fashion, Jesus warns that we cannot serve both God and wealth, and Paul warns against those whose god is their bellies (Phil 3:19).

Jesus does not condemn all economic activity, and Paul knows that we all must eat to live. Idolatry, again, is most often a matter of degree, and it is a degree of behavior, not mere belief. If a person claims to believe in the Christian God but spends the majority of his or her waking hours in obsessive pursuit of material goods, then his or her actual religion may not be Christianity. Nationalism is particularly susceptible to idolatry, because the demands it makes on its subjects are so intense, especially the demand that one be willing to lay down one's life on the nation's behalf. According to Carlton Hayes, the exclusivity of this demand distinguishes modern nationalism from medieval loyalties. Before modernity, people experienced conflicts among their many loyalties to locality and priest and lord and guild and family. "But nowadays, and herein lies the fundamental difference between us and our ancient and mediaeval and early modern forebears, the individual is commonly disposed, in case of conflict, to sacrifice one loyalty after another, loyalty to persons, places and ideas, loyalty even to family, to the paramount call of nationality and the national state."[33] This is why nationalism is rightly considered a "religion."

What Hayes does not mention here is the ideological apparatus that keeps us from seeing this exclusivity. We tend to view loyalty to God and Church and loyalty to the nation not as conflicting but as complementary. Brad Anderson has emphasized the ways in which Christian theology has been recruited to make loyalty to God and loyalty to the nation appear to be fully complementary. Sometimes God and country are melded into a seamless unity, and the nation is seen as sacred. As Anderson writes, drawing on the work of Anthony Smith, "Nationalism is itself a type of revivalist religion, driven by a particular 'cult of authenticity'—a sort of prophetic movement seeking the holiness (authenticity) of the nation—toward enacting a particular 'salvation drama' involving the nation as the divinely elected people of God, with whom God has instituted a unique covenant toward the end of global salvation (according to a particular conception)."[34] Sometimes, however, it is precisely because we see God and country as corresponding to two separate kinds of duty—one religious and the other secular—that we see them as complementary and not conflicting. We think we can give to both God and Caesar because they occupy two separate realms, religion and politics. But the biblical critique of idolatry makes clear that the lines are often much blurrier than we want to admit.

33. Hayes, *Essays on Nationalism*, 94–95.
34. Anderson, *Chosen Nation*, 59.

Here, I think that Anderson simply misunderstands my argument about the link between the creation of the modern category "religion" and the rise of nationalism. Anderson thinks that my emphasis on the creation of a new category of religion that is transcultural and transhistorical amounts to a "departicularized notion of religion"[35] that cannot account for the way that very particular Christian narratives are employed in the creation of nationalism. According to Anderson, I fail "to acknowledge the fact that some nationalist movements do not consider religion to be transhistorical or private at all. In these movements, the identity, mission, and destiny of the nation are actually being syncretized with specific features of a given faith tradition, that is to say, with quite *particular* historical and theological narratives."[36] But to point out that religion has come to be understood as transcultural and transhistorical is not to say that there exists some generic, departicularized religion that hovers above all particular cultures and times. It is rather to say that religion has been theorized in modernity as something present in all cultures, all times and places, in all their particularity. We have come to think in terms of "world religions," as if the distinction between the religious and the secular were a standard feature of all societies, as therefore natural and inevitable. But it is not; the religious/secular distinction is a peculiar Western, modern invention. It serves particular political ends, one of which is to minimize the apparent tension between one's "political" allegiances and one's "religious" allegiances, loyalty to the nation and loyalty to Christ.

Is Catholicism a Religion?

If we should be alert to the possibility that nationalism does not easily fit in the category of "secular," should we also be open to the possibility that Catholicism can go beyond its confinement to the sphere of religion? In his contribution to this volume, Brad Anderson writes about the patriotic appeals in the bishops' documents on religious liberty. I want to complement Anderson's analysis by also looking at the bishops' arguments on religious liberty but focusing specifically on the link between nationalism and the definition of Catholicism as a religion.

It might seem absurd to question whether or not Catholicism is a religion, but the debate over the HHS mandate is precisely about what counts as religion and what does not. The HHS mandate has been framed by its protagonists not as a restriction of religious liberty but as a clarification about

35. Ibid., 19.
36. Ibid., 28.

what counts as religion and what does not. Churches, synagogues, mosques, etc., are entitled as always to exemption from having to provide insurance coverage for services that violate their principles, based on the concept of free exercise of religion. But schools, hospitals, charities, and other agencies that are affiliated with such congregations have been redefined as not essentially religious, and therefore not exempt from the mandates under the principle of religious freedom, because they do not "serve primarily persons who share the[ir] religious tenets," according to the HHS.[37] As the U.S. Catholic bishops' blog comments, "HHS denies these organizations religious freedom precisely because their purpose is to serve the common good of society."[38] The government's position makes a distinction between church agencies that serve a religious function and those that serve a social function. The implication is that "religion" is not something that is essentially social.

The Justice Department took a similar position in the landmark case *Hosanna-Tabor v. EEOC*. The Equal Employment Opportunity Commission argued that the plaintiff in the case—a teacher at a Lutheran school—should not be covered by the "ministerial exemption" whereby religious organizations have more freedom to decide who works for them, because the plaintiff taught mostly "secular" subjects, such as math, social studies, art, and music, along with religion classes. The government's argument here again makes a sharp distinction between religion and the rest of life, even though the purpose of at least some church-related schools is not simply to tack a little religion onto an otherwise entirely secular curriculum but to see all of life through a Christian lens. In January 2012, the Supreme Court rejected the EEOC's argument that the ministerial exemption should apply only to those who "perform exclusively religious functions." The court's unanimous decision stated, "Indeed, we are unsure if any such employees exist. The heads of congregations themselves often have a mix of duties, including secular ones, such as helping to manage the congregation's finances, supervising purely secular personnel, and overseeing the upkeep of facilities."[39] Although the court seems to believe in the possibility of "purely secular" people, it casts doubt on the idea that "religion" could be kept entirely separate from the rest of life.

The Obama administration's position in issuing the HHS mandate is based on the idea that rights inhere in individuals, not groups. In this case, individuals have the right to contraception, a right that should be recognized

---

37. Quoted in USCCB, "Six Things Everyone Should Know."
38. Ibid.
39. *Hosanna-Tabor v. EEOC*, 565 U.S.___(2012) at 19.

by their employers in providing insurance coverage. Religious groups have no right to deny this right to individuals who work for them, even to individuals who claim membership in the sponsoring church. Because religion is inherently a matter of individual preference, religious bodies cannot claim rights. This logic is articulated by the *New York Times* editorial of February 10, 2012, which decried the "phony crisis" over religious freedom. According to the *Times*' editors,

> Churches are given complete freedom by the Constitution to preach that birth control is immoral, but they have not been given the right to laws that would deprive their followers or employees of the right to disagree with that teaching. If a religious body does not like a public policy that affects its members, it is free to try to change it, but it cannot simply opt out of society or claim a special exemption from the law.[40]

The same logic is at play in the Massachusetts federal court decision cited by the bishops in which the Bishops' Migration and Refugee Service was required to provide contraception and abortion services or lose its government contract. Individuals have a right to such services, and the church has no right to interfere with that right.[41]

The shift from the medieval ideal of a shared, substantive conception of the good to an individual and formal conception of freedom as the highest good is one of the hallmarks of a modern, liberal society. In his commentary on the *New York Times* editorial cited above, David Schindler has shown how John Locke's conception of rights, on which the Founding Fathers drew, is inherently individualistic.[42] Brad Gregory has recently traced this shift behind the Enlightenment to the Reformation. As he writes, "Because *individuals* disagreed about the meaning of God's word, *individuals* and not politically favored churches were and had to be the bearers of rights, beginning with the right to religious liberty."[43] The result would eventually be the modern conception of rights as inhering in individuals and the modern conception of religion as a matter of individual personal preference. "Leaving each person free to determine the good based on 'the word of God before him' and 'the mind of Christ within him' would prove to be *at one*

---

40. *New York Times*, "The Freedom to Choose Birth Control."

41. U.S. Conference of Catholic Bishops, "Our First, Most Cherished Liberty," 4.

42. Schindler, "Repressive Logic of Liberal Rights," 523–47.

43. Gregory, *Unintended Reformation*, 215. In his commentary on the current debate over religious freedom, David L. Schindler has shown how Locke's conception of rights, on which the Founding Fathers drew, also assumes that the individual is the bearer of rights.

and the same time the modern basis for protecting individual human beings against certain forms of coercion by the state, and the unintended road to the elimination of any shared notion of the good."[44] As Gregory notes, the result would be the subjectivization of morality. As he hints as well, the result was also the debilitation of any intermediate associations that stood between the state and the individual, because they were the only bearers of shared notions of the good. As Robert Nisbet argued, "The real conflict in modern political history has not been, as is so often stated, between State and individual, but between State and social group."[45]

If the bishops want to articulate a corporate right to freedom, the freedom of the church to be itself, they would certainly have ample theological grounds to do so. The patristic writers understood human creation in God's image to indicate that all people are created for communion with each other through their communion with God. The image of the Body of Christ so important in the New Testament ratifies the idea that the church is a corporate personality with a common end, not simply a collection of individuals. But the articulation of a right of religious freedom in America is usually done in a way that appeals not to theology but to putatively secular ideals available in principle to all. The problem is that the dominant secular discourse of rights sees both rights and religious preference as inhering in the individual. This dynamic can be seen clearly in the Supreme Court's resolution to the question of whether or not nontheists can claim conscientious objection to military service, which was open to people on "religious" grounds. Rather than define religion to exclude nontheists, the court offered the exemption to anyone holding a "sincere and meaningful belief which occupies in the life of its possessor a place parallel to that filled by the God of those admittedly qualifying for the exemption."[46] As legal scholar Marie Failinger comments, "The Court often uses the notion of freedom in a very atomistic way: religious freedom is the right of a person to select his or her religious faith and to choose what it will mean to him or her, whether his or her beliefs are shared by any other person, whether they grow out of any relationship with the external world including a transcendent being, whether they are based on a thoughtful argument or are simply the individual's whim."[47] In this light, the bishops' appeal to James Madison's idea that "the Religion then of every man must be left to the conviction and conscience of every man;

---

44. Ibid., 216.
45. Nisbet, *Quest for Community*, 109.
46. *United States v. Seeger*, 166.
47. Failinger, "Wondering after Babel," 94.

and it is the right of every man to exercise it as these may dictate"[48] can only serve to reinforce the idea that religion is a matter of personal preference. Religious rights, therefore, apply to individuals, not to corporate groups like the church, and the witness of the church as the Body of Christ is subordinated to the personal beliefs and preferences of individuals.

The second danger inherent in the idea that Christianity is a religion is that religion is defined in liberal society as a matter of beliefs about the otherworldly and only indirectly applies to the social and political. In Jefferson's terms, belief in one God or twenty has no immediate social effect. As I have indicated briefly in the genealogy above, the very modern Western concept of religion was born out of the desire to identify religion as precisely that which has to do with otherworldly concerns and not with the application of public power in "secular" matters such as politics and economics. The bishops have objected to the government's moves to declare the church's activity nonreligious precisely insofar as it has a social effect. They have also decried "the tendency to reduce the freedom of religion to the mere freedom of worship."[49] At the same time, however, they have continued to insist on the right to be "free in our conscience"[50] and have defined religious freedom as meaning that "all men are to be immune from coercion on the part of individuals or of social groups and of any human power, in such wise that in matters religious no one is to be forced to act in a manner contrary to his own beliefs."[51] The bishops are not wrong to claim the right of conscience and belief to be free of coercion, but insofar as religion is defined in terms of conscience and belief it is removed from the realm of the bodily, the world of health care and immigration policy and all those activities said to belong to the "secular," nonreligious realm. To resist the confinement of Christianity to concern with the otherworldly, we need a robust defense of the idea that our God is the God of all creation, and that the gospel is concerned with caring for the flourishing of the whole human person, body and soul. We need more than an appeal to freedom of belief and freedom of conscience; we need to question the modern terms under which Christianity is consigned to one side of the religious/secular dichotomy that has been constructed in liberal society. We need to ask, as Robert Shedinger puts it, "whether the concern so often expressed over the

---

48. Quoted in USCCB, "Our First, Most Cherished Liberty," 6.
49. Ibid., 9.
50. Ibid., 7.
51. Ibid., 8. Here the bishops are quoting from *Dignitatis Humanae*, §2.

politicization of Islam in the contemporary world ought to be replaced by a concern with the 'religionization' of Christianity."[52]

The bishops have chosen to defend the church by using one of the tools provided by American political culture, the concept of religious freedom. Rather than refuse the terms on which the debate is offered, they have sought protection by emphasizing the continuity between Catholic and American ideals. The third danger I see in this strategy is this: in emphasizing continuity, they will cease to challenge the assimilation of Catholicism to an American system that reflexively views Catholicism as a religion and therefore as a matter of personal preference.

In their statement on religious freedom, the bishops do recognize the prospect of unjust laws that Catholics must have the courage to disobey. They also cite Pope Benedict XVI's admonition that the laity should exhibit "a strong critical sense *vis-à-vis* the dominant culture" in America. The document is nevertheless filled with patriotic language about "our enlightened republic," "the land of the free, and a beacon of hope for the world." The prayer for the protection of religious liberty that was distributed in parishes throughout the country prays that "this great land will always be 'one nation, under God, indivisible, with liberty and justice for all.'" The bishops exhort lay Catholics "to be both engaged and articulate in insisting that as Catholics and as Americans we do not have to choose between the two."

It is not hard to sympathize with the bishops' attempts to win protection by appealing to the nation's best sense of its own ideals. The problem is that, in minimizing the tension between Catholicism and America, Catholics might too easily assume that Catholicism can be fitted into America as the particular into the universal. In other words, the way that the church and the nation-state have tended to make their peace in modernity is by assuming that a division of labor obtains in which the Christian's religious allegiance belongs to God and her political allegiance belongs to the nation. Religious allegiance in a liberal society has increasingly been defined since the mid-twentieth century as subjective, individual, and essentially apolitical, which is precisely the trivialization of Christian faith against which the bishops want to fight.

One final irony: the bishop who chairs the Bishops' Ad Hoc Committee on Religious Liberty is William Lori, archbishop of Baltimore. In 2005, he was bishop of Bridgeport, Connecticut. He was the bishop who fired Stephen Kobasa. The man now in charge of championing Catholics' freedom of conscience is the one who fired Stephen Kobasa for refusing, on gospel grounds, to display the American flag. This episode illustrates the danger

---

52. Shedinger, *Was Jesus a Muslim?*, 12.

that appealing to American values for protection will lead the church to offer its allegiance to America even when we do have to choose between the two.

To see Catholicism as religious and national loyalty as secular is to see them as essentially complementary and non-conflicting. Catholicism need not always conflict with national loyalty, but when it does, the religious/secular divide often makes it harder to see. To resist idolatry when we need to do so, we must see that national loyalty tends not to stay confined to a putatively secular sphere, and Catholicism ought not to be confined to a putatively religious sphere.

16

Imagining Identity/Community as Christian/Filipino: Implications for Doing Theology in East Asian Contexts

JOSE MARIO C. FRANCISCO, SJ

Introduction

Students of theology today can no longer speak about God without hearing each other. First, they and their work travel and cross boundaries with ease and speed, thanks to the global network of transport and communication. Second, they have come to understand themselves and their work as profoundly rooted in and shaped by their locations. Third, if, as is believed, God's communicative presence and action occur within all stretches of time and space, then they seek to be truly catholic by broadening their *locus theologicus* and relating what they say about God from their location to what others say from theirs.

As a result of these recent technological, anthropological, and theological perspectives, theological discourses are often identified by their origin, commonly referred to by the word "context." Theologians and their works bear labels such as "First World" or "Third World," "Western" or "Asian," and more recently, from the North or South.[1] As binary categories prone to reification, such labels are best considered heuristic pointers to ways of proceeding or styles of ethos constituted by particular landscapes and histories.

For instance, it has been commonplace to characterize the West in terms of the decline or privatization of religion,[2] and the East, espe-

---

1. Fabella and Sugirtharajah, *Dictionary of Third World Theologies*.
2. Casanova, *Public Religions in the Modern World*.

cially Asia, as being religious and spiritual.³ Moreover, such decline and privatization are thought to have been brought about by the processes of modernity and secularization as well as by concessions which religions, particularly Christianity, have surrendered to the modern global world. Even the rise of fundamentalist forms of different religious traditions has been explained in relation to these processes. In contrast, salvific religions are said to thrive in Asia and Africa because of the widespread and endemic forms of deprivation there.

These binary characterizations have been called into question on theoretical as well as empirical grounds. Students of religion have pointed to various types of modernity as well as different modalities of secularity that do not necessarily lead to the death or privatization of religion. Moreover, recent developments in the West show religious resurgence in the advocacy of religious groups in the political arena and the vigorous involvement of religions in civil society.⁴

It is within this general horizon that this essay examines issues of identity and community in relation to Catholicism in the Philippines. Its theoretical foundations lie in Benedict Anderson's insight regarding both identity and community of nations as imagined constructions,⁵ and its extension to that of the religious community. Though Anderson rightly points to differences between the construction of nation and religious community, the constructions in the Philippine case occurred within the same historical process beginning with the sixteenth-century entry of Spanish colonization. As a result, the role of sacred languages and their translation into the various vernaculars—elements identified by Anderson in the rise of the nation as distinct from the religious community⁶—came into play in the conflation of the body Catholic and the body politic which this essay calls the imaginary of the Philippines as "a Catholic nation."

The essay then proceeds to consider its implications for doing theology, not only in the Philippines but also in other East Asian contexts similarly dominated by particular religious traditions—for example, Islam in Indonesia and Malaysia, and forms of Buddhism throughout the entire region.

---

3. Rosales and Arevalo, *For All the Peoples of Asia*, 30.
4. Woodward et al., *Religions in the Modern World*.
5. Anderson, *Imagined Communities*, 6–7.
6. Ibid., 12–19.

Historical Formation of Christian Filipino Identity

The formation of Christian Filipino identity has been historic and multifaceted. As suggested in current studies on identity formation,[7] this identity emerged not through the identification of what is seen as essential elements but through a social process of construction based on diverse interacting forces such as social location and historical experience. Moreover, identity formation occurs in relation to what is consciously or implicitly considered "the other."

This formation starts with sixteenth-century Spanish colonization and engages the archipelagic geography of numerous islands. It began with the construction of native identity as colonized and as Christian, and then of the colonized into Filipino. Hence, this formation process could be appropriately described as translation, understood according to current studies not only as the transfer between languages but also as the mediation of social worlds across time and space.[8]

From Native to Colonized and Christian

The initial phase of this formation entailed the reduction (*reducción*) of *barangays*, relatively small settlements probably named after the kind of boat that natives used for transport.[9] This reduction followed the pattern of Spanish *pueblos*, towns with central and satellite communities—a geographical arrangement that facilitated pacification for Spanish colonial authorities and evangelization for religious orders assigned to different parts of the archipelago. Hence what were once discrete territories, some loosely connected by kinship and trade, became officially linked through the colonial government and had now been subsumed under the name *Las Islas Filipinas* after the Spanish King Philip II.

This translation of native space provided the geographical infrastructure for the more crucial translation of native languages. These languages of the Austronesian linguistic family were used primarily for oral communication and occasionally for short texts like contracts. Moreover, on account of their syllabic script, they proved difficult to learn and read for nonnatives. Thus, in accordance with its decision to evangelize in these languages rather than in Spanish as in the Americas, the colonial church translated these languages by transposing their script to the Roman alphabet, codifying their

---

7. Dunn, *Identity Crises*.
8. Francisco, "Fidelity in Translating Religious Practice."
9. Scott, *Barangay*, 4–6.

grammatical structure with Latin and Spanish patterns, and standardizing usage through dictionaries with native words given Spanish meanings.

For their preaching, missionaries borrowed native words like *binyag*, which meant originally the Muslim rite of purification, for Christian baptism, and employed Spanish rather than local vocabulary for central beliefs, such as *Dios* rather than *Bathala* for "God."[10] They also translated devotional and catechetical texts from Spanish and other European languages and, when already fluent in native languages, produced original religious works.

This translation of native space and language "sums up the thrust of Spanish colonization as both a political and a moral undertaking designed to reconstitute the natives as subjects of divine and royal laws. Bodies were to be 'reduced' to centralized localities subject to the letter of the law, just as Tagalog was to be 'reduced' to the grammatical terms of Latin in Castilian *artes*."[11] Thus emerged a new native identity as colonial subject and as Christian, based on "a hierarchical relationship between all things 'Spanish' (and therefore already 'Christian') and all things 'Tagalog' (yet to become 'Christianized')"[12] and best symbolized by the pamphlet *caton* that taught natives both literacy *and* praying.

Some resisted this identity. Larger organized settlements of indigenous or Muslim populations fought Spanish incursions. Others avoided reduction by returning to their traditional way of life in the mountains and were considered by the Spaniards *remontados*, apostates who abandoned both colonial civilization and religious faith.

Nevertheless, the Christian identity of the native deepened as the late medieval, post-Reformation Spanish Catholicism brought by missionaries increasingly took native form—first, on account of the use of native languages for Christian discourse, and second, through native participation. Natives called *fiscales* were recruited to instruct and console other natives through praying. Others who acquired more skills and greater knowledge in Christian practice through contact with missionaries produced native religious texts. Many participated in communal devotions that involved chanting or dramatizing religious texts in private and public spaces far removed from churches. All these created a native Christian discourse through which natives could pray in their voices and recognize themselves as Christians.

---

10. Francisco, "Interphasing Language with Religion and Nation," 233–34.
11. Rafael, *Contracting Colonialism*, 90.
12. Ibid., 90–91.

From Colonized to Filipino

The second moment in the formation of the Catholic Filipino identity involved the translation of the colonized into Filipino. With the long tenure of colonization in the archipelago and its changing economic, political, and social situation, different categories under the general rubric of "colonized" emerged through an entangled process involving ethnicity, location, and education that culminated in the late nineteenth century.

At first, the term "filipino" in its adjectival and noncapitalized form was generally applied to any inhabitant of *Las Filipinas*, though in certain contexts, it specifically referred to *creollos*, those of Spanish descent born in the islands and distinguished from those from the Spanish peninsula. However, it appeared in the nominative and capitalized form to include those under the category of "the colonized." For instance, the historian Floro Quibuyen notes that José Rizal, a nationalist educated in local Jesuit and Dominican colleges, said of his comrades in Spain, "They are creole young men of Spanish descent, Chinese mestizos, and Malayans; but we call ourselves only Filipinos."[13] Thus "the fundamental change in the meaning of 'Filipino' in the nineteenth century reflected the rapid transformation of the political demands of an anticolonial movement that was initiated by the ilustrados [the enlightened] but which eventually involved the masses—from secularization (1850s–1872) to assimilation (1880s) to separation (1890s)."[14] The shift in meaning of "Filipino" occurred in the contexts of both the debates within the ilustrado camp as they agitated for change and the colonial power's response to this agitation. Filipino identity arose out of this contestation within the ilustrado camp, as well as between it and the colonial power.[15] Therefore, "the Spanish ruling elite ends up referring to anyone outside their class—whether native, creole, or mestizo—as *Filipinos*."[16]

This integration of various groups came about because of the common experience of being under the colonial power and being influenced by common education in Jesuit and Dominican colleges. Native diocesan clergy opposed to the continued tenure of Spanish friars in parishes were educated with Chinese mestizos engaged in commerce and agriculture. Both had reason to oppose colonial policies and power.

Furthermore, the term "Filipino" would be extended to include precolonial natives: "Significantly, by 1889, Rizal had extended the term Filipino

---

13. Quibuyen, *Nation Aborted*, 76.
14. Ibid., 88.
15. Ibid.
16. Ibid., 83.

even further to apply not only to the present inhabitants of the Philippines, but also to precolonial natives."[17]

This identification among various groups as Filipino was aspirational: "A theme running through the *Noli-Fili* [Rizal's nationalist novels] is that an oppressed people may be disunited and without a voice, but through enlightened struggle, it can become a nation . . . In his July 27 letter to Mariano Ponce, Rizal spoke of 'our arduous mission which is the formation of the Filipino nation.'"[18] This aspiration finally took concrete form in the creation of the Filipino nation-state with the declaration of the 1898 Philippine Revolution.

This emergence of Filipino identity produced fissures in Catholic identity. Because of the dissociation of the Catholic Church from the Spanish colonial government brought about by the revolution and the anti-Catholic and anti-clerical sentiments among some nationalists, not all Filipinos identified themselves as Christians. However, there remained those who did, both among the educated such as Filipino diocesan clergy[19] as well as among ordinary people involved in various movements for change who saw their struggle against their colonizers as following Christ.[20] One can then say that by the end of the nineteenth century, native identity as Catholic and as Filipino had been formed.

Construction of the Philippines as Christian Nation

The impetus for imagining the Philippines as a Catholic nation began with Spanish colonization and then intensified during American occupation until the 1946 declaration of Philippine independence. With the defeat and departure of Spanish colonial forces, the Catholic Church became dissociated with civil government. Moreover, with the establishment of the Philippine Commonwealth under American imperialist power, the still-hispanized Church had to contend with the American culture's new language and social mores, the legal principle of the separation of church and state, and the evangelizing activity of Protestant churches and groups. Coeli Barry paints its situation thus: "In the Church's rendering of the American-era . . . the dominant trope has been one of loss: lost opportunities for the Church to re-integrate itself with secular powers and the threat of the loss of the nation

---

17. Ibid., 96.
18. Ibid., 82.
19. Schumacher, *Revolutionary Clergy*, 268–80.
20. Ileto, *Pasyon and Revolution*, 15–28.

to secularism, Protestantism, and breakaway religious movements."[21] Thus, from then onward, the Catholic Church cultivated in defense this imaginary of a Christian nation—an imaginary that was aligned with international and local geopolitical forces.

Construction through Discourse, Devotion, and Development

The Church's construction of this imaginary was achieved through official discourse, devotion, and social development. Numerous statements from the Catholic Welfare Organization (CWO), the forerunner of the post-Vatican II Catholic Bishops' Conference of the Philippines (CBCP), simply presumed the Philippines' Catholic character as a given and appropriated the title "Christian nation" without any reference to Protestant churches. For instance, its January 25, 1953, statement at the close of the First Plenary Council tells "our beloved clergy and people" that they "are a Catholic people, and as such are determined to live and die,"[22] and warns them about the fate of "once-Christian nations stricken with domestic strife."[23] Almost ten years later, in their February 2, 1964, letter on the Fourth Centenary of the Evangelization of the Philippines, they repeat the same message: "We will always consider the fact that we are the only Christian nation in the Orient as our badge of distinction in the whole Christian world."[24] Such a view of the Christian nation still finds expression in post-Vatican II CBCP statements, as in their July 9, 1970, statement regarding increasing violence: "The Philippines is a Christian and a democratic country. In the light of contemporary events, however, we begin to wonder if it is truly and fully so."[25]

Moreover, such statements about being not just a Christian nation but the only Christian nation in Asia were reinforced by issuing them for important religious occasions and devotional practices such as the Holy Year (1950–51), Marian Year (1954), and the Second Eucharistic Congress (1956). For example, the CWO said the following in connection with the 1954 Marian Year, the centenary of the dogmatic definition of the Immaculate Conception: "We ardently desire that our people, so profoundly in love with Mary since the divine light of the Gospel dawned upon them, should partake in a special degree, of the graces, which such dearly beloved Mother

21. Barry, "Polyglot Catholicism," 60.
22. Quitorio *Pastoral Letters*, 117.
23. Ibid., 118.
24. Ibid., 237.
25. Ibid., 330.

will shower in this year consecrated to her."[26] Further, it asked all priests "to enhance the devotion of the faithful toward the Mother of God by means of sermons, conferences, novenas, pilgrimages, and other means that their zeal might counsel them."[27]

Through these occasions and devotions, the Catholic Church strengthened the link between Christianity and nationhood as reflected in the following words from the CWO: "Love and cherish our Christian traditions and culture because they belong to the basic elements of our nationhood. Love and cherish our national symbols."[28]

Moreover, the Catholic Church accompanied official discourse and devotion with extensive involvement in social development. From its entry with Spanish colonization and beyond, it provided assistance in diverse fields like agriculture and construction as well as established social welfare institutions such as hospitals and orphanages, some of which still operate at present. In addition, it built an extensive network of educational institutions numbering at least 1,192 from primary to university levels.[29]

Given the historic and groundbreaking influence of the Second Vatican Council (1964-68) and the social upheavals related to President Ferdinand Marcos's tenure (1965-86), the Catholic Church played an important role on the frontiers of social development through discourse and involvement. Since its formal establishment in 1968, the CBCP issued no fewer than 170 statements, approximately two-thirds of which address social concerns. This quantity—perhaps the greatest from any local episcopal conference in the world—and the range of topics, from fundamental concerns like rural poverty to specific events like the 1994 Cairo International Conference on Population and Development,[30] highlight the Catholic Church's prominent role, among other social actors.

This official church discourse was accompanied by concrete responses to basic social needs and issues of injustice through parish communities and church-based organizations. Various efforts fostered economic activity through cooperatives of workers and farmers, promoted human rights, and contributed to the overthrow of the Marcos regime and the subsequent democratization process. All of these efforts, occasionally seen as competing with government programs, certainly strengthened the imaginary of a Christian nation now at work in social development.

26. Ibid., 138.
27. Ibid., 144.
28. Ibid., 227.
29. Moreno, *Church, State, and Civil Society*, 34.
30. Quitorio, *Pastoral Letters*, 818-19.

As the 1997 CBCP exhortation against Philippine politics asks rhetorically, "Why should this be so in a nation where the vast majority of the people are Catholic and Christian? Our faith in God has played a key role in major events of our history—even in a decidedly political matter like the People Power Revolution of EDSA. Yet politics as a whole has been, strangely, largely impervious to the Gospel. Our political culture denies, to our shame, our proud claim to the name Christian."[31]

Opposition to Independent Nationalism

The underside of constructing and cultivating this imaginary was the Church's opposition, especially right after Philippine independence, to forms of nationalism perceived to threaten this imaginary. The CWO's singular statement on nationalism—issued on December 3, 1958, and occasioned by the rise of a so-called National Progressive Movement that "has declared its avowed opposition to the Catholic Church"[32]—relates nationalism to the social nature of humankind, the search for the common good, and even the history of Israel and the gospel teaching of Jesus.[33] But it quickly condemns the misuse of nationalism and describes as "not genuine" the nationalistic movement that "disregard[s] the Christian moral standards" and "adopt[s] a hostile attitude towards foreigners, just because they are foreigners"[34]—this last point alluding to the nationalization of education that drew the Church's strongest opposition to independent nationalism.

The Church reacted to particular legal measures that either supported or threatened its control of the educational domain through which it passed on the Catholic faith to the youth and maintained its influence in Philippine society, especially under the circumstances of the American occupation. These measures involved religious instruction in public schools, nationalization of schools, and inclusion of nationalist publications in the general curriculum.

First, the Catholic Church pushed for legislation to provide religious instruction in public schools. Its January 25, 1953, CWO statement underlines "the Constitutional rights of our citizens concerning optional religious instruction in public schools."[35] In less than a month, a more strongly worded statement accuses three leading officials of the department of education

31. Quitorio, *CBCP on the Threshold*, 95.
32. Quitorio, *Pastoral Letters*, 225.
33. Ibid., 222–23.
34. Ibid., 224.
35. Ibid., 121.

of being members of "a secret Committee for the Elimination of Religious Instruction in Public Schools, organized by the Grand Lodge of Free and Accepted Masons of the Philippine Islands."[36]

Ten years hence, on June 6, 1965, the bishops supported the Mariano Cuenco Bill, "which authorizes public school teachers to teach religion in public schools voluntarily."[37] They marshaled all arguments from different perspectives—religious (parents' rights over children's education; lack of religion as the cause of criminality), constitutional (nonviolation of separation of church and state or of the rights of the minority), and various practical considerations (religious education as not divisive for students or an additional burden for public school teachers, as it is optional).[38]

In keeping with the constitutional provision on separation of church and state, the statement echoes what the earlier 1953 text states: "We Catholics seek no special privileges for ourselves or for our children in this matter of religious instruction."[39] But in the same breath, it condemns its adversaries on the same point: "To them the wall of separation between Church and State is to be a 'Berlin Wall,' a proof of opposition, enmity, and hatred, born of an essential opposition and antagonism."[40]

Only with the Cory Aquino presidency (1986–92) and its 1987 Constitution was the bishops' desire for greater support for religious instruction in public schools fulfilled. Hence, the CBCP supported the constitution's ratification in its November 21, 1986, statement.[41]

The second concern related to education was the proposal for nationalization of all schools. On January 28, 1959, church leaders issued a statement criticizing certain provisions of Congress bills (No. 38 in the Senate and Nos. 202, 222, and 381 in the Lower House) for nationalization. These provisions consist of the prohibition of non-Filipino citizens to head educational institutions, of nonnatural born Filipinos to teach social science subjects, and of less than 60 percent membership of governing bodies of schools to be noncitizens.[42]

The statement marshals cogent arguments against these provisions. It underscores the importance of professional training rather than ethnic origin as the basis for the competence and impartiality of educators. It further

36. Ibid., 122.
37. Ibid., 251.
38. Ibid., 252–57.
39. Ibid., 126.
40. Ibid., 257.
41. Ibid., 640–41.
42. Ibid., 209.

notes the presence of Filipino educators in Catholic schools, admittedly the majority but still insufficient for the needs, and praises the sacrifice of foreign missionaries.

However, it vilifies what it perceived to be the kind of nationalism behind the proposal: "This is precisely the brand of nationalism against which we want to warn our faithful. This is nothing but the old Nazi dogma of racism, the kind of nationalism that ignited the Second World War. We must realize that race and blood and the place where one was born have nothing to do with impartiality and truthfulness."[43]

What fueled this virulence is the issue of Filipinization of church personnel, one rooted in the Spanish colonial period and thought to have been resolved with the arrival of "non-Spanish foreign priests and nuns [through whom] the Church could simultaneously connect the Philippines with its Catholic past and do without evoking Spanish colonial associations."[44] But now these legislative proposals have resurrected this issue, and hence the Catholic Church protests, "We sincerely believe that by the natural development of our religious Orders and Congregations, the day will surely come when our Catholic educational institutions will be in the hands of Filipinos. But we cannot accept the idea that this process should be hastened by legislation."[45]

The third issue related to education involved the inclusion of nationalist books in the general curriculum—first, Rafael Palma's biography of Rizal, *Pride of the Malay Race*, and more significantly, Rizal's classic novels, *Noli me tangere* and *El Filibusterismo*. Regarding the first, the CWO wrote on January 6, 1950, the following condemnation: "We believe that we would seriously fail in our duty if we did not raise our voice of warning and protest against the attempt by the enemies of the Catholic name to impose on the young people in our public schools the reading of a book written by a well-known anti-Catholic, which is highly offensive to the religious sentiment of over 80 percent of the population of the Philippines."[46]

Its April 21, 1956, statement against the Rizal novels proclaimed in no uncertain terms, "We, the Catholic Philippine Hierarchy, maintain that these novels do contain teachings contrary to our faith and so, We are opposed to the proposed compulsory reading in their entirety of such books in any school in the Philippines where Catholic students may be affected. We cannot permit the eternal salvation of immortal souls, souls for which

43. Ibid., 216.
44. Barry, "Polyglot Catholicism," 60.
45. Quitorio, *Pastoral Letters*, 216.
46. Ibid., 53.

We are answerable before the throne of Divine Justice, to be compromised for the sake of any human good, no matter how great it may appear to be."[47]

John Schumacher's recent *Philippine Studies* article uncovers movements behind the text of the Church's statement.[48] As early as 1951, Jesuit historian Horacio de la Costa was asked to write a draft statement on Rizal for church leaders. His draft had five versions, revised as a result of interpellations on behalf of the church leaders, most likely from the Spaniard Fr. Jesus Cavanna, CM. In the final statement, only some paragraphs survive of the original twenty typewritten pages, and the revisions downplay the significance of Rizal and his novels and avoid attracting attention to Spanish religious orders. Such condemnation of his novels is ironic since, in their statement defending Catholic education, the bishops praise Rizal and other nationalists as having been "brought up in the Catholic Schools."[49]

In their defense of the imaginary of the Philippines as a Christian nation, the bishops linked any form of nationalism independent of the Church to those it considered enemies, both old and new.

The Church's strongest language was directed toward communism. Those against religious instruction in public schools are accused of "exploiting them with preternatural cunning, the evil genius of atheistic Communism,"[50] and of "hold[ing] up the Godless Communist nations as examples of countries that have eliminated many public vices without the need of religious instruction."[51]

In this fight against communism, the Philippine bishops were following the Church's program then to implement Catholic social teaching, most of which was directed against nineteenth-century European communism, and at the same time aligning themselves with the Philippine and American governments during the Cold War. Aside from critical statements, symbolic actions in the context of religious occasions were "were intended to revive the place of Catholicism in the daily life of its faithful" and "to celebrate the quintessential symbol of community for Catholics."[52] At the Second National Eucharistic Congress in 1954, the U.S.-supported President Magsaysay dedicated the nation to the Sacred Heart. Barry teases out the implications of this action: "In this Cold War climate, American-inspired anti-Communist ideologies resonated within the Church and assertions of the unique

---

47. Ibid., 194–95.
48. Schumacher, "The Rizal Bill of 1956," 529–53.
49. Quitorio, *Pastoral Letters*, 162.
50. Ibid., 125.
51. Ibid., 257.
52. Barry, "Limits of Conservative Church Reformism," 62.

role of the Philippines as the bastion of Christianity in Asia, which were the hallmark of these grand religious events, took on an added meaning."[53]

However, with late twentieth-century changes in the global situation such as the demise of European communism and the reinvention of Chinese communism, CBCP statements no longer focused on communism as an adversary. They, in fact, passed over in silence the local communist insurgency with which various government administrations have tried to come to terms through peace processes.

Official church discourse has instead concerned itself with a perspective that it called by different names—"liberalism," "a secular humanistic philosophy," and "a postmodern spirit." This adversary first appeared in the February 18, 1953, CWO statement against those "excluding religion from the national life in the name of a false liberalism,"[54] but has gained recent currency in statements against reproductive health legislation. The January 30, 2011, CBCP statement on the RH Bill indicts "a secularist, materialist spirit that considers morality as a set of teachings from which one can choose, according to the spirit of the age."[55] This adversary in their reckoning now constitutes the threat to the imaginary of the Philippines as a Catholic nation.

Doing Theology in East Asian Contexts

In the Philippines, to do theology—that is, "[to] mediate between a cultural matrix and the significance and role of a religion in that matrix"[56]—begins then with recognizing that the formation of identity and community, religious as well as national, occurred within one historical process with interweaving threads. As a result of this historical dynamic, imagining identity as Christian and as Filipino went hand in hand with imagining community as nation and Christian.

As discussed in the comprehensive *History of Southeast Asia*,[57] other East Asian contexts with dominant religious traditions are also characterized by analogous dynamics, though the religions involved differ according to context. While these traditions might not have ridden the waves of a single global movement as Christianity did with sixteenth-century coloniza-

53. Barry, "Polyglot Catholicism," 71.
54. Quitorio, *Pastoral Letters*, 125.
55. Catholic Bishops' Conference of the Philippines, "Choosing Life, Rejecting the RH Bill," par. 9.
56. Lonergan, *Method in Theology*, xi.
57. Tarling, *Cambridge History of Southeast Asia*.

tion, they arrived throughout the region with the movement of population and goods, and therefore also came to terms with new languages, cultures, and social structures. They survived and thrived to the extent that they were shaped by new contexts that they shaped in turn. Thus emerged, for instance, the various schools of Buddhism in the region or even the interaction of Islam with traditional religion or Hinduism in Indonesia. In the end, many of these traditions have become profoundly integrated within the national polity and local cultures, resulting in such commonplaces such as "to be Thai is to be Buddhist."[58]

Interrogation of Dominant View of Religion

Recognizing this interwoven formation of both religious and national identity and community opens the path toward interrogating the understanding of "religion" implicit in the existing dominant theological discourse developed by Christianity in early modern Europe, especially against heresy.[59]

The first element of this understanding—religion as an integrated system of beliefs, values, and practices with distinct boundaries distinguishing it from other religions—emerged, as Wilfred Cantwell Smith pointed out decades ago, through the encounter of the West with religions different from Christianity.[60] Moreover, in keeping with its emphasis on the rational, this view often privileged belief, the doctrinal content of religion, as the crucial linchpin that makes it different from others. This view is best seen as an ideal conceptualization of what religious adherents consider the "core" of their religion based on authoritative sources such as sacred texts.

Such a view proves inadequate for critical reflection on the historical experience of religious traditions in East Asian contexts where these traditions and contexts frequently influenced and shaped each other. Furthermore, though beliefs were part of these traditions, they were often not considered to be boundary-setting or even the core of religion. As Michael Budde discusses in the case of Christianity, "the borders of baptism" that constitute the Church create a more universal "polity against which nations and states look positively sectarian, parochial, and tribal."[61]

Applying this view of religion to East Asian religious traditions has created problematic issues, such as those involving conversion and syncretism. For instance, the authenticity of Filipino Christianity has been questioned

58. Keyes, "Why the Thai Are Not Christians," 259–83.
59. Zagorin, *How the Idea of Religious Toleration Came to the West*.
60. W. Smith, *The Meaning and End of Religion*.
61. Budde, *Borders of Baptism*, 76.

on account of a simplistic view of the relation between colonization and evangelization as well as an anachronistic view of conversion. Though colonization and evangelization were indeed intimately linked under the juridical agreement between the papacy and Spanish monarchy, integration between church and government was not total as shown in their periodic conflicts. Moreover, claiming that native religious practice did not count as authentic conversion is founded on a modern concept of conversion as a break freely chosen by the autonomous subject from one distinct state, "being non-Christian," to another, "being Christian."[62]

As mentioned earlier, the formation of native identity as Christian is better described not in terms of a discontinuous break from traditional religion but as the translation of Spanish Catholicism into a historical form that empowered natives to be Christian. In other East Asian contexts, "converted" Christians continue to acknowledge layers of their identity that are Hindu or Buddhist and have brought about the phenomenon of "multiple religious belonging."[63] Moreover, the traditional critique of syncretism in many religious traditions has been undermined by historical evidence; for instance, Christianity has always "borrowed" many elements from diverse sources as a means of translating Christian practice through different cultural codes and thus of forming new "hybrid" forms of religious identity.[64]

The second element in the dominant view of religion—as a domain independent of other social spaces and entities—also appears problematic with regard to East Asian religious traditions. Derived from nineteenth-century European sociological thinking, such a view looks at religion as an institution isolated from other social realities and, according to its twentieth-century lineage, foresees the decline and privatization of religion among individuals and societies due to the inevitable process of secularization.

Contrary to this "myth of secularization,"[65] religious traditions in East Asia as elsewhere are not institutions isolated from other social forces and entities; in fact, they are intimately linked with the cultures and politics of their contexts. For example, concomitant with imagining identity and community as Christian and Filipino, the religious was not divorced from but interacted with the racial, ethnic or cultural layers of personal and communal identities. Thus, structures involved in both the personal and the communal were notably homologous, but not identical: negotiating being

62. Hefner, *Conversion to Christianity.*
63. Cornille, *Many Mansions?*
64. Schreiter, *New Catholicity,* 62–83.
65. Casanova, *Public Religions in the Modern World.*

Christian with being native, colonial, or Filipino reflected negotiating being church with other social actors and forces.

Dis-imagining the Religious Nation

The interrogation of this dominant view of religion suggests an alternative approach to religion better suited to East Asian contexts. This approach makes an important distinction between a religious tradition's symbolic capital and its institutional nature. For instance, Filipino Christianity could be described as story—that is, the network of Christian symbols that function as a metanarrative in Philippine society—and as church, the institutional community of Christians.[66]

Such a distinction sheds better light on the role of religious traditions in society. In the Philippines, only 10 percent of baptized Catholics have regular contact with the Church,[67] but because of the extensive presence of the Christian story in lowland Philippine culture, the influence of Christianity is stronger, as manifested in the People Power Revolution that ended the Marcos regime[68] or even the 1896 Philippine Revolution against Spain in which the poor saw their revolutionary struggle in terms of Christ's Passion story.[69]

Moreover, this distinction unmasks the distorting implications of the concept of "a religious nation" and points to the need to dis-imagine it. It allows one to account for a religion's profound influence on society and culture through its symbolic capital as distinguished from its institutional role in the public sphere. To speak then of "a religious nation" conflates both the symbolic and the institutional influences of religion as well as religious community and nation.

It is true that, in the Philippines as elsewhere, the formation of religious community or church and of the nation commonly occurred within related historical processes—for instance, the construction of the Philippines as Christian, Thailand as Buddhist, or Indonesia and Malaysia as Islamic—regardless of the constitutional separation or establishment of religion in each case. Furthermore, because religious traditions originate within national or ethnic histories, the imaginary of a religious nation is reinforced. Such is especially the case with Christianity, which traces its lineage to Israel as

---

66. Francisco, "Christianity as Church and Story," 528–41.
67. Picardal, *Basic Ecclesial Communities in the Philippines*, 57.
68. Ibid., 172–86.
69. Ileto, *Pasyon and Revolution*.

"God's people"[70]—an image turned iconic by Catholicism's Second Vatican Council.

Though a theology of nationality such as Llywelyn's proves helpful in shifting paradigms from "redeemer nations to redeemed humanity,"[71] the temptation to re-create Christendom still appears irresistible. Its pull toward greater integration between religion and governance in general and the religious community and the nation in particular assumes greater legitimacy when such a close relationship leads to effective promotion of social justice. For example, many Catholics were undisturbed by the putting at the center of earlier EDSA People Power Revolution celebrations a Catholic Mass preceded by prayers led by leaders of other religions almost as a concession to the plurality of religions. Furthermore, though the official stand reflected in countless CBCP pastoral letters is to be politically involved only when moral issues are at stake, particular church leaders have crossed boundaries between the moral and the partisan political.

However, since these religious are open to and invite adherents from diverse backgrounds, the deconstruction of this imaginary is called for, especially because of its negative consequences. Twentieth-century examples include Catholic Spain under Francisco Franco, Northern Ireland with its interwoven religious, national, and class conflicts, and the Soka Gakkai phenomenon in postwar Japan. One finds more recent instances from Southeast Asia in studies such as *Conflict, Religion, and Culture*.[72]

Given this situation, dis-imagining the religious nation would facilitate the inclusion and empowerment of minority religious and ethnic groups who have been excluded by the historical construction of the religious state and the resulting dominance of some religions in particular contexts; examples of such groups are Muslims and indigenous peoples in the Philippines, Muslims in southern Thailand, and the many ethnic groups in Indonesia. Dissociating religion and nation could thus facilitate dialogue and collaboration between different religions.

Moreover, it would minimize conflict between religious communities and nation-states within whatever constitutional framework obtains in each context, since these institutions are distinct and independent but not isolated from each other, and all are concerned for the common good, especially in relation to family, health, and livelihood.

As an example, the long-standing controversy on reproductive health (RH) in the Philippines suggests the negative consequences of conflating

70. Buell, *Why This New Race?*
71. Llewelyn, *Toward a Catholic Theology*, 277–99.
72. Anceschi et al., *Conflict, Religion, and Culture*.

religion and nation. On May 1, 1976, the CBCP stated, "For centuries, Filipino life has been wedded to Catholicism; it has brought forth an outlook and practices that are both deeply Christian and deeply Filipino."[73] Given the continuing influence of this view, some Filipino Catholics opposed recent legislation on reproductive health. The January 30, 2011, CBCP statement asserts, "Far from being simply a Catholic issue, the RH bill is a major attack on authentic human values and on Filipino cultural values regarding human life that all of us have cherished since time immemorial."[74] This was followed by their March 2, 2010, statement in which they argued that "it is unjust that the taxes of the people including Catholics be used for purposes against their moral beliefs."[75]

Moreover, the imaginary of the Philippines as a Christian nation makes it difficult to recognize discourses from a domain other than the ecclesiastical—one resulting from "a process of functional differentiation and emancipation of the secular spheres—primarily the state, the economy, and science—from the religious sphere."[76] No CBCP statement acknowledged that others within Filipino society, including non-Catholic religious groups, could have contrary positions, and thus voices within the Catholic Church and outside it pointed to the principles of freedom of religion and conscience, the primacy of the common good and separation of church and state. Little dialogue within the Catholic Church as well as with government and other civil society and religious stakeholders occurred, and fragmentation took place within both the Catholic Church and the nation.

All these considerations ultimately lead to the fundamental question of where we, from East Asia and elsewhere, locate religious community. Religious traditions have historically employed geopolitical models to foster and structure religious community. Hence the traditional East Asian landscape is marked with networks of local churches, mosques, or temples. Within Christianity's extensive institutional differentiation, dioceses, parishes, and even the highly commended basic ecclesial communities are imitations of provinces, towns, and neighborhoods.

But given increased mobility and alternative connectivity as well as emerging forms of community in the contemporary landscape, including cyberspace, religious traditions are challenged to reimagine religious community other than being in the image and likeness of the nation. What specific configurations this community takes will certainly vary from religion

---

73. Quitorio, *Pastoral Letters*, 464.
74. CBCP, "Choosing Life, Rejecting the RH Bill."
75. Ibid.
76. Casanova, *Public Religions in the Modern World*, 19.

to religion and from place to place—hence, another instance when theologians from different contexts are compelled to converse with each other.

PART THREE

In Lieu of a Conclusion

17

Loyalties, Allegiances, and Discipleship: Facing the Challenges

MICHAEL L. BUDDE

Introduction

In attempting to conclude a volume like this, it seems no easy task to collect all the ideas, observations, insights, and exhortations we have shared. So many perspectives, so complex the relationships, so large the stakes—amid all this talk of multiple and competing identities, allegiances potentially in conflict, a plethora of claims on who and whose we are, it seems all too easy to throw up one's hands, or to wander off with the scholar's lament of "well, it's complex."

Too complex indeed. And yet, let us not let ourselves off so easily. The stakes continue to be high, both the problems and the opportunities remain significant, and the costs of deficient understandings of Christianity's claims amid those of nation, people, tribe, and state—to name just a few—remain immense in human terms. We need not review the human costs, for we can all produce a depressing list of millions killed or made to suffer due to the dynamics of collective identities armed and mobilized—whether it be in Europe during World War I, the colonization of the Americas and Africa, the wars of national liberation, or any number of violated places and peoples—just in the past century.

The sheer numbers of victims, and the opportunities to contribute to good in the world, make one claim on our continued attention and best efforts. Another derives from the hold collective identities have on people worldwide. No matter if one shows the crass instrumentalism behind the construction of many national borders, or the utter capriciousness of those features said to distinguish one group from its rivals, things like nationalism continue unabated, seemingly as strong as ever, even after centuries of mass death in the name of fatherland, mother country, or homeland.

We must be ever mindful, as many of the contributors here remind us, of the degree to which the construction of identities and loyalties taps into deep emotional and nonrational longings for friendship, meaning, and greatness. We misunderstand our world and ourselves if we ignore the extent to which the construction of emotion and sentiment is at the heart of what brings us here today.

We must also confront our inability to think of a world which is otherwise, in which the identities we wear and perform do not set us invariably in conflict from the outset from those defined as outside the range of one's people, as non-citizens, as tribal rivals, as outsiders, as threats to our security and destiny. Even suggesting that things could be otherwise seems irresponsible, idealistic, or simply idiotic. Thus is the world, thus have we made the world—as Robert Bolt once wrote—but also, thus has the world made us.

It is also difficult because so many of these identities enable good things in the world—a measure of security, the capacity for some sort of collective action, a range of limited goods that we cannot imagine living without but cannot imagine being provisioned by ways that do not presuppose the sort of strong, binding identities that simultaneously give rise to war and conquest, witch hunts, and ethnic cleansings. It is good to know from whom one comes; it is good to have ties of mutuality and reciprocity that make a difference in one's world; it is good to appreciate the dance of diversity and unity that one can see around us every day. But it is not good to presume blithely that one can have only the good things that strong political identities and allegiances produce without having to account for the ugly aspects that are irremovable from those same bonds.

All of this, let it be said, is even more difficult for those of us here because, in one way or another, we claim and are claimed by the designation "Christian." And that makes all the difference in the world, at least in this world. In case we've forgotten, let's revisit why all of this talk about identities, allegiances, and loyalties is especially important to Christians, and why anyone would bother to draw all of us together to struggle with these things.

We struggle with these issues because, no matter how we phrase it or what notes we emphasize, we expect more of the church—and thus ourselves—than what has been delivered thus far. Which is to say that, for all but the most accommodated forms of ecclesiology, something remains of the eschatological nature of the church—that it is called into being by God to act as some sort of exemplar, however imperfect, of what the world redeemed by Christ should look like. We have Acts 2 and 4 to give us one taste of what it means to be a new community gathered by the Holy Spirit: we have 1 Pet 2:9 calling us to be "a chosen race, a royal priesthood, a holy nation, God's own people, that you may declare the wondrous deeds of him who called you out of darkness into his marvelous light." We are told in no uncertain terms that the claims of the biological family are qualified by bonds to one's brothers and sisters in Christ; markers of status and hierarchy are set aside in a community in which "there does not exist among you Jew or Greek, slave or free, male or female. All of you are one in Christ Jesus" (Gal 3:28).

We struggle further because, and most fully because, we believe God has revealed God's self and God's ways in the world in the person of Jesus of Nazareth. Except for all but the most Unitarian-minded, or for those whose theological method substitutes something else, Jesus matters for what it means to be a Christian—somehow, some way, in some measure. And this Jesus raises questions not only about ends—calling people to follow him, to be his disciples and extend his work through time, to manifest the Kingdom of God via their life together—but also about means: making one's way in the world by loving one's enemies, returning good for evil, rejecting those sorts of power that presuppose lording it over others or that order can be built via the sword.

If none of this were true, we would have much less about which to worry when it comes to nationalism, ethnicity, or other forms of identity armed and on the march. But because it is true, even in ways we cannot always articulate, we feel the need to gather as Christians to explore our unease and push ourselves to a more adequate sense of how "being a Christian" can or should affect what we think, how we feel, and what we do with these other claimants on our bodies, our allegiances, and our dispositions. So many of our concerns would go away if we just lowered our expectations of the gathered community, if we just finished the process of fashioning a safer and more accommodated—and accommodating—Jesus. We see all around us many people and groups who have done just that—for whom Jesus is a patriot and champion of their own place in the universe, and for whom the church exists to assure us that however many people we have to kill to build or preserve order, we can still take comfort in being part of the new chosen people.

Now What?

If any of this rings true, if in fact we seem fated to continue with these seemingly intractable problems for many years to come, what do we do next? Such a question invites varied responses from pastors, and from congregational leaders and members. For those of us scholars whose work attends to the church in one way or another, where do we go and what do we do? While ours is not indispensable work in the big picture of the Kingdom, it may have a modest role to play; if we stay modest about ourselves, we may be allowed to make modest proposals from time to time. I take seriously the conclusion of our colleague Dorian Llywelyn that many of the topics we engage in this volume—nationhood, ethnicity, the claims of the modern state and nation-state—have generated only limited theological reflection thus far, especially in Catholic circles. Much more remains to be done, given that the materials currently at hand—in formal teaching materials of the church, for example—are rather sparse and limited.

Doubtless others might approach this question differently, but in a spirit of collegial encouragement I would like to humbly submit the following for your consideration—specifically a list of Dead Ends to avoid and Open Doors to explore. In the interests of time, I will limit myself to an abbreviated list—a few Dead Ends, and a few Open Doors.[1]

Dead Ends to Avoid

Family Metaphors and Large-Gauge Identities

As a volume like this makes clear, so much of the emotional power, resilience, and endurance of those ties that lead us to die and kill for those within the circle of "us" derives from deep metaphors that go largely unquestioned and reflexively affirmed. These are notions of family, of familial bonds and obligations, the sort of love shared by fathers and mothers, husbands and wives, spouses and children, brothers and sisters, and more. This is a source of referred power, in which the intensity and ferocity of those bonds are transferred to larger, impersonal groups—nations, tribes, states, peoples, and more. So much of the language of "imagined communities" that one encounters ad infinitum in the literature on nation-building itself is a transferral of the power of the family to more impersonal, more abstract, and more powerful entities.

---

1. Portions of the following section are derived in part from Budde, *Borders of Baptism*.

Nations as families, states as parental figures, citizens as brothers and sisters—all of this leads nowhere good. This is so for many reasons, but two of them merit notice briefly here. For one, real-world families are messy, imperfect places—nobody would think to idealize them with national monuments, anthems, heroic figures, sacred spaces and holidays—that nonetheless often demonstrate virtues that would be alien, if not anathema, to collectives that claim familial aura: virtues like forgiving wrongs rather than exacting retribution, providing second chances where none are merited, and redistributing from the haves to the have-nots without expectation of advantage or gain.

At the same time, family metaphors get Christian reflection on allegiances nowhere because the family itself is a notorious barrier to discipleship and the Way of the Cross. If you don't think so or have forgotten it, avail yourself of Matthew's Gospel—you don't have to deal with the whole thing; just limit yourself to chapter 10, if you'd like. There you would find Jesus instructing the apostles on their mission, authority, and calling. Jesus also warns them of the obstacles that await them and the persecution that will greet them as a consequence of following him. Such will not be random in its sources, says Jesus; rather, "Brother will betray brother to death, and a father his child; children will come forward against their parents and have them put to death" (10:21). Later in that chapter, Matthew's Jesus harkens back to Micah (7:6) in identifying the family as a prime obstacle to the gospel. And then, of course, there is Matt 10:34–39:

> Do not think that I have come to bring peace to the earth: it is not peace I have come to bring, but a sword. For I have come to set son against father, daughter against mother, daughter-in-law against mother-in-law; a person's enemies will be members of his own household.
>
> No one who prefers father or mother to me is worthy of me. No one who prefers son or daughter to me is worthy of me. Anyone who does not take his cross and follow in my footsteps is not worthy of me. Anyone who finds his life will lose it; anyone who loses his life for my sake will find it.

The family opposes discipleship in many ways, as Matthew and the other evangelists warn. It tempts one toward privileging blood relatives over all else, puts protecting family respectability and reputation above proclaiming the gospel, and counsels realism, practicality, and the safe path over the Way that may lead to exclusion, suffering, and martyrdom.

But Jesus doesn't stop here. In fact, he uses his destabilizing of family primacy to call into question other natural roles, allegiances, and responsibilities:

> When the other ten heard this they were indignant with the two brothers. But Jesus called them to him and said, "You know that among the gentiles the rulers lord it over them, and great men make their authority felt. Among you this is not to happen. No; anyone who wants to become great among you must be your servant, and anyone who wants to be first among you must be your slave, just as the Son of man came not to be served but to serve, and to give his life as a ransom for many." (Matt 20:24–28)

In other words, not only must followers of Jesus put being a disciple over being a good family person, this "being a disciple" may also render them unsuitable for exercising power in the secular realm. How can a disciple serve as a ruler, or even as a functionary in the ruler's apparatus, with Jesus's notion of legitimate and illegitimate power and its exercise? However much worldly power cloaks itself in the soft language of service, its institutions (consider the modern state and modern capitalism) presume the indispensability of the sort of power that Jesus calls upon his disciples to abjure.

Matthew on the family ought to make one forever suspicious of any sort of theology that privileges so-called natural institutions—the family, states, and the like—as among the self-evident goods to be embraced and celebrated by the church. Inasmuch as the nation is among these "natural" entities presumed to be good and valuable in and of themselves, and insofar as notions of "natural" community, cohesiveness, and identity underwrite much mainstream debate on borders and movement (especially in Christian circles, it must be said), then Matthew's scriptural assault on the family may have something to say in reframing the entire question for Christians and other interested people. For if even the family—an intricate and tangible source of identity—has value not solely on its own terms but to the extent that it serves the cause of discipleship, how much less claim on Christian practices of commonality, relatedness, and obligation should modern nations, peoples, tribes, ethnic communities, and states enjoy?

Nationalism Is Bad, Patriotism Is Good

Most of us want good things without bad things. We want delicious deep-dish pizza without calories or cholesterol. We want fit, tone bodies without the tedium and effort of exercise. And we want all the goodies that powerful allegiances like nationhood and peoplehood can deliver without any of the bad stuff.

Wishful thinking like this is more than simply an aspiration of everyday life—it is the stuff of careful reflection and learned reflection, like formal papal and church documents. It suffuses scholarly studies in ethics, political thought, and serious public opinion. In the writing of Pope Leo XIII, for example, nationalism is condemned as a form of idolatry, while patriotism is described as a virtue;[2] variations on this distinction reappear through formal Catholic documents in the twentieth century, and in the work of theologians of all stripes more often than can be counted, all with little or no attention to what distinguishes one from the other.

What all of these have in common is a depressing tendency to provide distinctions without criteria, typologies without metrics. That which we like we call "patriotism," or "sensible love of country." Those sentiments expressed by those we don't like are "nationalist," "extremist," or "jingoist" (these days, you could add "religious fanaticism," if such is your preference). The presumption is that, with all of this, one is dealing with categories that admit of degrees—some love of country, for example, is fine, but too much is bad: a little potassium chloride is good for you, too much will kill you.

But not everything is in this order of things. One can't get a healthy dose of plutonium, for example, even though more plutonium may well be worse than a little bit of it. The capacity of totalizing identities and allegiances—to one's people, tribe, nation, or state—should inspire no easy confidence that such can be imbibed in small doses, that most people can be "a little bit nationalistic" without harmful effect, or that such limited endorsement would be either welcomed or tolerated by the collectives in question (certainly not in extremis).

And even if one grants the possibility that meaningful distinctions here can be made—that "patriotism" is good but "nationalism" is bad—still, the question remains: what distinguishes one from the other? How is one to decide when conduct, belief, or conviction has passed from one to the other?

No self-evident criteria present themselves on secular grounds, and the Christian community seems paralyzed on how to proceed in discerning how much national, ethnic, or communal identification is too much. So let me offer one modest proposal: any identity that requires Christians to kill Christians from another group is illegitimate. Those sorts of identities put some other allegiance—to country, to peoplehood, to movement—over that loyalty that Christians owe to one another as members of the one Body of

---

2. See Llywelyn, *Toward a Catholic Theology*, 146.

Christ, created in baptism and renewed in Eucharist and manifested in the work of the church universal.

Immediately a criterion like this raises as many questions as it solves, which is a good thing. Do I presume that, while it is illegitimate for Christians to kill one another, they are free to follow political directives to kill non-Christians?

Since I believe that the refusal to kill anyone is a constitutive and not optional aspect of being a Christian, I would gladly say that Christians should not kill anyone. But for those who continue to hold to a Christian legitimation of lethal force in political endeavor, my proposed criterion would be a halfway measure, an interim guideline to judgment that may eventually lead the rest of the church to resolve the inconsistency by eventually condemning all killing on behalf of political allegiances.

Doubtless there are other ways to operationalize the theological intuition that whenever "being a Christian" is subordinated to another set of loyalties and allegiances that require lethal means in their construction or maintenance, something is amiss. Being a Christian should be the primary, formative identity against which others are measured and situated. But if you're being required to kill others in order to serve faithfully some collective or group, then perhaps you're being told which loyalty is meant to bow to the other.

"Faithful Citizenship": A U.S. Cul-de-sac

Elsewhere in this volume, Braden Anderson discusses the recent work of the U.S. Catholic bishops on Christianity and political responsibility. I would like to extend the conversation here and add my own reflections on a matter that is unlikely to fade anytime soon.

For those places where Catholic Christianity has had to prove its worth and convince a skeptical elite and public that it belongs, the document *Faithful Citizenship* is emblematic of a desire for full partnership between Catholicism and national identity. *Faithful Citizenship* is shorthand for *Forming Consciences for Faithful Citizenship*, a landmark 2007 statement voted on and approved by the Catholic bishops in the United States that reflects an unbreakable correspondence between being a Catholic Christian and being an American citizen. While most commentators read this document as a guide to Catholics in the political arena, I have written elsewhere about it as an ode to a Catholic self-understanding that is subordinated to the ethos of national belonging to the detriment of the integrity of the gospel and the Church.[3]

Documents like this are a curious sort of thing—the first two pages collapse the Church into the nation, with "We the nation," "we as society, we as country" being the categories of address—not we the Church, or we the followers of Christ, which would make more sense in a document addressed to Catholic Christians. One of the more curious things about this directive is that, while it goes to great lengths to deny that it "tells Catholics how to vote" (the specter of Vatican-controlled bloc voters being a cornerstone of American anti-Catholicism for centuries), it has no qualms about telling Catholics that they *must* vote—no matter how rotten or corrupt they may think the U.S. system to be, no matter how great the incompatibility between being a follower of Christ and a child of empire. They don't go as far as a Nigerian bishop a few years ago who threatened to excommunicate any Catholic who didn't vote in an election there, but the notion that Catholics might refuse participation in the civil religion ritual of voting for reasons of conscience seems abhorrent to the bishops.

Two things in particular mark this approach—embracing citizenship as self-evidently compatible with the demands of discipleship—as fruitless, if not incoherent. For one, for all the talk about the need for the Church to form its members' consciences in ways that allow them to pursue the common good with "principles" derived from the faith, directives like "Forming Consciences for Faithful Citizenship" are completely silent concerning the complete and abject failures of lay Christian formation in the United States (such is the case elsewhere in the world church, but that is another matter). The literature on all of this is overwhelming, the pastoral proofs are all but inescapable, and yet not a word in a document that trumpets "formation" as the linchpin of how Christianity is to make public life more adequately reflect those truths and goods derived from Scripture and the Christian tradition. The gap between the bishops' emphasis on lay formation and their record in lay formation is so vast that it is something akin to asking the Chicago Cubs how to win a World Series in baseball—the Cubs, like the Catholic Church, now think in terms of centuries, at least when it comes to success.

The second feature illustrating the futility that is the overly eager desire to harmonize nationalism and Catholicism can be seen when the U.S. bishops sounded the alarm in 2012 on "threats to religious liberty" afoot in the United States, threats so serious as to threaten the ability of Catholics to practice their faith free of government repression. A dispute with

---

3. Budde, *Borders of Baptism*, 96–100.

the Obama administration regarding provisions for contraceptive coverage in federal health care law was presented as religious liberty "under attack," part of the erosion of religious liberty worldwide that leads to arrest and martyrdom. To combat this assault on Catholicism, the bishops called for two weeks of prayer, church activities of all sorts, and mobilization of the faithful to stand with their bishops at this crucial time.

The "fortnight of freedom" was mostly a bust, a nonevent for most Catholics in most places. But why? Could it be that, among other reasons, Catholics in the United States are more deeply formed by American patriotic and nationalist identities than by their being members of the Body of Christ, a distinct and distinctive worldwide community, who confess Christ the King before all else? Perhaps the bishops have succeeded too well by half in convincing Catholic Americans that there is no contradiction between the gospel and the American Experiment, no disconnect between the Way of the Cross and the American Way of Life. If that is the case, as I suggest it is, then statements like this one on religious liberty (beginning as it does with a desiderata that pleads with readers to recall that Catholicism and Americanism should always be complementary and not in contradiction to one another) seem more pathetic than anything else. Having worked for more than a century to be more American than the Americans, the Catholic leadership seems stunned that the laity has taken them at their word and ignores alarmist cries about religious liberty as illogical and preposterous. More of this seems unlikely to make things any different.

A Few Open Doors Worth Exploring

Demoting Allegiances

It may be too modest a goal in some respects, but there may be something worthwhile in sustained efforts encouraging Christians to become more crassly instrumental about many of the expressly political allegiances and loyalties that claim them in emotionally deep and compelling ways. Until such time as more people start to believe and feel themselves more fundamentally oriented by the role of "disciple" instead of that of "American" or "Serbian" or "patriot" or "Hutu" or "Falangist," it might be worthwhile to work to defuse such rival claimants even if replacing them is not possible.

What I mean by this is to encourage a reception of political identities that is more utilitarian than affective. It means taking on the mindset of Mennonite residents in Latin America, for whom having church settlements in more than one country means that national identity is something they put on or take off as is most convenient when crossing borders, dealing with state authorities, or facilitating the transborder work of the church.[4] It is emphatically not an emotional investment—the emotionally resonant sense of "who and whose am I?" is as a member of the church universal, incarnated in a variety of countries and cultures. While they have not jettisoned national identities, they have significantly relativized them. You adopt national identities, cultural memberships, public obligations only to the extent that they are useful to the work of the church, and only so long as they remain modest in their demands. You live as good neighbors to your fellow countrymen (and women), you practice Christian hospitality toward those not part of your communion. But when one or another state demands military service or something similarly contrary to the gospel command to love enemies and refuse the sword, then one refuses. Or, like the Mennonites, one leaves. In all of this, allegiances are worn lightly, to be taken off when they become too burdensome.[5]

To some people, such a recommendation might seem selfish, a refusal to sacrifice on behalf of the political community, a lack of gratitude for the advantages conferred by membership in the national community or by citizenship in the state. Roman apologists made the same argument against the early Christians—that they were freeloaders, ingrates who benefited from the presence of the state but refused to support it via military service and worship of the gods. Origen's rebuttal to Celsus should be our answer today—that just by being what God wants it to be, the church contributes something crucial and irreplaceable to the world, and need not serve the empire on the empire's own terms in order to act "responsibly."[6] Perhaps the first open door to helping Christians think and act more adequately on matters of non-ecclesial communal identities is to encourage a spirit of selective "Christian freeloading," a deliberate campaign to de-sentimentalize such ways of situating themselves in the world. Perhaps we should make national identity more pedestrian, make citizenship more like membership in a club or part of an association of bird-watchers—useful for a certain range of pursuits, but nothing for which a sane person would be willing to kill.

Christian Formation as if We Meant It

Let me explain what I mean here, for I am speaking from experiences and contexts largely derived from advanced industrial countries (although my

4. See Canas Bottos, "Transformations of Old Colony Mennonites," especially 224–25.

5. Ibid. For a similar phenomenon, see the Ik tribe described by Bishop Paride Taban, 145–46.

6. See Hinson, *Understandings of the Church*, 63–66.

research continues to show me abundant evidence of comparable phenomena in all parts of the Catholic world). I refer to the dismal state of "Christian formation" in the Catholic world—and for a conference like the one that generated this volume, in which "transnational processes of Catholic formation" is in the subtitle, it is clear that more attention needs to be paid to this important matter.

It should not need to be said, but let me say it just as a reminder: no one is naturally or automatically a Christian, or an American, or a Kenyan, or a Brazilian, or a Muslim, or a Chinese. These identities are made, not born—they are the products and producers of affections, dispositions, desires, and habits that claim us and to which we respond. When this is done by political communities, it's usually called socialization; when it's done by the church, it's often called formation. Let me be more explicit in what I mean:

> [Formation] is a communal process similar to a craft apprenticeship, in which newcomers learn the explicit and tacit knowledge of practitioners by a process of imitation, then internalization, then innovation. Over time, if formation is successful, newcomers themselves become adept in encountering, imagining, and reasoning through Christian eyes, minds, and hearts. Christian practices of liturgy, religious education, prayer, and action are simultaneously practices of faith formation and products of communities themselves formed by the narratives, symbols, and examples of Jesus and his followers.

Stressing the centrality of formation in Christianity underscores two important points: that Christianity depends on collective, intensive practices distinct from the non-Christian world for its perpetuation; and that the process of "making Christians" is always a precarious matter, which can be undermined or diluted by other powerful institutions and processes of "formation." Consequently, formation is always intrinsically political, whether or not it is recognized as such. It requires institutional agents capable of inculcating their dispositions into human hearts and minds, often in opposition to actors attempting to do the same with different, sometimes conflicting, stories and symbols . . .

To be a people capable of loving its enemies, turning the other cheek, or seeing the inbreaking of the promised kingdom of God in the body of a crucified political enemy of the Roman Empire requires a more peculiar kind of formation. In every time and place, the church has formed a people capable of hearing and responding to the gospel of Jesus, the witness of the saints and martyrs, and the challenges of the prophets. Where formation has been neglected, undermined, or done poorly, evidence of such inadequacies appears as pathologies in the body of Christ and its practices, priorities, and affections.[7]

For most Catholic congregations in the advanced industrial world, we are a long way from the catechumenate or similar expressions of Christian formation taken seriously (we demand so much more from converts than we do cradle Catholics that it's no wonder the newcomers often find the born-into Catholics so depressingly accommodated and compromised).

If you want to see the data on what Catholic lay formation looks like in a place like the United States, look at what's being produced by people like David Campbell, coauthor of *American Grace* (2012) or the many works by Christian Smith, especially his groundbreaking *Soul Searching: The Spiritual Lives of American Teenagers* (2005). In the latter, it is the story of lay Catholic formation that merits an entire chapter to illustrate the worst and least effective of all communal attempts to pass on the faith to the next generation.[8] If you're in the mood for macrolevel research, wrap yourself up in the 2008 Pew Forum data that suggests that Catholics lose more members than any other group in the United States (one-third of persons raised Catholic leave the church) and that ex-Catholics constitute a full one-tenth of the national population.[9] And this is the industrial country that is "more religious" than post-Christian Europe, lest we forget.

I am aware that Christian faith is ultimately a gift, the work of the Holy Spirit and not sociologists or church workers armed with programs and guidebooks. But I am also aware that we come dangerously close to putting our Lord to the test if we continue to willfully make things more difficult and demand that He reverse our actions or inactions lest He be blamed for the outcomes. And it must be said that at least some of the public priorities of church leaders need to be reconsidered—even if I were convinced of the theological case against it, political opposition to same-sex marriage to me would not be a hill to die for, and certainly not on a par with the Resurrection or the scandal of Christians killing other Christians.

What would it look like to make the formation of disciples the pastoral priority of the Church, instead of simply giving them the scraps from the table? Smarter people than I would need to explore this, but it should be of major concern to those concerned with political theology, pastoral theology, ecclesiology, and intercultural theological exploration. This is an open

---

7. Budde and Brimlow, *Christianity Incorporated*, 60–61.

8. Smith and Denton, *Soul Searching*, ch. 6, "On Catholic Teens." See also Budde and Brimlow, *Christianity Incorporated*, 75–77.

9. Pew Research Center, "America's Former Catholics."

door inviting exploration—indeed, the door itself is falling off the hinges, crying out for attention. We should go through it together.

A Better Inculturation[10]

As I said earlier, I think Christian nonviolence means that Christians ought not to kill anybody—but the wholesale phenomenon of Christians killing one another with impunity remains a huge, perhaps insurmountable, obstacle to any sort of Christian credibility in the world. Why take seriously—whether in interreligious dialogues or anything else—anything coming from a religious movement whose members are willing to kill one another by the millions? And this coming from a movement that invites the world to embrace a Prince of Peace, calling for reconciliation and forgiveness rather than revenge and domination.

The third door through which I invite us to move is to think about these intertwined questions of Christianity and rival identities, especially those that presuppose lethality for the construction and maintenance of themselves, in a different way. More specifically, I'd like you to think about Christianity and contemporary allegiances as examples, for the most part, as matters of inculturation gone wrong.

Attention to inculturation has waxed and waned, but it remains a concern in Catholic circles worldwide—in missiology, contextual and systematic theologies alike, postcolonial and liberationist thought, and much more. One theme highlighted usefully in recent years concerns the recognition that inculturation is an ongoing process rather than a once-and-for-all phenomenon. It is not a finished work but one that requires ongoing renewal, rearticulation, and recommitment as host cultures and the Church both change and redefine one another as well as the notions of "cultures" and "church"; in this respect, it remains a constant both for churches in Europe and North America as well as for those in the many postcolonial regions of the world.

In all of this, it remains important to recognize that much damage was done to countless human beings, and to the witness of the gospel, by the forcible insertion of Christianity into human cultures during various eras of the past. This sort of inculturation at sword's point, suppressing preexisting peoples, beliefs, and communities in favor of a Christianity armed and aggressive, created a cultural milieu of a most particular sort. No one, least of

---

10. This section derives from my World Catholicism Week 2013 conference presentation, "Political Theology and the Church."

all leaders of the Catholic Church, should seek a return to any processes of inculturation that ally themselves with violence and death-dealing.

Much of the past seventy-five years has been spent coming to terms with the legacy of inculturation that comes by way of force, coercion, and power—in missiology, in the anti- and postcolonial movements, in the renewal movements surrounding the Second Vatican Council, and much more. How might the Church be true to its best self, how might it be a herald and foretaste of the Kingdom of God, without tying itself to forms of cultural and political habitation that presuppose the legitimacy of violence in the construction of identities and communities, and coercively regulated norms of order, belonging, and loyalty?

In our time, to repeat, the Church rejects the ambition of being an institution capable of structuring human affections and identities through force or by recourse to violent means. In this, may God be praised as room is made for a vision of religious liberty rooted both in individual conscience and a robust communal sense of cultural diversity and Christian discipleship.

For much of the so-called modern era, for imperial and colonial/postcolonial regions alike, perhaps the most powerful processes and ideologies of identity and belonging—of culturation and inculturation alike, if you will—have been those that seek to form peoples, nations, states, and homelands. If in the interests of time we confine ourselves to the powerful form of community known as national citizenship, we do well to see the violence built into the concept in its fundamentals and not its accidentals.

The power to exclude certain groups from national or political recognition should not be seen as an occasional or transitory phenomenon in political history, says social theorist Anthony Marx; rather, "exclusion is structural rather than fixed or tangential to nation-building."

Marx continues, noting that

> Nationalism is often purposefully exclusionary, with such exclusions emerging in fits and starts but encouraged or encoded to serve the explicit requirements for solidifying core loyalty to the nation. Rather than diversity precluding cohesion, diversity and selective allocations of nationalism and related rights may be the tools for building cohesion among the core that is included and demarcated.[11]

In addition,

> Much prior analysis has assumed that the imperative for encouraging national unity should be inclusive, but often this is not

11. Marx, "Nation-State and Its Exclusions," 107.

possible ... State elites make deals en route to nation-building, selecting whom to include, reward, and encourage loyalty from as the core constituency. To identify and consolidate the core, elites manipulate established antagonisms against some other group thereby excluded. And the core constituency so demarcated and reinforced may itself change over time according to shifting challenges and allegiances.[12]

While it might be comforting to assume that the process of willful exclusion is but a transitory matter, part of the labor pains of state- and nation-building to be superseded by a progressive incorporation of outside groups and former outsiders, such comfort might itself be transitory. Former outcasts may well be incorporated, provided they change themselves in accord with nationalist dictates and narratives, but other groups by necessity often become the objects of exclusion, definition-by-contrast, or similar binary negations. Such may be the fate of immigrants and refugees in our time, as well as other groups who by stipulation can be placed outside the parameters of accepted identity-description (terrorists, extremists, ethnically unassimilable communities, etc.). Such is emphasized by Adrian Oldfield in his reflections on citizenship in the modern world. As he notes,

> Citizenship is exclusive: it is not a person's humanity that one is responding to, it is the fact that he or she is a fellow citizen, or a stranger. In choosing an identity for ourselves, we recognize both who our fellow citizens are, and those who are not members of our community, and thus who are potential enemies. Citizenship cuts across both religious and secular universalism and involves recognizing that one gives priority, when and where required, to one's political community.[13]

While such does not always require unremitting hostility to others, to Oldfield, "It simply means that to remain a citizen one cannot always treat everyone as a human being."[14]

It means that states must retain the right, according to Peter Schuck and Rogers Smith, "to refuse consent to the membership of those who would disrupt their necessary homogeneity," however defined, in the interest of national unity.[15] As a political phenomenon, citizenship is distinction backed by force.

12. Ibid., 113.
13. Oldfield, "Citizenship and Community," 81.
14. Ibid.
15. Schuck and Smith, *Citizenship Without Consent*, quoted in Levinson, "Constituting Communities through Words," 1446.

In its embrace of nationalism, "peoplehood," and varied ethnic claims on identity and allegiance, I suggest, the Church again opts for another sort of inculturation at sword's point, in which Christianity mutes its call for peacemaking and reconciliation as it attempts to gain acceptance and incorporation among the diverse and varied cultures of the world. Such represents another variant on the now discredited agenda of inculturation by coercion, albeit one in which in most cases the violence is wielded on behalf of a non-Christian ideology to which the Church serves in a subordinate, not defining, role. Focusing on whether and to what extent dynamics of identity and allegiance reflect inculturation done well or poorly opens new conversations, makes available other tools, and allows for a dialogue in which all parts of the church must participate and share in fraternal correction and encouragement.

As one example of this, I recommend to you the counsel of Andrew Walls, who observes that the integrity and mission of the churches require the local and universal to exist in a dialectical interplay of creativity and correction. Walls describes this as the necessary complementarity of the "indigenizing principle" (guaranteeing that Christianity will adapt and embrace the best of all cultures worldwide, allowing for the faith to be "at home" in each culture) and the "pilgrim principle" (which makes Christianity transformative of all cultures worldwide rather than be absorbed by them).

> The Christian has all the relationships in which he was brought up, and has them sanctified by Christ who is living in them. But he also has an entirely new set of relationships, with other members of the family of faith into which he has come, and whom he must accept, with all their group relations (and "disrelations") on them, just as God has accepted him with his. Every Christian has dual nationality, and has a loyalty to the faith family which links him to those in interest groups opposed to that to which he belongs by nature . . .
>
> In addition . . . the Christian is given an adoptive past. He is linked to the people of God in all generations (like him, members of the faith family), and most strangely of all, to the whole history of Israel, the curious continuity of the race of the faithful from Abraham. By this means, the history of Israel is part of Church history, and all Christians of whatever nationality, are landed by adoption with several millennia of someone else's history, with a whole set of ideas, concepts, and assumptions which do not necessarily square with the rest of their cultural inheritance; and the Church in every land, of whatever race and

type of society, has this same adoptive past by which it needs to interpret the fundamentals of the faith. The adoption into Israel becomes a "universalizing" factor, bringing Christians of all cultures and ages together through a common inheritance, lest any of us make the Christian faith such a place to feel at home that no one else can live there; and bringing into everyone's society some sort of outside reference.[16]

In what I find to be a powerful and potent suggestion, Walls further notes that

> It is not possible to have too much of the localizing and indigenizing principle which makes the faith thoroughly at home, nor too much of that universalizing principle which is in constant tension with it, and which links that local community with its "domestic" expression of faith in the same Christ of Christians of other times and places. It is possible only to have too little of either.[17]

Can we really say that the evangelization of the world is better off with the sort of theo-ethnic alliances we have seen in so many places, with churches wedded or subordinated de jure or de facto to national identities or states? Or are these varied concordats like a vaccine against the good news—a weakened form of the gospel injected into the body politic of the world such that the world becomes resistant to the real thing? We have numerous examples of inculturation done well in the history of the church, and may it not be the case that many of these have much to teach us about the potential for fascinating diversity within an overarching ethos of peaceableness and noncoercive unity in Christ, across the borders and exclusions that human associations outside the gospel seem to require and presuppose?

A Final Door

This final door is one my brother Orobator has opened for us (see chapter 10 of this volume), and I will gladly be the first to pass through. I invite all of you to follow along.

In his insightful reflections, Father Orobator makes the helpful observation that the waters of baptism are themselves too thin to overcome the blood of familial and other bonds. The notion of baptism is too individualistic, too vertical by nature, to do the sort of lifting I hope it might someday

16. Walls, *Cross-Cultural Process*, 9.
17. Ibid., 30.

evoke from us as members of the Body of Christ. More adequate, he suggests, is a Eucharistic emphasis, wherein the blood of Christ breaks down barriers and gathers disparate peoples around the table, creating the sort of horizontal affections that might more adequately overcome the enmities of division and exclusion.

As I accept his invitation to move through this door, I offer a few observations: First, the notion of baptism that my friend Orobator discerns in my work is not one to which I subscribe—if I have given the impression that I see baptism as an individualistic exercise, a matter of private choice or affirmation, then doubtless the fault lies in failures in my powers of expression. In fact, my view of baptism is relentlessly communal, to my critics excessively so. A more adequate theology of baptism moving into the future, I suggest, is one that has much to learn from the notion of some practices of the early church, in which the community and its leaders demanded significant changes in a postulant's affections, practices—sometimes even occupation and groups of friends—before he or she might be admitted to the fellowship via baptism. Persons could even have their request for baptism deferred or rejected if the community believed them insufficiently aware of the demands that following Christ might put on them in a world in which Jesus is not always received as good news. If one wants to explore theologies of baptism that in practice trivialize or diminish the communal aspects of Christian membership, I encourage a rethinking of the practice of indiscriminate infant baptism, at least in advanced industrial countries and perhaps elsewhere—admittedly, an unusual perspective for someone who hopes to be heard as a member of the Catholic tradition.

Second, I welcome his insight that emphasis on the Eucharist is absolutely essential to an adequate Christian understanding of how to situate the varied roles, identities, and narratives that inhabit us. In fact, some of us have already begun to do so. The World Catholicism Week conference that was hosted by DePaul's Center for World Catholicism and Intercultural Theology in 2012 was titled "Real Presences: Eucharist, Society, and Global Catholicism"; it reflected an attempt by scholars from around the world to explore how Eucharistic sacramentality might help the Church think and act more adequately in a globalizing, pluralizing world.[18]

My own effort at that gathering was titled "Real Presences and False Gods: The Eucharist as Discernment and Formation." Most of the papers presented at that gathering have been published in the journal *Modern*

---

18. See the home page of World Catholicism Week 2012: http://las.depaul.edu/centers-and-institutes/center-for-world-catholicism-cultural-theology/World-Catholicism-Week/past-world-cath/Pages/2012.aspx

Theology.[19] I will avoid a rehash of that essay, but to show that I take seriously Orobator's recommendation, let me offer a couple of thoughts on which I invite your help, correction, and extension:

1. Theologian Gloria Schaab reminds us of the eschatological and transformative aspects of Eucharist, of the creation of a new people in and through the Eucharist who are charged with continuing the mission of Christ in the world—an eschatological picture of the church in every respect. As she notes,

> To be Eucharistic people is to be the presence of Christ, transformed by the whole of the Eucharistic event to take on the mind of Christ and to make the mission of Christ our own . . . The encounter with Christ in the Eucharist, far from being confined to the ecclesial or liturgical context, challenges those who partake of the Body of Christ in the context of the culture, the society, and the world in which the person of faith lives and moves and has being. In so doing the community of Christ's disciples carries forward the mission which Christ embodied in his own person, words, and actions.[20]

2. Given the long and tortured history of Christian theological debates on whether and how to understand the sacrificial nature of the Eucharist, it is odd that more attention has not been paid to the interactions and tensions between the sacrificial aspects of Christian Eucharist and the sacrificial aspects of war and nationalism. Both have generated an extensive literature, but relatively little that engages them simultaneously.

Amid the varied (and sometimes contentious) Christian reflections on Eucharist and sacrifice, the conviction that Christ's sacrifice brings peace remains undeniable. The extended reflection in Eph 2:12–22 is but one signal example; Matthew's account of the Last Supper, presenting Jesus's sacrifice as creating the New Covenant, is another.

A comparable sense fuels the Eucharistic theology of Alexander Schmemann and others, especially as the sacrifice of Christ brings good news to the world—in fact, it is love of enemies that is the "new" aspect of Jesus's proclamation, what he incarnates and recapitulates among his disciples.

> These words contain nothing less than an unheard-of demand for love toward someone whom we precisely *do not love*. That is why they do not cease to disturb us, to frighten us and, above

---

19. *Modern Theology* 30:2 (April 2014).
20. Schaab, "'As Christ, So We,'" 171.

all, to *judge* us, as long as we have not become thoroughly deaf to the gospel. Precisely because this commandment is unheard of and new, we for the most part substitute our own cunning human interpretations of it. Already for centuries, and apparently with a pure conscience, not only individual Christians but also whole churches have affirmed that in reality Christian love must be directed toward *one's own*—that to love essentially and self-evidently means to love neighbors and family, one's own people, one's own country—all those persons and things that we would usually love anyway, without Christ and the gospel . . . If coming to Christ signifies the fulfillment of his commandment, then, obviously, Christian love not only is not a simple increase, "crowning" and religious sanction of natural love, but is radically distinguished from it and even contraposed to it. It is really a *new* love, of which our fallen nature and fallen world are incapable and which is therefore impossible in it.[21]

The traditional understanding of Christ as the last sacrifice, completing and sealing the sacrificial system (whatever the contentious history of Christian reflections on the claim), has implications for how the Church should understand all other sacrificial systems and liturgical enactments. As the erstwhile mentioned Stanley Hauerwas suggests,

In the cross of Christ the Father has forever ended our attempts to sacrifice to God in terms set by the city of man. Christians have been incorporated into Christ's sacrifice for the world so that the world no longer needs to make sacrifices for tribe or state, or even humanity. Constituted by the body and blood of Christ, we may participate in God's kingdom so that the world may know that we, the church of Jesus Christ, are the end of sacrifice. If Christians leave the Eucharistic table ready to kill one another, we not only eat and drink judgment on ourselves, but we rob the world of the witness it needs in order to know that there is an alternative to the sacrifices of war.[22]

There is more to say, but suffice to say that we all need to walk through the door that Father Orobator has opened for us—to live more fully in the Eucharist as well as our common baptism, as we sort through the sometimes bewildering practices and stories that situate who and where we are along the Way.

---

21. Schmemann, *Eucharist*, 135–36.
22. Hauerwas, *War and the American Difference*, 68.

Bibliography

II Jornada Académica Iglesia-Revolución Mexicana: El Partido Católico Nacional, 1911–1914, Memorias. Guadalajara: Departamento de Estudios Históricos de la Arquidiócesis de Guadalajara, Universidad Autónoma de Guadalajara, 2012.
Abinales, Patricio N., and Donna N. Amoroso. State and Society in the Philippines. Lanham, MD: Rowman & Littlefield, 2005.
Adame Goddard, Jorge. "Significado de la coronación de la imagen de Nuestra Señora de Guadalupe en 1895." In La Iglesia católica en México, edited by Nelly Sigaut, 187–98. Zamora: El Colegio de Michoacán, 1997.
Agourides, Savas. "The Hope of the Orthodox Christian: Present and Future—a Simple Catechetical Lesson." Synaxi 52 (1994) 101–3 [in Greek].
———. "Religious Eschatology and State Ideology in the Tradition of Byzantium, of the Post-Byzantine Era and of the Modern Greek State." In Theology and Current Issues. Athens: Artos Zois, 1966.
AHAM, c. 46/exp. 37. Mora y del Río to the archbishops, Mexico City, n/d.
———. Ruiz y Flores to Mora y del Río, Morelia, 12 June 1912.
AHAM, c. 70/exp. 8. Circular, Mexico City, 3 January 1914.
AHAM, c. 79/exp. 21. Carta pastoral colectiva con ocasión del Monumento Nacional al Sagrado Corazón de Jesús en la "Montaña de Cristo Rey": Datos históricos del monumento actual y anteproyecto para la Basílica de Cristo Rey. Mexico City: Antigua Imprenta de Murguía, 1921.
AHAM, c. 90/exp. 26. Mora y del Río to El Heraldo de Cuba, Havana, 24 September 1914.
AHAM, c. 90/exp. 35. J. Ignacio Capetillo to Alberto Guillén, Mexico City, 8 January 1914.
AHAM, c. 91/exp. 30. Letters to various bishops, Mexico City, 1911.
AHAM, c. 91/exp. 62. Episcopal circular, Mexico City, 17 November 1913.
AHAM, c. 123/exp. 55. Letter from Victoriano Huerta to Mora y Río, Mexico City, 17 April 1913.
Allen, John L. "Benedict Sets about Reawakening Europe's Christian Roots." National Catholic Reporter, May 25, 2006. http://nationalcatholicreporter.org/word/pto52506.html.
———. "CELAM Update: 'Option for the Poor' Alive and Well in Latin America." National Catholic Reporter, May 21, 2007. http://ncronline.org/news/celam-update-option-poor-alive-and-well-latin-america.
———. The Future Church: How Ten Trends Are Revolutionizing the Catholic Church. New York: Doubleday, 2007.

"Anaphora [Eucharistic Prayer] of Saint Basil the Great." In *The Divine Liturgy: An Anthology for Worship*. Edited by Peter Galadza et al. Ottawa: Metropolitan Andrey Sheptytsky Institute of Eastern Christian Studies, 2004.

Anceschi, Luca, et al. *Conflict, Religion, and Culture: Domestic and International Implications for Southeast Asia and Australia*. Quezon City: Philippines-Australia Studies Network, Ateneo de Manila University Press, 2009.

Anderson, Benedict. *Imagined Communities: Reflections on the Origin and Spread of Nationalism*. Rev. ed. London: Verso, 1991.

Anderson, Braden P. *Chosen Nation: Scripture, Theopolitics, and the Project of National Identity*. Eugene, OR: Cascade, 2012.

Andjelović, Petar. *Vjerni Bogu, vjerni Bosni* [Faithful to God, Faithful to Bosnia]. Sarajevo: Rabic, 2000.

Andrade, Paulo Fernando Carneiro de. "As Religiões no Brasil e o Censo de 2010." *Debates do NER* 2:24 (2013) 93–98.

"Anti-celibacy Sect Wooing Kenyan Catholic Priests, Ex-seminarians." *Free Republic*, November 21, 2006. http://www.freerepublic.com/focus/f-religion/1742066/posts.

"Apostolic Constitutions," Book 8. In *The Ante-Nicene Fathers: Translations of the Writings of the Fathers Down to A.D. 325*, translated and edited by Alexander Roberts and James Donaldson, 7:485. Grand Rapids: Eerdmans, 1950.

Aquinas, Thomas. *On Law, Morality, and Politics*. Edited by William P. Baumgarth and Richard J. Regan. Indianapolis: Hackett, 1988.

———. *Summa Theologiae*. Lander, WY: Aquinas Institute for the Study of Sacred Doctrine, 2012.

Arenal Fenocchio, Jaime del. "Una devoción mariana francesa en México: Nuestra Señora del Sagrado Corazón." *Relaciones* 76 (1998) 161–94.

Arenas Guzmán, Diego. *El régimen del general Huerta en proyección histórica*. Mexico City: INEHRM, 1970.

Aristides. "Apology." Translated by D. M. McKay. In *Ante-Nicene Fathers: Translations of the Writings of the Fathers Down to A.D. 325: Original Supplement to the American Edition*, edited by Cleveland A. Coxe et al., 9:276. Grand Rapids: Eerdmans, 1979.

Armstrong, John A. *Ukrainian Nationalism*. 2nd ed. Littleton, CO: Ukrainian Academic Press, 1980.

Asad, Talal. *Formations of the Secular: Christianity, Islam, Modernity*. Stanford: Stanford University Press, 2003.

Aspe Armella, María Luisa. *La formación social y política de los católicos mexicano: La Acción Católica Mexicana y la Unión Nacional de Estudiantes Católicos, 1929–1958*. Mexico City: Universidad Iberoamericana, 2008.

Associated Press. "Poverty in Latin America Lowest in 3 Decades, UN Says." *Fox News Latino*, November 28, 2012. http://latino.foxnews.com/latino/lifestyle/2012/11/28/poverty-in-latin-america-lowest-in-3-decades-un-says/.

Athanasius. *On the Incarnation*. In *Patrologiae graecae* 25:192B, edited by J.-P. Migne. Stone Mountain, GA: Religion and Technology Center, 2003.

Augustine. *City of God*. Translated by Henry Bettenson. Harmondsworth: Penguin, 1972.

Avila, Oscar. "Obama's Census-Form Choice: 'Black.'" *Los Angeles Times*, April 4, 2010. http://articles.latimes.com/2010/apr/04/nation/la-na-obama-census4-2010apr04.

Azevedo, Marcelo C. de. *Dinâmicas atuais da cultura brasileira*. Estudos da CNBB 58. São Paulo: Paulinas, 1990.
Babić, Mile. "Kristološko utemeljenje tolerancije." *Forum Bosnae* 9-10 (2000) 287-320.
Banac, Ivo. *Cijena Bosne: članci, izjave i javni nastupi 1992-1995*. Sarajevo: Europa danas, 1996.
Barker, Philip W. *Religious Nationalism in Modern Europe: If God Be for Us*. New York: Routledge, 2009.
Barnard, Frederick M. *Herder on Nationality, Humanity, and History*. Montreal: McGill-Queen's University Press, 2003.
Barnes, Jane, and Helen Whitney. "John Paul II and the Fall of Communism." *Frontline/PBS*. http://www.pbs.org/wgbh/pages/frontline/shows/pope/communism/.
Barquín y Ruiz, Andrés. *Bernardo Bergoënd, S.J.* Mexico City: Jus, 1968.
———. *Cristo, Rey de México*. Mexico City: Jus, 1967.
Barranco, Bernardo. "Posiciones políticas en la historia de la Acción Católica Mexicana." In *El pensamiento social de los católicos mexicanos*, edited by Roberto Blancarte, 39-70. Mexico City: Fondo de Cultura Económica, 1996.
Barrington, Lowell W. "'Nation' and 'Nationalism': The Misuse of Key Concepts in Political Science." *PS: Political Science and Politics* 30 (1997) 712-16.
———. "Nationalism & Independence." In *After Independence: Making and Protecting the Nation in Postcolonial and Postcommunist States*, edited by Lowell W. Barrington, 3-30. Ann Arbor: University of Michigan Press, 2006.
Barry, Coeli M. "The Limits of Conservative Church Reformism in the Philippine Catholic Church." In *Religious Organizations and Democratization: Case Studies from Contemporary Asia*, edited by Tun-Jen Cheng and Deborah A. Brown, 157-79. Armonk, NY: M. E. Sharpe, 1991.
———. "Polyglot Catholicism: Genealogies and Reinterpretations of the Philippine Catholic Church." *Pilipinas* 32 (1999) 59-81.
Barth, Karl. *God in Action*. Translated by E. G. Homrighausen and Karl J. Ernst. 1936. Reprint, Eugene, OR: Wipf and Stock, 2005.
———. *The Humanity of God*. Richmond: John Knox, 1963.
Basil. "Epistle 161." PG 32, 629 B. In *A Select Library of the Nicene and Post-Nicene Fathers of the Christian Church: Second Series*, edited by Philip Schaff and Henry Wace, 8:214. Grand Rapids: Eerdmans, 1952.
Baum, Gregory. *Nationalism, Religion, and Ethics*. Montreal: McGill-Queen's University Press, 2001.
Bautista García, Cecilia Adriana. "Dos momentos en la historia de un culto: el origen y la coronación pontificia de la Virgen de Jacona (siglos XVII y XIX)." *Tzintzún* 43 (2006) 11-43.
Bavarian People's Party [Bayerische Volkspartei]. *Mitteilungen für die Vertrauensleute der Bayerischen Volkspartei* 7 (1933) 11:198.
———. Supplement to *Mitteilungen für die Vertrauensleute der Bayerischen Volkspartei*, 13th Annual National Conference [die 13. Ordentliche Landesversammlung der Bayerischen Volkspartei], Munich, November 15-16, 1930.
BBC News."Far Right Riles Austrian Church." May 22, 2009. http://news.bbc.co.uk/2/hi/europe/8063554.stm.
Becker, Winfried. "Die nationalsozialistische Machtergreifung in Bayern: Ein Dokumentarbericht Heinrich Helds aus dem Jahr 1933." *Historisches Jahrbuch* 112 (2012) 412-35.

Bediako, Kwame. *Theology and Identity: The Impact of Culture upon Christian Thought in the Second Century and in Modern Africa*. Oxford: Regnum, 1999.
Beiner, Ronald. *Civil Religion: A Dialogue in the History of Political Philosophy*. Cambridge: Cambridge University Press, 2011.
Bell, Edward. *The Political Shame of Mexico*. New York: McBride, Nast, 1914.
Bell, Seraphim. "Open Letter to His Eminence Archbishop Demetrios." January 5, 2004. http://www.orthodoxytoday.org/articles4/BellOpenLetter.php.
Bellah, Robert N. "Civil Religion in America." In *American Civil Religion*, edited by Donald E. Jones and Russell E. Richey, 21–44. San Francisco: Mellen Research University Press, 1990.
Bendyk, Myron. "Церкви Свято-Володимирового Хрещення" [Churches of St. Vladimir's Baptism]. April 12, 2011. http://ucu.edu.ua/eng/news/1418/.
Benedict XVI, Pope. "Address at the Inaugural Session of the Fifth General Conference of the Bishops of Latin America and the Caribbean." Address given at the Shrine of Aparecida, Brazil, May 13, 2007. http://www.vatican.va/holy_father/benedict_xvi/speeches/2007/may/documents/hf_ben-xvi_spe_20070513_conference-aparecida_en.html.
———. "Address at the Meeting with Catholics Engaged in the Life of the Church and Society." Address given at Freiburg im Breisgau, September 25, 2011. http://www.vatican.va/holy_father/benedict_xvi/speeches/2011/september/documents/hf_ben-xvi_spe_20110925_catholics-freiburg_en.html.
———. "Address at the Meeting with the Catholic Lay Faithful." Address given at Freiburg im Breisgau, September 24, 2011. http://www.vatican.va/holy_father/benedict_xvi/speeches/2011/september/documents/hf_ben-xvi_spe_20110924_zdk-freiburg_en.html.
———. "Homily at Eucharistic Celebration for the Opening of the Second Special Assembly for Africa of the Synod of Bishops." Homily delivered at Vatican Basilica, Vatican City, October 2009. http://www.vatican.va/news_services/press/sinodo/documents/bollettino_23_ii_speciale-africa-2009/02_inglese/b03_02.html#HOMILY_BY_THE_HOLY_FATHERk.
Benhabib, Seyla. *The Claims of Culture: Equality and Diversity in the Global Era*. Princeton: Princeton University Press, 2002.
Bennett, Georgette F. Letter to Rev. Ivo Marković, 18 April 1998.
Bergoglio, Jorge Mario, and Abraham Skorka. *On Heaven and Earth: Pope Francis on Faith, Family, and the Church in the Twenty-First Century*. Translated by Alejandro Bermudez and Howard Goodman. New York: Image, 2013.
Berkhoff, Karel C. *Harvest of Despair: Life and Death in Ukraine under Nazi Rule*. Cambridge, MA: Harvard University Press, 2004.
Berlatsky, Noah. "Bend Your Knee." *The Hooded Utilitarian: A Pundit in Every Panopticon* (blog). April 18, 2012. http://www.hoodedutilitarian.com/2012/04/bend-your-knee/.
Bibby, Reginald. *Beyond the Gods and Back: Religion's Demise and Rise and Why It Matters*. Lethbridge, AB: Project Canada, 2011.
Bjork, James. "Nations in the Parish: Catholicism and Nationalist Conflict in the Silesian Borderland, 1890–1922." In *Religion und Nation, Nation und Religion: Beiträge zu einer unbewältigten Geschichte*, edited by Michael Geyer and Hartmut Lehmann, 207–24. Göttingen: Wallstein, 2004.

Boff, Clodovis. "A originalidade histórica de Medellín." http://www.servicioskoinonia.org/relat/203p.htm.
Boff, Clodovis, and Jorge Pixley. *Opção pelos pobres*. Petrópolis: Vozes: 1987.
Boff, Leonardo, and Clodovis Boff. "A Concise History of Liberation Theology." In *Introducing Liberation Theology*. Maryknoll, NY: Orbis, 1987. http://www.landreform.org/boff2.htm.
Bokenkotter, Thomas S. *Church and Revolution: Catholics in the Struggle for Democracy and Social Justice*. New York: Image, 1998.
"The Borders of Baptism: Multiple Belongings and Transnational Processes of Catholic Formation." World Catholicism Week 2013 Web site. Center for World Catholicism and Intercultural Theology, DePaul University. No pages. Online: http://worldcath2013.depaul.edu/spirit/index.aspx.
Bouyer, Louis. *The Church of God: Body of Christ and Temple of the Spirit*. Translated by Charles Underhill Quinn. Chicago: Franciscan Herald, 1982.
Brading, David. *Mexican Phoenix: Our Lady of Guadalupe; Image and Tradition across Five Centuries*. Cambridge: Cambridge University Press, 2001.
Bradshaw, Paul F. *Eucharistic Origins*. Oxford: Oxford University Press, 2004.
Brass, Paul R. *Ethnicity and Nationalism: Theory and Comparison*. New Dehli: Sage, 1991.
Bremmer, Jan N. "Secularization: Notes Toward a Genealogy." In *Religion: Beyond a Concept*, edited by Hent de Vries, 432–37. New York: Fordham University Press, 2008.
Brighenti, Agenor. "A opção pelos pobres e a urgencia da missao: 40 anos de Medellín." http://www.missiologia.org.br/cms/ckfinder/userfiles/files/AgenorA2CMN.pdf.
Buciora, Jaroslaw. "Ecclesiology and National Identity in Orthodox Christianity." In *Orthodox Christianity and Contemporary Europe: Selected Papers of the International Conference Held at the University of Leeds, England, in June 2001*, edited by Jonathon Sutton, 29–38. Dudley, MA: Peeters, 2003.
Buconyori, Elie, ed. *Tribalism and Ethnicity*. Nairobi: AEA Theological and Christian Education Commission, 1977.
Budde, Michael L. *The Borders of Baptism: Identities, Allegiances, and the Church*. Eugene, OR: Cascade, 2011.
———. "Pledging Allegiance: Reflections on Discipleship and the Church after Rwanda." In *The Church as Counterculture*, edited by Michael L. Budde and R. W. Brimlow, 213–26. Albany: State University of New York Press, 2000.
———. "Political Theology and the Church." Paper presented at Ateneo de Manila University, Philippines, February 24, 2005.
Budde, Michael L., and Robert Brimlow. *Christianity Incorporated: How Big Business Is Buying the Church*. Grand Rapids: Brazos, 2002.
Buell, Denise Kimber. *Why This New Race? Ethnic Reasoning in Early Christianity*. New York: Columbia University Press, 2005.
Burdziej, Stanisław. "Voice of the Disinherited? Religious Media after the 2005 Presidential and Parliamentary Elections." *East European Quarterly* 42 (2008) 207–20.
Butler, Matthew. "La coronación del Sagrado Corazón de Jesús en la Arquidiócesis de México, 1914." In *Revolución, cultura, y religión: nuevas perspectivas en el siglo XX*, edited by Yolanda Padilla Rangel et al., 24–68. Aguascalientes: Universidad Autónoma de Aguascalientes, 2012.

———. "Transplanting the Eucharistic Seed: The Adoración Nocturna Mexicana in the 1920s." In *Local Church, Global Church: Catholic Activism in Latin America from Rerum Novarum to Vatican II*, edited by Stephen J. C. Andes and Julia G. Young, 53–90. Washington, DC: Catholica University of America Press, 2016.

———. "Trouble Afoot? Pilgrimage in Cristero Mexico City." In *Faith and Impiety in Revolutionary Mexico*, edited by Matthew Butler, 149–66. New York: Palgrave Macmillan, 2007.

Cacciottolo, Mario. "Papal Visit: Have Immigrants Saved the Catholic Church?" *BBC News*, September 12, 2010. http://www.bbc.co.uk/news/uk-11067661.

Campbell, David. *Writing Security: United States Foreign Policy and the Politics of Identity*. Minneapolis: University of Minnesota Press, 1998.

Canas Bottos, Lorenzo. "Transformations of Old Colony Mennonites: The Making of a Trans-Statal Community." *Global Networks* 8 (2008) 214–31.

Cantwell Smith, Wilfred. *The Meaning and End of Religion*. New York: Macmillan, 1962.

Carney, Jay. "Beyond Tribalism: The Hutu-Tutsi Question and Catholic Rhetoric in Colonial Rwanda." *Journal of Religion in Africa* 42 (2012) 172–202.

———. "Waters of Baptism, Blood of Tribalism?" *African Ecclesial Review* 50 (2008) 9–30.

Carrión, J. R. "La renovación solemne de la consagración de México al Divino Corazón de Jesús." In *El Mensajero del Corazón de Jesús. Órgano del Apostolado de la Oración y de la Guardia de Honor del Sagrado Corazón de Jesús en la República Mexicana*, Year XLI, Vol. LXIV (January 1914) 12–18.

Casanova, José. *Public Religions in the Modern World*. Chicago: University of Chicago Press, 1994.

Casaroli, Agostino. *The Martyrdom of Patience: The Holy See and the Communist Countries (1963–89)*. Translated by Marco Bagnarol. Toronto: Ave Maria Centre of Peace, 2007.

Castells, Manuel. *The Information Age: Economy, Society, and Culture*. Vol. 1, *The Rise of the Network Society*. Oxford: Blackwell, 2000.

Castro, Antonio Francisco B. de. "Jesuit Linguistic Battles ca. 1898–1932: Language, Power, and the Filipino Soul." *Philippine Studies* 58:1–2 (2010) 111–46.

Catechism of the Catholic Church. Mahwah, NJ: Paulist, 1994.

Catholic Bishops' Conference of the Philippines. "Choosing Life, Rejecting the RH Bill (A Pastoral Letter of the Catholic Bishops' Conference of the Philippines)." January 30, 2011. http://cbcponline.net/v2/?p=1151.

Catholic Church. *Annuarium Statisticum Ecclesiae* [Statistical Yearbook of the Church]. 1973.

———. *Annuarium Statisticum Ecclesiae* [Statistical Yearbook of the Church]. 2010.

———. *Code of Canon Law, Latin-English Edition*. Washington, DC: Canon Law Society of America, 1983.

Catholic Church, Congregation for the Doctrine of the Faith. "Instruction on Certain Aspects of the 'Theology of Liberation.'" *Acta Apostolicae Sedis* 76 (1984) 867–77. http://www.vatican.va/roman_curia/congregations/cfaith/documents/rc_con_cfaith_doc_19840806_theology-liberation_en.html.

Catholic News Agency. "Anti-celibacy sect attracts Catholic priests, ex-seminarians in Kenya." November 21, 2006. http://www.catholicnewsagency.com/news/anticelibacy_sect_attracts_catholic_priests_exseminarians_in_kenya/.

Cavanaugh, William T. *Being Consumed: Economics and Human Desire*. Grand Rapids: Eerdmans, 2008.
———. "If You Render Unto God What Is God's, What Is Left for Caesar?" *The Review of Politics* 71 (2009) 607–19.
———. *Migrations of the Holy: God, State, and the Political Meaning of the Church*. Grand Rapids: Eerdmans, 2011.
———. *The Myth of Religious Violence*. Oxford: Oxford University Press, 2009.
———. *Theopolitical Imagination: Discovering the Liturgy as a Political Act in an Age of Global Consumerism*. London: T. & T. Clark, 2002.
———. "The World Reconciled: Eucharist and Politics." Paper presented at World Catholicism Week 2012, DePaul University, Chicago, Illinois, April 16, 2012.
Ceballos Ramírez, Manuel. "Siglo XIX y guadalupanismo: de la polémica de la coronación y de la devoción a la política." In *Historia de la Iglesia en el siglo XIX*, edited by Manuel Ramos Medina, 317–32. Mexico City: Condumex, 1998.
"Centro de Estudiantes Católicos Mejicanos: Invitación." *El País*, January 9, 1914.
Chowning, Margaret. "The Catholic Church and the Ladies of the Vela Perpetua: Gender and Devotional Change in Nineteenth-Century Mexico." *Past & Present* 221 (2013) 197–237.
Christian Academic Circle. "Manifesto." *Nova prisutnost: časopis za intelektualna i duhovna pitanja* 7:2 (2009) 181–90.
Christian, William. *Visionaries: The Second Republic and the Reign of Christ*. Berkeley: University of California, 1996.
Chrysostom, John. *On Wealth and Poverty*. Translated by Catharine P. Ross. Crestwood, NY: St. Valdimir's Seminary Press, 1999.
Ćimić, Esad. "Bosanska raskrižja." In *Teorijski izazovi i dileme: Prilog sociologiji hrvatskog društva*. Zadar: Sveučilište u Splitu, 1996.
Cochrane, Arthur. *The Church's Confession under Hitler*. Philadelphia: Westminster, 1962.
Cohen, Lenard. "Bosnia's 'Tribal Gods': The Role of Religion in Nationalist Politics." In *Religion and the War in Bosnia*, edited by Paul Mojzes, 43–74. Atlanta: Scholars, 1998.
"Con gran solemnidad se consagró la C. de Puebla al S. Corazón de Jesús." *El País*, January 9, 1914.
Connolly, William. *Why I Am Not a Secularist*. Minneapolis: University of Minnesota Press, 1999.
Conquest, Robert. *The Harvest of Sorrow: Soviet Collectivization and the Terror Famine*. Oxford: Oxford University Press, 1986.
Cornille, Catherine, ed. *Many Mansions? Multiple Religious Belonging and Christian Identity*. Maryknoll, NY: Orbis, 2002.
Correa, Eduardo. *El Partido Católico Nacional y sus directores: explicación de su fracaso y deslinde de responsabilidades*. Mexico City: Fondo de Cultura Económica, 1991.
Correa Etchegaray, Leonor. "El rescate de una devoción jesuítica: el Sagrado Corazón de Jesús en la primera mitad del siglo XIX." In *Historia de la Iglesia*, edited by Manuel Ramos Medina, 369–80. Mexico City: Condumex, 1998.
Cullmann, Oscar. *Christ and Time: The Primitive Christian Conception of Time and History*. Translated by Floyd V. Filson. Revised ed. London: SCM, 1962.
Dann, Otto. *Nation und Nationalismus in Deutschland, 1770–1990*. 3rd ed. Beck'sche Reihe. Munich: C. H. Beck, 1996.

Davies, W. D. *The Gospel and the Land*. Berkeley: University of California Press, 1974.
De Bekker, Leander Jan. *The Plot against Mexico*. New York: Knopf, 1919.
De como vino Huerta y cómo se fue . . . apuntes para la historia de un regimen militar. Vol. 1, *Del cuartelazo a la disolución de las cámaras*. 1914. Reprint, Mexico City: El Caballito, 1975.
Delgado, Ricardo. *Aspecto agrario del gobierno del general Victoriano Huerta*. Guadalajara, 1951.
Denzinger, Heinrich. *Enchiridion symbolorum: definitionum et declarationum de rebus fidei et morum*. Barcelona: Herder, 1963.
"The Divine Liturgy of the Holy Apostle and Evangelist Mark, Disciple of the Holy Peter." In *The Ante-Nicene Fathers: Translations of the Writings of the Fathers Down to A.D. 325*, translated and edited by Alexander Roberts and James Donaldson, 7:555. Grand Rapids: Eerdmans, 1950.
Doerry, Martin, et al. "Theologian Hans Küng on Pope Benedict: Part 1—'A Putinization of the Catholic Church.'" *Spiegel Online International*, September 21, 2011. http://www.spiegel.de/international/world/theologian-hans-kueng-on-pope-benedict-a-putinization-of-the-catholic-church-a-787325.html.
Duling, Dennis C. "Recruitment to the Jesus Movement in Social-Science Perspective." In *Social Scientific Models for Interpreting the Bible: Essays by the Context Group in Honor of Bruce J. Malina*, edited by John J. Pilch, 132–75. Leiden: Brill, 2000.
Dunn, Robert G. *Identity Crises: A Social Critique of Postmodernity*. Minneapolis: University of Minnesota Press, 1998.
Durkheim, Émile. *The Elementary Forms of Religious Life*. Translated by Carol Cosman. Oxford: Oxford University Press, 2001.
Dymyd, Michael. Херсонеське таїнство свободи [The Chersonesus Mystery of Freedom], *Ecclesiology* [Еклезіологія], Vol. 1. Lviv: Svichado [Свічадо], 2007.
Eberts, Mirella W. "The Roman Catholic Church and Democracy in Poland." *Europe-Asia Studies* 50:5 (1998) 817–42.
The Economist. "The New Pope and the Ukrainian Greek Catholic Church." April 12, 2013. http://www.economist.com/blogs/easternapproaches/2013/04/ukraines-greek-catholic-church.
"Edicto Diocesano sobre la Solemne Consagración de la República al Sacratísimo Corazón de Jesucristo." *Gaceta Oficial del Arzobispado de México* 12:12 (December 15, 1913) 303–56.
Edwards, Lisa M. *Roman Virtues: The Education of Latin American Clergy in Rome, 1858–1962*. New York: Peter Lang, 2011.
Egbulem, Nwaka Chris. "African Spirituality." In *The New Dictionary of Catholic Spirituality*, edited by Michael Downey, 17–21. Bangalore: Theological Publications in India, 1995.
Eggersdorfer, Franz X. *Die Krise des staatlichen Lebens in Deutschland und die Ideenwelt der Bayerischen Volkspartei*. Flugschriften der Bayerischen Volkspartei, No. 1. Munich: Generalsekretariat der Bayerischen Volkspartei, 1929.
Ehrman, Bart D., ed. and trans. *The Apostolic Fathers*. 2 vols. Cambridge: Harvard University Press, 2003.
———. *Lost Christianities: The Battles for Scripture and the Faiths We Never Knew*. New ed. New York: Oxford University Press, 2005.
Elizondo, Virgilio P. *The Future Is Mestizo: Life Where Cultures Meet*. Rev. ed. Boulder: University Press of Colorado, 2000.

Elzo, Javier. *Los cristianos: ¿En la Sacristía o Tras la Pancarta? Reflexiones de un Sociólogo*. Madrid: PPC, 2013.
"En honor a Cristo Rey se verificará hoy una solemne manifestación en la capital." *El País*, January 11, 1914.
Espin del Prado, Orlando. "Evangelización y religiones negras: Propuesta de modelo de evangelizatión para la pastoral em la Republica Dominicana." PhD diss., Pontifícia Universidade Católica de Rio de Janeiro, 1984.
Espinosa, David. "'Restoring Christian Social Order': The Mexican Catholic Youth Association (1913–1932)." *The Americas* 59 (2003) 451–74.
Esquivel Obregón, Toribio. *Mi labor en servicio de México*. Mexico City: Botas, 1934.
"Ethnicity and Nationalism: A Challenge to the Churches." *The Ecumenical Review* 47 (1995) 225–31.
Fabella, Virginia, and R. S. Sugirtharajah, eds. *Dictionary of Third World Theologies*. Maryknoll, NY: Orbis, 2000.
Failinger, Marie A. "Wondering after Babel: Power, Freedom, and Ideology in U.S. Supreme Court Interpretations of the Religion Clauses." In *Law and Religion*, edited by Rex J. Ahdar, 81–109. Aldershot: Ashgate, 2000.
Fashole, Luke. "What Is African Christian Theology?" *African Ecclesial Review* 16 (1974) 383–88.
Faulhaber, Michael Kardinal. *Deutsches Ehrgefühl und katholisches Gewissen. Zur religiösen Lage der Gegenwart* 1. Munich: Dr. Franz A. Pfeiffer & Co., Nomos Verlagsges. mbH, 1925.
Faulk, Edward. *101 Questions and Answers on Eastern Catholic Churches*. New York: Paulist, 2007.
Ferry, Luc. *La révolution de l'amour: Pour una Spiritualité Laïque*. Paris: Editions 82, 2012.
Fichte, Johann Gottlieb. *Reden an die deutsche Nation*. Leipzig: Inselverlag, 1909.
Fisichella, Rino. *The New Evangelization: Responding to the Challenge of Indifference*. Leominster, UK: Gracewing, 2012.
Fitzgerald, Timothy. *Discourse on Civility and Barbarity: A Critical History of Religion and Related Categories*. New York: Oxford University Press, 2007.
Florovsky, Georges. "Antinomies of Christian History: Empire and Desert." In *Christianity and Culture*. Collected Works of Georges Florovsky 2. Belmont, MA: Nordland, 1974.
———. "Christianity and Civilization." In *Christianity and Culture*. Collected Works of Georges Florovsky 2. Belmont, MA: Nordland, 1974.
———. "The Church: Her Nature and Task." In *Bible, Church, Tradition: An Eastern Orthodox View*. Collected Works of Georges Florovsky 1. Belmont, MA: Nordland, 1972.
———. "Le Corps du Christ vivant. Une interprétation orthodoxe de l'Eglise." In *La Sainte Eglise Universelle*, edited by Georges Florovsky et al. Neuchâtel-Paris: Delachaux & Nestlé, 1948.
———. "On the Veneration of Saints." In *Creation and Redemption*. Collected Works of Georges Florovsky 3. Belmont, MA: Nordland, 1976.
———. "Revelation and Interpretation." In *Bible, Church, Tradition*, 17–36. Collected Works of Georges Florovsky 1. Belmont, MA: Notable & Academic Books, 1987.
———. "The Social Problem in the Eastern Orthodox Church." In *Christianity and Culture*. Collected Works of Georges Florovsky 2. Belmont, MA: Nordland, 1974.

Föllmer, Moritz. "The Problem of National Solidarity in Interwar Germany." *German History* 23 (2005) 202–31.
France, David. *Our Fathers: The Secret Life of the Catholic Church in an Age of Scandal.* New York: Broadway, 2004.
Francisco, Jose Mario C. "Christianity as Church and Story and the Birth of the Filipino Nation in the Nineteenth Century." In *World Christianities, c. 1815–1914*, edited by Sheridan Gilley and Brian Stanley, 528–41. Cambridge History of Christianity 8. Cambridge: Cambridge University Press, 2006.
———. "Fidelity in Translating Religious Practice: Illustrations from Filipino Christianity." *Kritika Kultura* 21–22 (2013–14). http://kritikakultura.ateneo.net/issue/no-2122/special-section-on-translation/fidelity-in-translating-religious-practice-illustrations-from-filipino-christianity.
———. "Interphasing Language with Religion and Nation: Illustrations from the Philippines." In *Language, Literature and Cultures in ASEAN: Unity in Diversity; Proceedings of the International Conference on the 40th Anniversary of ASEAN*, 230–46. Bangkok: Chulalongkorn University, 2011.
Fredriksen, Kaja Bonesmo. "Income Inequality in the European Union." OECD Economics Department Working Papers 952. April 16, 2012. http://dx.doi.org/10.1787/5k9bdt47q5zt-en.
Freyre, Gilberto, and Tomás Santa Rosa Júnior. *Casa-grande e senzala: formação da família brasileira sob o regime de economia patriarca.* Rio de Janeiro: Livraria José Olympio Editora, 1954.
Frisotti, Heitor. *Passos no diálogo: Igreja católica e religiões afro-brasileiras* [Steps Taken in Dialogue: The Catholic Church and the Afro-Brazilian Religions]. São Paulo: Paulus, 1996.
Fuss, Michael. "The Emerging Euroyâna." *The Way* 41 (2001) 136–47.
Galadza, Peter. "Eastern Catholic Christianity." In *The Blackwell Companion to Eastern Christianity*, edited by Kenneth Parry, 291–318. Oxford: Blackwell, 2007.
———. "The Reception of the Second Vatican Council by Greco-Catholics in Ukraine." *Communio: International Catholic Review* 27 (2000) 312–39.
———. "A Response to Sophia Senyk on Nationalism and Proselytism in Ukraine: An Outsider's *Inside* View." *Het Christelijk Oosten—Tijdschrift van het Institut voor Oosters Christendom te Nijmegen* 53 (2001) 125–42.
———. "Rome's Congregation for the Doctrine of the Faith and Ukrainian Ecumenism: A Plea for Clarity." *Logos: A Journal of Eastern Christian Studies* 51 (2010) 1–4.
———. "The Structure of the Eastern Churches: Bonded with Human Blood or Baptismal Water?" *Pro Ecclesia* 17 (2008) 373–86.
———. *The Theology and Liturgical Work of Andrei Sheptytsky (1865–1944)*. Orientalia Christiana Analecta 272. Rome: Pontificio Istituto Orientale, 2004.
Galeano, Eduardo. *El libro de los abrazos.* Madrid: Siglo XXI Editores, 2010.
Gamboa, Federico. *Mi diario: mucho de mi vida y algo de la de otros.* Vol. 6, *1912–1919.* Mexico City: Conaculta, 1995.
García Naranjo, Nemesio. *Memorias de Nemesio García Naranjo.* Vol. 7, *Mis andanzas con el general Huerta.* Monterrey: Talleres de "El Porvenir," n.d.
Garton Ash, Timothy. *The Polish Revolution: Solidarity.* New York: Scribner, 1984.
Gaudium et Spes, "The Pastoral Constitution on the Church in the Modern World." In *Documents of Vatican II*, edited by Austin P. Flannery. New rev. ed. Grand Rapids: Eerdmans, 1984.

German Bishops' Conference [Deutsche Bischofskonferenz]. "Nettoaufkommen an Kirchenlohn- und -einkommensteuer." http://www.dbk.de/fileadmin/redaktion/Zahlen%20und%20Fakten/Kirchensteuer/Kirchensteuer%20im%20gesamten%20Bundesgebiet/Diagramm-Kirchensteuer_1991-2012.pdf.

Geschäftsstelle des Lokalvereins. "Report on the 71st General Assembly of German Catholics in Essen" [Bericht über die 71. Generalversammlung der deutschen Katholiken in Essen]. August 31–September 5, 1932.

Gifford, Paul. *African Christianity: Its Public Role*. Bloomington: Indiana University Press, 1998.

Gorringe, Timothy. *Karl Barth: Against Hegemony*. Oxford: Oxford University Press, 1999.

Gourevitch, Philip. *We Wish to Inform You That Tomorrow We Will Be Killed with Our Families: Stories from Rwanda*. New York: Picador, 1998.

"Grandioso, imponente, y sublime fué el acto de la Consagración en la Catedral Angelopolitana." *La Nación*, January 8, 1914.

Grant, Michael. *The Roman Emperors: A Biographical Guide to the Rulers of Imperial Rome, 31 B.C.–476 A.D.* New York: Michael Grant, 1985.

Greek Orthodox Archdiocese of America. "Leadership 100 12th Annual Conference Honors Sarbanes, Tenet and Yanni—Reelects Anton Chairman." February 25, 2003. http://www.goarch.org/news/goa.news845.

Gregory of Nazianzus. *Against the Arians, and Concerning Himself (Oration 33)*. In vol. 7 of *A Select Library of the Nicene and Post-Nicene Fathers of the Christian Church: Second Series*, edited by Philip Schaff and Henry Wace, 332. Grand Rapids: Eerdmans, 1952.

———. *Epistle 101*. In Patrologiae graecae 37:181C–184A, edited by J.-P. Migne. Stone Mountain, GA: Religion and Technology Center, 2003. http://ezproxy.lib.ed.ac.uk/login?url=http:// phoenix.reltech.org/Ebind/docs/Migne/Migne.html.

———. *Oration 24*. In *Select Orations*. Translated by Martha Vinson. The Fathers of the Church 107. Washington, DC: Catholic University of America Press, 2003.

———. "Panegyric on His Brother St Caesarius (Oration 7)." In vol. 7 of *A Select Library of the Nicene and Post-Nicene Fathers of the Christian Church: Second Series*, edited by Philip Schaff and Henry Wace, 237. Grand Rapids: Eerdmans, 1952.

Gregory, Brad S. *The Unintended Reformation: How a Religious Revolution Secularized Society*. Cambridge: Harvard University Press, 2012.

Grosby, Steven. *Biblical Ideas of Nationality Ancient and Modern*. Winona Lake, IN: Eisenbrauns, 2002.

———. "The Category of the Primordial in the Study of Early Christianity and Second-Century Judaism." *History of Religions* 36 (1996) 140–63.

Gudziak, Borys. "'Besides Heaven, This Is the Only Place Where I Would Want to Be.' The Witness of the Greek Catholic Priest-Martyr of Majdanek, Blessed Omelian Kovch." http://risu.org.ua/en/index/expert_thought/analytic/48079/.

Gutiérrez, Gustavo. "Liberation Praxis and Christian Faith." In *Frontiers of Theology in Latin America*, translated by John Drury, edited by Rosino Gibellini, 1–33. Maryknoll, NY: Orbis, 1979.

———. *A Theology of Liberation: History, Politics, and Salvation*. Translated by Caridad Inda and John Eagleson. Maryknoll, NY: Orbis, 1973.

Halbertal, Moshe, and Avishai Margalit. *Idolatry*. Translated by Naomi Goldblum. Cambridge: Harvard University Press, 1998.

Hall, Stuart. "Negotiating Caribbean Identities." *New Left Review* 209 (1995) 3–14.
Harakas, Stanley. "Living the Orthodox Christian Faith in America." In *Martyria/ Mission: The Witness of the Orthodox Churches Today*, edited by Ion Bria, 153–58. Geneva: World Council of Churches, 1980.
Häring, Hermann, et al. "Creating Identity." *Concilium* 285 (2000) 173–328.
Harink, Douglas. *1 & 2 Peter*. Brazos Theological Commentary on the Bible. Grand Rapids: Brazos, 2009.
Hart, David Bentley. *Atheist Delusions: The Christian Revolution and Its Fashionable Enemies*. New Haven: Yale University Press, 2009.
Hauerwas, Stanley. *War and the American Difference: Theological Reflections on Violence and National Identity*. Grand Rapids: Baker Academic, 2011.
———. *Wilderness Wanderings: Probing Twentieth-Century Theology and Philosophy*. Boulder, CO: Westview, 1997.
———. *With the Grain of the Universe: The Church's Witness and Natural Theology*. Grand Rapids: Brazos, 2001.
Haupstaatsarchiv Bayern, Nachlaß Anton Pfeiffer, Vol. 325. In *Graue Eminenz der bayerischen Politik: Eine politische Biographie Anton Pfeiffers (1888–1957)*, edited by Christine Reuter. Neue Schriftenreihe des Stadtarchives München 17. Munich: UNI-Druck, 1987.
Hayes, Carlton J. H. *Essays on Nationalism*. New York: Macmillan, 1926.
Hebblethwaite, Peter. "From *Ostpolitik* to *Europapolitik*." *European Journal* 11 (1991) 59–72.
Hefner, Robert W. *Conversion to Christianity: Historical and Anthropological Perspectives on a Great Transformation*. Berkeley: University of California Press, 1993.
Heinz, Donald. "Clashing Symbols: The New Christian Right as Countermythology." *Archives de Sciences Sociales des Religions* 59 (1985) 153–73.
Herrero, Juan H. "Medjugorje: Ecclesiastical Conflict, Theological Controversy, Ethnic Division." In *Research in the Social Scientific Study of Religion*, vol. 10, edited by Joanne Marie Greer and David O. Moberg. Stamford, CT: JAI, 1999.
Herzog, William R. *Parables as Subversive Speech: Jesus as Pedagogue of the Oppressed*. Louisville: Westminster John Knox, 1994.
Hillman, Eugene. *Toward an African Christianity: Inculturation Applied*. New York: Paulist, 1993.
Hinson, E. Glenn, trans. and ed. *Understandings of the Church*. Philadelphia: Fortress, 1986.
Holanda, Sérgio Buarque de. *Roots of Brazil*. Translated by G. Harvey Summ. Notre Dame: University of Notre Dame Press, 2012.
Hosanna-Tabor Evangelical Lutheran Church and School v. EEOC, 565 U.S.___(January 11, 2012).
Huerta, Victoriano. *Memorias de Victoriano Huerta*. Mexico City: Ediciones "Vértice," 1957.
Hüffmeier, Wilhelm, ed. *Church, People, State, Nation: A Protestant Contribution on a Difficult Relationship; Report of the Discussions in the South and Southeast Europe Regional Group of the Leuenberg Church Fellowship*. Frankfurt am Main: Lembeck, 2002.
Hugelmann, Karl. "Das Abendland und der deutsche Nationalstaat." *Das Abendland: Deutsche Monatshefte für europäische Kultur, Politik und Wirtschaft* 1 (1925/26) 227–99.

Huntington, Samuel P. *The Clash of Civilizations and the Remaking of World Order*. New York: Simon & Schuster, 1996.
Hürten, Heinz. *Deutsche Katholiken 1918–1945*. Paderborn: Ferdinand Schöningh, 1992.
Hutchison, William R., and Hartmut Lehmann, eds. *Many Are Chosen: Divine Election and Western Nationalism*. Harvard Theological Studies 38. Minneapolis: Fortress, 1994.
Ignatieff, Michael. "Nationalism and the Narcissism of Minor Differences." In *Theorizing Nationalism*, edited by Ronald Beiner, 91–102. Albany: State University of New York Press, 1999.
Ignatius of Loyola. "Principle and Foundation." In *Spiritual Exercises of St. Ignatius Based on Studies in the Language of the Autograph*, edited and translated by Louis J. Puhl. Chicago: Loyola, 1952.
Ileto, Reynaldo C. *Filipinos and Their Revolution: Event, Discourse, and Historiography*. Quezon City: Ateneo de Manila University Press, 1998.
———. "Heroes, Historians, and the New Propaganda Movement, 1950–1953." *Philippine Studies* 58:1–2 (2010) 223–38.
———. *Pasyon and Revolution: Popular Movements in the Philippines, 1840–1910*. Quezon City: Ateneo de Manila University Press, 1979.
Instituto Nacional de Pastoral (Catholic Church—Conferência Nacional dos Bispos do Brasil), and Seminário "A Dinâmica da Cultura Brasileira Atual." In *Para onde vai a cultura brasileira?: desafios pastorais*. Col. Estudos da CNBB. São Paulo: Paulinas, 1990.
Irenaeus. *Five Books of S. Irenaeus, Bishop of Lyons, Against Heresies*. Translated by John Keble. Oxford: J. Parker, 1872.
Izuzquiza, Daniel. "Astérix y Obélix." *Vida Religiosa* 115 (2013) 52.
———. *Rincones de la ciudad: orar en el camino fe-justicia*. Madrid: Narcea, 2005.
Jakelić, Slavica. *Collectivistic Religions: Religion, Choice, and Identity*. Burlington, VT: Ashgate, 2010.
Jergović, Miljenko. "Mate Boban 1940–1997: Karadžić's 'Brother in Christ.'" *Bosnia Report* 19 (1997) 13–14.
John Paul II, Pope. *Ecclesia in Africa: Post-Synodal Apostolic Exhortation*. Nairobi: Paulines Africa, 1995. http://w2.vatican.va/content/john-paul-ii/en/apost_exhortations/documents/hf_jp-ii_exh_14091995_ecclesia-in-africa.html.
———. *Ut unum sint*. Vatican City: Libreria Editrice Vaticana, 1995. http://w2.vatican.va/content/john-paul-ii/en/encyclicals/documents/hf_jp-ii_enc_25051995_ut-unum-sint.html.
Jonas, Raymond. *France and the Cult of the Sacred Heart: An Epic Tale for Modern Times*. Berkeley: University of California Press, 2000.
———. *The Tragic Tale of Claire Ferchaud and the Great War*. Berkeley: University of California Press, 2005.
Juergensmeyer, Mark. *The New Cold War? Religious Nationalism Confronts the Secular State*. Berkeley: University of California Press, 1993.
Jukić, Jakov. *Lica i maske svetoga, Ogledi iz društvene religiologije*. Zagreb: Kršćanska sadašnjost, 1997.
Kahn, Paul. *Putting Liberalism in Its Place*. Princeton: Princeton University Press, 2005.
Kalaitzidis, Pantelis. "Church and Nation in Eschatological Perspective." In *Church and Eschatology*, edited by Pantelis Kalaitzidis, 339–73. Athens: Kastaniotis, 2003.

---. *Orthodox Christianity and Modernity: An Introduction*. Athens, Indiktos, 2007.

---. "Orthodoxy and Hellenism in Contemporary Greece." *St. Vladimir's Theological Quarterly* 54 (2010) 368–79.

---. *Orthodoxy and Modern Greek Identity: Ventures and Trajectories of a Controversial Relationship*. Athens: Indiktos, 2012 [in Greek].

---. "La relation de l'Église à la culture et la dialectique de l'eschatologie et de l'histoire." *Istina* 55 (2010) 7–25.

---. "The Temptation of Judas: Church and National Identities." *The Greek Orthodox Theological Review* 47 (2002) 357–79.

Kalaitzidis, Pantelis, and Nikolaos Asproulis. "Greek Religious Nationalism and the Challenges of Evangelization, Forgiveness, and Reconciliation." In *Just Peace: Orthodox Perspectives*, edited by Semegnish Asfaw et al., 201–21. Geneva: World Council of Churches, 2012.

Kantorowicz, Ernst. *The King's Two Bodies: A Study in Medieval Political Theology*. Princeton: Princeton University Press, 1957.

Karmiris, Ioannes. "Nationalism in the Orthodox Church." *Greek Orthodox Theological Review* 26 (1981) 171–84.

"Katholikentag in Frankfurt." *Kölnische Volkszeitung*, No. 636, September 7, 1921.

Katongole, Emmanuel. "A Blood Thicker than Tribalism: Eucharist and Identity in African Politics." Paper presented at World Catholicism Week 2012, DePaul University, Chicago, Illinois, April 16, 2012.

---. "Christianity, Tribalism and the Rwanda Genocide." In *A Future for Africa: Critical Essays in Christian Social Imagination*, 95–117. Scranton: University of Scranton Press, 2005.

---. "A Different World Right Here: The Church within African Theological Imagination." In *A Future for Africa: Critical Essays in Christian Social Imagination*, 153–84. Scranton: University of Scranton Press, 2005.

---. "Of Faces of Jesus and *The Poisonwood Bible*." In *A Future for Africa: Critical Essays in Christian Social Imagination*, 185–210. Scranton: University of Scranton Press, 2005.

---. "Identity, Community and the Gospel of Reconciliation: Christian Resources in the Face of Tribalism." Durham, NC: Duke Center for Reconciliation, 2009. https://divinity.duke.edu/sites/divinity.duke.edu/files/documents/cfr/identity-and-reconciliation.pdf.

---. *The Sacrifice of Africa: A Political Theology for Africa*. Grand Rapids: Eerdmans, 2011.

Katongole, Emmanuel, with Jonathan Wilson-Hartgrove. *Mirror to the Church: Resurrecting Faith after Genocide in Rwanda*. Grand Rapids: Zondervan, 2009.

Keleher, Serge. "Response to Sophia Senyk, 'The Ukrainian Greek Catholic Church Today: Universal Values versus Nationalist Doctrines.'" *Religion, State & Society* 31 (2003) 289–306.

Kelly, Anthony J. "Catholic Identity, Lost and Found." Aquinas Memorial Lecture given at the Australian Catholic University, Brisbane, Queensland, Australia, November 23, 2009. https://library.acu.edu.au/find/other_collections_and_catalogues/special_collections/?a=220311.

Kembo-Sure, Edward. *Literacy, Language, and Liberty: The Cultural Politics of English as Official Language in Africa*. Moi University Inaugural Lecture 19:2. Eldoret, Kenya: Moi University Press, 2013.

Kennedy, John F. "Address of Senator John F. Kennedy to the Greater Houston Ministerial Association." Address given at Rice Hotel in Houston, Texas, September 12, 1960. http://www.jfklibrary.org/Asset-Viewer/ALL6YEBJMEKYGMCntnSCvg.aspx.

Kessler, Christi, and Jürgen Rüland. *Give Jesus a Hand! Charismatic Christians: Populist Religion in the Philippines*. Quezon City: Ateneo de Manila University Press, 2008.

Keyes, Charles F. "Why the Thai Are Not Christians: Buddhist and Christian Conversion in Thailand." In *Conversion to Christianity: Historical and Anthropological Perspectives on a Great Transformation*, edited by Robert W. Hefner, 259-83. Berkeley: University of California Press, 1993.

Klaiber, Jeffrey L. *Religion and Revolution in Peru, 1824-1976*. Notre Dame: University of Notre Dame Press, 1977.

Klein, Gotthard. *Der Volksverein für das katholische Deutschland, 1890-1933: Geschichte, Bedeutung, Untergang*. Veröffentlichungen der Kommission für Zeitgeschichte. Reihe B, Band 75. Paderborn: Ferdinand Schöningh, 1996.

Knight, Alan. "The Mentality and *Modus Operandus* of Revolutionary Anticlericalism." In *Faith and Impiety in Revolutionary Mexico*, edited by Matthew Butler, 21-56. New York: Palgrave Macmillan, 2007.

———. *The Mexican Revolution*. 2 vols. Lincoln: University of Nebraska Press, 1991.

Kovalenko, Lesia. *Соціяльно зорієнтовані документи УГКЦ (1989-2008)* [Documents of the UGCC Related to Social Questions: 1989-2008]. Lviv: Institute of Religion and Society [Інститут релігії та суспільства], 2010.

Krawchenko, Bohdan. *Social Change and National Consciousness in Twentieth-Century Ukraine*. London: Macmillan, 1985.

Krivocheine, Basil. "Catholicity and the Structures of the Church." *Saint Vladimir's Theological Quarterly* 17 (1973) 41-52.

Kulenović, Tarik. "Pripreme za rat i početak rata u Bosni i Hercegovini 1992 godine." *Polemos* 1.1 (1998) 89-112.

Küng, Hans. *Ist die Kirche noch zu retten?* Munich: Piper, 2011.

Labunka, Miroslav, and Leonid Rudnytzky. *The Ukrainian Catholic Church, 1945-1975: A Symposium*. Philadelphia: St. Sophia Religious Association of Ukrainian Catholics, 1976.

Langle Ramírez, Arturo. *El militarismo de Victoriano Huerta*. Mexico City: UNAM, 1976.

Larkin, Emmet. "The Devotional Revolution in Ireland, 1850-1875." *American Historical Review* 77 (1972) 625-52.

Latin American Episcopal Council. *Medellín: conclusiones (segunda conferencia general del Episcopado Latinoamericano, Bogotá, 24 de Agosto; Medellín, Agosto 26-Septiembre 6; Colombia-1968* [Medellín: Conclusions (Second General Conference of the Latin American Episcopate, Bogotá, August 24; Medellín, August 26-September 6; Colombia-1968)]. Bogotá: Secretariado General del CELAM, 1974. http://issuu.com/celam/docs/medellin/1?e=0.

Lehnert, Marek. "Poland: The Controversy Involving Radio Maryja." *Vatican Insider/La Stampa*, August 8, 2012. http://vaticaninsider.lastampa.it/en/world-news/detail/articolo/polonia-poland-radio-maria-19562/.

Leo XIII, Pope. *The Chief Duties of Christians as Citizens: Sapientiae Christianae*. New York: Paulist, 1941.

———. *On Civil Government: Diuturnum*. New York: Paulist, 1942.

Leustean, Lucian, ed. *Representing Religion in the European Union: Does God Matter?* New York: Routledge, 2013.

Levinson, Sanford. "Constituting Communities through Words That Bind: Reflections on Loyalty Oaths." *Michigan Law Review* 84 (1986) 1440–70.

Leys, Collin. *Underdevelopment in Kenya: The Political Economy of Neo-Colonialism* London: Heinemann, 1975.

Lightfoot, J. B., and J. R. Harmer, trans. *The Apostolic Fathers: Greek Texts and English Translations.* Edited by Michael W. Holmes. 2nd ed. Grand Rapids: Baker, 1998.

Lilla, Mark. *The Stillborn God: Religion, Politics, and the Modern West.* New York: Knopf, 2007.

Lima Vaz, Henrique C. de. "Igreja-reflexo vs. Igreja-fonte." *Cadernos Brasileiros* 46 (1968) 17–22.

Llywelyn, Dorian. *Sacred Place, Chosen People: Land and National Identity in Welsh Spirituality.* Cardiff: University of Wales Press, 1999.

———. *Toward a Catholic Theology of Nationality.* Lanham, MD: Lexington, 2010.

Loades, David, and Katherine Walsh. *Faith and Identity: Christian Political Experience.* Studies in Church History 6. Oxford: Blackwell, 1990.

Locke, John. *A Letter Concerning Toleration.* Indianapolis: Bobbs-Merrill, 1955.

Lohfink, Gerhard. *Does God Need the Church? Toward a Theology of the People of God.* Translated by Linda M. Maloney. Collegeville, MN: Liturgical, 1999.

Londoño-Vega, Patricia. *Religion, Culture, and Society in Colombia: Medellín and Antioquia, 1850–1930.* Oxford: Clarendon, 2002.

Lonergan, Bernard. *Method in Theology.* London: Darton, Longman & Todd, 1971.

Longman, Timothy. *Christianity and Genocide in Rwanda.* Cambridge: Cambridge University Press, 2009.

Lori, William E. "Homily for Rosary Pilgrimage." Homily given at the National Shrine of the Immaculate Conception, Washington, DC, October 14, 2012. http://www.usccb.org/issues-and-action/religious-liberty/archbishop-lori-homily-rosary-pilgrimage-october-2012.cfm.

Lossky, Vladimir. "Catholic Consciousness: Anthropological Implications of the Dogma of the Church." In *In the Image and Likeness of God*, edited by John H. Erickson and Thomas E. Bird, 183–94. Crestwood, NY: St. Vladimir's Seminary Press, 1974.

———. *In the Image and Likeness of God.* Edited by John H. Erickson and Thomas E. Bird. Crestwood, NY: St. Vladimir's Seminary Press, 1985.

Loureiro, Gabriela. "'Bento XVI mudou a ideia do que é ser papa,' diz historiador." VEJA. February 16, 2013. http://veja.abril.com.br/noticia/mundo/%E2%80%98bento-xvi-mudou-a-ideia-do-que-e-ser-papa%E2%80%99.

Lovrenović, Ivan. *Bosna-kraj stoljeća.* Zagreb: Duriex, 1996.

———. "Rat 1992–1995 i nakon njega: Ima li buducnosti?" *Jukić* 26/27 (1996/1997) 211–33.

Lucić, Ljubo. "Govor u Bosansko-hercegovačkom parlamentu." *Svjetlo riječi* (September 1993).

———. "Oporuka mrtvog franjevca." *Svjetlo riječi* (February 1994).

Maalouf, Amin. *In the Name of Identity: Violence and the Need to Belong.* Translated by Barbara Brey. New York: Arcade, 2001.

MacGregor, Josefina. "Una perspectiva del Régimen Huertista a través de sus declaraciones." *Anuario de Historia* 11 (1983).

Mach, Zdzisław. "The Roman Catholic Church in Poland and the Dynamics of Social Identity in Polish Society." In *The Religious Roots of Contemporary European Identity*, edited by Lucia Faltin and Melanie J. Wright, 117–33. London: Continuum, 2007. http://www.humanityinaction.org/files/279-The_Roman_Catholic_Church_in_Poland_and_the_Dynamics_of_Social_Identity_in_Polish_Society.pdf

MacIntyre, Alasdair. *The Religious Significance of Atheism*. New York: Columbia University Press, 1966.

Magaš, Branka, and Ivo Žanić, eds. *The War in Croatia and Bosnia-Herzegovina, 1991–1995*. London: Cass, 2001.

Magesa, Laurenti. *Anatomy of Inculturation: Transforming the Church in Africa*. Maryknoll, NY: Orbis, 2004.

Mahieu, Stephanie, and Vlad Naumescu, eds. *Churches In-Between: Greek Catholic Churches in Post-Socialist Europe*. Berlin: Max Planck Institute for Social Anthropology, 2008.

Mamdani, Mahmood. *Citizen and Subject: Contemporary Africa and the Legacy of Late Colonialism*. Princeton: Princeton University Press, 1996.

———. *When Victims Become Killers: Colonialism, Nativism, and the Genocide in Rwanda*, Princeton: Princeton University Press, 2001.

Mancisidor, José. "El huertismo." *Historia Mexicana* 3 (1953) 34–51.

"La Manifestación de Ayer en Homenaje a Cristo Rey, Resultó Verdaderamente Grandiosa y sin Precedente en la República." *El País*, January 12, 1914.

Markešić, Luka. *Svjetlo riječi* (September 1996) 9.

Marković, Rev. Ivo. Letter to Georgette F. Bennett, 27 April 1998.

Markus, Vasyl. "A Century of Ukrainian Religious Experience in the United States." In *The Ukrainian Experience in the United States: A Symposium*, edited by Paul Robert Magocsi, 105–28. Cambridge: Harvard Ukrainian Research Institute, 1979.

Martin, David. *The Future of Christianity: Reflections on Violence and Democracy, Religion and Secularization*. Surrey, UK: Ashgate, 2011.

Martin, James. *This Our Exile: A Spiritual Journey with the Refugees of East Africa*. Maryknoll, NY: Orbis, 1999.

Marvin, Carolyn, and David W. Ingle. "Blood Sacrifice and the Nation: Revisiting Civil Religion." *Journal of the American Academy of Religion* 64 (1996) 767–80.

———. *Blood Sacrifice and the Nation: Totem Rituals and the American Flag*. Cambridge: Cambridge University Press, 1999.

Marx, Anthony. *Faith in Nation: Exclusionary Origins of Nationalism*. New York: Oxford University Press, 2003.

———. "The Nation-State and Its Exclusions." *Political Science Quarterly* 117 (2002) 103–26.

Marynovych, Miroslav. *Українська Ідея і Християнство або коли гарцюють кольорові коні Апокалипсису* [The Ukrainian Idea and Christianity, or When the Colored Horses of the Apocalypse Prance]. Київ: Дух і Літера [Spirit and Letter], 2003.

Mazzini, Giuseppe. *Opere Politiche*. Turino: UTET, 2005.

Mbiti, J. S. *African Religions and Philosophy*. Nairobi: Heinemann, 1969.

Meier, John P. *A Marginal Jew: Rethinking the Historical Jesus*. 4 vols. New York: Doubleday, 1991–2009.

Menke, Martin. "'Thy Will Be Done': Nationalism and Faith in German Catholicism." *Catholic Historical Review* 91 (2005) 300–320.

"Message of the Primates of the Orthodox Church during Their Synaxis-Assembly at the Phanar, Christmas 2000 AD." http://www.orthodoxa.org/GB/patriarchate/documents/noel_2000GB.htm.

Meyer, Jean. *La cristiada*. Vol. 2. Mexico City: Siglo XXI, 1973–74.

Meyer, Michael. *Huerta: A Political Portrait*. Lincoln: University of Nebraska, 1972.

Miłosz, Czesław. *Native Realm: A Search for Self-Definition*. Translated by Catherine S. Leach. New York: Doubleday, 1968.

Mitschke-Collande, Thomas von. *Schafft sich die Katholische Kirche ab? Analysen und Fakten eines Unternehmensberaters*. Munich: Kösel, 2012.

Moheno, Querido. *Mi actuación política después de la decena trágica*. Mexico City: Botas, 1939.

Mojzes, Paul. "The Camouflaged Role of Religion in the War in Bosnia and Herezgovina." In *Religion and the War in Bosnia*, edited by Paul Mojzes, 74–99. Atlanta: Scholars, 1998.

Moock, Wilhelm. "Christentum und Nation." *Hochland* 30 (1932) 233–43.

Moreno, Antonio F. *Church, State, and Civil Society in Postauthoritarian Philippines: Narratives of Engaged Citizenship*. Quezon City: Ateneo de Manila University Press, 2006.

Moreno Chávez, José Alberto. "Devoción y cultura católica en la Arquidiócesis de México, 1880–1920." PhD diss., El Colegio de México, 2010.

———."Devoción política: el culto al Sagrado Corazón de Jesús en perspectiva comparada (Francia, España, y México)." Unpublished manuscript.

Morsey, Rudolf. *Die deutsche Zentrumspartei, 1917–1923*. Beiträge zur Geschichte des Parlamentarismus und der politischen Parteien 32. Düsseldorf: Droste, 1966.

———. *Der Untergang des politischen Katholizismus: Die Zentrumspartei zwischen christlichem Selbstverständnis und "Nationaler Erhebung" 1932–33*. Stuttgart: Belser, 1977.

Motiuk, David. *Eastern Christians in the New World: An Historical and Canonical Study of the Ukrainian Catholic Church in Canada*. Ottawa: Saint Paul University, 2005.

Motyl, Alexander J. *The Turn to the Right: The Ideological Origins and Development of Ukrainian Nationalism, 1919–1929*. New York: Columbia University Press, 1980.

Myhill, John. *Language, Religion, and National Identity in Europe and the Middle East*. Discourse Approaches to Politics, Society, and Culture 21. Philadelphia: John Benjamins, 2008.

New York Times. "The Freedom to Choose Birth Control." February 10, 2012. http://www.nytimes.com/2012/02/11/opinion/the-freedom-to-choose-birth-control.html.

Nichols, Aidan. *Rome and the Eastern Churches: A Study in Schism*. Rev. ed. San Francisco: Ignatius, 2010.

Niebuhr, H. Richard *Christ and Culture*. New York: Harper, 1956.

Niebuhr, Reinhold. *Reinhold Niebuhr on Politics: His Political Philosophy and Its Application to Our Age as Expressed in His Writings*. Edited by Harry R. Davis and Robert C. Good. New York: Scribner, 1960.

Nisbet, Robert A. *The Quest for Community*. London: Oxford University Press, 1953.

Nongbri, Brent. *Before Religion: A History of a Modern Concept*. New Haven: Yale University Press, 2012.

Norwegian Nobel Committee. "Announcement: The Nobel Peace Prize for 2012." Oslo, October 12, 2012. http://nobelpeaceprize.org/en_GB/laureates/laureates-2012/announce-2012.

Nowicka, Wanda. "Roman Catholic Fundamentalism against Women's Reproductive Rights in Poland." *Reproductive Health Matters* 4 (1996) 21–29.

Nyairo, Joyce. "'Modify': *Jua Kali* as a Metaphor for Africa's Urban Ethnicities and Cultures." In *Urban Legends, Colonial Myths: Popular Culture and Literature in East Africa*, edited by James Ogude and Joyce Nyairo, 125–54. Asmara: African World Press, 2007.

Obeifuna, Albert Kanene. Intervention delivered during Session 4 at the First Special Assembly for Africa of the Synod of Bishops, Vatican City, April/May 1994. http://www.afrikaworld.net/synod/obiefuna.htm.

Odalo, Bob. "Rebel Priests Await Milingo Visit." *Daily Nation*, August 6, 2009. http://www.nation.co.ke/News/-/1056/608302/-/view/printVersion/-/10vgouf/-/index.html.

O'Dogherty Madrazo, Laura. "El ascenso de una jerarquía eclesial intransigente, 1890–1914." In *Historia de la Iglesia en el Siglo XIX*, edited by Manuel Ramos Medina, 179–98. Mexico City: Condumex, 1998.

———. *De urnas y sotanas: el Partido Católico Nacional en Jalisco*. Mexico City: Conaculta, 2001.

Okolo, Chukwudum Barnabas. "The African Experience of Christian Values: Dimensions of the Problematic." In *Identity and Change: Nigerian Philosophical Studies I*, edited by Theophilus Okere, 173–86. Washington, DC: Council for Research in Values and Philosophy, 1996. http://www.crvp.org/book/Series02/II-3/chapter_xi.htm.

Oldfield, Adrian. "Citizenship and Community: Civic Republicanism and the Modern World." In *The Citizenship Debates*, edited by Gershon Shafir, 75–89. Minneapolis: University of Minnesota Press, 1998.

O'Leary, Cecilia. *To Die For: The Paradox of American Patriotism*. Princeton: Princeton University Press, 1999.

O'Shaughnessy, Edith. *Intimate Pages of Mexican History*. New York: George H. Doran, 1920.

"Página que *La Nación* Bondadosamente Destina al Comité Organizador del Homenaje Nacional a Jesucristo Rey." *La Nación*, January 8, 1914.

Palma, Rafael. *The Pride of the Malay Race: A Biography of José Rizal*. New York: Prenctice-Hall, 1949.

Pannenberg, Wolfhart. *Human Nature, Election, and History*. Philadelphia: Westminster, 1977.

Papathanasiou, Athanasios N. "The Postmodern Revival of Polytheism in the Name of Christian Adherence to the Faith of the Fathers: A Paradox in Our Modern Ecclesiastical Situation." *Panta ta Ethni* [All Nations] 108 (2008) 3–7.

Papathomas, Grigorios. "Culturalisme ecclésiastique: l'aliénation de la culture et l'anéantissement de l'eglise." *Année canonique* 51 (2009) 61–67.

Paul VI, Pope. *Dogmatic Constitution on the Church: Lumen Gentium*. Boston: Pauline, 1990.

Pawliczko, Ann Lencyk, ed. *Ukraine and Ukrainians throughout the World: A Demographic and Sociological Guide to the Homeland and Its Diaspora*. Toronto: University of Toronto Press, 1994.

Perica, Vjekoslav. *Balkan Idols: Religion and Nationalism in Yugoslav States.* Oxford: Oxford University Press, 2002.

Perlez, Jane. "As a Priest Gives Poles Hate Radio, Rome Stirs." *New York Times*, December 14, 1997. http://www.nytimes.com/1997/12/14/world/as-a-priest-gives-poles-hate-radio-rome-stirs.html.

Perreau-Saussine, Emile. *Catholicism and Democracy: An Essay in the History of Political Thought.* Translated by Richard Rex. Princeton: Princeton University Press, 2011.

Petrà, Basilio. *Due Carismi: Preti Celibi e Preti Sposati.* Assisi: Cittadella Editrice, 2011.

Petras, David M. *Eastern Catholic Churches in America.* Parma, OH: Office of Religious Education, Diocese of Parma, 1987.

Pew Forum on Religion and Public Life. *Global Christianity: A Report on the Size and Distribution of the World's Christian Population.* Washington, DC: Pew Forum on Religion and Public Life, December 2011. http://www.pewforum.org/files/2011/12/Christianity-fullreport-web.pdf.

———. *Tolerance and Tension: Islam and Christianity in Sub-Saharan Africa.* Washington, DC: Pew Forum on Religion and Public Life, 2010. http://www.pewforum.org/2010/04/15/executive-summary-islam-and-christianity-in-sub-saharan-africa/.

Pew Forum on Religion and Public Life and Pew-Templeton Global Religious Futures Project. *The Future of the Global Muslim Population: Projections for 2010–2030.* January 2011. http://pewforum.org/The-Future-of-the-Global-Muslim-Population.aspx.

Pew Research Center. "America's Former Catholics." June 13, 2008. http://www.pewresearch.org/daily-number/americas-former-catholics.

Phan, Peter. "Multiple Religious Belonging: Opportunities and Challenges for Theology and Church." *Theological Studies* 64 (2003) 495–519.

Picardal, Antonio L. *Basic Ecclesial Communities in the Philippines: Ecclesiological Perspective.* Rome: Pontifica Gregoriana, Facultas Theologiae, 1995.

Pius X, Pope. "A Nuestros Venerables Hermanos los Arzobispos y Obispos de la República Mexicana, Pío Papa X." Rome, November 12, 1913. AHAM, c. 91/exp. 57.

Pius XI, Pope. *Caritate Christi compulsi.* Libreria Editrice Vaticana. http://w2.vatican.va/content/pius-xi/en/encyclicals/documents/hf_p-xi_enc_03051932_caritate-christi-compulsi.html.

———. *Non abbiamo bisogno.* Libreria Editrice Vaticana. http://www.vatican.va/holy_father/pius_xi/encyclicals/documents/hf_p-xi_enc_29061931_non-abbiamo-bisogno_en.html.

Plekon, Michael. "The Church, the Eucharist and the Kingdom: Towards an Assessment of Alexander Schmemann's Theological Legacy." *St. Vladimir's Theological Quarterly* 40 (1996) 119–43.

Plutarch. *Lives.* Vol. 1. Translated by Bernadotte Perrin. Cambridge: Harvard University Press, 1917.

Popovich, Justin. "The Inward Mission of Our Church." In *Orthodox Faith and Life in Christ*, translated by Asterios Gerostergios, 23–24. Belmont, MA: Institute for Byzantine and Modern Greek Studies, 2005.

Pospishil, Victor J. *Ex Occidente Lex: From the West, the Law; The Eastern Catholic Churches under the Tutelage of the Holy See of Rome.* Cartaret, NJ: St. Mary's Religious Action Fund, 1979.

Prieto Laurens, Jorge. *Anécdotas históricas de Jorge Prieto Laurens.* Mexico City: Costa-Amic, 1977.
———. *Cincuenta años de política mexicana: memorias políticas.* Mexico City: Editora Mexicana de Periódicos, Libros, y Revistas, 1968.
Procko, Bohdan P. *Ukrainian Catholics in America: A History.* Washington, DC: University Press of America, 1982.
Prunier, Gérard. *The Rwanda Crisis 1959-1994: History of a Genocide.* New York: Columbia University Press, 1995.
Puhl, Jan. "Polish Populists: Papal Reprimand for Catholic Radio." *Spiegel Online International,* May 2, 2006. http://www.spiegel.de/international/polish-populists-papal-reprimand-for-catholic-radio-a-413976.html.
Pulcini, Theodore."Toward an Acceptable Byzantine Catholic Ecclesiology." *Diakonia* 15 (1980) 5-22.
Quibuyen, Floro C. *A Nation Aborted: Rizal, American Hegemony, and Philippine Nationalism.* Quezon City: Ateneo de Manila University Press, 1999.
Quitorio, Pedro C. *CBCP on the Threshold of the Next Millennium.* Manila: Catholic Bishops' Conference of the Philippines, 1999.
———. *Pastoral Letters, 1945-1995.* Manila: Catholic Bishops' Conference of the Philippines, 1996.
Rafael, Vicente L. *Contracting Colonialism: Translation and Christian Conversion in Tagalog Society under Early Spanish Rule.* Quezon City: Ateneo de Manila University Press, 1988.
Ramet, Pedro, ed. *Catholicism and Politics in Communist Societies.* Durham: Duke University Press, 1990.
Ramírez Rancaño, Mario. "La república castrense de Victoriano Huerta." *Estudios de Historia Moderna y Contemporánea de México* 30 (2005) 167-213.
Ratzinger, Joseph. *Kirche-Zeichen unter den Völkern: Schriften zur Ekklesiologie und Ökumene, Erster Teilband.* Freiburg: Herder, 2010a.
———. *Kirche-Zeichen unter den Völkern: Schriften zur Ekklesiologie und Ökumene, Zweiter Teilband.* Freiburg: Herder, 2010b.
Ray, Benjamin C. *African Religions: Symbol, Ritual, and Community.* 2nd ed. Upper Saddle River, NJ: Prentice Hall, 2000.
Reich Chancellery Archives [Akten der Reichskanzlei]. Letter from Minister of Finance to Secretary Pünder, February 25, 1930 [Der Reichsminister der Finanzen an Staatssekretär Pünder. 25. Februar 1930]. Müller Cabinets [Kabinett Müller] 2, No. 454. http://www.bundesarchiv.de/aktenreichskanzlei/1919-1933/0000/ma3/ma32p/kap1_1/kap2_80/para3_1.html.
———. "Ministerial Meeting on October 9, 1924 [Ministerbesprechung vom 9. Oktober 1924]." Marx Cabinets [Kabinette Marx] 1/2, No. 321. http://www.bundesarchiv.de/aktenreichskanzlei/1919-1933/0000/ma3/ma32p/kap1_1/kap2_80/para3_1.html.
Richter, Reinhard. *Nationales Denken im Katholizismus der Weimarer Republik.* Theologie 29. Münster: LIT, 2000.
Rittner, Carol, et al., eds. *Genocide in Rwanda: Complicity of the Churches.* St. Paul, MN: Paragon House, 2004.
Rius Facius, Antonio. *De don Porfirio a Plutarco: Historia de la ACJM.* Mexico City: Jus, 1958.

Roberson, Ronald. *The Eastern Christian Churches: A Brief Survey*. 7th ed. Rome: Orientalia Christiana, 2007.

Rodríguez, Miguel. "El Sagrado Corazón de Jesús: imágenes, mensajes, y transferencias culturales." *Secuencia* 74 (2009) 147–68.

Rosales, Gaudencio B., and C. G. Arevalo, eds. *For All the Peoples of Asia: Documents from 1970-1971*. Quezon City: Claretian, 1992.

Ross, Stanley. "Victoriano Huerta visto por su compadre." *Historia Mexicana* 12 (1962) 296–321.

Rothschild, Matthew. "Catholic High School Teacher Forced Out over Flag." *The Progressive*, October 17, 2005. http://www.progressive.org/mag_mc101705.

Roy, Olivier. *Holy Ignorance: When Religion and Culture Part Ways*. New York: Columbia University Press, 2010.

Ruiz y Flores, Leopoldo. "Instrucción Pastoral sobre los Deberes de los Católicos en Política, Pronunciada por el Illmo. Sr. Arzobispo Dr. Don Leopoldo Ruiz y Flores en la Función Religiosa Celebrada por el Partido Católico Nacional en la Catedral de Morelia, 20 de febrero de 1912." ALNDLR: caja 1, ff. 1–7.

———. *Recuerdo de Recuerdos: Autobiografía del Excmo. y Rdmo. Sr. Dr. Don Leopoldo Ruiz y Flores*. Mexico City: Buena, 1942.

Runciman, Steven. *The Byzantine Theocracy*. Cambridge: Cambridge University Press, 1977.

Ruppert, Karsten. *Im Dienste am Staat von Weimar: Das Zentrum als regierende Partei in der Weimarer Demokratie, 1923-1930*. Düsseldorf: Droste, 1992.

Russkiy Mir Foundation Press Service. "Patriarch Kirill: Russkiy Mir and the Russian Orthodox Serve to Unite Nations and Confessions." November 3, 2010. http://russkiymir.ru/en/news/135562/.

Sánchez, Pedro J. *Episodios eclesiásticos de México (contribución a nuestra historia)*. Mexico City: Impresora Barrié, 1948.

Sandbrook, Richard. *Proletariats and African Capitalism: The Kenyan Case, 1960-1972*. Cambridge: Cambridge University Press, 1975.

Schaab, Gloria L. "'As Christ, So We': Eucharist as Liturgy." *Liturgical Ministry* 18 (Fall 2009) 171–81.

Schindler, David L. "The Repressive Logic of Liberal Rights: Religious Freedom, Contraceptives, and the 'Phony' Argument of the *New York Times*." *Communio* 38 (2011) 523–47.

Schineller, Peter. "African Christianity in the 21st Century: Hope of the Future or Remnant of the Past?" Lecture delivered at Weston Jesuit School of Theology, Boston, Massachusetts, March 4, 1999. http://www.loyolajesuit.org/peter_schineller/resources/WESTON%20LECTURE.doc.

Schmemann, Alexander. *The Eucharist: Sacrament of the Kingdom*. Translated by Paul Kachur. Crestwood, NY: St Vladimir's Seminary Press, 2003.

———. *For the Life of the World: Sacraments and Orthodoxy*. Crestwood, NY: St Vladimir's Seminary Press, 1998.

———. "The Missionary Imperative." In *Church, World, Mission: Reflections on Orthodoxy in the West*, 135–36. Crestwood, NY: St. Vladimir's Seminary Press, 1979.

———. *Of Water and the Spirit: A Liturgical Study of Baptism*. Crestwood, NY: St. Vladimir's Seminary Press, 1984.

Schmitt, Carl. *Political Theology: Four Chapters on the Concept of Sovereignty*. Translated by George Schwab. Chicago: University of Chicago Press, 2005.
Schönhoven, Klaus. *Die Bayerische Volkspartei, 1924–1932*. Kommission für Geschichte des Parlamentarismus und der politischen Parteien. Düsseldorf: Droste, 1972.
Schreiter, Robert J. *The New Catholicity: Theology between the Global and the Local*. Maryknoll, NY: Orbis, 1997.
Schuck, Peter H., and Rogers M. Smith. *Citizenship Without Consent: Illegal Aliens in the American Polity*. New Haven: Yale University Press, 1985.
Schumacher, John N. *Revolutionary Clergy: The Filipino Clergy and the Nationalist Movement, 1850–1903*. Quezon City: Ateneo de Manila University Press, 1981.
———. "The Rizal Bill of 1956: Horacio de le Costa and the Bishops." *Philippine Studies* 58 (2011) 529–53.
Scott, William Henry. *Barangay: Sixteenth-Century Philippine Culture and Society*. Quezon City: Ateneo de Manila University Press, 1994.
"Se Efectuó la Solemne Consagración de la República Mejicana al Sagrado Corazón de Jesús para Impetrar la Paz." *El País*, January 7, 1914.
Second Special Assembly for Africa of the Synod of Bishops. "Message to the People of God." October 23, 2009. http://www.vatican.va/roman_curia/synod/documents/rc_synod_doc_20091023_message-synod_en.html.
Segunda carta pastoral del Ilmo. y Revmo. Sr. Dr. y Mtro. D. Francisco Orozco y Jiménez, 50 Arzobispo de Guadalajara, con motivo de la solemne consagración de la República Mexicana al Sacratísimo Corazón de Jesús. Guadalajara: Tip. de "El Regional," 1913.
Seligman, Adam. "Particularist Universalism: A Response to Abdullahi Ahmed An-Na'im." *Common Knowledge* 11 (2005) 81–88.
Seligman, Adam, et al. *Ritual and Its Consequences: An Essay on the Limits of Sincerity*. Oxford: Oxford University Press, 2008.
Sells, Michael. *The Bridge Betrayed: Religion and Genocide in Bosnia*. Berkeley: University of California Press, 1996.
———. "Crosses of Blood: Sacred Space, Religion, and Violence in Bosnia-Herzegovina." *Sociology of Religion* 64 (2003) 309–31.
Senyk, Sophia. "A Response to a Response: Several Comments on Peter Galadza's Position." *Het christelijk Oosten—Tijdschrift van het Institut voor Oosters Christendom te Nijmegen* 51 (1999) 143–48.
———. "The Ukrainian Greek Catholic Church Today: Universal Values versus Nationalist Doctrines." *Religion, State & Society* 30 (2002) 317–32.
———. "A Victim to Nationalism: The Ukrainian Greek Catholic Church in Its Own Words." *Het christelijk Oosten—Tijdschrift van het Institut voor Oosters Christendom te Nijmegen* 51 (1999) 167–87.
Seuss, Paulo. "Inculturação, desafios, caminhos, metas" ["Inculturation, Challenges, Paths and Goals"]. *Revista Eclesiástica Brasileira* 49/193 (1989) 81–126.
Shedinger, Robert F. *Was Jesus a Muslim? Questioning Categories in the Study of Religion*. Minneapolis: Fortress, 2009.
Sherman, William L., and Richard E. Greenleaf. *Victoriano Huerta: A Reappraisal*. Mexico City: Centro de Estudios Mexicanos, 1960.
Shilling, Chris, and Philip A. Mellor. "Durkheim, Morality and Modernity: Collective Effervescence, Homo Duplex and the Sources of Moral Action." *The British Journal of Sociology* 49 (1998) 193–209.

Shorter, Aylward. *Christianity and the African Imagination: After the African Synod; Resources for Inculturation*. Nairobi: Paulines, 1996.

Sibomana, André. *Hope for Rwanda: Conversations with Laure Guilbert and Hervé Deguine*. Translated by Carina Tertsakian. London: Pluto Press, 1999.

Sieyès, Joseph Emmanuel. *Qu'est-ce que le Tiers état?* Paris: Éditions du Boucher, 2002. http://www.leboucher.com/pdf/sieyes/tiers.pdf.

Smith, Anthony D. *Chosen Peoples*. Oxford: Oxford University Press, 2003.

———. *The Cultural Foundations of Nations: Hierarchy, Covenant, and Republic*. Malden, MA: Blackwell, 2008.

———. "Culture, Community, and Territory: The Politics of Ethnicity and Nationalism." *International Affairs* 72 (1996) 445–58.

———. *The Ethnic Origins of Nations*. Oxford: Blackwell, 1986.

———. "The Formation of National Identity." In *Identity*, edited by Henry Harris, 129–53. Oxford: Clarendon, 1995.

———. *The Nation in History: Historiographical Debates about Ethnicity and Nationalism*. Hanover, NH: Brandeis University Press, 2000.

———. *National Identity*. Reno: University of Nevada Press, 1991.

———. *Nationalism and Modernism: A Critical Survey of Recent Theories of Nations and Nationalism*. London: Routledge, 1998.

Smith, Wilfred Cantwell. *The Meaning and End of Religion: A New Approach to the Religious Traditions of Mankind*. New York: Macmillan, 1962.

Snyder, Timothy. *Bloodlands: Europe between Hitler and Stalin*. New York: Basic Books, 2010.

Soares, Afonso. *Sincretismo e inculturação: pressupostos para uma aproximação teológico-pastoral às religiões afro-brasileiras buscados na epistemologia de Juan Luis Segundo* [Syncretism and Inculturation: Searching for the Presuppositions of a Theoretical-Pastoral Approach to Afro-Brazilian Religions in the Epistemology of Juan Luis Segundo]. São Bernardo do Campo: UMESP, 2001.

Sobrino, Jon. *Fuera de los pobres no hay salvación*. San Salvador: UCA Editores, 2008.

"La Solemne Coronación al S. Corazón de Jesús: Indicaciones que para la Ceremonia Hace el Señor Dean de la Catedral." *El País*, January 5, 1914.

"La Solemne Coronación del S. Corazón de Jesús: Se Efectuará en la Catedral de Méjico, al Igual que en Todos los Templos de la Nación." *El País*, January 6, 1914.

"La Solemne Coronación del Sagrado Corazón de Jesús en este C. y las Ceremonias que Tuvieron Lugar." *El País*, January 11, 1914.

"Las Solemnidades de la Consagración de la Rep. al Sagrado Corazón de Jesús, en Guadalajara." *El País*, January 9, 1914.

Solic, Mirna. "The Other Bosniaks." *Central Europe Review* 4:4 (2002). http://www.ce-review.org/02/4/CERbookCroatsJB.html.

Standard Digital News. "Kenya: Celibacy Debate Back as Church Seeks New Pope." February 23, 2013. http://www.zambianews.net/index.php/sid/212778389.

Steber, Martina. "'. . . Daß der Partei nicht nur die äußere, sondern auch innere Gefahren drohen:' Die Bayerische Volkspartei im Jahre 1933." In *Das Jahr 1933: Die nationalsozialistische Machteroberung und die deutsche Gesellschaft*, edited by Andreas Wirsching, 70–91. Dachauer Symposien zur Zeitgeschichte 9. Göttingen: Wallstein, 2009.

Stehkämper, Hugo. *Konrad Adenauer als Kirchentagspräsident 1922: Form und Grenze politischer Entscheidungsfreiheit im katholischen Raum*. Veröffentlichungen der

Kommission für Zeitgeschichte B:21. Adenauer-Studien IV. Mainz: Matthias-Grünewald, 1977.
Steil, Carlos, and Rodrigo Toniol. "O catolicismo e a igreja católica no brasil à luz dos dados sobre religião no censo de 2010." Universidade Federal do Rio Grande do Sul, 2013. http://www.seer.ufrgs.br/index.php/debatesdoner/article/view/43576.
Steinberg, Leo. *The Sexuality of Christ in Renaissance Art and in Modern Oblivion.* Chicago: University of Chicago Press, 1983.
Strassberg, Barbara. "Changes in Religious Culture in Post [World] War II Poland." *Sociological Analysis* 48 (1988) 342–54.
Suess, Paulo. "Inculturação, desafios, caminhos, metas." Revista Ecclesiástica Brasileira 49 (1989) 81–126.
Tapia Méndez, Aureliano. *José Antonio Plancarte y Labastida, profeta y mártir.* Mexico City: Jus, 1973.
Taracena, Alfonso. *La verdadera revolución mexicana: segunda etapa (1913 a 1914).* Mexico City: Jus, 1960.
Tarling, Nicholas, ed. *The Cambridge History of Southeast Asia.* Cambridge: Cambridge University Press, 1999.
Taylor, Charles. *A Secular Age.* Cambridge: Belknap Press of Harvard University Press, 2007.
Taylor, Justin. "La fraction du pain en Luc-Actes." In *The Unity of Luke-Acts,* edited by Jozef Verheyden, 281–95. Leuven: Peeters, 1999.
Teresa of Ávila. *The Interior Castle.* New York: Paulist, 1979.
———. *The Life of Teresa of Ávila.* London: Penguin, 2004.
Tillich, Paul. *Systematic Theology.* Vol. 1. Chicago: University of Chicago Press, 1951.
Tischleder, Peter. *Die Staatslehre Leos XIII.* Mönchen Gladbach: Volksverein, 1925.
Tischner, Józef. *Marxism and Christianity: The Quarrel and the Dialogue in Poland.* Washington, DC: Georgetown University Press, 1987.
———. *The Spirit of Solidarity.* Translated by Marek B. Zaleski and Benjamin Fiore. San Francisco: Harper and Row, 1984.
Torres Septién, Valentina."Guanajuato y la resistencia católica en el siglo XX." In *Integrados y marginados en el México posrevolucionario. Los juegos de poder local y sus nexos con la política nacional,* edited by Nicolás Cárdenas García and Enrique Guerra Manzo, 83–119. Mexico City: Miguel Angel Porrúa/UAM, 2009.
Torres Septién, Valentina, and Yves Solís. "De Cerro a Montaña Santa: La Construcción del Monumento a Cristo Rey (1919–1960)." *Historia y Grafía* 22 (2004) 113–54.
Traslosheros, Jorge. "Señora de la historia, madre mestiza, reina de México: la coronación de la Virgen de Guadalupe y su actualización como mito fundacional de la patria, 1895." *Signos Históricos* 7 (2002) 105–30.
Treviño, José Guadalupe. *Antonio Plancarte y Labastida, Abad de Guadalupe.* 2nd ed. Mexico City: La Cruz, 1948.
Tuñón Pablos, Esperanza. *Huerta y el movimiento obrero.* Mexico City: El Caballito, 1982.
United States v. Seeger, 380 US 163 (1965).
United States Conference of Catholic Bishops. *Forming Consciences for Faithful Citizenship: A Call to Political Responsibility from the Catholic Bishops of the United States.* Rev. ed. Washington, DC: USCCB, 2011.

———. "Six Things Everyone Should Know about the HHS Mandate." *USCCBlog* (blog), February 6, 2012. http://usccbmedia.blogspot.com/2012/02/six-things-everyone-should-know-about.html?spref=tw.

United States Conference of Catholic Bishops, Ad Hoc Committee for Religious Freedom. "Our First, Most Cherished Liberty: A Statement on Religious Liberty." 2012. http://www.usccb.org/issues-and-action/religious-liberty/upload/Our-First-Most-Cherished-Liberty-Apr12-6-12-12.pdf.

Urrutia Martínez, Cristina. *Aureliano Urrutia: del crimen político al exilio*. Mexico City: Tusquets, 2008.

Valenzuela, Georgette. "Entre el poder y la fe: El Partido Nacional Cooperatista. ¿Un Partido católico en los años veinte?" In *El camino de la democracia en México*, edited by Patricia Galeana, 199–220. Mexico City: UNAM-Instituto de Investigaciones Jurídicas, 1998.

Van der Borght, Eddy. "Uniting Europe as a Challenge to the Future of National Churches." In *Charting Churches in a Changing Europe: Charta Oecumenica and the Process of Ecumenical Encounter*, edited by Tim and Ivana Noble et al., 105–25. Amsterdam: Rodopi, 2006.

Vassiliadis, Petros. *Lex Orandi: Studies in Liturgical Theology*. Thessaloniki: Paratiritis, 1994 [in Greek].

Veer, Peter van der, and Hartmut Lehmann. *Nation and Religion: Perspectives on Europe and Asia*. Princeton: Princeton University Press, 1999.

Velikonja, Mitja. *Religious Separation and Political Intolerance in Bosnia-Herzegovina*. Translated by Rang'ichi Ng'inja. College Station: Texas A&M University Press, 2003.

Vincent, Andrew. *Nationalism and Particularity*. New York: Cambridge University Press, 2002.

Volf, Miroslav. Review of *The Bridge Betrayed: Religion and Genocide in Bosnia*, by Michael Sells. *The Journal of the American Academy of Religion* 67 (1999) 250–53.

Volk, Ludwig. *Akten Kardinal Michael von Faulhabers, 1917–1945*. Vol. 1, *1917–1934*. Veröffentlichung der Kommission für Zeitgeschichte, Series A, vol. 17. Mainz: Mathias-Grunewald, 1975.

Wall, Robert W., and Eugene E. Lemcio. *The New Testament as Canon: A Reader in Canonical Criticism*. Journal for the Study of the New Testament Supplement Series 76. Sheffield: JSOT, 1992.

Walls, Andrew F. *The Cross-Cultural Process in Christian History*. Maryknoll, NY: Orbis, 2002.

———. "The Ephesian Moment: At a Crossroads in Christian History." In *The Cross-Cultural Process in Christian History*, 72–81. Maryknoll, NY: Orbis, 2002.

Walton, Nicholas. "Polish Cardinal Tackles Radical Radio." *BBC News*, October 1, 2002. http://news.bbc.co.uk/2/hi/europe/2289567.stm.

Ware, Kallistos. "L'unité dans la diversité. La vocation orthodoxe en Europe occidentale." In *Service Orthodoxe de Presse* 77 (April 1983) 14.

Wartburg, Walther von. "Saeculum, séculariser." In *Französisches etymologisches Wörterbuch*, 11:44–46. Basel: Zbinden, 1964.

Wa Thiong'o, Ngugi. "Preface." In *Decolonizing the Mind: The Politics of Language in African Literature*, ix–xii. 1986. Reprint, Nairobi: East African Educational Publishers, 2004.

Weigel, George. *Evangelical Catholicism: Deep Reform in the Twenty-First Century Church.* New York: Basic Books, 2013.
Wells, Sam. *Improvisation: The Drama of Christian Ethics.* Grand Rapids: Brazos, 2004.
Wiesemann, Falk. *Die Vorgeschichte der nationalsozialistischen Machtübernahme in Bayern 1932–1933.* Beiträge zu einer historischen Strukturanalyse Bayerns im Industriezeitalter 12. Berlin: Duncker and Humblot, 1975.
Williams, Derek. "The Making of Ecuador's *Pueblo Católico*, 1861–1875." In *Political Cultures in the Andes, 1750–1950,* edited by Jacobsen Nils and Cristóbal Aljovín de Losada, 207–29. Durham: Duke University Press, 2005.
Williams, Raymond. *Keywords: A Vocabulary of Culture and Society.* New York: Oxford University Press, 1976.
Wolff, Larry. *The Vatican and Poland in the Age of the Partitions: Diplomatic and Cultural Encounters at the Warsaw Nunciature.* Boulder, CO: East European Monographs, 1988.
Wolin, Sheldon. *Politics and Vision.* Princeton: Princeton University Press, 2004.
Woodward, Linda, et al. *Religions in the Modern World: Traditions and Transformations.* London: Routledge, 2002.
World Council of Churches Commission on Faith and Order. "Ethnic Identity, National Identity, and the Search for Unity." http://www.wcc-coe.org/wcc/what/faith/kuala-docs13-makarios.pdf.
Wright-Rios, Edward. *Revolutions in Mexican Catholicism: Reform and Revelation in Oaxaca, 1887–1934.* Durham: Duke University Press, 2009.
Yazbeck Haddad, Yvonne. *Not Quite American? The Shaping of Arab and Muslim Identity in the United States.* Waco: Baylor University Press, 2004.
Yeago, David. "Messiah's People: The Culture of the Church in the Midst of the Nations." *Pro Ecclesia* 6 (1997) 146–71.
Young, Crawford. "The Heritage of Colonialism." In *Africa in World Politics: Post-Cold War Challenges,* edited by John W. Harbeson and Donald S. Rothchild, 23–37. Boulder, CO: Westview, 1995.
Young, Julia G. "*Cristero* Diaspora: Mexican Immigrants, the U.S. Catholic Church, and Mexico's *Cristero* War, 1926–1929." *The Catholic Historical Review* 98 (2012) 271–300.
Zagorin, Perez. *How the Idea of Religious Toleration Came to the West.* Princeton: Princeton University Press, 2003.
Žanic, Ivo. "Hercegovački rat i mir." *Erasmus* 23 (1998) 84–92.
Zimmer, Sven-Oliver. "Nation und Religion: Von der Imagination des Nationalen zur Verarbeitung von Nationalisierungsprozessen." *Historische Zeitschrift* 283 (2006) 617–56.
Zizioulas, John. *Being as Communion: Studies in Personhood and the Church.* Crestwood, NY: St. Vladimir's Seminary Press, 1985.
———. "Déplacement de la perspective eschatologique." In Giuseppe Alberigo et al., *La Chrétienté en débat: Histoire, formes et problèmes actuels, Colloque de Bologne (11–15 mai 1983).* Paris: Cerf, 1984.
Zubrzycki, Geneviève. *The Crosses of Auschwitz: Nationalism and Religion in Postcommunist Poland.* Chicago: University of Chicago Press, 2006.

Subject/Name Index

Adventures of Asterix and Obelix, The, 75–76
Africa
    Christianity as causing alienation from the self in, 190
    effect of modern worldview upon, 190
    impact of Christianity upon education in, 189
    indigenous worldview of, 184–87
    legacy of colonialism in, 183, 187–90
    modern education system in, 191
    tension between Christianity and Islam in, 170
    tension between different forms of Christianity in, 171–72
    tension between kin-centered and faith-centered identity in, 173
African Religion
    influence on African forms of Christianity and Islam, 169–70.
    See also Reformed Catholic Church
African Synod
    1994, 174, 198
    2009, 176
Augustine, Saint, 37, 83, 92, 265–66. See also *City of God*
Auschwitz, 3–4, 28, 91, 134, 263. *See also* National Socialism
Bandera, Stepan, 134

baptism
    and Eucharist, as mutually reinforcing, 178–79 (*see also* Eucharist)
    and tribalism in Rwanda, 14–15, 19–21, 24, 26–27, 78
    as indicating new communal identity, 30, 32, 40, 75–76, 139, 141–44, 156–57, 173–74, 177–79, 308, 319
    in the Greek Orthodox Church, 155–57
    of infants, 154–55
Barmen Declaration, The, 56
Barth, Karl, 53–58, 61–62
    Christocentrism of, 56
    early recognition of dangers presented by Nazism, 58
Bavarian People's Party, 94–103
    accusations against German Center Party of being bad Catholics, 100–101
    as championing uniqueness of Bavarian identity, 96–98
    challenges in defining national and religious interests, 102
    mistrust of Berlin's influence, 97
    split with German Center Party, 95
    view of Bavaria as last bastion of Catholicism in post-WWI Germany, 102
    view of love of fatherland as basis for Christian international order, 99
Benedict XVI, Pope, 41, 71, 82–84, 119, 170, 204, 208, 211, 277

Borders of Baptism Conference, 2, 36, 40, 42, 46, 79, 139, 214
Borders of Baptism, 2, 7, 10, 14, 24–25, 79, 91, 127, 129, 132, 147, 173–74, 179, 292, 304, 309. See also Budde, Michael
Bosnia and Herzegovina
    Franciscan community in, 105
    "Silver Bosnia" province, 117
Bosniak Muslims, 110–12
Bosnian Franciscans
    peacemaking and tolerance of, 117 (*see also* Marković, Father Ivo)
    peacemaking as due to universality of values and faith, 118
Budde, Michael, 14, 24–24, 78–79, 91, 105, 127, 129, 132, 134, 147, 174, 179, 292. See also *Borders of Baptism*
capitalism, corrosive effect upon spirituality of, 73, 78–79, 85, 137, 306
Catholicism
    Africa, contemporary state of, 174
    Africa, influence upon African politics, 174–77
    Africa, missionaries in, 172
    as challenging relegation of religion to sphere of otherworldly, 276–78
    collectivistic form as answer to problem of exclusionary nationalism, 105
    detraditionalization, 210–11
    Europe, as losing dominant role in global Church, 87–89
    Europe, future responses to secularism, 90 (*see also* secularism and tension with religion)
    Europe, tension with secularism, 89 (*see also* secularism and tension with religion)
    impact of appointment of Pope Francis on Latin America, 212–13 (*see also* Francis, Pope)
    implications of changing status in modern society, 272–78
    Poland, as united with secular Poles through shared enemy of communist Russia, 115
    population changes worldwide, 209–11
    probability of losing material and constitutional privileges in Europe, 86–87
    Roman Catholic contempt toward Eastern Catholics, 137
    versus Catholicity, 181–82
Chagall, Marc, 65
Christ, Jesus
    as perfect human, 42
    eschatological mission given by, 46
    Christian Church as collective Christian being, 38
    as metahistorical, 148
    beliefs as having political implications, 52
    communal basis in both baptism and Eucharist, 142
    depolitization of, 52
    early communities as neither Jew nor Gentile, 146–47
    eschatological anarchism of, 149–50
    eschatological character of, 60–62
    ethics of, 52
    quasi-personal identity of, 33
Council of Chalcedon, 42–43
Christology, 40, 42–44, 118
    four heretical versions of, 42–44
City of God, 92, 265–66. See also Augustine, Saint
diversity
    celebration of, 136
    methods for fostering of, 138
Durkheim, Emile, 120, 269–70
Eastern Orthodox Church

association with local and
national traditions, 159
decline of, 162
ecclesial sense of belonging v.
societal sense of belonging,
160
history of salvation v. history of
national revival, 164–65
need for recognizing difference
between baptismal and
ethnocultural communities,
166–67
negative effects of Hellenism
upon, 163–65 (*see also*
Hellenism)
Ephesian moment, 20–22. See also
Paul, Saint
Eucharist
and baptism, as mutually
reinforcing, 40, 141–42, 144,
146, 157, 160, 178–79, 308,
319 (*see also* baptism)
as both local and universal, 76,
153, 163
differences between Roman
Catholic and Eastern
Catholic views on, 137–39,
142–43, 155, 165
role in early Christian
communities, 147
European Union
ambiguities of project, 67
extreme political right, 81
financial crisis, 68
reverse missionary activities
in, 87
false consciousness, 60
Faulhaber, Cardinal Michael, 96–98,
102
Florovsky, Father Georges, 144–46,
148–49, 156–57
Francis, Pope, 8, 84, 90, 126, 136,
176, 199
impact on Catholicism in Latin
America, 212–13 (*see also*
Catholicism)
French Revolution, 50, 78, 80, 82,
89, 92

German Center Party, 94–103
nationalism as service to all
German people, 95–96
split with Bavarian People's
Party, 95
view of Bavarian People's Party
as excessively nationalistic,
99
Gregory of Nazianzus, 41, 150–51
Hellenism, 160–65. *See also* Eastern
Orthodox Church
Heraclitus, 30–31, 34
heresies, as faith in search of
understanding, 44
Herzegovinian Franciscans, 111, 117
Huerta, General Victoriano, 214,
236, 242, 244
non-attendance at 1914
consecration, 216
relationship with Catholic
clergy, 216–17
John Paul II, Pope, 82–83, 89, 108,
124, 178
visit to Poland as giving rise to
Solidarity, 114
See also Radio Maryja
kenosis, 246
kerygma, 136, 150, 162
Kigali, Muslim population of, 25
Kobasa, Stephen, 262–64, 277
koinonia, 28, 32, 128, 137, 139
Kolbe, Saint Maximilian, 263
Kovch, Father Emilian, 139–40
Latin America
consecrations as Catholic-style
republicanism, 221 (*see also*
Mexico, 1914 consecration
to the Sacred Heart of Jesus)
effect of poverty upon, 202–3
Latin American Conference of
Bishops (CELAM), 204
Leo XIII, Pope, 96–97, 205, 221,
228, 307
liberalism, 49-50, 54–55, 78, 220,
235, 291. *See also* secularism
and tension with religion
liberation theology, 204–5

as ecclesial practice rather than
purely academic practice,
206
as expanding range of interests
after fall of Berlin Wall,
208–9
as placing the poor at the center
of Christian life, 204–5
as sharing the life of the poor,
206–7
Marković, Father Ivo, 117
as exemplifying radical nature
of Bosnian Franciscan's
peacemaking status, 117 (*see
also* Bosnian Franciscans)
martyrdom, as threat to the state, 49
Mary, as queen of the Croats, 110
Međugorje pilgrimage site, 104, 110
Bosnian-Croat nationalistic
symbolism of, 112
collectivistic meanings of, 110
religious nationalism of
Franciscans, 117, 120
Mexico, 1914 consecration to the
Sacred Heart of Jesus, 214,
220–22
as both Mexicanized and
Romanized, 227
as containing the roots of
Cristero Rebellion, 244–45
as decentralized, 231
as denial of comprises made
during Porfirian years, 231
as indicating the state's
submission to the Church,
215
as national project of a
Catholicized social order,
243–45
as response to modernity,
217–18
as stained by partisanship, 243
ceremony of, 242–43
colonial origins of, 220
effects of, 235
in Mexico City, 231–34
intended healing character of,
228

nonpartisan nature of, 240–41
organization of, 238
social and anti-secular aspects
of, 228–30
See under Latin America; Pius
X, Pope,
Michnik, Adam, 116
Milingo, Emanuel, 193–94, 196
modern society
as embracing materialism,
individualism, and
consumerism, 190–91
as individualistic, 274
as relegating religion to
individual sphere, 48
monoculture, 136
nation-states, as effective sacrificial
agents, 50
National Socialism
rise of, 103
death camps, 139 (*see also*
Auschwitz)
nationalism
and the American Christian
Right, 252
as contradicting the Christian
salvation narrative, 260–61
as requiring a threat as
condition of possibility, 258
authentication as central process
of, 250
by omission, 255–56
Christian origins of, 267–68
definitions of, 249
difference from patriotism, 135
different meanings for
oppressors or oppressed, 135
dis-imagining the religious
nation, 294–97
links with Catholicism in
America, 272
Philippines, problems arising
from, 287–91
Polish, and links to Catholicism,
106
problems for religion caused
by, 93

religious aspects of, 262–65,
    268–72
neoclericalism, 90
New Atheists, 53
Niebuhr, Reinhold, 43, 52–53, 182
Nietzsche, Friedrich, 23, 49, 61
Niyitegeka, Sister Félicité, 25–26
Nyamata, Rwanda, 13–14
Nyere, Julius, 176
ontology, 35
Ostpolitik, 125–26
parishes, traditional model
    in Europe, need for
    transformation of, 85
Parmenides, 30–31
particularism, 39, 45, 163
Paul, Saint, 15–16, 19–21, 25, 27,
    36, 145, 179, 195, 271. *See
    also* Ephesian moment;
    transformation
Pentecost, 136, 142, 145, 148
Pentecostalism, 1, 169, 171–172,
    175, 178, 200, 209–11
Pius IX, Pope, 220
Pius X, Pope, approval of
    consecration plans, 226–227.
    See also under Mexico, 1914
    consecration to the Sacred
    Heart of Jesus
Pius XI, Pope, 131, 205, 263
pluralism, challenge of, 8, 32, 70–71,
    76–77, 105, 107–8, 210, 222
Popular Association for Catholic
    Germany, 95
Radio Maryja, 104, 106–7, 110, 113
    Catholic censure against
    xenophobia of, 108 (*see also
    under* John Paul II, Pope)
    nationalistic agenda of, 108–9,
    120
    naturalistic assumptions about,
    48
    See also Rydzyk, Father Tadeusz
Reformed Catholic Church (RCC),
    193–194
    conflict with practice of celibacy,
    195
    See also African Religion

religio, 265–66
Ruiz y Flores, Leopoldo, 223–27
Rydzyk, Father Tadeusz, 107-8. *See
    also* Radio Maryja
secularism and tension with
    religion, 57, 70, 72–73, 76,
    78, 80–82, 84, 101, 105, 218,
    259, 285.
    See also Catholicism; liberalism;
    and Taylor, Charles
Solidarity movement, 5, 105, 114,
    117, 120
    as presenting vision of
    Polishness that transcended
    politics, 116
    as social phenomenon, 115
    Catholic influence on, 114
Symphonia, 141, 157
Taylor, Charles, 80, 121. *See also*
    secularism and tension with
    religion
Theodosius, 92, 154
theology
    as faith in search for
    understanding, 28
    character of modern forms of,
    48
Theopolitics, 246–47, 255, 260
Teresa of Ávila, Saint, 45
Thomas Aquinas, Saint, 18, 36, 38
Tischner, Father Józef, 107, 115–16
transformation, two styles of
    according to Paul, 15–16.
    See also Paul, Saint
tribalism, modern forms of, 15
Trinity
    as coincidence of opposites, 38
    as combining diverse and
    autonomous elements within
    an essential unity, 37
    as supreme model of loving, 37
Ukrainian Greco-Catholic Church
    (UGCC), 123
    Catholicity of, 127, 129
    nationalism of, 131–34
    origins of term, 124
    Russian opposition to, 126

sacrifice of interests by Catholic Church in talks with Russia, 126
U.S. Conference of Catholic Bishops (USCCB), 252, 259
Forming Consciences for Faithful Citizenship, 252–54, 256–57
Weimar Republic, 94–103
Vatican II, 7, 82–83, 130–31, 137, 192, 198, 203–6, 212, 285–86, 295, 315

Scripture Index

Acts
2	303
2:8–12	128
4	303

Colossians
1	261
1:15–18	182
1:17	181
2	261
3:10–11	145
3:11	153

1 Corinthians
7	195
10:16–17	146
12:12–13	145

2 Corinthians
10:5	138
11:22	145

Ephesians
2:5–6	21
2:6–19	129
2:12–22	320
2:13–22	21
2:15	20
2:18	20
3:17–19	72
4:4	20
4:5-6	20–21
4:15–16	21

Exodus
16	76

Galatians
3:26–29	145
3:28	40, 129, 153, 303
5:10	173
5:22–24	31

Genesis
1:28	46
2:7	36

Hebrews
3:1–3	35
5:8	35
13:14	148

Isaiah
31:1	270
31:3	270
57:21	237

1 John
2:2	147
5:6	179

John

1:1	181–82
6:68	167
10:16	147
11:52	147
12:20–23	162
14:6	58
17:11	37
18:33–38	91
19:34	139

Joshua

24:15	91

Luke

2:10	141
6	206
14:26	35

Mark

12:13–17	91
12:25	41
12:50	35
19:12	41

Matthew

5	206
10:21	305
10:34–39	305
19:29	35
20:24–28	306
20:28	181
28:19	139, 146, 260
28:19–20a	46

Micah

7:6	305

1 Peter

	260–61
2:9	303
2:11	148, 158

Philippians

2	261
3:5	145
3:19	271
3:20	148, 256
4:8	135

Psalms

103:1	41
145	234

Romans

6:4	75
10:12–13	145
11:1	145
12:1	16, 25
12:2	13, 15, 16, 19, 27, 76

Revelations

7:9	26
14:6	129

1 Timothy

3:2	195

www.ingramcontent.com/pod-product-compliance
Lightning Source LLC
Chambersburg PA
CBHW032012300426
44117CB00008B/1002